M000198231

Predictive Analysis with SAP®

 **PRESS**

SAP PRESS is a joint initiative of SAP and Galileo Press. The know-how offered by SAP specialists combined with the expertise of the Galileo Press publishing house offers the reader expert books in the field. SAP PRESS features first-hand information and expert advice, and provides useful skills for professional decision-making.

SAP PRESS offers a variety of books on technical and business-related topics for the SAP user. For further information, please visit our website: *www.sap-press.com*.

Bjarne Berg and Penny Silva
SAP HANA: An Introduction (2nd Edition)
2013, 527 pp., hardcover
ISBN 978-1-59229-865-5

Jonathan Haun, Chris Hickman, Don Loden, and Roy Wells
Implementing SAP HANA
2013, 837 pp., hardcover
ISBN 978-1-59229-856-3

Xavier Hacking and Jeroen van der A
Getting Started with SAP BusinessObjects Design Studio
2014, 468 pp., hardcover
ISBN 978-1-59229-895-2

John MacGregor

Predictive Analysis with SAP®

The Comprehensive Guide

Galileo Press

Bonn • Boston

Galileo Press is named after the Italian physicist, mathematician, and philosopher Galileo Galilei (1564–1642). He is known as one of the founders of modern science and an advocate of our contemporary, heliocentric worldview. His words *Eppur si muove* (And yet it moves) have become legendary. The Galileo Press logo depicts Jupiter orbited by the four Galilean moons, which were discovered by Galileo in 1610.

Editor Katy Spencer
Copyeditor Pamela Siska
Cover Design Graham Geary
Photo Credit Fotolia.com/45245762/© Melanie Mertens
Layout Design Vera Brauner
Production Kelly O'Callaghan
Typesetting Publishers' Design and Production Services, Inc.
Printed and bound in the United States of America, on paper from sustainable sources

ISBN 978-1-59229-915-7

© 2014 by Galileo Press Inc., Boston (MA)
1st edition 2014

Library of Congress Cataloging-in-Publication Data
MacGregor, John (Product manager)
Predictive analysis with SAP : the comprehensive guide / John MacGregor.
pages cm
Includes bibliographical references and index.
ISBN-13: 978-1-59229-915-7
ISBN-10: 1-59229-915-6
ISBN-13: 978-1-59229-917-1 (e-book : alk. paper)
ISBN-13: 978-1-59229-916-4 (e-book : alk. paper) 1. Data mining. 2. Forecasting--Data processing.
3. Forecasting--Statistical methods. 4. SAP ERP. I. Title.
QA76.9.D343M34 2014
006.3'12--dc23
2013037972

Contents at a Glance

Dear Reader,

At first glance, the practice of predictive analysis is seemingly all about number crunching, bar graphs, and equations. In short, Math with a capital "M". As I read and developed this title, I came to realize that beyond the multitude of algorithms, and in between the covariates and variables lies the true, practical business value of predictive analysis.

Our fantastic author, John MacGregor, has dug deep into his wealth of knowedge in order to produce a title that simplifies the complex predictive analysis process, reduces the painful points surrounding managing multiple data sources, and shows you how to navigate different types of predictive analyses. Beyond the expansive wealth of information shared, John's writing style and approach is informative, help-ful, and down-to-earth. He will skillfully show you all that predictive analysis has to offer. Don't blame us if you pick up some math along the way.

As always, we appreciate your business and welcome your feedback. What did you think about *Predictive Analysis with SAP—The Comprehensive Guide*? Your comments and suggestions are the most useful tools to help us improve our books for you, the reader. We encourage you to visit our website at *www.sap-press.com* and share your feedback.

Katy Spencer
Editor, SAP PRESS

Galileo Press
Boston, MA

katy.spencer@galileo-press.com
www.sap-press.com

Contents

11 Classification Analysis 313

PART IV Classification Analysis

12 Classification Analysis—Regression 327

Introduction

At first glance, the practice of predictive analysis is seemingly all about formulas and math. However, beyond the multitude of algorithms lies the real business value of predictive analysis. From defining the objectives of the analysis through to the application of algorithms and their deployment in business processes, today's businesses are now deriving significant benefits from the use of predictive analysis.

SAP is at the forefront of these exciting new opportunities. From the development of the in-database algorithms in the SAP HANA Predictive Analysis Library and the integration of the open source statistical tool R, through to the client tool, SAP Predictive Analysis for the definition, visualization and running of predictive analysis processes, SAP provides business users with the tools to leverage massive amounts of data in real time, to anticipate business changes, and to drive smarter, more strategic decision making. The reach of predictive analysis solutions has expanded considerably across a wide diversity of industries, delivering predictive capabilities to data analysts, business users, and decision makers.

This book presents the core concepts of predictive analysis through case studies, simple examples, and algorithm descriptions. Accompanied by a business explanation to support an understanding of the practical application, along with the strengths and the weaknesses of each algorithm, you will understand how to develop a business driven predictive analysis strategy.

Structure of This Book

The book is organized into five parts, starting with the practical aspects and then moving on to the more advanced considerations for predictive analysis. The parts are organized as follows:

► Part I: Predictive Analysis Overview (Chapter 1 and Chapter 2)
► Part II: Predictive Analysis Applied (Chapter 3 through Chapter 7)
► Part III: Predictive Analysis Categories (Chapter 8 through Chapter 11)

- Part IV: Classification Analysis (Chapter 12 through Chapter 14)
- Part V: Advanced Predictive Analysis (Chapter 15 through Chapter 17)

The first and second parts have a business focus, reviewing predictive analysis as a process and the specific SAP tools that can be leveraged to support this process. These chapters present the best practices for using the predictive assets of SAP, and when conducting such analysis, choosing which algorithms to use when, avoiding potential pitfalls and practical case studies across multiple industries.

Once we develop that foundational understanding, we shift our focus to the various predictive analysis categories and the predictive algorithms that are generally applied within those categories in Parts III, IV, and V. Association analysis, cluster analysis, classification analysis and time series analysis are the most common analysis categories and each will be featured, along with the overall topic of outlier analysis. In addition, a chapter is devoted to text analysis, a topic of growing importance.

To tie all these concepts together, the book closes with customer case studies that demonstrate the application of these concepts in detail for different industries, from simple to complex applications of predictive analysis.

Target Audience

This book is written for several different audiences based on their various needs to understand predictive analysis. This title is aimed at business users, business analysts, and the data analysts who work with the data directly, plus the decision makers empowered to translate predictive analysis into improved business processes. The book is written from a practical business approach. Application developers will be interested in the in-database predictive analysis capabilities of SAP HANA, and our title gives many examples of SAP HANA's Predictive Analysis Library SQLScript. The content is relevant to a diverse set of industries, including CRM/marketing, financial, insurance, telecommunications, and retail, given that the predictive analysis process itself is applicable across all industries. As a reader, you will find our content particularly useful if you fall into any one of the following categories:

- You want to a business driven focus for understanding what predictive analysis is and how it can be useful.
- You want to know more about the subject of predictive analysis.

▶ You want to see where predictive analysis has been successfully applied.

▶ You want to learn what SAP has to offer in the predictive space.

▶ You want to understand the process for predictive analysis.

▶ You want to learn more about predictive analysis algorithms, but not all the mathematical detail.

▶ You want to understand the key concepts behind the algorithms.

▶ You want to explore the data visualizations available.

▶ You want an understanding of what is involved in, and what is available for, initial data analysis.

▶ You want an understanding of how to choose which algorithm to use when.

▶ You want to learn how to avoid the pitfalls and potential mines awaiting the unwary data miner.

▶ You want to learn what applications SAP is building that contain predictive capabilities and what those capabilities are.

▶ You want a thorough understanding of the tools available from SAP for predictive analysis; specifically SAP Predictive Analysis, the in-database data mining in SAP HANA, and the integrations of the R open source statistics language.

▶ You want an understanding of what are text analysis and text mining, and their benefits.

▶ You want to see where and how SAP customers are using the predictive assets offered by SAP.

How to Use This Book

Given that the book appeals to many audiences, it has been designed so that sections are interconnected yet can be read independently. You can read from start to finish or simply progress straight to the chapters of specific interest. The details regarding algorithms have been written to help educate, not to vainly try to impress the reader with the author's knowledge. The objective is to demystify much of the mystique that surrounds predictive analysis and describe it in a comprehensible manner.

Ancillary Materials

You will note throughout the chapters that we mention the SAP PRESS product page and the code listings that are found therein. These listings are intended to help facilitate your using the SAP HANA Predictive Analysis Library (PAL). To access these files, please visit the SAP PRESS product page: *http://www.sap-press.com/H3317*. The files are available in the Additional Resources section and comprise the full code for the examples of the PAL in the book. To run the code, you will need to check user permissions and environment variables; however, the code is self-contained and includes any data sets and parameter settings required for the analysis.

Conclusion

We hope that you enjoy this book and benefit from it as much as we enjoyed creating it. The insights derived from predictive analysis are providing significant benefits in an age when there is no shortage of data that can provide competitive advantage and, more generally, improve our lives.

Acknowledgments

First and foremost, I wish to acknowledge my wonderful wife Shemin, without whose continuous encouragement and support, I would not have been able to produce this book.

I would also like to thank my manager, Alan Southall, for his support of my writing of the book.

The predictive journey in SAP began with my colleagues and good friends in SAP P&I Bengaluru, India, where we built our first version of SAP Predictive Analysis. It was a pleasure, and a lot of fun, to work with Shyamakrishna Kattepur, Sreejith Viswanathan, Venkatesh Vaidyanathan, Vishwanath Belur, Ashok Kumar KN, Ajay Kumar Gupta, Abanindra Nath Sarkar, Unmesh Sreedharan, Girish Kalasa Ganesh Pai, and Sujit Ramesh A.

In parallel, I must also acknowledge the contribution of two people who have since left SAP, but whose strong legacy remains and who led these developments, namely Rick Lui with the SAP Predictive Analysis Library, and Caro Ge with the R Integration for SAP HANA, and of course their manager, Wen-Syan Li. More recently, Xiaowei Xu and his development team provided invaluable help.

My thanks also go to Markus Fath and Markus Doehring for their assistance with the chapter on Text Analysis.

For the chapter on Customer Applications in SAP, my thanks go to Michael Haft, Christine Preisach, Klaus Vogelgesang, Tobias Hoppe-Boeken, Carsten Heuer, Niels Schmitt, Valerie Tardif, Alan Miller, Andreas Vogel, Helmut Linde, Joerg Brunner, Wolfgang Schuetz, Stephan Kreipl, Yue Chen, Anna Linden, Achim Becker, Charles Vogt, and Alex Liu.

I should also acknowledge the contributions of Karl Rexer of Rexer Analytics and Gregory Piatesky-Shapiro of KDnuggets.com for their predictive analysis surveys and their permission in reprinting their survey results found throughout Chapter 1 and beyond.

I would also like to thank Katy Spencer from SAP PRESS, who was my very diligent Acquisitions Editor, and Pamela Siska, who was the Copy Editor. And of course, thanks is owed to SAP PRESS themselves for accepting my proposal to write the book.

Finally, there is a whole group of people, really too many to mention, who have proactively pushed predictive in SAP and who have been a part of my journey. I thank you.

PART I
Predictive Analysis Overview

This chapter introduces the topic of predictive analysis and includes sections on its definition, its value, and application. The chapter concludes with a review of the latest hot topics in predictive, the challenges, and the main factors for success.

1 An Introduction to Predictive Analysis

Predictive analysis is a hot topic, aligned with the explosive growth in data. Management is about the future, not the past, so the more that we can prepare for the future, the more efficient and competitive we will be.

SAP has made significant investments in predictive analysis, ranging from the development of in-database predictive algorithms in SAP HANA, through to the support of the open source statistics language R and the development of SAP Predictive Analysis for the definition, visualization, processing, and deployment of predictive analysis processes. In addition, many groups within the SAP Business Suite, Industry and Line of Business Solutions are incorporating predictive analysis capabilities into their applications.

We start this chapter by looking at the various definitions of predictive analysis, the value that it provides to business, and the users of predictive analysis. Predictive analysis can also be defined in terms of its applications, which we will describe and then group into five broad areas, from which we can classify the many algorithms of predictive analysis. It is important to recognize that predictive analysis is not just about algorithms – far from it. Therefore, we review the predictive analysis process in total. Finally, we look at some of the hot topics and trends, and conclude with a section on the challenges and criteria for success when undertaking predictive analysis projects.

1.1 Definitions of Predictive Analysis

Predictive analysis can be simply defined as quantitative analysis that supports the making of predictions. Predictions of, for example, product sales, costs, headcount, key performance metrics, customer churn, creditworthiness, cross-selling and up-selling opportunities, market campaign response, anomalies and possible fraud. It is a relatively new term, but it's not a new topic, given its foundation on such disciplines as statistical analysis, machine learning and operations research. Until recently it was usually referred to as data mining and to a lesser extent as knowledge discovery. There is even a debate as to whether it is predictive analysis or predictive analytics. Although the terms are interchangeable, we will use the term analysis, as analytics often refers to reports rather than analysis. However, as with all phrases and terms, it is what it means that is important, not so much what it is called.

Wikipedia has become a reputable resource for definitions and understanding, particularly in the world of quantitative analysis. Wikipedia cites predictive analytics as an area of statistical analysis in which you extract information from data to predict patterns and trends. This can then be used to predict an unknown, be it past, present or future; for example identifying fraud that has been committed or as it is actually occurring, through to forecasting future sales. The heart of predictive analytics is finding the relationship between known variables and a predicted variable, using past occurrences. This relationship is then used to predict an unknown outcome. Naturally, in such an analysis the quality of the data analysis and the assumptions made, will greatly affect the accuracy and usability of the predictions. (Reference: *http://en.wikipedia.org/wiki/Predictive_analytics*.)

The Gartner Group provides a good definition of data mining in their "Magic Quadrant for Customer Data Mining Operations" report:

> ...the process of discovering meaningful new correlations, patterns and trends by sifting through large amounts of data stored in repositories, using pattern recognition technologies as well as statistical and mathematical techniques.

The qualification that the data be large amounts is rather misleading as predictive analysis is also concerned with analyzing even small amounts of data, which is, after all, the very essence of statistical sampling and inferential statistics.

Given that predictive analysis encompasses many quantitative analysis disciplines, a Venn diagram may help describe their contribution and overlap. You can debate the detail, but Figure 1.1 makes the key point that predictive analysis is a synergy of interdisciplinary approaches, a corollary of which is that the best predictive analysis project teams are interdisciplinary.

The key takeaway from Figure 1.1 is that each profession brings a slightly different approach to problem solving. Statisticians have a strong background in data analysis using such methods as inferential statistics, regression, and multivariate methods in general. Operational researchers have more of a background in optimization methods and simulation, while data miners are generally associated with the methods of artificial intelligence and extracting information from very large data sets. There are, of course, overlaps and the boundaries are definitely fuzzy.

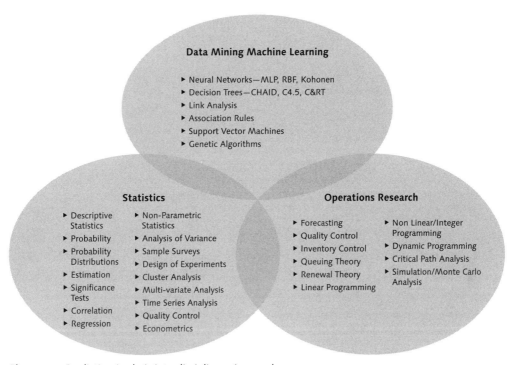

Figure 1.1 Predictive Analysis Interdisciplinary Approach

Predictive analysis is an analytic process starting from data selection, acquisition and exploration, through to visualization and analysis, validation (and possibly the reiteration of the whole process), and finally dissemination and implementation in improved business processes. We will discuss this further in the following sections, notably Section 1.7.

Definitions can sometimes be rather academic. We can also define predictive analysis in terms of what it is used for, as described in Section 1.4, and by looking at what value it brings to business.

1.2 The Value of Predictive Analysis

Management is about the future, so the more insight we can obtain about the future, the better the management of that future should be, provided of course that our insights are accurate. The better our insight into the future, the greater the potential for competitive advantage. This is reflected in the diagram in Figure 1.2, which shows the progression from simply reporting the past to predicting the future and the resultant increased competitive advantage.

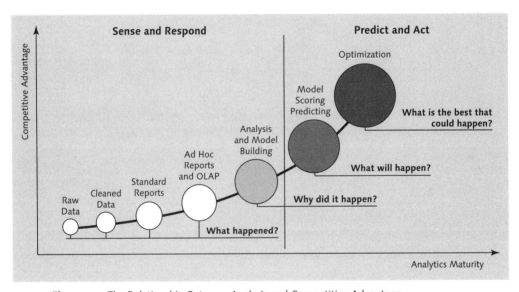

Figure 1.2   The Relationship Between Analysis and Competitive Advantage

Karl Rexer of Rexer Analytics, in his annual Data Miner Survey asked respondents to rate their use of predictive analysis from very low to very high, and also their company performance from much worse than peers to much better. Karl Rexer would never claim that this survey is solid scientific analysis, but the results are interesting and lead to a broad conclusion. From the answers of over 1,300 respondents in 2011, Rexer constructed the graphic shown in Figure 1.3, which suggests that the greater the use of analysis, the better the company performance. What is also interesting is that only 12% of the respondents rated their company as having very high analytic sophistication. As Karl Rexer concluded: there is room for improvement, and it matters!

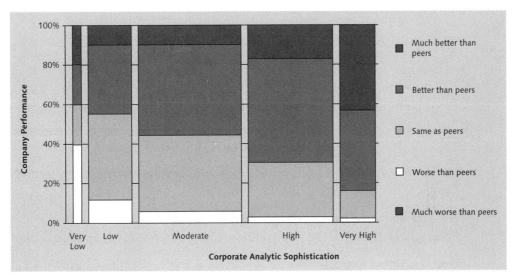

Figure 1.3 Rexer Analytics Data Miner Survey 2011 – Usage and Benefits

The results of a recent survey by Ventana Research titled "Predictive Analytics: Improving Performance by Making the Future More Visible" (2012), showed that:

▸ 55% use predictive analytics to create new revenue opportunities.

▸ 68% who use predictive analytics claimed a competitive edge.

▸ 86% asserted that predictive analytics will have a major positive impact.

▸ Nearly a third believe it could be transformative in their organization.

It's hard to provide actual numbers of increased revenue or profitability, as they are usually company confidential. Furthermore, the measurement of the benefit is itself difficult, as theoretically it is the difference between what happened from using predictive analysis, compared to what would have happened had it not been used, with the latter, of course, being unknown.

IDC Research, in their white paper titled "The Business Value of Predictive Analytics" published in 2011, reported:

- An asset management firm increased its marketing offer acceptance rate by 300%.

- An insurance company identified fraudulent claims 30 days faster than before.

- A bank was able to identify 50% of fraud cases within the first hour.

- A communications company increased customer satisfaction by 53%.

IDC Research went on to state:

- The return on investment (ROI) of business analytics solutions that incorporate predictive analytics is about 250%, significantly higher than the 89% ROI of projects focused only on information access and internal productivity gains.

- Benefits of predictive analytics projects are sustained over long periods of time, and those that rely more on analytics tend to be more competitive.

- Predictive analytics projects result in many intangible, or difficult to quantify benefits, that give further impetus to investment in these solutions.

IDC concluded that a growing body of market research shows that predictive analytics can positively impact the profitability and competitiveness of an organization.

Figure 1.4 shows examples of how predictive analysis can deliver business value across all aspects of a business.

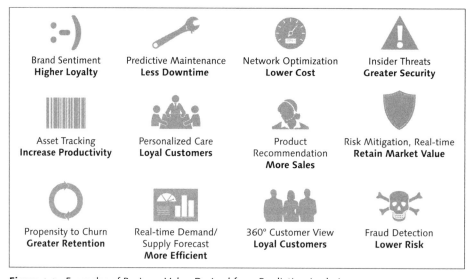

Figure 1.4 Examples of Business Value Derived from Predictive Analysis

The fact that the market for predictive analysis software is estimated at over $2 billion and growing strongly shows how relevant it is to businesses today. Furthermore, the value of predictive analysis is reflected in the significant number of people whose careers are based on it, namely statisticians, data scientists, data miners, operations researchers, market researchers, etc.

In the next section we look at all the user personas of predictive analysis.

1.3   User Personas

There is a wide spectrum of users of predictive analysis, ranging from the data scientist to the consumer of business applications that incorporate predictive analysis. Figure 1.5 shows three broad groups, from the relatively small group of data scientists, who represent less than 1% of an organization's headcount, through to the data analysts, and then the vast majority of business users, who would not build predictive models but who would like to use the outputs of predictive models.

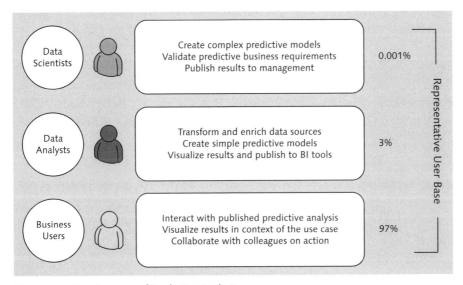

Figure 1.5   User Personas of Predictive Analysis

The term data scientist is a relatively new term and encompasses the more traditional terms of statistician, data miner, and operations researcher. Data scientists have the knowledge and experience to build predictive models and would follow all the steps of a predictive analysis process: data collection and validation; model exploration and selection; prediction and implementation. We discuss the process of predictive analysis in more detail in Section 1.7.

Data analysts may work with models built by data scientists or through an interface such as a wizard to explore and analyze data for a specific application such as a marketing campaign, a product segmentation analysis, or a churn analysis. They generally possess numerate skills but they don't want to get into questions such as which specific predictive algorithm should they use. They want guidance in performing the analysis and an interface that is easy to use. A typical user might be a market researcher, a market campaign manager, an investment analyst, or a sales analyst.

Business users simply want the benefits of predictive analysis embedded in their business processes. They want to see the output of the analysis. The term business user could be slightly misleading, as it also includes general consumers of information derived from predictive analysis. They could be passive consumers or interactive. An example of the former is a user who follows the product recommendations of a website. An example of the latter is a call center operative suggesting cross-selling opportunities depending upon the attributes of the caller.

We can map these user personas to the predictive products in SAP that will be described in detail throughout this book (see Figure 1.6).

The data scientist would use the Predictive Analysis Library in SAP HANA (PAL), which is a library of in-database predictive analysis algorithms in SAP HANA. They might also use the R Integration for HANA or the R integration for SAP Predictive Analysis. R is a popular open source statistics language for data scientists.

The business analyst is targeted by SAP Predictive Analysis (PA), given its simple and effective user interface for defining predictive analysis processes. PA also includes the capability for data exploration with its integration to SAP Lumira, previously known as Visual Intelligence (VI), plus data visualizations to support specific algorithms. Data visualization is attractive to all user personas.

The final group of users is those who use business applications with embedded predictive content. SAP is investing significant resources in putting predictive into its business applications. Examples include SAP Audience Discovery and Targeting; SAP Customer Value Intelligence; SAP Account Intelligence; SAP Fraud Management and SAP B2C Product Recommendations.

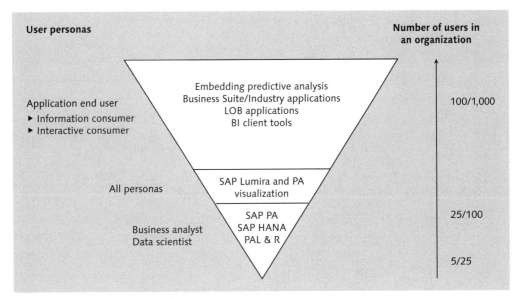

Figure 1.6   User Personas of Predictive Analysis Mapped to SAP Products

These are the users of predictive. The obvious next question is: what are they all doing?

1.4   Applications of Predictive Analysis

Predictive analysis has a huge range of applications. We start by looking at the applications in terms of the broad questions that they are trying to answer.

There are five main questions, as shown in Figure 1.7.

1. **What are the trends in the historical data and can we use them to project the data?** This is the major application area of time series analysis and, in particular, demand or sales forecasting. It includes any application where we have some historical data points and we want to project them.

2. **What are the key influencers of an event or outcome?** Perhaps the best known example of this is churn analysis, where we want to try to find the key reasons customers stop purchasing a product. It includes applications such as looking for which customers are more likely to respond to a marketing campaign. Then

there are applications trying to identify occurrences of fraud based on a predictive model.

3. **Are there any significant segments or groups in the data which we can focus on?** Typical applications include designing specific product promotions, targeted sales plays, and specific strategies for groups of sales outlets.

4. **What are the associations or links between products?** The best examples of this are market basket analysis and recommendation engines. People who bought this product also bought these products; if you like this song, you may also like these other songs; if you watched this video you may like these; if you know this person, you may also know these people.

5. **What anomalies exist in the data; what is unusual? Are they errors or are they actual variations that need to be included in our analysis?** Examples of applications using anomaly detection are data validation, manufacturing process control and fraud management.

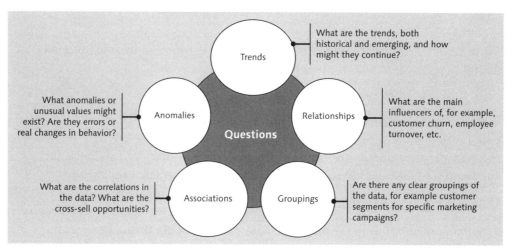

Figure 1.7 The Five Main Questions of Predictive Analysis

We can look at applications of predictive analysis by industry and by line of business. Figure 1.8 shows examples by industry, such as retail, banking, and utilities.

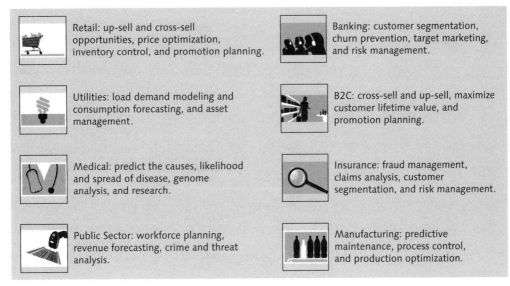

Retail: up-sell and cross-sell opportunities, price optimization, inventory control, and promotion planning.

Banking: customer segmentation, churn prevention, target marketing, and risk management.

Utilities: load demand modeling and consumption forecasting, and asset management.

B2C: cross-sell and up-sell, maximize customer lifetime value, and promotion planning.

Medical: predict the causes, likelihood and spread of disease, genome analysis, and research.

Insurance: fraud management, claims analysis, customer segmentation, and risk management.

Public Sector: workforce planning, revenue forecasting, crime and threat analysis.

Manufacturing: predictive maintenance, process control, and production optimization.

Figure 1.8 Applications of Predictive Analysis by Industry

Figure 1.9 offers examples of applications of predictive analysis by line of business, such as marketing, finance, production, and sales.

Marketing is a major area of application of predictive analysis, given its close association with the interactions with customers. Knowing their attributes, attitudes, and their propensity to respond to product offers, is paramount to the success of business.

You can well argue that business is in the end all about profit and loss, and therefore applying predictive analysis in the field of finance is highly relevant.

Of course business is about making things, so doing that in an optimal manner is another rich area for the application of predictive analysis. Aligned to this process is the delivery of those products through the supply chain, an area that has received considerable focus from operational researchers.

According to the Rexer Analytics Data Miner Survey 2011 and the response to the question "In what fields do you typically apply data mining?" (shown in Figure 1.10), data mining (predictive analysis) is everywhere, and from a business perspective, primarily in CRM/Marketing and Finance.

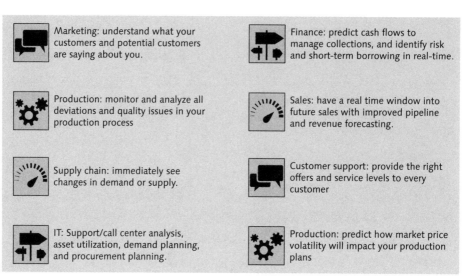

Figure 1.9 Applications of Predictive Analysis by Line of Business

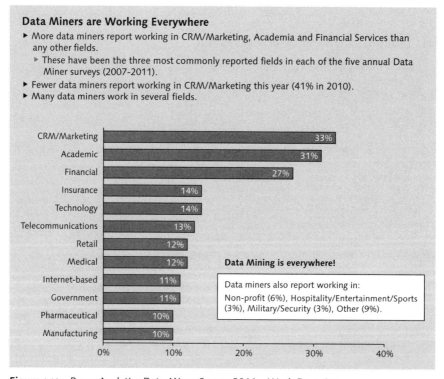

Figure 1.10 Rexer Analytics Data Miner Survey 2011 – Work Domains

As you can see from this section, applications of predictive analysis are widespread. However, if we go back to the broad questions that we are trying to answer through the use of predictive analysis, then perhaps we can group or define classes of applications to provide some structure to our understanding.

1.5   Classes of Applications

In the previous section we listed five broad questions that predictive analysis is trying to answer. Now we can use these five questions to define five groups or classes of applications. Each class of application is represented in Figure 1.11, describing the structure of the data for each analysis.

We review the following classes of applications that form predictive analysis:

1. Time Series Analysis
2. Classification Analysis
3. Cluster Analysis
4. Association Analysis
5. Outlier Analysis

1.5.1   Time Series Analysis

In this group we use past data points as the basis for projecting future ones. The data is a variable, such as sales or headcount or telemetry readings, with a series of values over time. We use historical patterns in the known data to make predictions about future values. We can represent this class of application as shown in Figure 1.11 (1. Time Series Analysis).

1.5.2   Classification Analysis

This is the largest group of applications of predictive analysis. In general terms we wish to predict a variable using the data of other variables that we believe affect the values of the variable that we are trying to predict. The variable that we wish to predict is variously known as the output variable, the target variable, or the dependent variable. The latter name comes from the assertion that it depends on the values of the independent variables or input variables. We can represent this class of application as shown in Figure 1.11 (2. Classification Analysis). Examples of classification analysis include churn analysis, target marketing to those most likely to respond, predictive maintenance and price optimization.

1.5.3 Cluster Analysis

This class of application is concerned with grouping the data into clusters or segments that have similar attributes. We can represent this class of application as shown in Figure 1.11 (3. Cluster Analysis). It is often used to subset a large data set, as we may be able to better understand the attributes of the smaller subsets. With large data sets, the relationships in the data can be harder to find and may even cancel each other out. Whereas by focusing on subsets we may more easily find patterns in the data and explanations for any relationships. We also cluster data so that we can focus on specific groups within a dataset. The best example of this is customer segmentation where we want to develop specific sales strategies for particular customer groups.

1.5.4 Association Analysis

This class of applications looks for associations between things, with the best known example being the analysis of shopping baskets and the prediction that people who purchased this product are most likely to purchase these other products. We can represent this class of application as shown in Figure 1.11 (4. Association Analysis) with the first column representing the transaction IDs, and the second column the actual purchases. The format is sometimes referred to as till-roll format. The associations do not necessarily need to be products in shopping baskets, whether in a retail store or an ecommerce application. They could be between people in a social network. In general, it is the analysis is of a collection of things in some container. Other examples include the analysis of telecom services purchased by subscribers; financial policies held by households; telephone calling patterns; visitor paths through a website.

1.5.5 Outlier Analysis

This class of application of predictive analysis looks for the unusual and the unexpected: unusual in the sense that values in a data set are very different from other values, and unexpected in the sense that the values are very different from what was predicted. The outliers could be as a result of errors in the data or genuine variations in the data, which the predictive model needs to take into account.

Outliers can have a significant effect on the predictions from a predictive model, so it is important to try to identify them. Outlier or anomaly detection has a major application in the area of fraud detection. This class of application occurs in the context of all the other classes of predictive applications; for example, detecting unusual values in a time series, investigating where fitted values in a model are very different from actual, identifying data records that do not belong to any cluster, and observing unusual purchase combinations.

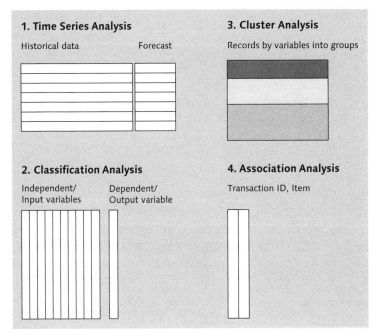

Figure 1.11 The Structure of Data for Analysis

Aligned to the classes of applications of predictive analysis is a grouping of the algorithms used in predictive analysis.

1.6 Algorithms for Predictive Analysis

The algorithms used in predictive analysis can be grouped by the classes of application as described in the previous section. For time series analysis, algorithms include single, double and triple exponential smoothing, plus regression models of a variable by time.

Algorithms for classification analysis are by far the biggest group and include the very popular subgroup of decision trees. Multivariate regression models are also very popular for classification analysis, plus neural networks.

Algorithms for cluster analysis include the well-known K-Means algorithm and, for association analysis, there is the equally popular Apriori algorithm.

Outlier detection algorithms range from simple statistical tests such as the Inter-Quartile Range Test to "reverse" cluster analysis in the sense of looking for objects far away from cluster centers.

These algorithms are explored in detail in Parts III, IV, and V of this book.

According to the Rexer Analytics Data Miner Survey 2011 and the response to the question "What algorithms/analytic methods do you typically use?", the top three are regression, decision trees, and cluster analysis. The full list is shown in Figure 1.12.

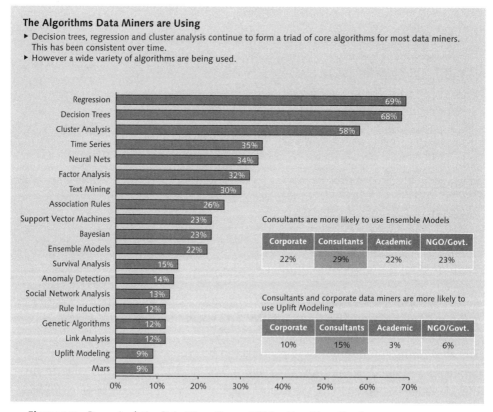

Figure 1.12   Rexer Analytics Data Miner Survey 2011 – Algorithms Used

The website *www.kdnuggets.com* conducts regular polls of its readers and is another valuable source of information on predictive analysis. In November 2011 it conducted a poll on the question "Which methods/algorithms did you use for data analysis in 2011?" with 311 responses. The responses confirmed the finding of the Rexer Analytics survey that the top three are decision trees, regression, and clustering. The full list is shown in Figure 1.13.

Method	Percentage
Decision Trees/Rules (186)	59.8 %
Regression (180)	57.9 %
Clustering (163)	52.4 %
Statistics (descriptive) (149)	47.9 %
Visualization (119)	38.3 %
Time series/Sequence analysis (92)	29.6 %
Support Vector (SVM) (89)	28.6 %
Association rules (89)	28.6 %
Ensemble methods (88)	28.3 %
Text Mining (86)	27.7 %
Neural Nets (84)	27.0 %
Boosting (73)	23.5 %
Bayesian (68)	21.9 %
Bagging (63)	20.3 %
Factor Analysis (58)	18.7 %
Anomaly/Deviation detection (51)	16.4 %
Social Network Analysis (44)	14.2 %
Survival Analysis (29)	9.32 %
Genetic algorithms (29)	9.32 %
Uplift modeling (15)	4.82 %

Figure 1.13 KDnuggets Poll – Which Methods/Algorithms Do You Use?

For all these classes of applications of predictive analysis and algorithms, there is a common and important process for conducting the analysis. Predictive analysis isn't just about algorithms.

1.7 The Predictive Analysis Process

The process for predictive analysis is essentially very simple:

1. Define the objectives of the analysis. What are the desired outcomes from the project? Define a project plan. Identify participants, timelines and resources.

2. Identify data requirements and sources. Acquire and validate the data. Conduct an initial data exploration. Perhaps perform some data transformations such as sampling, binning or rescaling the data in preparation for model building.

3. Build a model or models. This is where the algorithms are applied to the data and their parameters chosen to provide the best fit. It may include the concept of training the model on part of the data and then testing the model on the other unused or "unseen" part of the data. The models are evaluated in terms of goodness of fit, robustness and usability.

4. Deploy the model in a business application. This is sometimes called model scoring. It may involve integrating with a business rules application to provide further business context. It also includes monitoring model performance over time.

5. Reiterate to any stage of the process. This is an important point. The predictive analysis process is rarely a single pass through a sequential series of steps. The development of a model often highlights the need for additional data, further data transformations and alternative analyses.

This process is shown in Figure 1.14.

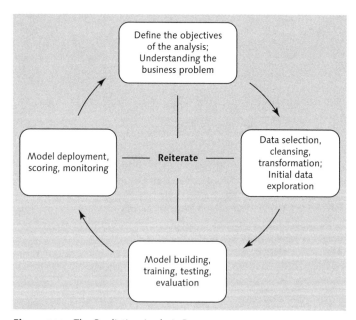

Figure 1.14   The Predictive Analysis Process

It is generally agreed that most of the time in this process is spent on data selection, acquisition and preparation. Business users are generally wary of predictive analysis, as they associate it with statistics, mathematics and algorithms. However, in reality, predictive analysis is mainly about data and identifying what is needed, how it can be measured, where it can be obtained from, and how good is it.

According to the Rexer Analytics Data Miner Survey and the response to the question "What percentage of time do you spend on the various tasks of data mining?", respondents reported that only 20% of their time is spent on the actual modeling step of data mining, whereas accessing and preparing data takes up the most time. See Figure 1.15.

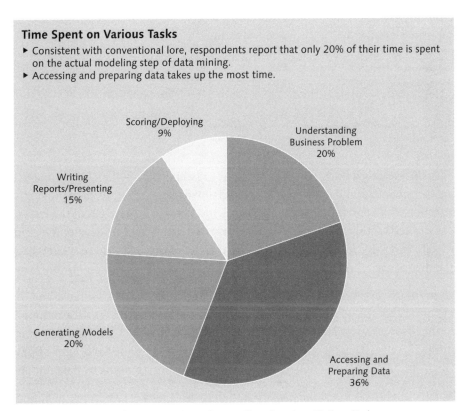

Time Spent on Various Tasks
- ▶ Consistent with conventional lore, respondents report that only 20% of their time is spent on the actual modeling step of data mining.
- ▶ Accessing and preparing data takes up the most time.

Scoring/Deploying 9%
Understanding Business Problem 20%
Writing Reports/Presenting 15%
Generating Models 20%
Accessing and Preparing Data 36%

Figure 1.15 Rexer Analytics Data Miner Survey: Time Spent on Various Tasks

So far we have looked at the most common applications of predictive analysis; however, it is also interesting to look at some of the more recent hot topics and trends.

1.8   Hot Topics and Trends

Predicting the future should be easy for predictive analysts! The 366 respondents to the KDnuggets (*www.kdnuggets.com*) poll "Hottest Analytics/Data Mining Topics in 2012", rated the top three as Big Data, Analytics in the Cloud and Hadoop, and Social Analytics. The full list is shown in Figure 1.16.

Of course we should add our own – predictive at SAP is now a very hot topic!

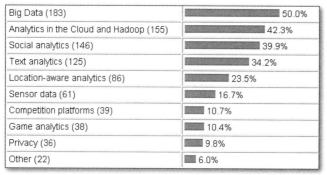

Big Data (183)	50.0%
Analytics in the Cloud and Hadoop (155)	42.3%
Social analytics (146)	39.9%
Text analytics (125)	34.2%
Location-aware analytics (86)	23.5%
Sensor data (61)	16.7%
Competition platforms (39)	10.7%
Game analytics (38)	10.4%
Privacy (36)	9.8%
Other (22)	6.0%

Figure 1.16   KDnuggets Poll – Hot Topics in Data Mining

Big data is certainly a hot topic. We live in the era of big data, with it being amassed from everywhere and in particular from social networks, sensor data, commercial transactions, and communications. A staggering statistic is that 90% of the data in the world today was collected in just the past two years. Recent developments in hardware and software enable the detailed analysis of this data. There is overlap of the topics, as social analytics and sensor data are themselves examples of Big Data.

In terms of predicting the future of predictive, Karl Rexer's 2011 survey asked the question "What do you envision as the primary future trends in data mining?" with the responses shown in Figure 1.17. The results broadly follow the hot topics identified in the KDnuggets 2012 survey, plus a belief of wider adoption of data mining, although the latter may be more a case of wishful thinking by data miners.

Predictive analysis is not some magic wand that we can wave to predict the future. Predictions are estimates, not facts. They are inherently uncertain and it is important that all predictions come with a statement of our confidence in them. In our final section of this chapter, we review the challenges and also identify some critical factors for success.

Future Trends in Data Mining

▸ Survey respondents shared their ideas about future trends in data mining (an open-ended survey question).
▸ Many data miners think that there will be wider adoption of data mining in the future.
▸ Future visions of data mining are stable: the top three items are the same as last year.

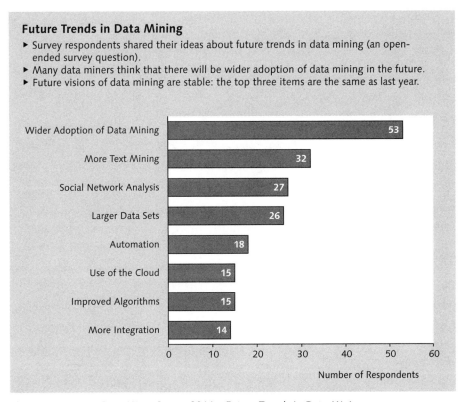

Figure 1.17   Rexer Data Miner Survey 2011 – Future Trends in Data Mining

1.9   Challenges and Criteria for Success

Data mining hell was once described by Tom Khabaza, a founding member of the Clementine data mining product, the first predictive workbench, as "We have some data – just don't ask me where. Now tell us all that we do not know." In contrast, data mining heaven was described as "We have a clear business objective, defined success criteria, a multidisciplinary team, relevant and quality data, an iterative process, and finally an action plan." The hardest part is the relevant and quality data, plus a reasonable amount of it. This is the main challenge for predictive analysis.

Other challenges include the time and effort required for some projects, which may be substantial compared to the benefits. It can be a challenge to get the findings from the analysis accepted and implemented by management, who may be skeptical, political, and uncooperative. If management does not understand the analysis, then they are very unlikely to implement its findings.

In Chapter 5 we discuss these challenges as well as how to meet them and minimize their impact. When mining for gold, there is no guarantee that we will find it, and when mining data for interesting patterns to use to make predictions, there is no guarantee that we will find any.

As part of meeting the challenges of predictive analysis, there are some critical factors to help maximize the chances of success, in other words, the critical success factors for predictive:

1. Manage expectations. Predictive analysis is not guaranteed to find anything interesting or accurately predict the future. If you over promise, then you are likely to under deliver and consequently be seen as having failed.

2. Analyze for real business benefit. Predictive analysis should not be an academic exercise within a business context. It should address real business problems with potentially substantial benefits. There is little point in analyzing problems with little benefit.

3. Work as a team. As we saw in the section on the predictive analysis process, predictive is not just about algorithms. Much of it is about identifying relevant data, acquiring it and preparing it for analysis. Business domain knowledge is an invaluable addition to any project.

4. Data scientists will be an important part of a team undertaking a predictive analysis project; however, other skills will add valuable input to a project.

5. Use sensitivity analysis to explore the robustness of a solution. Experiment with different data sets, different models and model parameters to see how robust or stable the model solution is. If slight changes in inputs to a model result in major changes to the solution, then you need to be very wary when implementing the findings of the model.

6. From analysis to action. The benefit from predictive analysis comes when it is used to improve a business process; otherwise, it is mainly an academic exercise.

These factors are explored further in Chapter 5.

A final, and hopefully amusing, conclusion to this chapter comes from the New York Criminal Code. The Old Criminal Code of New York considered prediction a criminal offence: "Persons who pretend to predict the future shall be considered disorderly and will be liable to a fine of $300 or 3 months in jail."

1.10 Summary

In this chapter we began our introduction to predictive analysis starting with definitions of the subject, augmented by an overview of its application by industry, by line of business and by the questions the analysis tries to answer. We looked at the user types and the benefits of predictive analysis. Then we examined classes of predictive analysis, the algorithms used, and the process of predictive analysis. The chapter concluded with a review of the latest hot topics in predictive, the challenges and the main factors for success.

In the next chapter we look at the predictive analysis products in SAP, their functionality and inter-relationship.

This chapter introduces you to the various products in SAP that support predictive analysis and provides an overview of their functionality and their relationship to each other.

2 An Overview of the Predictive Analysis Products in SAP

SAP has made significant investments in the area of predictive analysis, from in-database data mining in SAP HANA, to a modern user interface for the definition, visualization and execution of predictive analysis processes. Many of the industry and line of business groups in SAP are investing in embedding predictive functionality into their business applications. These investments have resulted in SAP now being recognized by Forrester as a leader in big data predictive analysis in their report "The Forrester Wave™: Big Data, Predictive Analytics Solutions."

The predictive assets of SAP range from data sources, data preparation, predictive algorithms, developer tools, a predictive analysis workbench for the definition, execution, visualization and sharing of analyses; to industry and line of business applications with embedded predictive functionality. These assets, shown in Figure 2.1, support every stage of the predictive analysis process as was described in Section 1.7.

The data sources naturally include SAP HANA, which is the main data source for our new predictive products. The analysis can be in-database in SAP HANA whereby the data remains in the database and is not copied out to a separate process, or the data can be read from SAP HANA for merging with other non-HANA data, prior to analysis. The data can be read from Hadoop via SAP Data Services with the ability to load and read large volumes of data into and out of SAP HANA, from and to Hadoop. You can use SQL for a target data source, plus CSV and XLS. You can acquire data from SAP BusinessObjects universes that reside on the XI 3.x and BI 4.x platform.

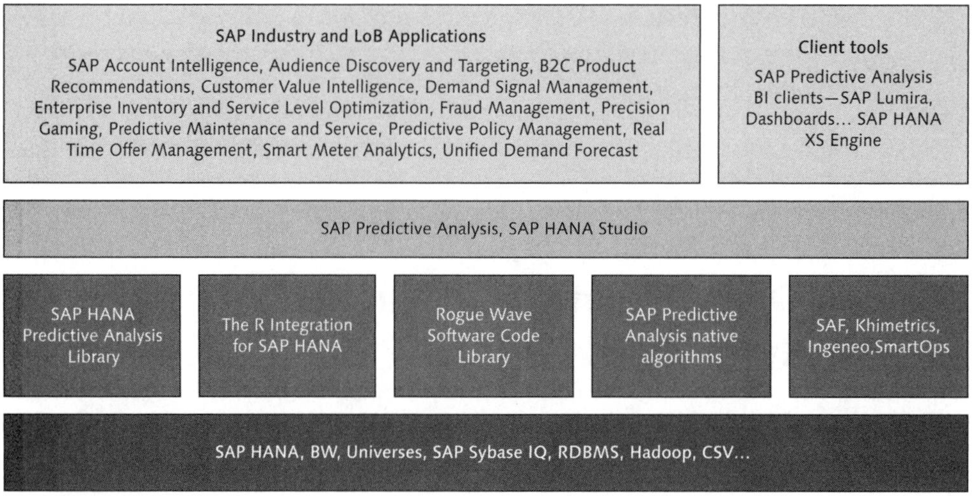

Figure 2.1 SAP Predictive Analysis Assets

At the heart of the predictive assets are the predictive analysis algorithms, and at their core is the Predictive Analysis Library (PAL) in SAP HANA. The PAL is a built-in C++ library to perform in-database data mining and statistical calculations, designed to provide excellent performance on large data sets. SAP HANA SQLScript is an extension of SQL that includes enhanced capabilities enabling developers to define complex application logic inside database procedures; however, it is difficult and in general impossible to define predictive analysis logic with procedures. For example, an application may need to perform a cluster analysis on a huge customer table. It is impossible to implement the analysis in a SQLScript procedure using even the simple K-Means algorithm. The PAL provides functions that can be called from within HANA SQLScript procedures to execute predictive analysis algorithms. The PAL is described in more detail in the next section and examples of the PAL are given throughout the book.

The R Integration for SAP HANA enables the use of the R open source environment in the context of SAP HANA. R is a software environment/programming language for statistical computing with over 3,500 add-on packages. It is widely used for a variety of statistical analysis such as linear and non-linear modeling, statistical tests, time series analyses, classification and clustering. It is said to contain more algorithms and packages than the combined total of SAS, SPSS, and Statistica. The R Integration for SAP HANA establishes a communication channel between HANA and R for the fast exchange of data. By providing the R-operator as a custom operator in the calcModel of the SAP HANA calculation engine, the user is able to embed R script within HANA SQLScript and submit the entire query to SAP HANA. The R Integration for SAP HANA is described in more detail in Section 2.2 and examples are given in later chapters of this book.

Within SAP HANA, there is Rogue Wave's IMSL numerical library of mathematical and statistical functions, which may be used as a basis to create further analytic functions for SAP. There are also some simple algorithms, created in and referred to as SAP Predictive Analysis Native Algorithms, which were created for when neither the PAL nor R is available (for example, when a user has a CSV file and no access to SAP HANA or R and wishes to perform very simple analyses). Finally, regarding predictive analysis algorithms, as SAP has made various company acquisitions, the algorithms developed by those companies have become part of the predictive assets of SAP specific to their domain. For example: SAF in the domain of demand forecasting; Khimetrics in the domain of campaign management and price optimization; Ingeneo in the domain of real-time offer management, now known by the acronym RTOM; and, more recently, SmartOps in the domain of inventory and service-level optimization.

The algorithms in the PAL and the R Integration for SAP HANA can be invoked from SAP Predictive Analysis (PA), a client tool for the definition, exploration, execution, and visualization of predictive analyses, and the subsequent dissemination of the results. It is fully integrated with SAP Lumira, for data acquisition, data manipulation and visualization capabilities, plus the sharing of the analysis. PA includes specific visualizations for predictive analysis, such as a decision tree viewer, a cluster analysis viewer and an interactive tag cloud for association analysis. PA also includes support for specific algorithms in R through user friendly dialogues for the less experienced user. Figure 2.2 shows the welcome screen of PA. We devote a whole chapter (Chapter 7) to PA, given its importance as the user interface to the PAL and R, and overall support for the predictive analysis process. We include many examples from PA throughout the book.

The business benefits of predictive analysis come when it is incorporated into business processes. To that end, SAP is embedding predictive in many of its industry and line of business applications. This is now a major activity within SAP and already specific business applications containing predictive functionality have been released, for example, SAP Audience Discovery & Targeting, SAP Account Intelligence, SAP Customer Value Intelligence, SAP B2C Product Recommendations, SAP Demand Signal Management, SAP Enterprise Inventory and Service Level Optimization, SAP Fraud Management, SAP Real Time Offer Management, SAP

Smart Meter Analytics, and SAP Unified Demand Forecast. We go into more detail on these applications in Chapter 6.

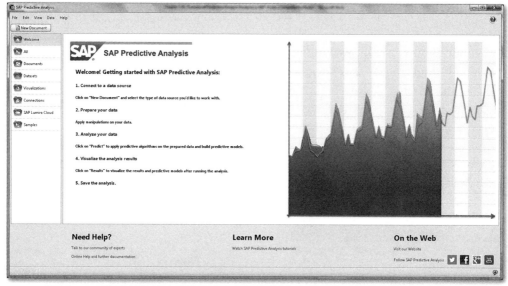

Figure 2.2 The Welcome Screen of PA

In Chapter 1 we made the key point that predictive analysis is not just about algorithms. Therefore, reflecting this idea within SAP, we have further assets supporting the overall predictive analysis process, as shown in Figure 2.3, which is an expansion of Figure 2.1.

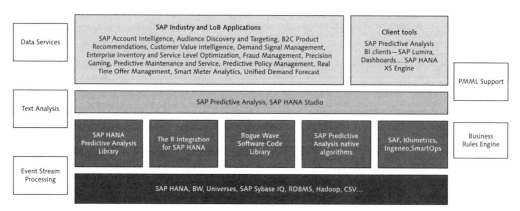

Figure 2.3 SAP Assets Supporting the Overall Predictive Analysis Process

In terms of input to the predictive analysis process, SAP Data Services delivers an enterprise-class solution for data integration, data quality management, text analytics, data profiling, and metadata management – prerequisites for data preparation priori to data analysis. SAP supports predictive analysis on unstructured sources through the combination of SAP Data Services and SAP HANA. SAP Data Services includes advanced text data processing capabilities to pre-process unstructured sources such as extract entities and facts, in order to create useful structured data that can be stored and analyzed using SAP HANA. This extends to pre-processing of unstructured sources via Hadoop. SAP HANA also supports native full text search with advanced text data processing capabilities. Data can be streamed into SAP HANA using SAP Sybase Event Stream Processor.

In terms of output from the predictive analysis process, as well as exporting the predicted results to a database table or file, SAP predictive products support the export of predictive models using the Predictive Modeling Markup Language (PMML), which is an industry standard for defining and sharing models between applications. In addition, SAP Business Rules in HANA may be used to augment model rules emanating from predictive models, which is an important check on the validity of business rules purely derived from predictive models.

Now that we have a broad understanding of the predictive assets in SAP and the products available, we will look at each of these elements in further detail. This chapter covers the four main ones:

▶ The SAP HANA Predictive Analysis Library

▶ The R Integration for SAP HANA

▶ SAP Predictive Analysis

▶ SAP Business Applications with Predictive Analysis

2.1   The Predictive Analysis Library in SAP HANA

As indicated earlier in this chapter, the PAL is a collection of predictive analysis algorithms that execute in-database to provide excellent performance on large data sets. Importantly, the data is not extracted out of SAP HANA to a separate analysis server. The algorithms are called from within HANA SQLScript procedures and we will give a simple example shortly. They can be grouped together using the classes of applications as defined in Section 1.5, and as shown in Figure 2.4, which is the list of algorithms in SAP HANA SPS06.

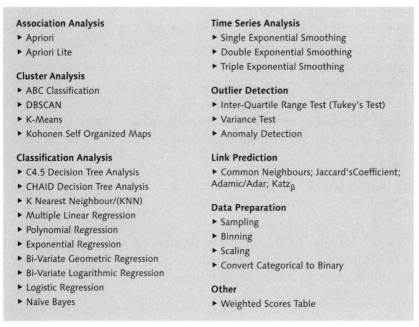

Association Analysis
▸ Apriori
▸ Apriori Lite

Cluster Analysis
▸ ABC Classification
▸ DBSCAN
▸ K-Means
▸ Kohonen Self Organized Maps

Classification Analysis
▸ C4.5 Decision Tree Analysis
▸ CHAID Decision Tree Analysis
▸ K Nearest Neighbour/(KNN)
▸ Multiple Linear Regression
▸ Polynomial Regression
▸ Exponential Regression
▸ Bi-Variate Geometric Regression
▸ Bi-Variate Logarithmic Regression
▸ Logistic Regression
▸ Naïve Bayes

Time Series Analysis
▸ Single Exponential Smoothing
▸ Double Exponential Smoothing
▸ Triple Exponential Smoothing

Outlier Detection
▸ Inter-Quartile Range Test (Tukey's Test)
▸ Variance Test
▸ Anomaly Detection

Link Prediction
▸ Common Neighbours; Jaccard'sCoefficient; Adamic/Adar; $Katz_\beta$

Data Preparation
▸ Sampling
▸ Binning
▸ Scaling
▸ Convert Categorical to Binary

Other
▸ Weighted Scores Table

Figure 2.4 The Predictive Analysis Algorithms in the PAL

In addition to the five standard groupings of association analysis, cluster analysis, classification analysis, time series analysis and outlier detection, we have link prediction, which is the start of a new group of simple algorithms for social network analysis. The other group of algorithms is for data preparation, an important step in the predictive analysis process. These algorithms support in-database processing along with the predictive analysis algorithms. Finally, there is the weighted scores table, which is more of a data manipulation algorithm used after an analysis for scoring records based on the weights and scores of the attributes of variables.

The PAL is essentially table-based in the sense that for each algorithm we have three tables – an input table containing the data for the analysis, a parameter or control table containing the various parameter settings for the algorithm, and an output table or tables for the output or results of the analysis.

The SQLScript containing the PAL first comprises code to generate the specific procedure; then the definition of the tables for the data input, parameter settings and results; and finally, the calling of the procedure. The procedures are defined in what is called the Application Function Library (AFL) schema. The PAL is one of several AFLs in SAP HANA. The technical details of AFLs are fully explained in Chapter 2 of the SAP HANA Predictive Analysis Library (PAL) Reference Manual, which is available at SAP Help: *http://help.sap.com/hana/SAP_HANA_Predictive_Analysis_Library_PAL_en.pdf.*

2.1.1 PAL Workflow and Business Example

As always, a simple example is the best way to understand the process. We will use linear regression to fit a straight line through a series of data points. Assume that we have the data as shown in Figure 2.5 in tabular and graphical form. In our example we have just two variables, the Period and the Value, and we wish to find the linear regression line of best fit using the model Value = A_0 + A_1 * Period, where A_0 and A_1 are the model parameters, respectively known as the intercept and slope of the line.

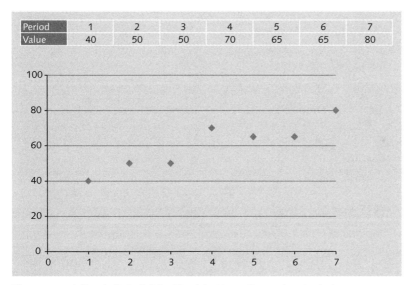

Period	1	2	3	4	5	6	7
Value	40	50	50	70	65	65	80

Figure 2.5 A Simple Data Set for Bivariate Linear Regression Analysis

In the PAL, the algorithm name is Multiple Linear Regression and the associated function name is LRREGRESSION. The main elements of the SQLScript are shown in Listing 2.1. The full code is available in the file SAP_HANA_PAL_Chapter_2_Introductory_Example_SQLScript on the SAP PRESS website.

```
-- Define the schema and the procedure generator
SET SCHEMA _SYS_AFL;
call SYSTEM.afl_wrapper_generator('palLR','AFLPAL','LRREGRESSION',PDA
TA);

-- Define the input data
CREATE COLUMN TABLE  DATA_TAB ( "ID" INT,"Value" DOUBLE,"Period"
DOUBLE);
INSERT INTO DATA_TAB VALUES (1,40,1);
INSERT INTO DATA_TAB VALUES (2,50,2);
INSERT INTO DATA_TAB VALUES (3,50,3);
INSERT INTO DATA_TAB VALUES (4,70,4);
INSERT INTO DATA_TAB VALUES (5,65,5);
INSERT INTO DATA_TAB VALUES (6,65,6);
INSERT INTO DATA_TAB VALUES (7,80,7);

-- Define the parameter or control table values
CREATE LOCAL TEMPORARY COLUMN TABLE #CONTROL_TAB ("Name" VARCHAR(100),
"intArgs" INT, "doubleArgs" DOUBLE,"strArgs" VARCHAR(100));
INSERT INTO #CONTROL_TAB VALUES ('THREAD_NUMBER',8,null,null);
INSERT INTO #CONTROL_TAB VALUES ('PMML_EXPORT',1,null,null);

-- Call the procedure and display the results
CALL palLR(DATA_TAB, "#CONTROL_TAB", RESULTS_TAB, FITTED_TAB,
SIGNIFICANCE_TAB, PAL_PMMLMODEL_TAB) with overview;
SELECT * FROM RESULTS_TAB;
SELECT * FROM FITTED_TAB;
SELECT * FROM SIGNIFICANCE_TAB;
```

Listing 2.1 Simple Example of the PAL Based on LRREGRESSION

The PAL LRREGRESSION data input table for our example comprises three columns, the first containing the item IDs or record names, and the second and third columns containing the numeric values for the variables Value and Period.

The parameter table specifies the number of threads to be used in the analysis, 8 in our example, plus if PMML output is required with the value set at 1.

The output tables comprise the model (RESULTS_TAB), the fitted data (FITTED_TAB), the significance of the model fit (SIGNIFICANCE_TAB), and the model PMML (PMMLMODEL_TAB), shown in Figure 2.6, Figure 2.7, Figure 2.8, and Figure 2.9 respectively.

The model result is shown in Figure 2.6, with the coefficients for the linear regression giving a model of Value = 36.4285 + 5.8929 * Period.

SELECT * FROM RESULTS_TAB		
	ID	Ai
1	0	36.4285...
2	1	5.89285...

Figure 2.6 The PAL LREGRESSION Model Coefficients

The fitted data is shown in Figure 2.7. This gives us the regression line as shown in the chart in Figure 2.10.

SELECT * FROM FITTED_TAB		
	ID	Fitted
1	1	42.3214...
2	2	48.2142...
3	3	54.1071...
4	4	60.0
5	5	65.8928...
6	6	71.7857...
7	7	77.6785...

Figure 2.7 The PAL LRREGRESSION Model Fitted Data

The significance of the model is shown in Figure 2.8 with the two model quality statistics of R Squared (R2) and the F Value (F). We go into the details of this in Chapter 12. However for now, suffice it to say that a value of R2 of 0.84549 is very significant, as is the F value of 27.3618. You can also see from Figure 2.10 that a linear line is a good fit of the data.

SELECT * FROM SIGNIFICANCE_TAB		
	NAME	VALUE
1	R2	0.84549...
2	F	27.3618...

Figure 2.8 The PAL LRREGRESSION Model Quality Measures

Finally, the PMML output for the linear regression model is shown in Figure 2.9. Note the model coefficients of the intercept 36.4286 and the slope of the line 5.89286.

```
<PMML version="4.0" xmlns="http://www.dmg.org/PMML-4_0"
xmlns:xsi="http://www.w3.org/2001/XMLSchema-instance" >
<Header copyright="SAP" >
<Application name="PAL" version="1.0" />
</Header>
<DataDictionary numberOfFields="2" >
<DataField name="Value" optype="continuous" dataType="double" />
<DataField name="Period" optype="continuous" dataType="double" />
</DataDictionary>
<RegressionModel modelName="Instance for regression"
functionName="regression" algorithmName="LinearRegression"
targetFieldName="Value" >
<MiningSchema>
<MiningField name="Value" usageType="predicted"/>
<MiningField name="Period" />
</MiningSchema>
<ModelExplanation>
<PredictiveModelQuality targetField="Value" dataUsage="training" r-
squared="0.845497" >
</PredictiveModelQuality>
</ModelExplanation>
<RegressionTable intercept="36.4286">
<NumericPredictor name="Period" exponent="1" coefficient="5.89286"/>
</RegressionTable>
</RegressionModel>
</PMML>
```

Figure 2.9 The PAL LREGRESSION PMML Output

We have found the line of best fit using the PAL LRREGRESSION function, which is shown in Figure 2.10, along with the regession line, the model parameters, and the model quality statistic R Squared.

The key point of the PAL is that the data does not leave SAP HANA. It is not extracted to a separate server for analysis and thus avoids slow data transfers. Plus, SAP HANA provides high calculation performance for large data volumes. There are some situations where the data volumes may not be high and where the performance for building a model is not critical, in which case SAP HANA provides the integration to the R open source statistical analysis language and programs. Furthermore, R is a very comprehensive source of predictive analysis algorithms, supporting the creation of user-defined algorithms by the open source community, and thus additionally provides the user of SAP HANA with an incredibly comprehensive range of predictive analyses, all definable and deployable from within SAP HANA.

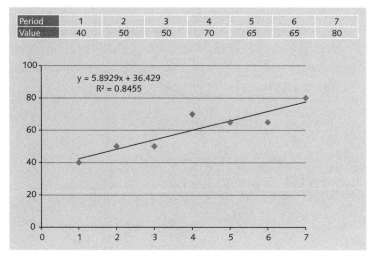

Period	1	2	3	4	5	6	7
Value	40	50	50	70	65	65	80

Figure 2.10   The Regression Line of Best Fit

2.2   The R Integration for SAP HANA

The R open source statistics language and its 3,500 plus packages or algorithms is the most popular predictive analysis tool with, according to the Rexer Analytics 2011 Data Mining Survey, close to half of all data miners (47%) using it. It is becoming more popular each year, according to the Rexer survey, in which R users reported as preferring it for being free, open source, and having a wide variety of algorithms. Many people also cited R's flexibility and the strength of the user community. By supporting the use of R from within SAP HANA, we offer the breadth of algorithms available to customers, along with the depth of specific algorithms from a performance perspective from the PAL.

The high level architecture for the predictive assets in SAP is shown in Figure 2.11. At the core is the SAP HANA Platform with the PAL and the R Integration, both native to SAP HANA. SAP HANA Studio provides a development environment, while business analysts and data scientists use the client tool SAP Predictive Analysis. In addition, there is the SAP Extended Application Services XS engine, and applications with embedded predictive content that work on top of SAP HANA. Then, of course, there are various data sources to bring data into SAP HANA.

R resides on a separate server, side by side with SAP HANA. Data stored in SAP HANA tables is passed to the R server and transformed into R data vectors or data frames, which is the data format used by R. R script code is embedded in SAP HANA SQLScript and is also passed over to R for processing on the R server. The results, in the form of R data vectors or data frames, are transferred back to SAP HANA, which then converts it back to an SAP HANA table. All the communication, data transfer and transformation tasks are performed by the SAP HANA Platform.

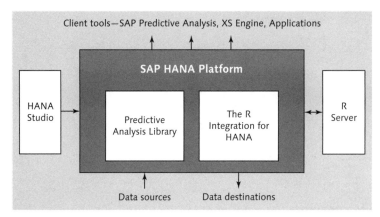

Figure 2.11 A High Level Architecture of the Predictive Assets in SAP

2.2.1 R Integration Worked Business Example

Just as when we introduced the PAL, a simple worked example of the R Integration for SAP HANA is the best way to provide an understanding of the whole process. The reference manual for the R Integration for SAP HANA can be found at: *https://help.sap.com/hana/hana_dev_r_emb_en.pdf*.

The SQLScript containing the R script first comprises code to generate the specific procedure; then the definition of the input tables and output tables; and finally the calling of the procedure. The main elements of the SQLScript are shown in Listing 2.2 and Listing 2.3. The full code is available in the file SAP_HANA_R_Chapter_2_Introductory_Example_SQLScript on the SAP PRESS website.

```
-- The R procedure within HANA SQLScript
CREATE PROCEDURE KMEANS_R_PROC(IN input1 KMEANS_DATA_T, IN parameters
KMEANS_CONTROL_T, OUT result KMEANS_RESASSIGN_T, OUT centers KMEANS_
CENTERS_T)

LANGUAGE RLANG AS
BEGIN
```

```
groupNumber <- parameters[parameters$NAME == 'GROUP_NUMBER', 'INTARGS']
if (is.na(groupNumber)) stop("Group Number is NULL")
iterMax <- parameters[parameters$NAME == 'MAX_ITERATION', 'INTARGS']
if (is.na(iterMax)) iterMax <- 100

kmeansResult <- kmeans(input1, groupNumber, iter.max=iterMax, nstart=5)
centersCoord <- kmeansResult$centers[kmeansResult$cluster,]
    V000_diff = input1$V000 - centersCoord[,'V000']
    V001_diff = input1$V001 - centersCoord[,'V001']
    centers <- as.data.frame(
    cbind(CENTER_ID=1:groupNumber,kmeansResult$centers))
    result <- data.frame(ID=input1$ID,
        CENTER_ASSIGN=kmeansResult$cluster,
        DISTANCE=sqrt(V000_diff * V000_diff + V001_diff * V001_diff)
)
END;
```
Listing 2.2 The R Script in SAP HANA – Part 1

In this example we perform a cluster analysis using the R kmeans algorithm with the data coming from the SAP HANA table KMEANS_DATA_T and another table containing the control parameters defined in the SAP HANA table KMEANS_CONTROL_T. The key line in the procedure is LANGUAGE RLANG AS, which means that between the BEGIN and END statements, the code is R script and that will be processed on the R server.

The rest of the procedure, as shown in Listing 2.3, comprises data input, the control parameters of the number of clusters, four in our example, and the maximum iterations for the algorithm, 20 in our example, and finally calling the procedure.

```
-- Data input for the cluster analysis
INSERT INTO KMEANS_DATA_TAB VALUES (0 , 0.5, 0.5);
INSERT INTO KMEANS_DATA_TAB VALUES (1 , 1.5, 0.5);
INSERT INTO KMEANS_DATA_TAB VALUES (2 , 1.5, 1.5);
INSERT INTO KMEANS_DATA_TAB VALUES (3 , 0.5, 1.5);
INSERT INTO KMEANS_DATA_TAB VALUES (4 , 1.1, 1.2);
INSERT INTO KMEANS_DATA_TAB VALUES (5 , 0.5, 15.5);
INSERT INTO KMEANS_DATA_TAB VALUES (6 , 1.5, 15.5);
INSERT INTO KMEANS_DATA_TAB VALUES (7 , 1.5, 16.5);
INSERT INTO KMEANS_DATA_TAB VALUES (8 , 0.5, 16.5);
INSERT INTO KMEANS_DATA_TAB VALUES (9 , 1.2, 16.1);
INSERT INTO KMEANS_DATA_TAB VALUES (10, 15.5, 15.5);
INSERT INTO KMEANS_DATA_TAB VALUES (11, 16.5, 15.5);
```

```
INSERT INTO KMEANS_DATA_TAB VALUES (12, 16.5, 16.5);
INSERT INTO KMEANS_DATA_TAB VALUES (13, 15.5, 16.5);
INSERT INTO KMEANS_DATA_TAB VALUES (14, 15.6, 16.2);
INSERT INTO KMEANS_DATA_TAB VALUES (15, 15.5, 0.5);
INSERT INTO KMEANS_DATA_TAB VALUES (16, 16.5, 0.5);
INSERT INTO KMEANS_DATA_TAB VALUES (17, 16.5, 1.5);
INSERT INTO KMEANS_DATA_TAB VALUES (18, 15.5, 1.5);
INSERT INTO KMEANS_DATA_TAB VALUES (19, 15.7, 1.6);

INSERT INTO KMEANS_CONTROL_TAB VALUES ('GROUP_NUMBER',4,null,null);
INSERT INTO KMEANS_CONTROL_TAB VALUES ('MAX_ITERATION',20,null,null);

-- Calling the R procedure
CALL KMEANS_R_PROC(KMEANS_DATA_TAB, KMEANS_CONTROL_TAB, KMEANS_
RESASSIGN_TAB, KMEANS_CENTERS_TAB) WITH OVERVIEW;
SELECT * FROM KMEANS_RESASSIGN_TAB;
```
Listing 2.3 The R Script in SAP HANA – Part 2

The results are returned to SAP HANA and shown in the table KMEANS_REAS-SIGN_TAB, as shown in Figure 2.12, with the input data for each record, its assigned cluster number and the distance from the individual record to its cluster center.

KMEANS_RESASSIGN_TAB.ID					
	ID	V000	V001	CENTER_ASSIGN	DISTANCE
1	0	0.5	0.5	3	0.74966...
2	1	1.5	0.5	3	0.72249...
3	2	1.5	1.5	3	0.66483...
4	3	0.5	1.5	3	0.69426...
5	4	1.1	1.2	3	0.17888...
6	5	0.5	15.5	4	0.74966...
7	6	1.5	15.5	4	0.69426...
8	7	1.5	16.5	4	0.66483...
9	8	0.5	16.5	4	0.72249...
10	9	1.2	16.1	4	0.17888...
11	10	15.5	15.5	2	0.68410...
12	11	16.5	15.5	2	0.79246...
13	12	16.5	16.5	2	0.74027...
14	13	15.5	16.5	2	0.62289...
15	14	15.6	16.2	2	0.35777...
16	15	15.5	0.5	1	0.76026...
17	16	16.5	0.5	1	0.83546...
18	17	16.5	1.5	1	0.67675...
19	18	15.5	1.5	1	0.58137...
20	19	15.7	1.6	1	0.53665...

Figure 2.12 The Results Table in SAP HANA from R KMeans

The R Integration for SAP HANA provides a huge amount of flexibility and comprehensiveness in terms of predictive analysis. It is easy to invoke from SAP HANA and simply requires the R code to be included along with the data and any parameters from the HANA tables.

Using the PAL requires knowledge of SQLScript, while using open source R requires knowledge of R. Not everyone has these skills or wishes to learn them in order to use and benefit from predictive analysis. This is where SAP Predictive Analysis (PA) comes in as a user interface for the business analyst and data scientist, for the definition of predictive analysis processes based on the PAL and the R Integration for SAP HANA.

2.3   SAP Predictive Analysis

SAP Predictive Analysis (PA) is a client tool for the definition and execution of predictive analysis processes, whether they are on the in-database PAL in SAP HANA or, for example, on predictive algorithms in R, or the analysis of non-HANA data sources such as SAP BusinessObjects Universes, XLS or CSV file. PA is fully integrated with SAP Lumira, for data acquisition, data manipulation and visualization capabilities, plus the sharing of the analysis. PA fully supports the entire predictive analysis process as defined in Section 1.7. We describe the product in detail in Chapter 7; however, for now, we give an introductory example.

When you invoke PA, you see the Welcome Screen as shown in Figure 2.2. We start this example by creating a NEW DOCUMENT, which then prompts for the data source as shown in Figure 2.13. PA keeps track of data sources that have been accessed recently.

You select the most recent data source, namely CUSTOMERS.xlxs, which is then displayed in preview form as shown in Figure 2.14.

An important point to note here is that if you had selected SAP HANA Online as the data source, then a dialogue would have opened to enable you to access tables in SAP HANA and then apply the in-database PAL algorithms plus a selection of R algorithms executed from SAP HANA. By selecting any other data source, you are performing an out-of-database analysis or, as it is referred to in PA, an in-process analysis.

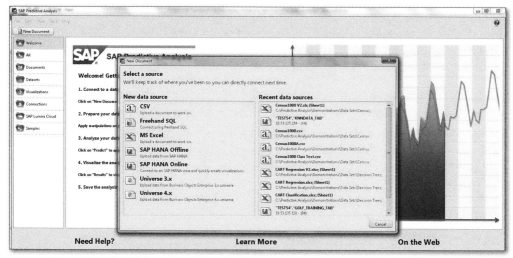

Figure 2.13 The Welcome Screen and Select a Data Source in PA

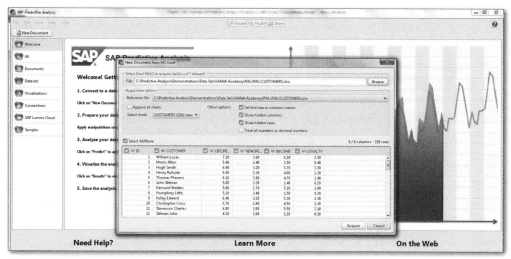

Figure 2.14 Data Source Preview in PA

In our example we have data for 150 records, which contain customer names and, for each customer, their lifetime spend, new or recent spend, income and a loyalty index. If you are happy with the preview of the data, you then acquire all the data and move to the screen as shown in Figure 2.15.

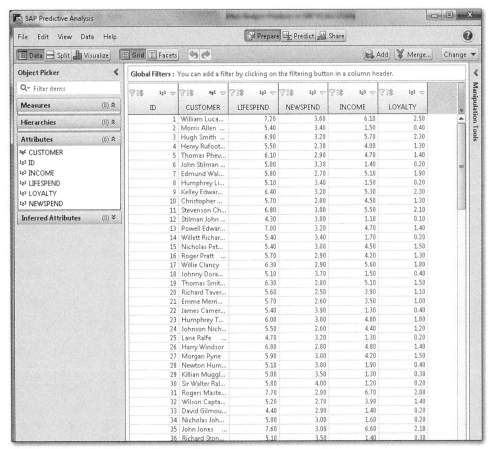

Figure 2.15 The Initial Prepare View of PA

You are now in the heart of PA, with the main views shown at the top of the screen of PREPARE, PREDICT, and SHARE, which, as the names suggest, are used to prepare the data prior to analysis, providing a comprehensive range of data views, manipulations and exploratory visualizations; the actual definition of the predictive analysis process, including all the predictive algorithms and specific data visualizations; and finally, the ability to share the analysis with others through, for example, publishing to SAP StreamWork or SAP Lumira Cloud.

In this simple example, the objective of our analysis is to see whether there are any clusters or groups of customers, based on their spending, income and loyalty, that we could then specifically target in a marketing campaign.

In the PREPARE view you can perform an initial data analysis or exploration. We can explore that data in a classic data grid view as shown in Figure 2.15, or in a facet view, where the data is shown for each column by distinct count, so that you can see the distibution of the values of each variable as shown in Figure 2.16.

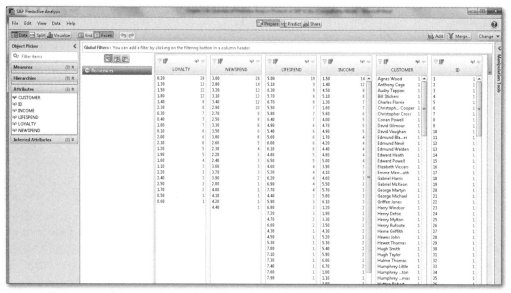

Figure 2.16 The Facet View in the Prepare View of PA

You can visualise the data in either the GRID or FACET view, and optionally split the view between table and chart. Figure 2.17 shows a visualization of the data in a bubble plot, with income on the x-axis, lifespend on the y-axis, and loyalty represented by the size of the bubble for each customer. This shows that there are two clear groups or segments in the data and perhaps more within the larger group. You can drill into the chart and filter or exclude data points for more detailed review of the data.

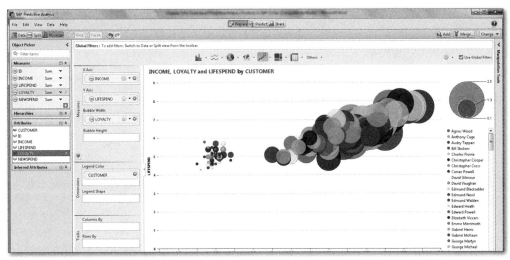

Figure 2.17 An Example Visualization in the Prepare View – Bubble Plot

After an initial data exploration, we move to the PREDICT view. Within PREDICT, there are two views – DESIGNER and RESULTS. If you run the data source component, you can then open the RESULTS view, where you can view the data in a statistical summary chart, a scatter matrix chart and a parallel coordinates chart. We show these in Figure 2.18, Figure 2.19, and Figure 2.20 respectively.

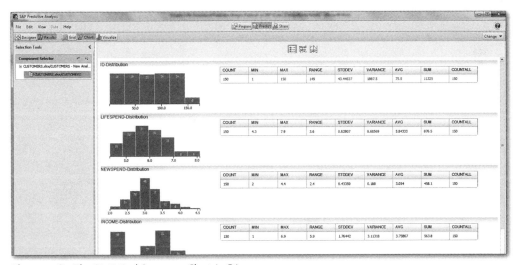

Figure 2.18 The Statistical Summary Chart in PA

The statistical summary chart shows a histogram for each numeric variable in the data set, plus summary statistics such as the average, variance, minimum and maximum values.

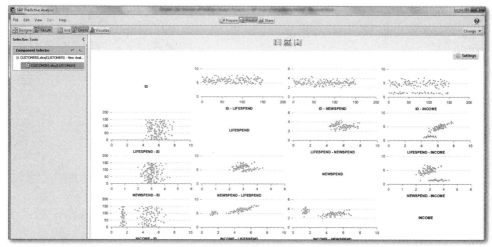

Figure 2.19 A Scatter Matrix Chart in PA

The scatter matrix chart shows pairwise scatter charts for every combination of numeric variables in the data set or any selected subset. You can see in Figure 2.19 that LIFESPEND and INCOME are positively correlated, that is, as one increases, so does the other. The INCOME and LOYALTY scatter plot highlights two strong clusters.

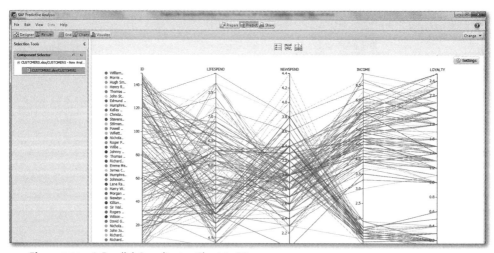

Figure 2.20 A Parallel Coordinates Chart in PA

The parallel coordinates chart draws a line for each record in the data set based on its value for each of the displayed numeric variables. You can use the chart to look for patterns in the data such as groupings and conversely outliers, with the latter occuring where a record follows a path very different from others. In the chart shown in Figure 2.20 there appear to be two groupings of the data and two records with very high LIFESPEND clearly different from the rest, which may be worth investigating before proceeding with any further analysis.

In the RESULTS view you can also select VISUALIZE and again a comprehensive chart library is available. An example is shown in Figure 2.21 of a box plot of the data, which will highlight any outliers in the data.

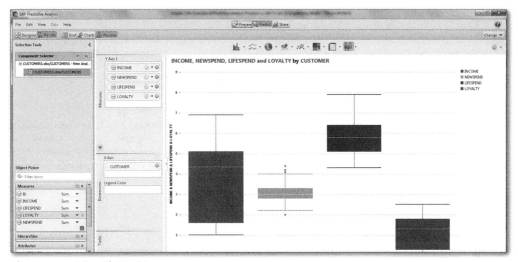

Figure 2.21 A Box Plot in PA

In the box plot shown in Figure 2.21, outliers are detected in the variable NEWS-PEND, which should be investigated further.

The DESIGNER VIEW within the PREDICT view is where you access and apply the predictive analysis algorithms to the data, plus perform any data preparation such as sampling or filtering of the data, save your models, and finally write the results of the analysis back to an SAP HANA table or to relational databases or to files such as CSV.

In this example, the objective of our analysis is to see whether there are any clusters or groups of customers, based on the customer data set, which we could specifically target in a marketing campaign. To do this, you can use the R component in PA for the K-Means clustering algorithm. PA includes a selection of R algorithms with specific dialogues created to simplify their use, for example, apriori for association analysis, multiple linear regression, exponential smoothing for time series analysis, and neural networks for classification analysis. Figure 2.22 shows the analysis and the connected components of the analysis representing the data flow through the analysis.

If the data had been sourced from SAP HANA Online, then the PAL algorithms would have been available for inclusion in the analysis.

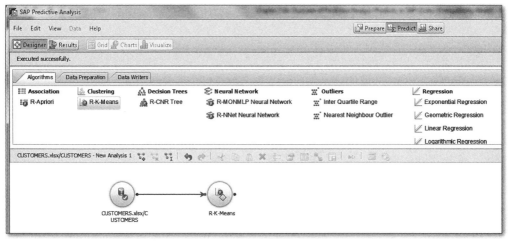

Figure 2.22 The Cluster Analysis in PA Using the R K-Means Algorithm

When you select the R K-Means component, you can define its properties as shown in Figure 2.23, where we have selected the variables for the analysis: Lifespend, Newspend, Income and Loyalty. They are refered to as the independent variables or columns. We have also set the Number of Clusters or Groups to be 5 in our example.

After you have run this analysis, you can switch to the Results view and from the Grid view see the assignment of each record to a cluster number as shown in Figure 2.24.

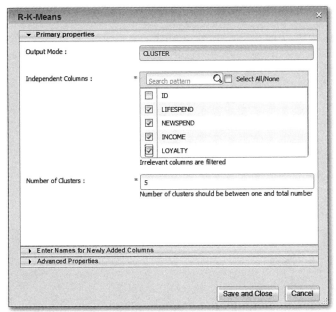

Figure 2.23 The R K-Means Component Dialogue in PA

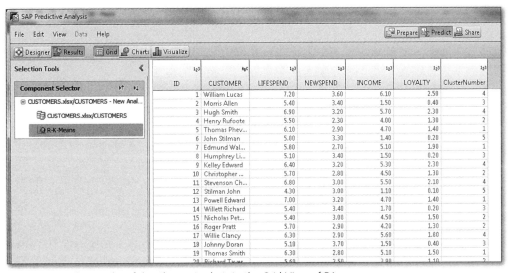

Figure 2.24 The Results of the Cluster Analysis in the Grid View of PA

You can also select the CHART option to see the CLUSTER VIEWER, as shown in Figure 2.25.

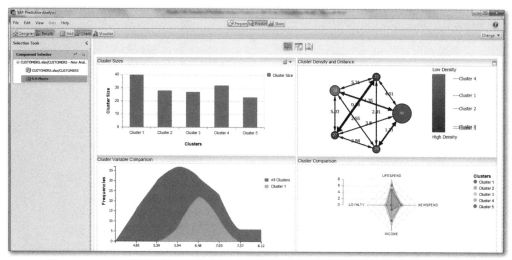

Figure 2.25 The Cluster Viewer in PA

The CLUSTER VIEWER comprises four charts for exploring the results of the analysis. It shows the size of each cluster, the between cluster centre distances and the cluster densities, and comparisons of each variable for each cluster compared to all the data. Cluster analysis is fully explored in Chapter 10.

Finally, in the analysis we might save all the input and results data to a database table and also perhaps filter the data for a specific cluster and write that data to a file in preparation for a marketing campaign. The components to do this are shown in Figure 2.26.

The final view in PA is SHARE, shown in Figure 2.27, where we can disseminate our analysis to others using SAP StreamWork, SAP Explorer, or SAP Lumira Cloud.

The Predictive Anaysis Library, the R Integration for SAP HANA, and SAP Predictive Analysis can all be used to develop and deploy predictive analysis in business applications. We see the wider use and major benefits of predictive analysis, when it is embedded in business processes. In the next section we give an overview of examples of this within SAP, with a more detailed look in Chapter 6.

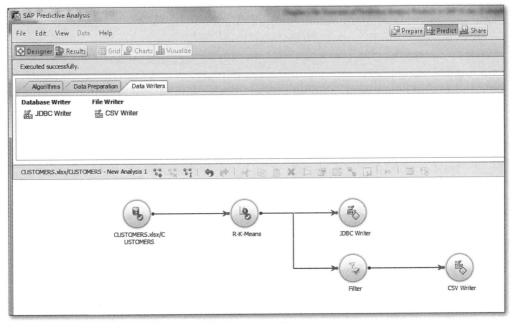

Figure 2.26 Writing the Results Data to a Table and to a File

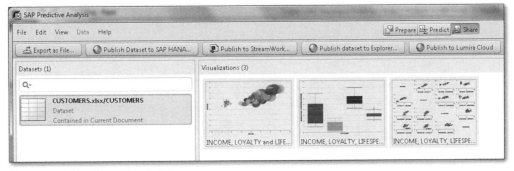

Figure 2.27 The Share View in PA

2.4   SAP Business Solutions with Predictive Analysis

If you accept the maxim that management is about the future, not the past – and most people do – then for business applications to be relevant, they need to contain some predictive elements. That's not to diminish the importance of historical reporting and analytics, but to see why predictive analysis is growing in relevance to decision making. Reflecting this trend is the ever increasing number of business applications in SAP either currently containing predictive content or planning to. Table 2.1 lists examples along with the associated predictive analysis solution.

SAP Solutions	Predictive Use
SAP Account Intelligence	Product recommendations, churn probability, customer lifetime value
SAP Affinity Insight	Association analysis by store/product hierarchies
SAP Audience Discovery and Targeting	Customer segmentation, product affinity scoring
SAP B2C Product Recommendations	Product cross-sell and up-sell opportunities
SAP BPC Predictive Forecasting	Revenue and expense forecasting
SAP Credit Insight	Predict credit risk and rating
SAP Customer Value Intelligence	Customer classification, churn probability, customer lifetime value
SAP Demand Signal Management	Improved forecasting and optimized replenishment planning
SAP Enterprise Inventory and Service Level Optimization	Inventory and service level optimization
SAP Fraud Management	Detecting the unusual and unexpected
SAP Labor Demand Planning	Forecasting resource requirements
SAP Precision Gaming	Converting free to paying users with real time offers
SAP Predictive Maintenance and Service	Predictive maintenance
SAP Pricing Simulation	Pricing simulation
SAP Real Time Offer Management	Real time offer management
SAP Sales Intelligence	Sales forecasting
SAP Smart Meter Analytics	Demand planning and performance benchmarking
SAP Unified Demand Forecast	Demand forecasting

Table 2.1 SAP Business Solutions with Predictive Content

We will review some of these solutions in more detail in Chapter 6; however, by way of introduction, we briefly look at two here. First, at a group of business solutions that come under the umbrella of SAP Customer Engagement Intelligence (CEI), namely SAP Account Intelligence, SAP Audience Discovery and Targeting, and SAP Customer Value Intelligence; second, the business solution SAP Smart Meter Analytics.

CEI is part of the new High Performance Applications (HPA) powered by SAP HANA. Predictive analysis is built into CEI to identify product recommendations for cross-sell and up-sell opportunities, to estimate customer buying propensity, customer segmentation for target marketing, and customer lifetime value analysis. The analysis is based on the Predictive Analysis Library, the R Integration for SAP HANA, and SAP Predictive Analysis.

Figure 2.28 shows a screen shot from SAP Customer Value Intelligence, which uses customer segmentation and product recommendations to create groups of customers and targeted sales initiatives.

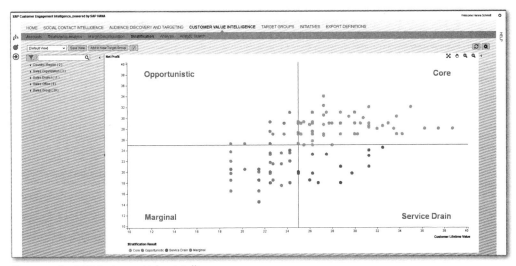

Figure 2.28 SAP Customer Value Intelligence

Figure 2.29 shows a screen shot from SAP Audience Discovery and Targeting, which provides high volume, real-time customer segmentation to identify the right audience by segmenting huge volumes of data using interactive visualizations and predictive analysis.

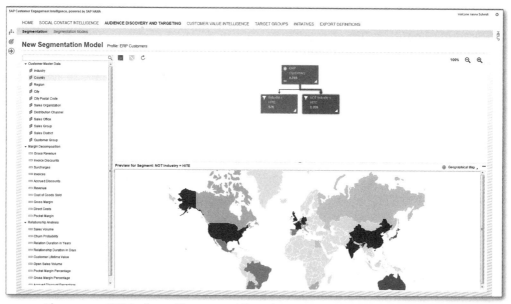

Figure 2.29 SAP Audience Discovery and Targeting

SAP Smart Meter Analytics (SMA) is an application built on the SAP HANA platform that enables utility companies to turn massive volumes of smart meter data into powerful insights and actions, by understanding consumption behavior and consumption patterns. SMA segments customers based on their consumption behavior and general master data. It also enables energy efficiency benchmarking for peer group comparisons and to identify any outliers in terms of energy consumption for further investigation.

Figure 2.30 shows how customer energy usage can be analyzed at any level of granularity, aggregation, or dimension.

Figure 2.31 shows how advanced customer segmentation can be performed enabling the precise segmentation of customers based on their consumption patterns.

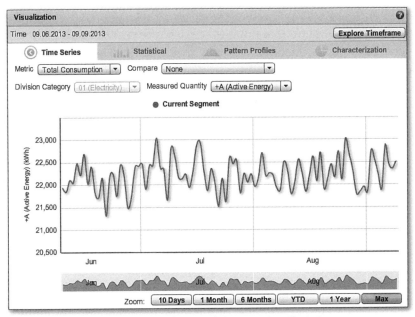

Figure 2.30 SAP Smart Meter Analytics and Consumption Clustering

ID	+A (Active Energy) (%)	Daily profiles (%)	Profile Shape
● 1	87 %	83 %	
● 3	13 %	17 %	
● 6	0 %	0 %	
● 7	0 %	0 %	
● 8	0 %	0 %	

Figure 2.31 SAP Smart Meter Analytics – Benchmarking Using Regression Analysis

These applications and others are more fully described in Chapter 6.

2.5 Summary

In this chapter we introduced the various products in SAP that support predictive analysis and provided an overview of their functionality and their relationship to each other within the overall context of the predictive assets in SAP. We started with the in-database predictive algorithms of the Predictive Analysis Library (PAL) in SAP HANA, then introduced the R Integration for SAP HANA, showing worked examples of both. We then described the new SAP Predictive Analysis (PA) product, again through a worked example, as this is the best way to get an understanding of any product's functionality. Finally, we briefly reviewed the new business applications being created in SAP that contain predictive content and briefly focused on two, SAP Customer Engagement Intelligence and SAP Smart Meter Analytics.

In the next part, Predictive Analysis Applied, we will review algorithm selection, data mining, data exploration, and the SAP applications that support predictive analysis. In the next chapter we look at the first stages of any predictive analysis, namely, initial data exploration in conjunction with the overall topic of data preparation.

PART II
Predictive Analysis Applied

This chapter covers the important topic of initial data exploration in conjunction with the overall topic of data preparation for predictive analysis.

3   Initial Data Exploration

An initial exploration of the data to be used in an analysis is one of the most important steps in predictive analysis. The quality of any analysis is directly related to the quality of the input data. The old adage of garbage in, garbage out applies as much today as at any time, in fact perhaps more, given the huge amounts of data available for analysis. There is the danger that we just collect everything we can, then throw some algorithms at it, and hope that our predictive model will sort out everything and provide some useful predictions. The hardest part of predictive analysis is trying to identify what data might be useful, then finding out where it might be available, and then reviewing it, understanding it, and validating it. If the key variable that affects an outcome is not identified and therefore not incorporated into our analysis, our analysis is going to be poor and potentially spurious.

Dr. Chris Chatfield, an eminent statistician and author, states in his book *Problem Solving: A Statistician's Guide*:

> *Initial Data Analysis is an essential part of nearly every analysis... and I strongly encourage its more systematic and thorough use.*

As an aside, his book is unique in that it discusses how to solve problems using statistical analysis, but is not just another statistics textbook. The phrases Initial Data Analysis, Initial Data Exploration, and Exploratory Data Analysis are all interchangeable. We will use the phrase Initial Data Exploration (IDE), to emphasize the role of exploring the data, prior to analysis.

Chatfield then defines the various parts of initial data exploration in terms of:

▶ Reviewing the structure of the data. How many variables? How many records? What are the types of data: numeric, text, binary, etc.? As we saw in Section 1.5, the structure of the data affects the type of analysis that we can perform.

▶ The quality of the data. This is of paramount importance. An understanding of how the data was collected is required.

▶ A key aspect of data quality is the identification and handling of any data errors, outliers and missing values.

▶ Using descriptive statistics to summarize and get a feel for the data, for example, averages, variances, maximum and minimum values, the distribution of the data.

▶ Data visualization. They say a picture is worth a thousand words and we all prefer to view a chart rather than a table of data. From standard charts, such as bar, pie, line and scatter, to box plots, scatter plot matrices and parallel coordinate charts, the visualization needs to be as interactive as possible to support true exploration.

▶ Modifying the data, for example, transforming variables, binning data, forming new variables, and estimating missing observations.

John Tukey was an American mathematician and who has been described as the father of modern exploratory data analysis and data visualization. He is credited with inventing the box plot, first published in his book, *Exploratory Data Analysis*.

The book contains many excellent passages. Here is one that stands out:

> To learn about data analysis, it is right that each of us try many things that do not work — that we tackle more problems than we make expert analyses of. We often learn less from an expertly done analysis than from one where, by not trying something, we missed an opportunity to learn more.

This may be counter-intuitive, given that we all tend to operate under pressure to get results and to complete things. Why would we do things that might not work? However, by trying different approaches, we may uncover some unique approaches and opportunities. It is one of the reasons that teams conducting predictive projects are often more successful when they are multidisciplinary and not just algorithm experts.

In the rest of this chapter we discuss the various data types used in predictive analysis as they generally define the types of analysis that we can conduct. We then present a major section on data visualization for data exploration. This is where the merging of SAP Lumira and SAP Predictive Analysis completed the total picture for predictive with data access, exploration, visualization, analysis and collaboration, all in the one product. The remaining sections of this chapter are concerned with data preparation: specifically, sampling, scaling and binning of data. We conclude with a section on outliers, as they are often identified during initial data exploration and it is important to discuss how we treat them. Throughout the chapter, examples are given from both the PAL and PA.

3.1 Data Types

There are two main types of data: qualitative and quantitative. Qualitative data is expressed by means of a natural language description, as opposed to in terms of numbers. In statistics, it is often used interchangeably with the term categorical data. Examples are your favorite color is blue, height is tall, your blood type, and your gender. The data values are non-numeric categories. The categories may have a structure to them. When there is no natural ordering of the categories, we call these nominal categories. Examples might be gender, race, religion, or sport. When the categories can be ordered, they are called ordinal variables, for example, small, medium, and large. Note that the distance between these categories is not measurable or quantifiable.

Quantitative data is a numerical measurement expressed in terms of numbers rather than by means of a natural language description. However, not all numbers are continuous and measurable, for example, post codes and tax codes are numbers, but not something that we can add or subtract. A quantitative variable can be either discrete, such as the number of students receiving an "A" in a class, or continuous, such as salary, weight, height; these are equivalent to integer and continuous respectively.

Within these two main data types there can be binary variables, either categorical, such as yes or no; stay or leave; constant or improved; or numeric, for example, 0 or 1. There is also the specific data type of date, which can be expressed in various date formats or as a numeric value. Qualitative variables are also referred to as categorical, text or string variables. Quantitative variables are also referred to as numeric.

For each variable in an analysis, it is important to know its type. For example, a linear regression model cannot directly predict non-numeric values, some decision tree models require the target variable to be non-numeric, logistic regression is analogous to linear regression but can take a categorical target field as well as a numeric one. Some statistical tests are sensitive to the type of data available, so it is necessary to identify the data types that you have before choosing a test.

In the PAL, the data types reflect database types. For categorical variables, we have the string or varchar data type, and for numeric variables, we have integer and double. In PA, the data types support those of the PAL, plus a date data type. PA also supports converting data types as appropriate and reformatting date fields. Figure 3.1 shows an example in PA, based on the CUSTOMERS.xlxs, as described in Chapter 2.

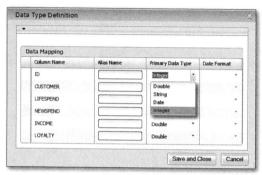

Figure 3.1 Data Type Definition in PA

Where an algorithm accepts only numeric data (for example K-Means only works on numeric data), if the input data is categorical, it can be converted to numeric using the CONV2BINARYVECTOR function in the PAL. A simple example will help to explain the conversion.

Suppose we have a table of data as shown in Table 3.1.

ID	Fruit	Vegetable
1	Apple	Peas
2	Banana	Beans
3	Banana	Carrots
4	Apple	Peas
5	Banana	Carrots

Table 3.1 Table of Categorical Data

Then CONV2BINARYVECTOR will create new variables for every distinct value, for every categorical variable in the input table. Table 3.1 will be converted to Table 3.2. The numeric columns F1 and F2 are created for the categorical variable Fruit, while the numeric columns V1, V2 and V3 are created for the categorical variable Vegetable.

ID	Fruit	Vegetable	F1	F2	V1	V2	V3
1	Apple	Peas	1	0	1	0	0
2	Banana	Beans	0	1	0	1	0
3	Banana	Carrots	0	1	0	0	1
4	Apple	Peas	1	0	1	0	0
5	Banana	Carrots	0	1	0	0	1

Table 3.2 Table of Categorical Data Converted to Numeric

Converting categorical variables to numeric variables can also be performed in PA using the Formula component and an if clause such as IF ([Fruit] == 'Apple') THEN (1) ELSE (0).

Before concluding our discussion of data types, there are two other related topics. First, as well as creating numeric variables from categorical variables, there is a generic requirement to be able to construct new variables from existing variables. For example, the ratio of telephone calls over the weekend compared to during the week may be more useful in a model than using the two variables separately.

One final data type to consider is missing value. Missing values can arise in a data set for a variety of reasons, such as mistakes, a reluctance to provide confidential information in a survey, or the values may simply not be available. Data records containing missing values can be ignored; imputed, whereby they are replaced with substituted values perhaps from similar records; or interpolated from within the range of a discrete set of known data values. Such approaches and overall data quality validation are probably better done in SAP Data Services or other tools, prior to bringing the data into the PAL or PA. In the next section we describe and illustrate many of the visualizations and associated interactions that are available in PA for initial data exploration.

3.2   Data Visualization for Data Exploration

It is generally accepted that we get a better understanding of data through visual representation, rather than through lists or tables of data. Even a simple example, as shown in Figure 3.2, shows the power of data visualization over data lists or tables. The data represents phone calls made between eight people, with the time and date. Compare your analysis using the table, where it is hard to see any patterns, with that of the diagram, which clearly shows the call traffic and the most frequently called pairings and groups of callers.

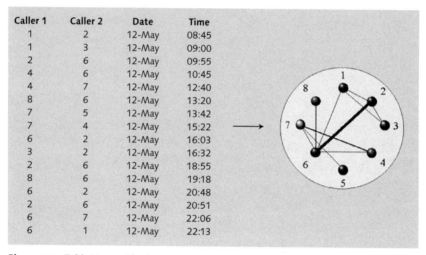

Caller 1	Caller 2	Date	Time
1	2	12-May	08:45
1	3	12-May	09:00
2	6	12-May	09:55
4	6	12-May	10:45
4	7	12-May	12:40
8	6	12-May	13:20
7	5	12-May	13:42
7	4	12-May	15:22
6	2	12-May	16:03
3	2	12-May	16:32
2	6	12-May	18:55
8	6	12-May	19:18
6	2	12-May	20:48
2	6	12-May	20:51
6	7	12-May	22:06
6	1	12-May	22:13

Figure 3.2   Table Versus Chart

We take for granted the existence of line charts, bar charts, pie charts and area charts, but someone had to have the original idea of inventing them. That someone was William Playfair, who in 1786 published the first versions of these charts in his seminal book titled *The Commercial and Political Atlas*. As always, the greatest inventions are the ones that are obvious – in hindsight. The book is available in reprint from Cambridge University Press.

Many of the visualizations are reproduced in the acclaimed book by Edward Tufte titled *The Visual Display of Quantitative Information*. Playfair was also wise enough to realize that charts can be designed to mislead:

As to the propriety and justness of representing sums of money, and time, by parts of space, tho' very readily agreed to by most men, yet few seem to comprehend that there may possibly be some deception in it, of which they are not aware ....

Tufte devotes a whole chapter in his book to graphical integrity, with many excellent illustrations. He also discusses one of his favorite topics: minimizing chart junk, in other words, removing unnecessary embellishments of charts. His book is well worth reading and includes in Chapter 1, "Graphical Excellence", on page 41, what he believes to be the best statistical chart ever drawn, which was created by Charles Minard in 1861 to show the devastating losses suffered in Napoleon's Russian campaign of 1812. By way of contrast, Tufte also includes in Chapter 5, "Chart Junk", on page 118, "the worst graphic ever to find its way into print."

We presented many of the data visualizations available in PA in Chapter 2. Figure 3.3 shows all the chart types available from the PREPARE view and VISUALIZE tab of PA.

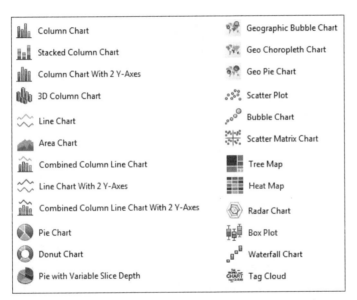

Figure 3.3 Chart Types in the Prepare View Visualization Tab of PA

The field selector in the Visualize tab includes support for trellis charts, also called lattice diagrams, and thus we can layout multidimensional data using various panels on the page. In addition, filters may be applied to subset the data and then, with the support of drill down in the chart, visual interaction enables full data exploration. To illustrate this, we have extended the Customer.xlsx data set to include a variable Region (North, South, East and West) plus a variable Churn Probability (High, Medium, Low), and then filtered the data to just view the North and South regions, as shown in Figure 3.4.

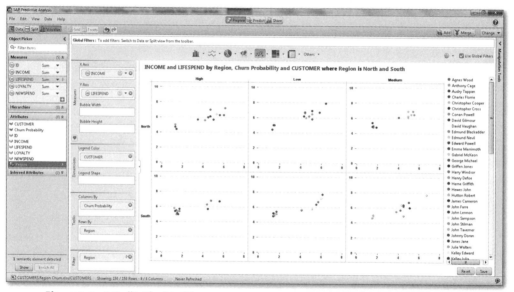

Figure 3.4 A Trellis Chart in PA

You can see from Figure 3.4 that there are broadly two clusters in the data. In the North region, the data is fairly similar across the three churn probabilities of High, Medium, and Low; in the Medium region, the clusters are tighter. In the South region, there appears to be an outlier in the second cluster in the Medium group, which we can drill into by selecting the cluster in the chart and highlighting the specific value as shown in Figure 3.5.

To help drive your imagination, here are examples of some of the other visualizations that can be created in PA. Figure 3.6 shows a line chart, with a moving average and forecast.

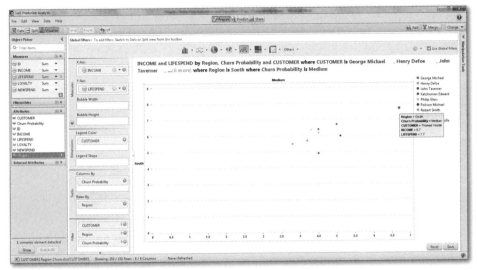

Figure 3.5 Drill Down into the Trellis Chart in PA

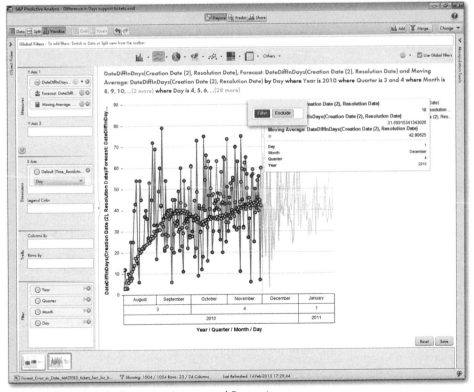

Figure 3.6 A Line Chart, Moving Average and Forecast

PA fully supports geographic visualizations such as the geographic bubble chart, the geographic choropleth chart, and the geographic pie chart, with an example of the latter shown in Figure 3.7.

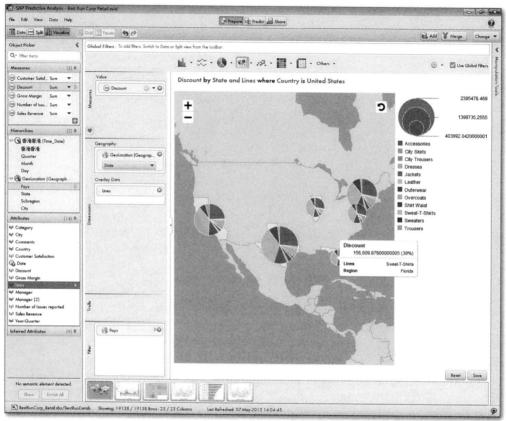

Figure 3.7 A Geographic Pie Chart in PA

Using a bar chart we can produce win loss charts as shown in Figure 3.8.

From the PREPARE view in PA, we can move to the PREDICT view, where we can continue with our initial data exploration. Within the PREDICT view there are two views: DESIGNER, for defining the predictive analysis process, and RESULTS, for viewing the results of the analysis. In the RESULTS view, we can view the data in a statistical summary chart, a scatter matrix chart, and a parallel coordinates chart, as shown in Chapter 2, Figures 2.18, 2.19, and 2.20 respectively.

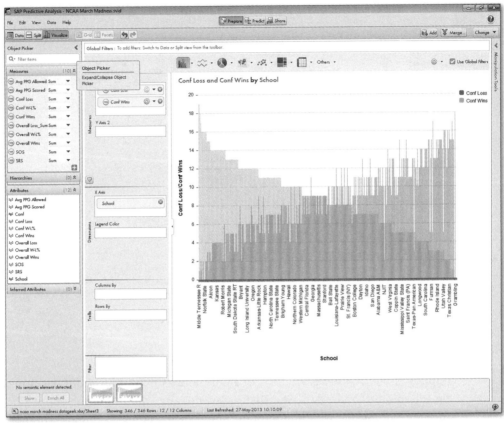

Figure 3.8 A Win Loss Chart in PA

Again, we can drill into our charts, so, for example, when using the parallel coordinates chart, we can select a group of records, as shown in Figure 3.9, where the selected records are highlighted, while the rest of the data set is shown in the background. We can drill right down to individual records.

So far we have discussed initial data exploration; however, of equal importance is the associated topic of data preparation, prior to an analysis. Therefore, in the next three sections of this chapter, we introduce the major topics of data preparation for predictive analysis: sampling, scaling, and binning.

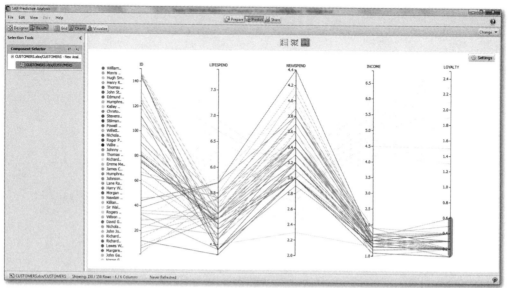

Figure 3.9 Drill Down into the Parallel Coordinates Chart in PA

3.3 Sampling

Sampling is the creation of a subset of all of the data from which inferences may be made about all of the data. Statisticians refer to all of the data as the population, hence the expression "sampling from the population." Sampling is done where the cost of obtaining all the data is unjustified. It may be that all the data cannot be obtained, for example, when an entity has to be changed or destroyed to obtain data. Sampling is done where we may want to initially explore the data using a variety of analyses before focusing in on a particular one, and looking at all of the data is initially unnecessary. An important qualification is that the sample is representative of all of the data.

Sampling is also used in a predictive analysis technique called cross-validation. In its simplest form we create a subset of the data to build or train a model, and then use the remaining data to test the model. The idea is that the test data is not used by the model during its creation, so that we can measure how good the model is on new or unseen data. A model may produce a good fit of the data that it is given, whereas on new data it performs poorly. This is referred to as model overfitting, where we have fitted an excellent model using the training data but have a poor model for the test data. We will discuss this topic further in the chapter on regression analysis, although it applies to all predictive models.

Sampling can be used for a simple train then test split of the data, known as holdout, through to k-fold cross-validation where the data set is divided into k subsets, and the holdout method is repeated k times. Each time, one of the k subsets is used as the test set and the other k-1 subsets are amalgamated to form a training set, from which the average error across all k trials is computed. A variant of this method is to randomly divide the data into a test and training set k different times. All these methods use sampling and are known to produce more robust models.

In the PAL there are eight sampling methods, invoked from the function called SAMPLING:

1. First N

2. Middle N

3. Last N

4. Every Nth

5. Simple random with replacement

6. Simple random without replacement

7. Systematic sampling

8. Stratified sampling

The first four are self-explanatory. The fifth method, simple random with replacement, is just random sampling of N or N% of all of the records, with replacement. In other words, the selected record is also returned back to all of the data for potentially further selection. In the sixth method, simple random without replacement, a record can only be selected once, as there is no replacement.

In method seven, random sampling is given a little structure. It is sometimes called interval sampling. A systematic sample is created by firstly determining the sampling interval (k), by dividing the number of units in the population by the desired sample size. For example, to select a sample of 100 from a population of 500, you would need a sampling interval of *500 ÷ 100 = 5*. Therefore, k is set to 5, so that you select one record out of every five records to end up with a total of 100 records in your sample. Then, given a random number between one and k, called the random start, this would be the first number included in your sample. Using the example above, you would randomly select a number between 1 and 5 from a table of random numbers. If you chose 4, the fourth unit in the data set would be the first unit included in your sample; if you chose 3, your sample would start with the third record. Then select every kth record, in this case every fifth, after that first number. For example, the sample might consist of the following units to make up a sample of 100: record 3 (the random start), 8, 13, 18, 23, 28, etc. A worked example in the PAL will help explain further.

Figure 3.10 shows the data in the table DATA_TAB. The 25 records comprise the population or all the data, from which we wish to select samples.

	EMPNO	GENDER	INCOME
	SELECT * FROM DATA_TAB		
1	1	male	4000.5
2	2	male	5000.7
3	3	female	5100.8
4	4	male	5400.9
5	5	female	5500.2
6	6	male	5540.4
7	7	male	4500.9
8	8	female	6000.8
9	9	male	7120.8
10	10	female	8120.9
11	11	female	7453.9
12	12	male	7643.8
13	13	male	6754.3
14	14	male	6759.9
15	15	male	9876.5
16	16	female	9873.2
17	17	male	9889.9
18	18	male	9910.4
19	19	male	7809.3
20	20	female	8705.7
21	21	male	8756.0
22	22	female	7843.2
23	23	male	8576.9
24	24	male	9560.9
25	25	female	8794.9

Figure 3.10 Input Data for the Example of Sampling

The main elements of the SQLScript are as shown in Listing 3.1 with the full code available in the file SAP_HANA_PAL_SAMPLING_SYSTEMATIC_Example_SQLScript on the SAP PRESS website.

```
-- The procedure generator

call SYSTEM.afl_wrapper_generator ('SAMPLING_TEST','AFLPAL','SAMPLING',
PDATA);

-- The Control Table parameters
```

```
INSERT INTO #CONTROL_TAB VALUES ('SAMPLING_METHOD',6,null,null);
INSERT INTO #CONTROL_TAB VALUES ('SAMPLING_SIZE',5,null,null);

-- Assume the data has been stored in table DATA_TAB as shown in Figure
3.10

-- Calling the procedure

CALL SAMPLING_TEST(DATA_TAB, "#CONTROL_TAB", RESULT_TAB) WITH OVERVIEW;

SELECT * FROM RESULT_TBL;
```
Listing 3.1 The PAL SQLScript for Systematic Sampling

We have used sampling method 6 in the code, as the numbering of the methods in the function starts from 0. Software developers have a habit of starting their numbering from 0, whereas most people start counting from the number 1. We selected a sampling size of 5. The output is shown in Figure 3.11, with 5 records, incrementing with a sampling interval of 5, derived from the calculation 25/5, starting randomly from record 2.

SELECT * FROM RESULT_TAB		
RESULT_EMPNO	RESULT_GENDER	RESULT_INCOME
2	male	5000.7
7	male	4500.9
12	male	7643.8
17	male	9889.9
22	female	7843.2

Figure 3.11 The Results Table from Systematic Sampling

If we rerun the code, we get the new output as shown in Figure 3.12.

SELECT * FROM RESULT_TAB		
RESULT_EMPNO	RESULT_GENDER	RESULT_INCOME
3	female	5100.8
8	female	6000.8
13	male	6754.3
18	male	9910.4
23	male	8576.9

Figure 3.12 The Results Table from Systematic Sampling when Rerun

This time the random start is 3. The sample interval is still 5, and the sample size is 5.

The final sampling method available in the PAL is stratified sampling. There may be attributes that divide up a data set or population into subpopulations or groups or strata. This should be accounted for when we select a sample from the population in order that we obtain a sample that is representative of the population. This is achieved by stratified sampling, which involves taking samples from each stratum or subgroup of a population. When we sample a population with several strata, we generally require that the proportion of each stratum in the sample be the same as in the population. Stratified sampling techniques are generally used when the population is heterogeneous, or dissimilar, where certain homogeneous, or similar, subpopulations or strata can be isolated. Simple random sampling is appropriate when the entire population from which the sample is taken is homogeneous.

PA also supports sampling, with the Sample component available in the DATA PREPA-RATION tab in the PREDICT view. The sampling can be in-database in SAP HANA or on non-SAP HANA data sources. Figure 3.13 shows the Sample component in PA on a SAP HANA data source.

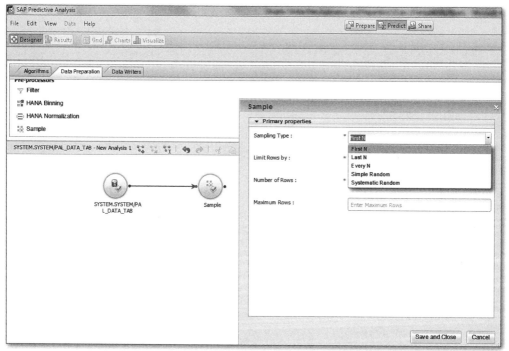

Figure 3.13 The Sample Component in PA

In the next section we present another important topic in the data preparation phase of predictive analysis, Scaling.

3.4   Scaling

Scaling of data is used prior to running a predictive algorithm when we wish to ensure that each variable in the model is given equal weight on input to the model by defining a common data scale for all the variables. For example, we may wish to scale all the input data to fall within a specified range, such as, -1.0 to 1.0, or 0.0 to 1.0. Another scaling method is to normalize or standardize the data using a z-score, whereby a variable is rescaled to have a mean of zero and a standard deviation of one. The calculation is defined as the mean of the variable subtracted from the value for each record, resulting in a mean of the standardized variable of zero, divided by the standard deviation, which results in a standard deviation of one. A value of 0.5 indicates that the value for that record is half a standard deviation above the mean, while a value of -2 indicates that a record has a value two standard deviations less than the mean.

Scaling or normalization is particularly useful for classification algorithms involving neural networks, or distance measurements such as nearest neighbor classification and clustering, where differently scaled data, for example some variables in millions and some in tens or hundreds, can bias the analysis. Thus there is a need for a common scale across the numeric variables.

The PAL supports three methods, called from the function SCALINGRANGE:

▶ Min-max normalization.

▶ Z-Score normalization

▶ Normalization by decimal scaling

For the following examples of scaling, assume that we have the table DATA_TAB in SAP HANA with the values as shown in Figure 3.14.

1. In general, to scale data in the range A to B, we use the formula

   $(B - A) * (X_i - Min\ X_i) / (Max\ X_i - Min\ X_i) + A$

2. For A = 0 and B = 1, this simplifies to

   $(X_i - Min\ X_i) / (Max\ X_i - Min\ X_i)$

SELECT * FROM DATA_TAB			
	ID	X1	X2
1	1	6.0	9.0
2	2	12.1	8.3
3	3	13.5	15.3
4	4	25.4	28.7
5	5	10.2	19.8
6	6	33.3	40.6
7	7	24.4	24.3
8	8	60.6	75.3
9	9	72.5	87.6
10	10	35.6	48.5

Figure 3.14 The Input Data Table for Scaling in the PAL

The main elements of the SQLScript are shown in Listing 3.2, with the full code available in the file SAP_HANA_PAL_SCALING_MIN_MAX_Example_SQLScript on the SAP PRESS website.

```
-- The procedure generator

call SYSTEM.afl_wrapper_generator ('SCALINGRANGE_TEST','AFLPAL','SCALIN
GRANGE',PDATA);

-- The Control Table parameters

INSERT INTO #CONTROL_TAB VALUES ('SCALING_METHOD',0,null,null);
INSERT INTO #CONTROL_TAB VALUES ('THREAD_NUMBER',2,null,null);
INSERT INTO #CONTROL_TAB VALUES ('NEW_MAX',null,1.0,null);
INSERT INTO #CONTROL_TAB VALUES ('NEW_MIN',null,0.0,null);

-- Assume the data has been stored in table DATA_TAB as shown in Figure
3.14

-- Calling the procedure

CALL SCALINGRANGE_TEST (DATA_TAB,"#CONTROL_TAB",RESULT_TAB) with
overview;
SELECT * FROM RESULT_TAB;
```
Listing 3.2 The PAL SQLScript for Scaling

In our first example, we will scale the data from 0 to 1, by setting the parameter NEW_MAX to 1 and NEW_MIN to 0. The result of the scaling is shown in Figure 3.15, with the maximum value of each variable set to 1, and the minimum value set to 0.

```
SELECT * FROM RESULT_TAB
```

	ID	X1_SCALED	X2_SCALED
1	1	0.0	0.0088272...
2	2	0.0917293...	0.0
3	3	0.1127819...	0.0882723...
4	4	0.2917293...	0.2572509...
5	5	0.0631578...	0.1450189...
6	6	0.4105263...	0.4073139...
7	7	0.2766917...	0.2017654...
8	8	0.8210526...	0.8448928...
9	9	1.0	1.0
10	10	0.4451127...	0.5069356...

Figure 3.15 The Results of Scaling in the PAL

The z-score normalization or scaling in the PAL is called by setting the SCAL-ING_METHOD control parameter to 1, and within that there are three options, specified by the Z_SCORE_METHOD parameter:

▸ 0: Mean and standard deviation

▸ 1: Mean and mean absolute deviation

▸ 2: Median and median absolute deviation

If we set the Z_SCORE_METHOD to 0, and the input table is as shown in Figure 3.14, the results are as shown in Figure 3.16, where the data has been scaled to have a mean of zero and standard deviation of 1.

```
SELECT * FROM RESULT_TAB
```

	ID	X1_SCALED	X2_SCALED
1	1	-1.381267...	-1.226155...
2	2	-1.020577...	-1.258253...
3	3	-0.937795...	-0.937270...
4	4	-0.234153...	-0.322817...
5	5	-1.132923...	-0.730924...
6	6	0.2329706...	0.2228539...
7	7	-0.293282...	-0.524578...
8	8	1.8472090...	1.8140132...
9	9	2.5508514...	2.3780264...
10	10	0.3689687...	0.5851063...

Figure 3.16 Z- Score Normalization in the PAL

Finally, if we set the SCALING_METHOD to 2, normalization by decimal scaling, the result is as shown in Figure 3.17. The method finds the largest number and then scales the data by moving the decimal point of the values, so that the maximum absolute value for each attribute is less than or equal to 1. In our worked example, for variable X1, the largest value is 72.5, so all the values are scaled by 10 power 2, so that they are all less than or equal to 1. If the maximum value had been 725.0, then the scaling factor would have been 10 power 3.

SELECT * FROM RESULT_TAB			
	ID	X1_SCALED	X2_SCALED
1	1	0.06	0.09
2	2	0.121	0.083
3	3	0.135	0.153
4	4	0.254	0.287
5	5	0.102	0.198
6	6	0.3329999...	0.406
7	7	0.244	0.243
8	8	0.606	0.753
9	9	0.725	0.8759999...
10	10	0.3560000...	0.485

Figure 3.17 Scaling Data in the PAL

PA also supports scaling with the Normalization component available in the Data Preparation tab in the PREDICT view. The scaling can be in-database in SAP HANA or on non-SAP HANA data sources. Figure 3.18 shows the Normalization component in PA on a SAP HANA data source using the PAL Normalization function.

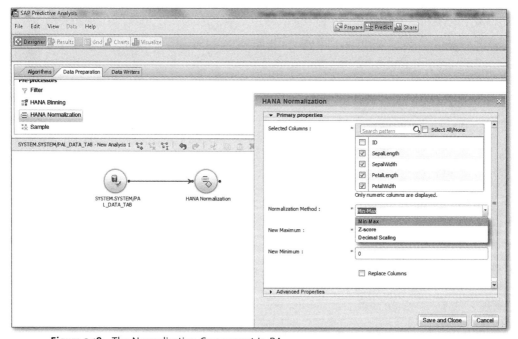

Figure 3.18 The Normalization Component in PA

In the next section we review the final data preparation function: Binning.

3.5 Binning

Binning of data is used prior to running certain predictive algorithms as a way of trying to reduce the complexity of the model. Complex models are not necessarily the best models, as they are less likely to be understood by management and consequently less likely to be used. Statisticians refer to the concept of parsimony, defined as the simplest plausible model with the fewest possible number of variables. In other words, keep it simple if you can. A good example of this is when constructing decision trees based on variables with many numeric values, each branch of the tree would have to consider each numeric value, which could lead to very large and complex decision trees that are impractical to implement in any decision making process. Binning of numeric data is sometimes referred to as the discretization of continuous data.

Binning may be used when there are very large amounts of data, so that it can be summarized or grouped for visualization. Constructing histograms for example requires data binning. An approach to visualizing thousands of data points involves binning the data first, for subsequent interactive drill down to the details.

Typically, data is binned or discretized into partitions or groups of k equal intervals, or k% of the total data, or into equal amounts or frequencies. The method involves calculating the range values for each bin, then assigning the records to that bin, and then determining the value for that bin, called smoothing.

The PAL function, BINNING, supports four methods:

1. Equal widths based on the number of bins
2. Equal widths based on the bin width
3. Equal number of records per bin
4. Mean/Standard Deviation bin boundaries

There are also three methods for smoothing:

1. Smoothing by bin means, whereby each value in a bin is replaced by the mean value of the bin.

2. Smoothing by bin medians, whereby each bin value is replaced by the bin median.

3. Smoothing by bin boundaries, whereby the minimum and maximum values in a given bin are identified as the bin boundaries. Each bin value is then replaced by its closest boundary value.

For the following example of binning, assume that we have the table DATA_TAB in SAP HANA with the values as shown in Figure 3.19.

	ID	TEMPERATURE
1	0	6.0
2	1	12.0
3	2	13.0
4	3	15.0
5	4	10.0
6	5	23.0
7	6	24.0
8	7	30.0
9	8	32.0
10	9	25.0
11	10	38.0

Figure 3.19 The Input Data for Binning in the PAL

The main elements of the SQLScript, shown in Listing 3.3 are as follows, with the full code available in the file SAP_HANA_PAL_BINNING_Example_SQLScript on the SAP PRESS web site.

```
-- The procedure generator

call SYSTEM.afl_wrapper_generator ('BINNING_TEST','AFLPAL','BINNING',PD
ATA);

-- The Control Table parameters

INSERT INTO #CONTROL_TAB VALUES ('BINNING_METHOD',0,null,null);
INSERT INTO #CONTROL_TAB VALUES ('SMOOTH_METHOD',0,null,null);
INSERT INTO #CONTROL_TAB VALUES ('BIN_NUMBER',4,null,null);

-- Assume the data has been stored in table DATA_TAB as shown in Figure
3.19

-- Calling the procedure
```

```
CALL BINNING_TEST(DATA_TAB, "#CONTROL_TAB", RESULT_TAB) with overview;
SELECT * FROM RESULT_TAB;
```
Listing 3.3 The PAL SQLScript for Binning

In our example, we have selected the first binning method, again starting the numbering from zero, of equal widths based on the number of bins, which we set to 4, and smoothing by bin means. The bin widths are (max – min) / k, which in our example becomes *(38 – 6) / 4 = 8*, so the bin ranges are *>=6 to <14; >=14 to <22; >=22 to <30; >=30 to <=38*. Therefore, the first bin contains the values 6, 12, 13 and 10, which has a mean of 10.25. The second bin contains just the value of 15. The third bin contains the values 23, 24 and 25, with a mean value of 24. The fourth and final bin, contains the values 30, 32 and 38, with a mean value of 33.33. This result is as shown in Figure 3.20.

	ID	BIN_NUMBER	PRE_RESULT
1	0	1	10.25
2	1	1	10.25
3	2	1	10.25
4	3	2	15.0
5	4	1	10.25
6	5	3	24.0
7	6	3	24.0
8	7	4	33.333333333...
9	8	4	33.333333333...
10	9	3	24.0
11	10	4	33.333333333...

Figure 3.20 The Results Table from Binning Data in the PAL

The question arises: which binning method should you choose? The answer partly resides in your response to the question: which method appeals? There is no best method in the sense of an optimal one. The best approach is to try different binning and smoothing methods and see what impact that has on the model. If the model is robust to changes in binning, the decision of which method to choose is not so important. If the model solution does vary significantly, the data needs to be looked at in detail to try and understand the reasons for the variations.

In the final section of this chapter, we look at the important topic of outlier detection within the context of initial data exploration.

3.6 Outliers

Outliers in data can significantly affect an algorithm's performance, the model's parameters, and the confidence of its predictions. An important part of initial data exploration is to look for outliers or unusual values in the data, to try and determine their cause, and to decide what to do about them. Outliers may be detected visually, for example, in scatter plots, although this doesn't easily scale for large data volumes. The most popular visualization for outlier detection is the Box Plot as shown in Figure 3.21. For each numeric variable, the "box" in the chart represents the upper and lower quartiles drawn using the y-axis scale, with the white line in the box representing the median value. The "fences" above and below the box represent a factor times the interquartile range, and then the dots outside the fences represent the outliers.

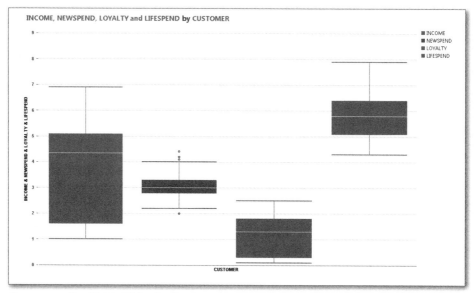

Figure 3.21 Box Plot in PA for Outlier Detection

The visual detection of outliers is limited in terms of data volume and dimensions. There are specific algorithms for outlier detection available in both the PAL and PA, namely the Variance Test, the Inter-Quartile Range Test, the K Nearest Neighbour Outlier Test, and Anomaly Detection using Cluster Analysis. The important topic of outlier analysis is discussed in detail in Chapter 8.

3.7   Summary

In this chapter we covered the important topics of initial data exploration and data preparation for predictive analysis. The quality of any analysis is directly related to the quality of the input data. The main focus of the chapter was how you can use data visualization for data exploration, with PA providing a rich set of capabilities, from a standard chart library through to specific data visualizations such as trellis charts, statistical summary charts, scatter plot matrices and parallel coordinate plots. We then discussed the associated topic of data preparation for analysis, and specifically sampling, scaling and binning. Finally, we introduced the concept of outliers, which, because of its importance in predictive analysis, has a whole chapter devoted to it: Chapter 8.

In the next chapter we address the main question that concerns most people with little knowledge or experience of predictive analysis: which algorithm should I use when?

In this chapter we address one of the more common questions for the less experienced user of predictive analysis: Of all the many algorithms available, which ones do I use when?

4   Which Algorithm When?

It is rather a daunting task for less experienced users to decide which algorithm they should use in an analysis. When you consider that R contains over 3,500 packages or algorithms, it can indeed be overwhelming. In this chapter we address the question of which algorithm to use when, by first describing the main factors to consider in selecting an algorithm. We then present a matrix of the class of problem by the type of data, and, in each cell of the matrix, we list the appropriate algorithms and model output. Finally, we look at how we measure the accuracy of an algorithm, and we conclude by producing a general set of rules to help you decide which algorithm to use when.

4.1   The Main Factors When Selecting an Algorithm

Two main factors drive this decision:

1. What do you want to do? For example: group the data, look for associations in the data, or predict a series of data values.

2. What data do you have and what are the attributes of that data? For example: numeric, categorical, Boolean, etc.

From this you may then apply an algorithm or selection of algorithms and the question becomes: which one gives the best fit? This is a key question in itself, as there can be several criteria, and in some cases, for example as in cluster analysis, best fit is a subjective measure because there is no best clustering in the sense of optimizing model parameters to predict a target variable. In addition to the question of which algorithm gives the best fit, there is the important consideration of how useful the derived model is in practice. Complexity does not necessarily equate to usefulness.

In terms of the first question, we can develop the list presented in Figure 1.1, and create a new diagram as shown in Table 4.1 of Task, Algorithm Category, and Example Algorithms.

Task	Algorithm Category	Example Algorithms
Summary statistics	Descriptive statistics	Mean, median, variance…
Outlier detection	Statistical tests	Variance test, IQR test, anomaly detection…
Preparation of the data for analysis	Data preparation	Sampling, scaling, binning…
Statistical inference	Sampling theory	T tests, F tests, ANOVA…
Relationships, cause and effect	Correlation and regression	Multiple linear regression, non-linear regression…
Clustering or grouping data	Cluster analysis	ABC Analysis, K-Means, Kohonen SOMs…
Time series forecasting	Time series analysis	Exponential smoothing, regression…
Association or affinity analysis	Association analysis	Apriori
Prediction, model building	Classification analysis	Decision trees, neural networks, regression…
Social network analysis	Network analysis	Jaccard's coefficient, common neighbors…
Optimization	Optimization	Linear and non-linear programming
Risk analysis, modelling	Simulation	Monte Carlo analysis

Table 4.1 Predictive Analysis Tasks, Algorithm Categories, and Examples

In Table 4.1 we see, for example, that if our task is to look for unusual values or outliers as identified as outlier detection, then we could use algorithms such as the Variance test and the Inter-Quartile Range test. If our task is to build a predictive model whereby we wish to predict a variable using the data of other variables (the prediction, model building task), such as in churn analysis or target marketing, then examples of groups of algorithms that we could use are decision trees, neural networks and regression models. Within these three groups, there are many algorithms that we will discuss shortly; however, at the individual algorithm level, the decision of which algorithm to use is primarily one of which algorithm best fits the data, in addition to considerations such as how easy it will be to deploy the results of the analysis into a business process.

In terms of the question, "What data do you have and what are its attributes?", we ask this question because some algorithms work only with numeric data, some also support categorical data, and others are specifically designed to work with categorical target data.

The list in Table 4.1 can itself be somewhat overwhelming for the less experienced user; however, fortunately, we can broadly say that there are five main classes of application in predictive analysis, which we describe below.

4.2   Classes of Applications and Algorithms

Algorithms in predictive analysis may be broadly classified into the five groups we presented in Section 1.5. As always, there are exceptions to any general or broad statement. However, this simple and generally valid classification helps with understanding which algorithm to use when. The five groups:

1. Association analysis, where we look for associations or affinities in the data.
2. Segmentation or cluster analysis, where we look to segment or group the data into similar clusters.
3. Classification analysis, where we wish to classify or predict new data based on a model built by an algorithm. We wish to predict a variable using the data of other variables that we believe affect the values of the variable that we are trying to predict. This is the largest group of algorithms in predictive analysis.
4. Time-series analysis, where we use data with an inherent periodicity to predict values for future time periods.
5. Outlier analysis, where we look for unusual values in the data.

In association analysis, the most well-known algorithm is Apriori. It is very easy to understand and we describe it in detail in Chapter 9. Other algorithms in this group are variations of Apriori that try to solve the potentially long processing times, as the data volumes for association analysis can be huge. Other association algorithms related to Apriori account for multiple purchases by the same entity over time, sometimes referred to as sequential analysis, and analyses within hierarchies such as product purchases by region or store.

In segmentation or cluster analysis, the most popular algorithm is K-Means. It is also a very simple algorithm and is described in detail in Chapter 10. As you may note, simplicity and popularity are positively correlated. Naturally, people tend to trust and use what they understand. Other algorithms in this group range from the very simple ABC Analysis through to the complex Kohonen Self Organizing Maps, both of which are described in Chapter 10.

Classification analysis has the largest group of algorithms, reflecting the importance of the topic. To many people, this is what predictive analysis is all about – using an algorithm to build a model of the relationship between a target or output or dependent variable, and the values of one or more input or independent variables, and then from that model, predict or score new data. This group of algorithms can be subdivided into regression algorithms, decision tree algorithms, neural network algorithms, and others. We devote a whole part of this book to classification analysis, specifically Part IV.

Regression analysis is a major topic in the field of statistical analysis. It is essentially the fitting of a model, either linear or non-linear, of the form Y is a function of X_1, $X_2...X_N$, where Y is the dependent variable and X_i are the independent variables, which minimizes the difference between the fitted data and the actual data. The most common regression algorithms are bivariate linear and non-linear regression, multiple linear regression, polynomial regression and logistic regression. The latter is specifically designed for Boolean dependent or target variables, and is therefore popular for churn analysis, predicting the probability of success or failure of a medical treatment, or predicting a customer's propensity to repay a loan or default. Regression analysis is covered in depth in Chapter 12.

Decision trees are another major group of algorithms within classification analysis. Figure 1.12 from the Karl Rexer 2011 survey showed that regression analysis and decision trees are the two most popular groups of predictive analysis algorithms. Decision trees recursively split the data, starting with the most divisive split of the input variable values compared to the target variable, and continuing until various stopping criteria are met. The result is a tree of decisions that produces rules to define the relationships between the input and target variables. The attraction of decision trees is that their output is in terms of rules that may be easy to understand and consequently to implement in business processes. Decision trees are covered in depth in Chapter 13.

Neural networks are designed to resemble a simplified model of the way the human brain processes information. They are complex and work by simulating a large number of interconnected simple processing units that resemble abstract versions of neurons, core components of the human nervous system. The processing units are arranged in layers typically with three parts: an input layer, with units representing the input variables; one or more hidden layers; and an output layer, with a unit or units representing the output variable. The units are connected with varying connection strengths or weights. Input data is presented to the first layer, and values are propagated from each neuron to every neuron in the next layer. Eventually, a result is delivered from the output layer. The network learns by examining individual records, generating a prediction for each record, and making adjustments to the weights whenever it makes an incorrect prediction. This process is repeated many times, and the network continues to improve its predictions until one or more of the stopping criteria have been met. PA supports two neural network algorithms, sourced from R, namely the Monmlp package, a multi-layer perceptron neural network and the Nnet package, a feed-forward neural network.

Further discussion on this topic is beyond the scope of this book; however, if you are keen to learn more, please see this link: *http://cran.r-project.org/*. Neural networks are complex and the basis of their solution is not as clear as that of, for example, a decision tree. They are sometimes referred to as "black box" models in that data goes in and results come out, but without any clear explanation. However, they can produce very good model fits for complex relationships.

The final group of algorithms is just a catch-all for other classification algorithms. Of specific interest to us is the K-Nearest Neighbor (KNN) algorithm, which is very simple and elegant in concept. It is a method for predicting or classifying objects based on their similarity or closeness to other objects in the training data, with the prediction being the average classification or value of those closest cases. KNN is among the simplest of all machine learning algorithms: an object is classified by a majority vote of its neighbors, with the object being assigned to the class most common amongst its K-Nearest Neighbors. The algorithm is discussed in detail in Chapter 14.

Our fourth group of algorithms covers the topic of time series analysis. This is another major group of algorithms given the relevance of time series forecasting to business applications. Many algorithms are designed for time series analysis. You could simply apply them all and choose the one with the best fit, for example, the minimum sum of squares of actual versus fitted. The data is generally either constant, has a trend, or is seasonal. You can therefore consider single, double, or triple exponential smoothing, for these three patterns respectively. For data that is stationary or has a trend, you could also use bivariate linear and non-linear regression. This topic is covered in detail in Chapter 15.

Our final group of algorithms is outlier analysis. Here we are looking for the unusual and probably the best known algorithm is the Inter-Quartile Range test, which is the basis of the Box Plot, as discussed in Section 3.6. The Variance test can also be used, based on the simple concept of unusual data being a long way from the average of the data. Anomaly Detection finds local outliers in a data set based on the clusters within the data set, and values which are a long way from the cluster centers are deemed to be outliers. This topic is covered in detail in Chapter 8.

Clearly knowledge of algorithms is beneficial, but it is not mandatory in order to benefit from predictive analysis. You could simply try all the algorithms in a group and see which provides the best fit and use that. Furthermore, you don't have to really understand an algorithm in depth to benefit from its use. This is a contentious point, of course, as data scientists will naturally propose the need for their domain expertise, and that is clearly beneficial. Perhaps an analogy is that while not many of us know how airplanes manage to fly, we still use them (although the analogy is not perfect, as our confidence to fly comes from observing its rate of success).

In this discussion it is important to remember that, first, a major challenge for predictive analysis is identifying data for analysis, getting it, checking it, and preparing it for analysis. Finding the very best model is good, but not the main challenge. Second, moving from analysis to implementation in business processes is the other big challenge.

In the next section we further explore which algorithm to use when, through relating the class of problem and algorithm group, with the attributes of the data which also determine the choice of algorithm, and then give examples of appropriate algorithms and their output.

4.3 Matrix of Application Tasks, Variable Types and Output

Table 4.2 presents, for each class of problem and algorithm group, the appropriate specific algorithms, depending on the input and output data types.

Class of Problem and Algorithm Group	Input or Independent Variables	Output or Target or Dependent Variable	Algorithms
Association	Categorical	Categorical	Apriori, Apriori Lite
Cluster	Numeric	N/A	K-Means, ABC Analysis, Kohonen SOMs
Classify— Regression	Numeric	Numeric	Multiple Linear & Non-Linear Regression
Classify— Regression	Numeric/ Categorical	Numeric/ Categorical	Logistic Regression
Classify—Decision Trees	Numeric/ Categorical	Numeric/ Categorical	C4.5, CHAID
Classify—Neural Networks	Numeric/ Categorical	Numeric/ Categorical	Neural Network
Classify—Other	Numeric	Numeric/ Categorical	K Nearest Neighbour
Time Series Analysis	Numeric	Numeric	Exponential Smoothing, Regression
Outlier Detection	Numeric	N/A	IQR, Variance Test, Anomaly Detection

Table 4.2 Class of Application, Variable Type and Algorithm

The main points to note are that for regression models, the data types do affect the choice of algorithm, and the restrictions that apply when we have categorical data for either the input or output variables. As we saw in Section 3.2, categorical data can be transposed to numeric data; however, when the underlying data is categorical, then algorithms that inherently support categorical data are preferable to those that do not. Also, continuous numeric data can be binned into categorical data, e.g., less than X, is low, greater than Y is high, otherwise medium. The N/A in the cluster analysis target variable cell reflects the fact that it does not have a target variable, which is sometimes referred to as undirected data mining or unsupervised learning.

The output from an algorithm can also affect our choice of which algorithm to use when. Table 4.3 shows the output from each class of problem and algorithm group.

Class of Problem and Algorithm Group	Algorithms	Output
Association	Apriori, Apriori Lite	Association rules with support, confidence and lift
Cluster	K-Means, ABC Analysis, Kohonen SOMs	Cluster groupings, cluster quality
Classify—Regression	Multiple Linear & Non-Linear Regression	Best fit regression equation
Classify—Regression	Logistic Regression	Best fit logistic curve, probabilities of outcomes
Classify—Decision Trees	C4.5, CHAID	Decision tree and rules with confidence level
Classify—Neural Networks	Neural Network	Black box model for prediction
Classify—Other	K- Nearest Neighbour	Classification of new data
Time Series Analysis	Exponential Smoothing, Regression	Best fit and projected values
Outlier Detection	IQR, Variance Test, Anomaly Detection	Detected outliers

Table 4.3   Class of Application, Algorithm, and Output

A major benefit and key reason for using decision trees, is that they output rules, which may then be embedded into business processes. Some data scientists dislike neural networks as they have a "black box" approach to analysis, in the sense that data is just input, the results are output. However, the reasons for the results are not clear. Other data scientists, especially those with an artificial intelligence (AI) background, like neural networks as they can give excellent results, even when the data has a complex structure. Statisticians tend to prefer regression models as the statistical theory supporting regression algorithms is extensive and includes methods to determine the confidence of predictions. All predictions should have an accompanying statement on the degree of confidence of the prediction.

Finally, of course, the choice of algorithm is also determined by how good they are at making predictions. We discuss this topic in the next section.

4.4   Which Algorithm Is the Best?

In order to decide which algorithm to use when, we could just apply all the appropriate algorithms to the data and choose the best one. It's a logical and sensible approach. It does however raise the question: What is best and how do we measure it? The answer to this question varies by algorithm group.

For association analysis, the choice of algorithms in the PAL is between Apriori and Apriori Lite, with the latter being a subset of the former, given that it is restricted to finding single pre and post rules. The choice has therefore more to do with the rule requirements and performance, as Apriori Lite will be faster than the generic Apriori but is restricted in terms of the rules extracted from the data.

For cluster analysis, the concept of what is best is difficult to define. For ABC Analysis, we cannot really say that different values of A, B or C are better or worse. It's up to the user to choose what is best for them, and there is no concept of a best model fit. The K-Means algorithm does not necessarily provide a better cluster analysis than Kohonen Self Organizing Maps (Kohonen SOM), and vice versa. K-Means is easier to understand; hence its popularity. However, although Kohonen SOMs are complex, they are more flexible in that the assignment of records to a cluster is less forced, in the sense that K-Means has to have K clusters, whereas Kohonen SOMs do not predetermine the number of clusters. There are cluster quality measures such as the Silhouette, as described in Chapter 10; however, these measures are more indicators of quality than definitive calculations. The best approach is to try both K-Means and Kohonen SOMs, with varying cluster numbers, to explore the solutions in order to decide which is the most appropriate for the application.

The concept of best algorithm varies within each subgroup of classification analysis. However, fundamentally there are two types of prediction from classification models – numeric or categorical – and naturally measures of best, vary within these two types. For numeric predictions, the most common measure is the sum of the square of actual minus fitted for each data point, also called the residual error. It can also be presented as the Mean Squared Error (MSE). There is the associated square root of the MSE, to bring the scale back to that of the original data (RMSE). Regression analysis, which produces numeric predictions, also uses statistical measures of goodness of fit, for example, R Squared, Analysis of Variance (ANOVA) and the F Value. Categorical predictions are generally evaluated using what is called classifier confusion matrices, which are essentially matrices of how often each category is correctly predicted and how often it is incorrectly predicted. Based on the matrix, there are then model quality measures, such as Sensitivity or True Positive Rate, and Specificity or True Negative Rate. For binary classification models, we can plot and compare model performance in gain and lift charts. All these model quality measures are discussed in detail in Part IV, Classification Analysis.

For time series analysis, the same measures of model quality apply as for numeric predictions in classification analysis, except that the analysis is over time periods.

For the outlier tests, the Variance test and Inter-Quartile Range (IQR) test are used to look for overall outliers in the data set. The Variance test is trivial and well-known but it is biased by the outliers themselves. Hence, the more popular IQR test, which uses the median and quartiles, and thus the measure to identify an outlier is not affected by the actual outliers. The Anomaly Detection algorithm is used to find local outliers in the data set. We discuss these algorithms in detail in Chapter 8.

Recent developments in predictive analysis have proposed using several algorithms for a particular class of problem and then using an average of their predictions, called ensemble modeling. It has been shown to lead to more robust models than those of individual algorithms. As such, the choice of which algorithm to use when becomes which group of algorithms to use when, and then amalgamating or ensembling the algorithm predictions. This is particularly relevant in decision tree analysis, where we may not wish to choose between, for example, the C4.5 and CHAID algorithms, but rather use them both independently and then ensembled, and compare their quality.

4.5   A Set of Rules for Which Algorithm When

From the above, we can construct as set of rules to help in the selection of the algorithms available in the PAL and in PA.

If you are looking for associations in the data, and if –

▶ All multiple item associations are wanted, then use Apriori.

▶ Only single pre and post item rules are wanted, then use Apriori Lite.

▶ If performance with Apriori is too slow, then try Apriori Lite sampling.

If you are looking for clusters or segments in the data, and if –

▶ The cluster sizes are user defined, then use ABC Analysis.

▶ The desired number of clusters is known, use K-Means.

▶ The number of clusters is unknown, use Kohonen SOMs.

If you are looking to classify data and the target variable is numeric and if there is only one independent numeric variable and if –

▶ A linear relationship is considered, use Bivariate Linear Regression.

  ▶ Else if –

  A non-linear relationship, use Bivariate Exponential or Geometric or Natural Logarithmic Regression

  ▶ If more than one independent numeric variable –

  Use Multiple Linear and Non-Linear Regression for linear and non-linear models, respectively.

If you are looking to classify data and the variables are categorical or a mixture of categorical and numeric, and if –

▶ Output of decision tree rules is desired, then use either C4.5 or CHAID or CNR Tree and choose the best fit.

▶ Output of the probability of an outcome is preferred, then use Logistic Regression.

▶ If model quality is of primary concern, and model understanding less so, then use Neural Networks and choose the best fit.

If you are looking to classify data and the target variable is numeric or categorical, and the input variables are numeric, and a simple approach is preferred, then use K Nearest Neighbor.

If you are looking to predict time series data, and if the data is –

▸ Constant or stationary, then use Single Exponential Smoothing.

▸ If a trend, then use Double Exponential Smoothing.

▸ If seasonal, then use Triple Exponential Smoothing.

You can also use bivariate linear and non-linear regression for stationary and trend data. You could use polynomial regressions for seasonal data, but there is a strong chance of overfitting the data, a topic discussed in Chapter 12.

If you are looking for outliers or unusual values, and if you are looking for global outliers, then use the Variance and IQR tests. If there are significant outliers, then the IQR test is preferable. If you are looking for local outliers, then try Anomaly Detection.

We should reemphasize that these rules are by no means definitive. They are guidelines for the less experienced user. Experienced users will review many potential algorithms and from experience, probably focus in on specific ones for specific applications.

4.6   Summary

In this chapter we addressed the question of which algorithm to use when, by first examining the main factors driving the decision, namely, what do you want to do and what data do you have? We then looked at the broad classes of tasks and applications, associating algorithms with each class. We reviewed the concept of what is best, in terms of algorithm fit, and finally presented a series of broad rules to guide the less experienced user in addressing the question of which algorithm to use when.

In the next chapter we look at many of the practical issues that arise when we apply these algorithms in predictive analysis, and where we need to be careful, as of course, predicting the future is not easy!

Following on from our introduction to predictive analysis and the products from SAP, we now look at some of the challenges of predictive analysis.

5   When Mining, Beware of Mines

Predictive analysis does not guarantee that we can successfully and consistently predict the future. In this chapter we examine the various myths surrounding predictive analysis, for example, that it is all about algorithms and no business understanding is required. We then discuss some of the major pitfalls awaiting the unwary data analyst, such as model overfitting and how to minimize its impact, correlation among the independent variables, and statistical correlation versus genuine cause and effect. To help explain these issues in a straightforward manner, simple examples will be given as demonstrations of the difficulties. We conclude the chapter on a more positive note by describing the critical factors for achieving success when undertaking predictive analysis.

5.1   Data Mining Heaven and Hell

This may be a bit of a contentious section heading, but it helps to highlight the contrasting situations of a predictive analysis project that will most likely fail versus one that has a far better chance of succeeding. Tom Khabaza, a founding member of the Clementine data mining product team, the developer of the first predictive workbench, and a highly experienced data miner has defined data mining hell as the statements of:

▸ "We have some data – just don't ask me where."

▸ "Now tell us all that we do not know."

It is a classic situation, not entirely restricted to predictive analysis. Organizations collect masses of data and not always with regard to how useful it might be, or, perhaps more importantly, to what decisions might be improved by collecting the data. Of course, there is a major need to collect data for reporting purposes; however, it sometimes feels like a matter of bragging rights: who can build the largest data store, who is analyzing the largest data sets. It's like an insurance policy; let's store everything because you never know when you might need it. There is, of course, some sense in this; however, it would be interesting if we also stored data with metadata defining its purpose and the possible decision making it is designed to support.

One of the hardest tasks in predictive analysis is identifying the variables that might affect an outcome and then finding data that provides information regarding those variables. Take churn analysis, for example: Why do customers leave? Is it because they found a better deal elsewhere? How do we measure that? We can include all the variables we wish in a model; however, if the ones that really affect the outcome are not included, we will not be able to build a very useful model.

Telling us all that we do not know brings back memories of the famous British comedy series "Yes, Prime Minister" and the legendary civil servant retort of Sir Humphrey:

> How can I tell you what you do not know Prime Minister, as I do not know what you do not know, and neither do you know what you do not know, so you cannot tell me what I should tell you, so I don't know!

It is also interesting how sometimes, when things are discovered, people say, "Oh, I knew that" – another example of the wonders of hindsight management. There is also the interesting conundrum that if you don't know what you are looking for, then how will you know when you have found it?

In contrast, Tom provides his view of data mining heaven as:

- Clear business objectives
- Defined success criteria
- Multi-disciplinary team
- Relevant and quality data
- An iterative process
- An action plan

Successful predictive analysis projects start with a clear definition of the objectives of the analysis. This may seem fairly obvious, but spending time really thinking about this, as opposed to rushing into a project, can pay dividends throughout a project. Part of the objective of an analysis is defining the criteria for success, preferably in quantitative terms. Having a multidisciplinary team helps to bring different perspectives to a project, be they data scientists, business analysts, market researchers, or experts from finance, operations, customer support or marketing, for example. Relevant and quality data is the main prerequisite of successful predictive analysis projects, and, as we saw in Chapter 3, the importance of initial data analysis and preparation can never be understated. The whole process of predictive analysis is an iterative one. Often having analyzed some data we realize we need more data, instigating further analysis, or, having identified an interesting relationship, we may then want to explore that in more detail. Finally, data mining heaven is when the results of the analysis are translated into action via an improved business process, and in Chapter 17, we give many examples of this in the description of customer applications.

In the next section we present five common myths of predictive analysis, which, if avoided, will lead to more successful projects.

5.2 Five Myths

Myths can gain credibility over time and can be propagated by biased parties, so it is important to recognize some of the major ones in the field of predictive analysis, and thereby avoid them. We will look at five of the most common misconceptions held about predictive analysis:

1. Predictive Analysis is all about algorithms.
2. Predictive Analysis is all about accuracy.
3. Predictive Analysis requires a data warehouse.
4. Predictive Analysis is all about vast quantities of data.
5. Predictive Analysis is done by predictive experts.

5.2.1 Myth No.1. Predictive Analysis is all about Algorithms

This myth comes mainly from people who love algorithms and usually live in an academic world. There is nothing wrong with that, and indeed we need these people, but we need to put algorithms in context. To say that all you need for predictive analysis is good algorithms is clearly wrong, and to equate advances in predictive with advances in algorithms tells only part of the story. We saw in

Figure 1.15 that, based on the Rexer Analytics Survey, only 20% of the predictive analysis process is devoted to generating models. Predictive analysis involves a lot of things: defining project goals, then the key part involving acquiring, understanding and preprocessing the data, then evaluating, presenting and deploying the results of analysis, as well as modeling. This myth is dangerous and can deter business analysts from trying to use predictive analysis, so it needs to be rejected. The risk of believing this myth is that in any real project no useful results would be produced. Of course, algorithms are important and the more they are understood, the better. Perhaps there is an analogy: we certainly need an engine in a car, but we can't leave out the steering wheel, the fuel, the brakes, etc.

5.2.2   Myth No. 2. Predictive Analysis is all about Accuracy

This myth is somewhat controversial in that we have discussed various measures of model quality and surely we want the best one. The myth really comes from the word "all." We need to be careful that we do not spend our time and resources continuously refining a model in order to get the very last level of precision, and ask ourselves if the costs of obtaining the very best model match the extra benefits. Some degree of predictive accuracy tells us that we have discovered an interesting pattern in the data, but the usefulness of that pattern does not depend on the accuracy of the model. Usefulness is influenced by many things including whether the model is understandable and deployable in a business process. Statisticians use the word "parsimony" to define the best model as the simplest plausible model with the fewest possible number of variables. A similar concept is Occam's Razor, a principle of parsimony, which states that among competing hypotheses, the hypothesis with the fewest assumptions should be selected. The risk of believing this myth is that predictive analysis results are of no practical use with the algorithms unusable by people with business problems to solve

5.2.3   Myth No. 3. Predictive Analysis Requires a Data Warehouse

This myth comes from the assertion that we need to get a data warehouse built before we can do any predictive analysis. Certainly, predictive analysis will benefit from well organized data that is relatively clean and easy to access. The data warehouse should also include in its design thoughts of potential analyses and the requisite data for that analysis. Data warehouses are generally designed for management reporting and not for data analysis. A lack of a data warehouse should not be a reason for postponing predictive analysis. Rather, it should be an opportunity to include requirements for data analysis in the design of the data warehouse.

5.2.4 Myth No. 4. Predictive Analysis is all about Vast Quantities of Data

We live in the age of Big Data and, clearly, predictive analysis has an important role in analyzing that data. Furthermore, the ever increasing performance of computers means that we can start analyzing data volumes that were previously impossible. However, we should not forget that predictive analysis is still very relevant for even very small volumes of data. Statistical analysis includes the important topic of statistical inference, where data volumes can be very small, yet the value of the analysis can be very high. Often, the overall data volumes may be very high, but the data needed for analysis is much lower. For example, in market basket analysis, we probably have millions of records available for analysis; however, the analysis may be relevant only within a product hierarchy or an individual store or a specific time period. If we are analyzing small businesses and their credit risks, we might start with a loans database of millions of loans, from which we extract just business loans, then small business loans, then small business loans defaulting. We have gone from millions of records to only hundreds or thousands. In churn analysis, the number of customers actually leaving is hopefully small; otherwise, it may be too late for the analysis! Out of the millions of customer records, the number of leavers is a small percent, and then in any analysis, we should balance the data for analysis between leavers and stayers, so that we do not bias or swamp the analysis with the attributes of stayers, when we are actually trying to find the attributes of leavers. So from millions of data records, we may actually analyze just thousands. This is not to say that large data volume data analysis is not relevant. Of course it is and it is becoming even more relevant. It's just to say not to forget that the analysis of small data volumes may also be beneficial.

5.2.5 Myth No. 5. Predictive Analysis is done by Predictive Experts

This is true, but it is not the only use case. It depends on what is meant by "done." Statisticians certainly do predictive analysis, as do operations researchers and data scientists. When a prospective purchaser is browsing a website and product recommendations are given based on their browsing history, interests, other purchases, etc., they are "doing" predictive analysis (well maybe "using" is a better word). When market researchers use a market segmentation product via a series of wizards, they are 'doing' predictive, although they are not predictive experts. The danger of this myth is that predictive expertise is seen as a prerequisite for doing predictive analysis, when the main expertise that is required is business domain expertise, if business benefits are to be derived. Of paramount importance is business knowledge. Predictive analysis is best performed by someone who has that business knowledge or, as a minimum, in combination with the analyst. A corollary of this is that a predictive analysis tool needs to also support business users. There's a nice phrase "Data miners need hard hats more than white coats" attributed to Tom Khabaza and amusingly shown in Figure 5.1. Data mining is more about insight and useful suggestions than about mathematical certainty.

Figure 5.1 Data Miners Need Hard Hats More Than White Coats

We have presented five myths of predictive analysis. We now present five pitfalls that should be avoided when performing predictive analysis. We use five as it's a convenient number, not that it is a magic number. There are naturally more than five myths and pitfalls, but we focus on the main ones.

5.3   Five Pitfalls

A pitfall is defined as an unapparent source of trouble or danger, so we should try to avoid them. Here are five pitfalls to avoid when using predictive analysis.

5.3.1   Pitfall No. 1: Throwing in Data without Thinking

Rational thinking would suggest that this is foolish; however, some data scientists argue that you should "throw in everything" and let a smart algorithm work out the important variables. This is heresy to most statisticians and operations researchers, as it is counter to the predictive analysis process that we discussed in Chapter 1. It is related to Myth No. 4, which was that predictive analysis is all about vast quantities of data. To be fair, some data scientists do passionately believe that they have the algorithms to sort out the noise from the signal, and that you should not reject any data by prejudging the model. However, people with a statistics and operations research background find this approach counterintuitive, dangerous, and just plain lazy, throwing in every data item you can think of, without thinking.

5.3.2   Pitfall No. 2: Lack of Business Knowledge

Business knowledge of the application area that is being analyzed is crucial to guide the predictive analysis process toward useful results and to understand and use those results once found. It follows that teams undertaking predictive projects need to be interdisciplinary and synergistically combine business knowledge with analysis knowledge. It's why the data mining hell of "Here is the data, go away and mine it and come back with the answers" does not work. The people with the business knowledge need to be involved at every stage of the predictive analysis process. Predictive analysis can be viewed by those with the problem as a threat to their integrity and position. Management may ask why they didn't think of the solution before, with hindsight management coming to fore once again. By working with the business executives with the business problem or opportunity, there is a much greater chance that the results of the analysis will find themselves implemented into a predictive process. SAP's consulting group, Performance and Insight Optimization (PIO), always involve the customer and work in parallel with those with the business knowledge of the application area when conducting predictive assignments.

5.3.3   Pitfall No. 3: Lack of Data Knowledge

Predictive analysis requires a lot of detailed questions about the data, for example, questions regarding its authenticity, its source, and the provider. There are questions of interpretation: What is it actually measuring? Has the data come from a sample or a survey? Was it unbiased? Friendly faces are more likely to be asked to fill out our surveys, but that becomes a survey of friendly people. Is the sentiment analysis just the analysis of the sample of complainers, rather than also the majority of supporters? The former tend to voice their concerns; the latter just expect the service and therefore see no need to say anything. Have we in fact just surveyed people with complaints? Clearly there are questions of quality: Are IDs unique? Can there be more than one record per customer? What does the code 99 mean? Sometimes this information is hard to come by. If the data comes from samples, are they biased? If the data is ordered and we sample the first N, we will have a very biased sample. Data knowledge is critical to the success of predictive analysis.

5.3.4   Pitfall No. 4: Erroneous Assumptions

Life is full of these. Even with a lot of data knowledge, we can be misled. Simple assumptions need checking, for example: no customer can hold both types of account, or no case will contain more than one event of this type, or only the following codes will be present, etc. This checking can be difficult, as even the data experts can be mistaken, especially regarding legacy and outsourced data. Assumptions regarding the data need to be checked and verified before depending upon them, by questioning the sources.

5.3.5   Pitfall No. 5: Disorganized Project

This final point is self-explanatory, so maybe we should leave it at that, other than to say that applying predictive analysis done in an ad hoc manner, with no clearly defined goals and no deployment plans, will most probably lead to unfocussed, inefficient processes, with poor and unusable results.

Examples are always better than paragraphs of explanation, so we will now demonstrate some of the practical difficulties of predictive analysis using some simple examples.

5.4   Further Challenges and Resolution

In this section we discuss and demonstrate four common difficulties encountered in predictive analysis:

1. Cause and effect. A good mathematical relationship between variables does not necessarily mean that there is a cause and effect relationship.

2. Lies dammed lies and statistics. A well-known phrase that we illustrate using four data sets that have identical simple statistical properties yet when plotted are clearly very different.

3. Model overfitting. We can sometimes produce an excellent model based on the data set that it is given, but which performs very poorly when it is used for predicting new data.

4. Correlation between the independent variables. Statisticians have a word for this – multicollinearity, which sounds very complex, but really it's the challenge of having highly correlated independent variables, so a model could equally choose either or some combination.

5.4.1 Cause and Effect

One of the key questions in predictive analysis is that when we find a good mathematical relationship between variables, does it follow that there is a casual relationship? There was a recent headline in the press: "If you speak English, you're more likely to have a heart attack." We know that the causal link is nonsense – well, we hope so! Translating mathematical relationships into cause and effect relationships is a major topic, and one we may be tempted to ignore if finding a relationship is particularly difficult and we are grateful to have at least found something. Then there is the opposite situation, where a mathematical relationship is dismissed, without further examination, such as the tobacco companies' dismissal of any link between smoking and cancer.

A famous example is shown in Figure 5.2, which shows on the x-axis the number of babies born in Sweden and on the y-axis the number of storks arriving in Sweden. You can see that there is a clear mathematical relationship, so should we conclude that storks deliver babies!

This topic is summarized well by Gerard E. Dallal, Chief, Biostatistics Unit at Tufts University, Boston, USA, who states:

Statistics alone can never prove causality, but it can show you where to look.

Note this further comment by Dr. Dallal:

A good statistician will point out that causality can be proven only by demonstrating a mechanism.

Figure 5.2 Storks and Babies

Regarding our English-speaking heart attack example, you can hear Professor Hans Rosling of TED and Gapminder fame, and Sir Michael Marmot, Professor of Epidemiology, University College London, discuss this example and more at this URL:

http://www.open.edu/openlearn/science-maths-technology/mathematics-and-statistics/statistics/the-joy-stats-meaningless-and-meaningful-correlations/

Professor Sir Michael Marmot makes the important point:

> *Correlations do not replace human thought. A good scientist should try as hard as they can to disprove it, break it down, and refute it. If it withstands all those efforts at demolishing it, then there may be something in the correlation.*

Note the "may be."

5.4.2 Lies, Damned Lies, and Statistics

This famous phrase is attributed to the 19th-century British Prime Minister Benjamin Disraeli:

> *There are three kinds of lies: lies, damned lies, and statistics.*

There is some debate as to who actually came up with the phrase and some recognize the author Mark Twain as the person who made it popular.

Related Reading

For a related and fun read, Darrel Huff wrote the book *How to Lie with Statistics* (first published in 1954), which has become one of the best-selling statistics books in history, with over one and a half million copies sold in the English-language edition. In Chapter 3 we referred to Edward Tufte's seminal book *The Visual Display of Quantitative Information* with its chapter on graphical integrity – another excellent book.

One of the most abused statistics is the comparison with the average, and the shocking revelation, for example, that 50% of our salesmen have below average performance! 50% of our retail outlets show below average sales revenue! Only 50% of our product profit margins are above average!

One of the best examples of the dangers of looking only at statistical measures is known as Anscombe's quartet. In 1973, the statistician Francis Anscombe demonstrated the importance of graphing data before analyzing it, and the effect of outliers on statistical properties. Anscombe's quartet comprises four data sets that have the same simple statistical properties but are clearly very different when graphed.

Each data set consists of two variables, X and Y, for eleven data points. The values for the four data sets are shown in Table 5.1.

Dataset 1		Dataset 2		Dataset 3		Dataset 4	
X	Y	X	Y	X	Y	X	Y
10	8.04	10	9.14	10	7.46	8	6.58
8	6.95	8	8.14	8	6.77	8	5.76
13	7.58	13	8.74	13	12.74	8	7.71
9	8.81	9	8.77	9	7.11	8	8.84
11	8.33	11	9.26	11	7.81	8	8.47
14	9.96	14	8.10	14	8.84	8	7.04
6	7.24	6	6.13	6	6.08	8	5.25
4	4.26	4	3.10	4	5.39	19	12.50
12	10.84	12	9.13	12	8.15	8	5.56
7	4.82	7	7.26	7	6.42	8	7.91
5	5.68	5	4.74	5	5.73	8	6.89

Table 5.1   The Four Data Sets in Anscombe's Quartet

The simple statistical measures and linear regression line with goodness of fit statistic R2 are the same for all four data sets, as shown in Table 5.2.

Statistical Measure	Value
Mean of each X variable	9
Variance of each X variable	10
Mean of each Y variable	7.5
Variance of each Y variable	3.75
Correlation between each X and Y variable	0.816
Linear regression line	y = 3 + 0.5x
Goodness of fit R2	0.67

Table 5.2   The Statistical Measures for Anscombe's Quartet

However, if we plot each data set, we can see that they are all very different.

Data set 1 is plotted in Figure 5.3.

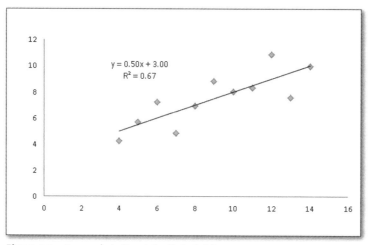

Figure 5.3   Anscombe's Quartet – Data Set 1

Data set 2 is plotted in Figure 5.4, and although clearly different from data set 1, the equation for the linear regression line is the same, Y = 0.5 X + 3.0, as is the goodness of fit statistic, R Squared value of 0.67.

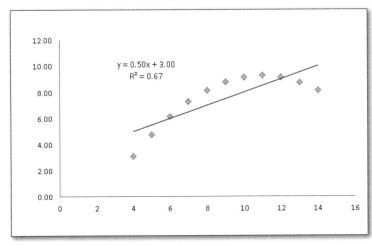

Figure 5.4   Anscombe's Quartet – Data Set 2

Data set 3 is plotted in Figure 5.5, and although clearly different from data sets 1 and 2, the equation for the linear regression line is the same, Y = 0.5 X + 3.0, as is the goodness of fit statistic, R Squared value of 0.67.

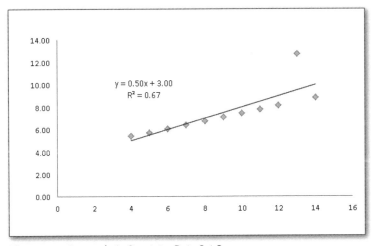

Figure 5.5   Anscombe's Quartet – Data Set 3

Data set 4 is plotted in Figure 5.6, and although clearly different from data sets 1, 2 and 3, the equation for the linear regression line is the same, Y = 0.5 X + 3.0, as is the goodness of fit statistic, R Squared value of 0.67.

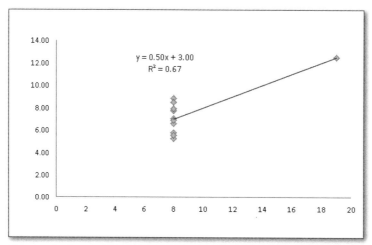

Figure 5.6 Anscombe's Quartet – Data Set 4

Data set 4 also clearly shows the effect of outliers on a model and the danger of blindly applying an algorithm. With the outlier removed, the line of best fit would be very different.

The above analysis underlines the importance of understanding the data before applying any algorithms.

5.4.3 Model Overfitting

Model overfitting is where a model provides an excellent fit to the data it is given, referred to as the training data, but is a poor predictor of new data. The overfitting refers to the fact that we have done too good a job of fitting the training data, perhaps by introducing too many input or independent variables, at the expense of the model's predictive accuracy. Overfitting usually occurs when a model is overly complex, such as having too many parameters relative to the number of data points. This problem is best illustrated using regression analysis and specifically polynomial regression.

Figure 5.7 shows a data set with a range of values for seven data points.

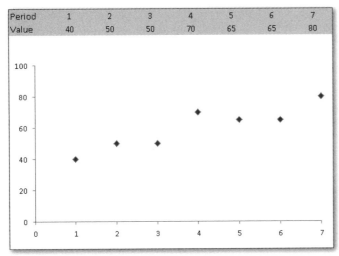

Period	1	2	3	4	5	6	7
Value	40	50	50	70	65	65	80

Figure 5.7 A Simple Data Set for Analysis

Now we can fit a bivariate linear regression model to this data, as shown in Figure 5.8. The value of R Squared of 0.8455 represents a good model fit as we can see in the chart.

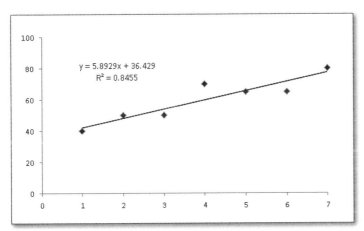

$y = 5.8929x + 36.429$
$R^2 = 0.8455$

Figure 5.8 A Bivariate Linear Regression Line Fitted to the Data

If we now fit a polynomial regression of three degrees, a cubic equation, as shown in Figure 5.9, we have improved the model, which shows an increased value of R Squared of 0.8665, but at the expense of model complexity.

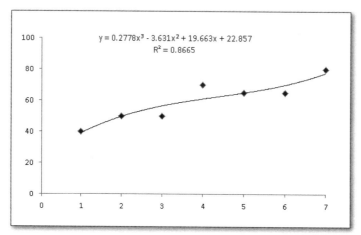

Figure 5.9   A Polynomial Regression Curve Fit to the Power 3

We can take this to the extreme, by fitting a polynomial of degree equal to the number of data points, less one, therefore six, in our example. The curve fit is shown in Figure 5.10, where we have a perfect fit and a value of R Squared at its maximum value of 1.

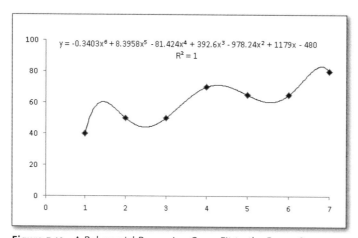

Figure 5.10   A Polynomial Regression Curve Fit to the Power 3

We now have a perfect model, but also a very complex model. Worse still, if we project the data using the six degree polynomial equation, the value for the projection of Y, given X=8 is -250.89, and for X=9 is -2,209.68, as shown in Figure 5.11, which is clearly nonsense.

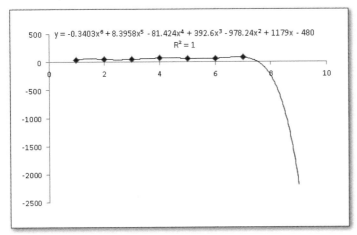

Figure 5.11 Projections for the Polynomial Regression

As with all risks, there should be recommendations on how to mitigate them. In order to avoid overfitting, the most important recommendation is to use a proportion of the available data to train the model and the rest of the data, sometimes called unseen or hold out data, to test the model. This is a key methodology in predictive analysis and a particularly important one in classification analysis and time series analysis, as the above example has shown. There are many extensions to the train and test method, such as repeatedly dividing the data into the two groups, but using various sampling methods to determine and vary the selected data, and then combining the resultant models. This is known as cross-validation. Additional techniques include "early" stopping of model iterations in an attempt to avoid overly complex models, and in decision tree models, "pruning" of the tree to reduce complexity, when the complexity of the tree does not add sufficient gains in performance. Essentially we test the model's ability to generalize by evaluating its performance on a set of data not used for training, with the proviso that the test data is typical of the unseen data that a model will encounter.

5.4.4 Correlation between the Independent Variables

Strong correlation between two or more independent variables is referred to by statisticians as multicollinearity. For example, in a multiple regression model, the existence of multicollinearity means that the model could easily choose either of the highly correlated variables and still get an equivalent goodness of fit. It is hard to untangle their separate effects on the dependent variable because when one variable increases or decreases, the other increases or decreases at the same time, as shown in Figure 5.12. Parameter estimates may change erratically in response to small changes in the model or the data. Multicollinearity does not reduce the predictive power or reliability of the model as a whole, at least within the sample data itself, but it affects calculations regarding individual predictors. That is, a multiple regression model with correlated predictors can indicate how well the entire bundle of predictors predicts the outcome variable, but it may not give valid results about any individual predictor, or about which predictors are redundant with regard to others.

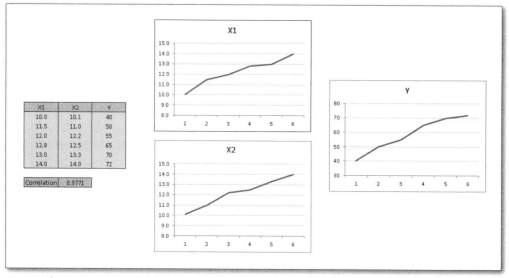

Figure 5.12   Example of Multicollinearity

In Figure 5.12 we see that X1 and X2 are highly positively correlated, with a correlation coefficient of 0.9771, so in finding a model to describe the relationship between Y and the independent variables, X1and X2, it is hard to differentiate between them, as they are so closely related.

A high degree of multicollinearity can also cause problems in matrix inversion, which is required for computing the regression coefficients, and can make the results of that inversion inaccurate.

In mitigation, you could try to obtain more data, particularly if the data sets are small, and then perhaps the correlation will be less. Sampling might help, in that subsets of the data may not exhibit multicollinearity. Perhaps you could omit one of the correlated variables; however, the question would be which one to omit and the danger is that it might be the real causal variable. Of course, examining the independent variables that are highly correlated would be very worthwhile. You could just leave the model as is, as the presence of multicollinearity does not affect the effectiveness of prediction, provided that the same pattern of multicollinearity in the new data is the same as in the data that was used to build the regression model.

We have discussed the difficulties that can be encountered in predictive analysis, so in the next section we turn the topic around, and discuss the key factors for success in predictive projects.

5.5 Key Factors for Success

The five key factors for success are:

1. Managing expectations.
2. Analyzing for a real business benefit.
3. Working as a team.
4. Using sensitivity analysis.
5. Shifting from analysis to action.

We start with perhaps the most important one – managing expectations. Data mining does not guarantee finding gold! So be careful what you promise. It is perhaps a little cynical to say that promising four things and delivering three is seen as a failure, whereas promising two things and delivering three is heroic! Of course, promising three things and delivering three is ideal. However, given that there is no guarantee of finding something useful, some caution is advisable.

Analyzing for real benefit is an obvious point but not always observed. Sometimes the intellectual challenge takes over from the practical challenge. This is also why following the process for predictive analysis is important and agreeing the first steps in the process of defining the objectives of the analysis, the business case, and the desired outcomes from the project.

Working as a team is important, in particular including those who have business domain expertise together with data analysts. A successful project is one that translates into improved business processes, and that is much more likely if the owners of the process are involved in the project. Change is always a challenge and is best achieved in a cooperative environment.

Sensitivity analysis is essentially questioning the assumptions made in developing an analysis, to see the impact that changes to those assumptions have on the results of the analysis. It is often referred to as what-if analysis. It is a very important influencer of success. If relatively small changes in the assumptions cause large changes in the results, then the solution is unstable, and needs to be considered carefully. Model robustness is a key measure of usefulness.

Finally, the ultimate measure of success is that our analysis leads to action, and improved business processes. This is not easy and requires cooperation with management, who will need convincing of the benefits, an easier task if they are part of the analysis team.

We conclude this chapter with a quotation from Professor George Box, Professor Emeritus of Statistics at the University of Wisconsin:

> *All models are wrong, but some are useful.*[1]

They are wrong in the sense of predicting the unknown, and perhaps Box should have said the majority of models are wrong, but then the quotation would have less impact. However, even if only some models are useful, they can deliver very substantial benefits.

5.6   Summary

In this chapter we looked at some of the challenges of predictive analysis, contrasting date mining heaven and hell. We presented five myths and five pitfalls to look out for in predictive analysis. We then augmented the discussion with specific examples, such as the apparent relationship between the increased number of babies born in Sweden and the increased number of storks arriving in Sweden. We presented the famous Anscombe's Quartet to show how important it is to understand the data before crunching it through algorithms. We concluded the chapter on a more positive note with a discussion of the key factors for success when conducting predictive projects.

In the next chapter we build on the content of our first five chapters and look at it in terms of the many applications of predictive analysis in SAP solutions.

---

1 Box, G. E. P., and Draper, N. R., (1987), *Empirical Model Building and Response Surfaces*, John Wiley & Sons, New York, NY.

This chapter describes the various uses of predictive analysis in SAP business applications.

6   Applications in SAP

SAP is making significant investments in predictive analysis and the embedding of analysis in business applications. The chapter is divided into subsections, one for each application, and after an introduction, we will describe the application, the current and planned use of predictive analysis in the application, and the benefits. These applications cover SAP solution offerings across SAP ERP, industry solutions, and line of business applications. At the time of writing, these are the products available. The following applications are described:

▸ SAP Smart Meter Analytics

▸ SAP Customer Engagement Intelligence

▸ SAP Enterprise Inventory and Service-Level Optimization

▸ SAP Precision Gaming

▸ SAP Affinity Insight

▸ SAP Demand Signal Management

▸ SAP On-Shelf Availability

▸ SAP Product Recommendation Intelligence

▸ SAP Credit Insight

▸ SAP Convergent Pricing Simulation

In the following sections, we will look at each application, the current and planned use, and the benefits.

6.1   SAP Smart Meter Analytics

SAP Smart Meter Analytics (SMA) is designed for real-time analysis of the massive volumes of meter readings created by utility companies. It provides a highly granular analysis of end customers' consumption behavior, thereby providing a deep understanding of their requirements to better manage and predict the demand for energy. Furthermore, it provides customers with self-help energy management tools, which support them in managing their use of energy.

6.1.1 Application Description

SMA consists of a utility oriented data model and analytic components. The data model contains the meter readings as time series data in combination with the master data objects with different extensible attributes.

One of the key features of the analytic components is the powerful customer insights, providing instant aggregated data to analyze customer energy usage at any level of granularity, aggregation, or dimension, as shown in Figure 6.1.

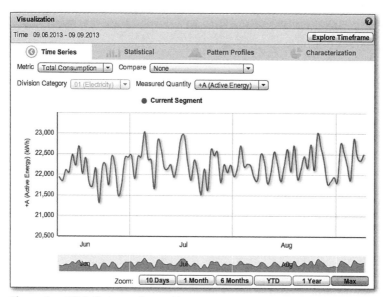

Figure 6.1 SMA Customer Energy Usage

Another key feature is the advanced customer segmentation enabling the precise segmentation of customers based on consumption patterns, as shown in Figure 6.2.

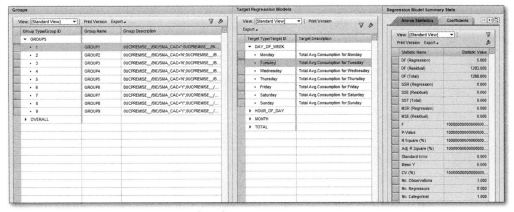

ID	+A (Active Energy) (%)	Daily profiles (%)	Profile Shape
1	87 %	83 %	
3	13 %	17 %	
6	0 %	0 %	
7	0 %	0 %	
8	0 %	0 %	

Figure 6.2 SMA Customer Segment Consumption Patterns

Energy efficiency benchmarking is provided to enable the comparison of energy usage of customers against peers, and root cause analysis to improve their energy efficiency, as shown in Figure 6.3.

Figure 6.3 SMA Customer Energy Benchmarking

Finally, the application provides access to insights for end customers to empower them with self-service access to energy usage.

6.1.2 Current and Planned Use of Predictive Analysis

SAP Smart Meter Analytics uses regression analysis to conduct energy efficiency benchmarking to compare the energy usage of customers against peer groups based on statistically predicted consumption. Users can generate different benchmarking analyses by changing model attributes such as sales square footage, opening hours, climate zone, etc.

For extracting typical pattern profiles from smart meter data, SMA uses the K-Means clustering algorithm to calculate the pattern profiles or clusters. The algorithm analyzes typical load profiles in a huge amount of meter data to summarize it and categorize the user behavior.

6.1.3 Benefits

The benefits delivered by SMA include:

▶ Increase the adoption of tariffs for demand side management programs by precisely segmenting and targeting customers.

▶ Reduce direct energy costs via more accurate load forecasts based on energy consumption patterns.

▶ Achieve energy savings and emission targets via more effective energy efficiency programs.

▶ Increase revenue by up-selling and cross-selling new energy services.

▶ Reduce revenue loss via increased transparency into smart meter data and benchmarking of accounts.

▶ Increase customer satisfaction and retention by providing direct access to energy usage insights.

6.2 SAP Customer Engagement Intelligence

Sales, marketing and customer service professionals struggle to access and analyze the large amounts of internal customer data stored in disparate systems within their organizations, as well as external social media data beyond the reach of their IT systems. Often they must rely on outdated information, which can cause them to miss out on profitable cross-sell and up-sell opportunities, or incomplete information, which can lead them to rely on only gut instincts when making strategic decisions, such as offering incentives to engage customers and prospects.

The SAP Customer Engagement Intelligence (CEI) solution is a set of applications powered by SAP HANA designed to enable real-time insight from customer data, which allows for highly personalized and targeted initiatives that can help grow both revenue and profit for organizations. SAP Customer Engagement Intelligence leverages powerful text analysis and predictive engines within SAP HANA to bring the power of advanced natural language processing and complex predictive algorithms directly to the fingertips of marketing, sales and service executives in an intuitive, practical and user-friendly way without the need for data scientists and PhDs.

6.2.1 Application Description

SAP Customer Engagement Intelligence consists of four fully integrated applications:

► SAP Audience Discovery and Targeting
► SAP Social Engagement Intelligence
► SAP Customer Value Intelligence
► SAP Account Intelligence

First, SAP Audience Discovery and Targeting (ADT) is an analytic application to enable marketing managers to engage customers and help convert prospects to profitable customers by running advanced segmentations on large target populations and distilling insights into focused and personalized marketing campaigns.

Intuitive visualizations help the marketing expert segment out of millions of customers the best ones for a campaign. Predictive models score customers on the fly, using the most recent data based on a comprehensive customer profile incorporating sales and financial information, as well as social media sources. For example, business analysts can train models, which are seamlessly used by marketing experts to calculate buying propensity, churn rates or run cluster analysis for customer segmentation, as shown in Figure 6.4.

Figure 6.4 SAP Audience Discovery and Targeting

Second, CEI includes SAP Social Engagement Intelligence (SEI), which allows organizations to leverage real-time sentiment and contact insights from social media and internal company-owned sources. With this application, key influencers are identified and targeted, new leads and opportunities are generated, and overall service levels and customer loyalty are improved. A net promoter and activity score is calculated for each customer, as shown in Figure 6.5.

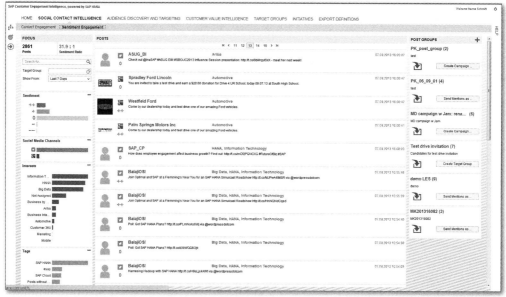

Figure 6.5 SAP Social Engagement Intelligence

Third, CEI includes SAP Customer Value Intelligence (CVI), which is an analytic application that gives sales and marketing managers real-time insight into the true value of their customers based on ERP Sales and Distribution and Financial data. A customer lifetime value and churn rate are calculated and visualized for customer stratification and in a customer score card. Personalized product recommendations are offered for cross- and up-selling with closed loop execution into the CRM backend, as shown in Figure 6.6.

Finally, CEI includes SAP Account Intelligence (AI), which is a mobile application that offers mobile sales teams real-time customer insights and personalized selling recommendations. From any location, they can create target lists, increase the effectiveness of their sales visits, and seize sales opportunities, as shown in Figure 6.7.

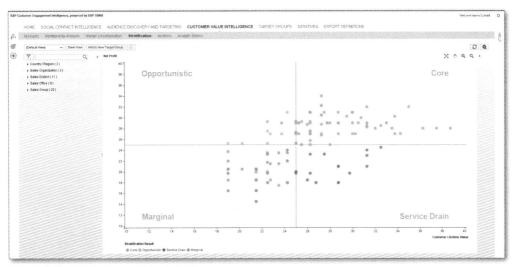

Figure 6.6 SAP Customer Value Intelligence

Figure 6.7 SAP Account Intelligence

6.2.2 Current and Planned Use of Predictive Analysis

The analysis of customers provides a variety of areas and use cases to apply predictive functionality, and thereby to identify patterns in customer behavior. Figure 6.8 shows the various predictive use cases supported in SAP Customer Engagement Intelligence.

- Classify and understand customer behavior
  - Customer Clusters (e.g., retention and defection pattern)
  - RFM Analysis and RFM Scoring (for segmentation)
- Customer Acquisition
  - Contact Scoring/Market Basket Analysis/Contact Segmentation
- Customer Value
  - Cross-/Up-selling/Campaign targeting (channel optimization)/Revenue forecasting (e.g., time trend analysis)
  - Customer Lifetime Value
  - Buying Propensity Scoring
- Customer Retention
  - Churn scoring/Campaign optimization (optimized retention offer)
  - Customer attributes, which have high impact on customer churn/retention/loyalty/satisfaction.
- Success Reporting/Control Groups
  - Calculate success rates per campaign as well as per Predictive Model for target groups and control groups.
  - Show overall the best campaigns and predictive models

Figure 6.8 Predictive Features in SAP Customer Engagement Intelligence

Companies that invest in predictive today face two main challenges. First, the data foundation for predictive algorithms needs to be set up, which means data needs to be extracted and combined from many different sources. The data need to be flat, in that there is no header-item hierarchy, and it should have an appropriate quality, e.g., not too many missing values, outliers, etc. Customer data can be very heterogeneous, unspecific and from soft sources as well as hard facts. Second, once such a data mart for predictive purposes is available, a skilled expert, such as a statistician or data scientist, has to assess the business problem and the available data, chose an appropriate predictive approach, and run the predictive method with a specific tool to produce a prediction. Finally, the data scientist needs to communicate to the business people the predicted result and convince them that it has a significant benefit for business decisions, which will improve and supplement best practice procedures.

In CEI, the predictive functionality is directly and seamlessly integrated into business processes, which can be consumed, understood and worked on by business people, who have little or no idea about predictive analysis. The predictive UI and functionality for business people is designed to be very easily used by marketing, sales and customer service people.

With SAP HANA the application built in predictive functionality is offered to overcome the above challenges. SAP HANA is the database, where data from all different sources is integrated on a very granular level. With CEI, a data foundation is shipped with preconfigured data structures on the customer level, which are consumed by predictive algorithms. This data model can be extended by customers to be enriched with additional data specific to their industry and business.

The steps to run predictive applications in SAP Customer Engagement Intelligence are summarized in Figure 6.9.

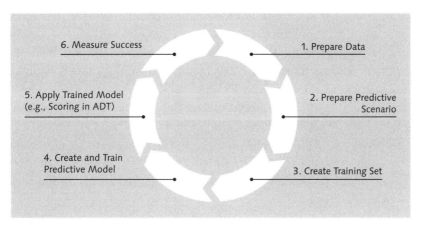

Figure 6.9 Steps to Run Predictive in SAP CEI

The six steps to run Predictive in SAP CEI are described as follows:

1. For data preparation, the shipped HANA Data Views can be used as a template and enriched by any data that is available to support the predictive use case. This would be done in HANA Studio and related tools, for example, to replicate the data. An extensibility guide is available. The HANA Data Views shipped for predictive analysis already contain the CRM Business Partner Master Data, the

CRM transactional data, e.g., activities, leads, opportunities, sales and service data as well as ERP Sales and Distribution transactional data, e.g., revenue, pocket margin, external customer satisfaction data, and other information. The data preparation task is typically done by a data analyst.

2. The predictive scenario is defined by the data analyst for the specific use case at the beginning, for example, the buying propensity using a specific statistical implementation such as logistic regression based on the PAL, on a specific data source.

3. The training set is a target group derived in ADT by a couple of segmentation steps. The training set contains those customers who are considered to have the relevant historical information as a basis for model training. The training set is also part of the header of the predictive model.

4. The predictive model for a certain predictive scenario specifies the target object, such as the product in focus for the buying propensity calculation, together with the target variable, the 0-1 variable, which will be included in the logistic regression. The training set, which is an ADT Target Group to be used to train the models, is selected. Once the header of the predictive model is specified, the status is converted from NEW to IN PREPARATION and various models with different explanatory variables can now be fitted to the training set. The model fit quality can be rated by the Gini coefficient and the Gain chart or Lorenz curve. The best fitting model can be chosen and published to the business process, e.g., buying propensity in ADT. In addition, the business analyst can define the applicable scope, i.e., the context in which a predictive model is valid, for example, the buying propensity for a certain product may only be valid for a certain geographic region.

5. The published trained model for a certain product can now be used in ADT to score the customers and to include those customers who have the highest probability to buy into the target group for a marketing campaign.

6. Finally, success reporting is offered to demonstrate that the applied predictive feature has a real benefit, which is then immediately visible to the business users. If the results are not as expected, then the business users see this right away and can interact with the business analyst to understand what can be improved. This creates trust in working with predictive models integrated into business scenarios. For example, marketing campaigns will be run on an

optimized target group, which was created based on buying propensity scoring and on one or more control groups selected at random or based on best practice. The success report shows response rates, resulting presales activities and sales data for the optimized target group in comparison with the control group.

6.2.3 Benefits

The application offers a variety of opportunities to apply predictive analytics, to help optimize customer relationships and business results. Predictive analysis involves a high investment at the beginning of a project and requires specific knowledge, specific tools, specific data treatment and acceptance by the business users.

With SAP HANA CEI, this can be obviated by combining data preparation and predictive infrastructure into one database, and by offering fully integrated predictive model management to support the deployment of predictive results directly into the business processes. With an intuitive UI, the business user can immediately understand and interact with predictive information and even see the direct benefit when looking into success reports. Predictive in CEI offers an agnostic infrastructure in standard software to seamlessly integrate predictive processes into business applications, which is very flexible and extendable in all aspects.

6.3 SAP Enterprise Inventory & Service-Level Optimization

SAP Enterprise Inventory and Service-Level Optimization (EIS) determines the right inventory and service level targets for real-world supply chains to enable enterprises to capture more sales and simultaneously reduce working capital. EIS models the supply chain as a multistage network that consists of products, distributions and manufacturing locations, vendors, and customers that affect and depend on each other. With its comprehensive data model, it captures the realities and complexities of global enterprises. With its sophisticated predictive analytics, EIS quantifies the uncertainty and risk from demand, supply, and production variability. EIS analyzes this massive data volume and uses proprietary algorithms to determine the right service level targets to achieve a profitable balance between expected costs and revenues. In addition, EIS right-sizes inventory targets to achieve service level targets with the lowest working capital investment. EIS is designed to run as part of Sales and Operations Planning processes as well as to support supply chain continuous improvement processes with powerful what-if analysis capabilities.

6.3.1 Application Description

The application is designed around the fundamental supply chain needs of under-standing the supply chain and its drivers. At its core, EIS models the supply chain from the master and transaction data found in SAP's business applications. EIS also extracts past transactions, such as shipments and sales, supplier deliveries, stock transfers, and actual production data, recorded as time series, to quantify the inherent variability between plans and realities and the corresponding risk to service goals. These inputs can often come from disparate systems with different functions. It is essential to understand how all these inputs come together to form a model of the supply chain. Functionality to visualize the network is embedded in the application, as shown Figure 6.10, to help make sense of all of the drivers of supply chain costs and performance.

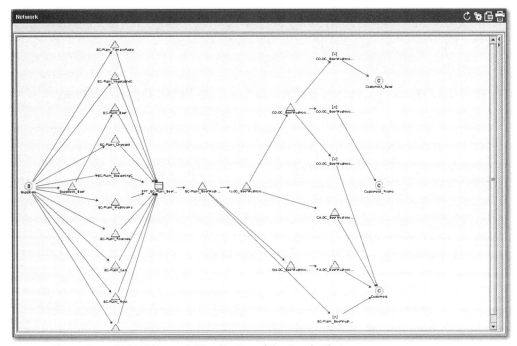

Figure 6.10 SAP EIS Network Visualization of the Supply Chain

Reports describing the data imported from source systems are as shown in Figure 6.11.

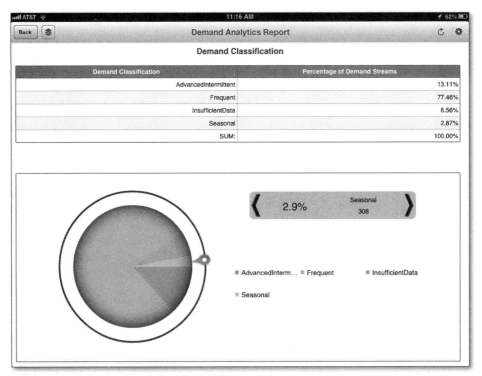

Figure 6.11 SAP EIS Demand Classification and Analysis

Perceived variations between planned and actual replenishment drivers, as shown in Figure 6.12, provide visibility into the drivers of service and inventory, and ultimately help the understanding and adoption of recommendations.

Variations between forecasts and actual sales or between planned and actual lead times, whether due to planning errors or uncertainty, are a source of risk that needs to be understood, mitigated, and, if possible, corrected. Gauges report the current variability metrics and can trigger alerts when key indicators are out of tolerance, as shown in Figure 6.13.

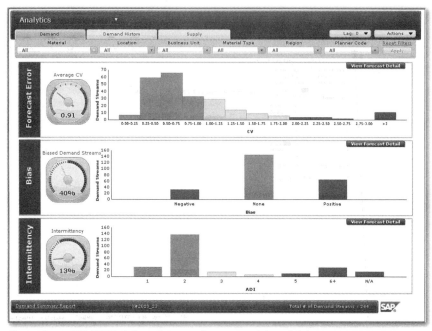

Figure 6.12 SAP EIS Variations Between Forecast and Actual Sales

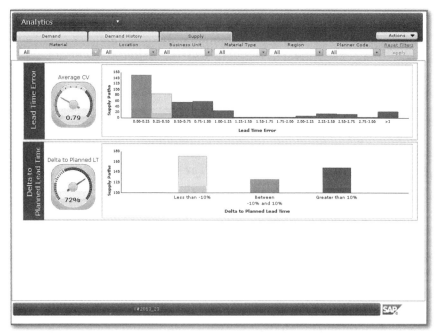

Figure 6.13 SAP EIS Variations Between Planned and Actual Lead Times

EIS utilizes probability models to characterize the uncertainty due to demand quantity or timing variability, lead times and production. EIS then applies proprietary stochastic multistage inventory optimization algorithms to recommend the right level of inventory at the right time, in the right place, across the entire supply chain. By also factoring all replenishment complexities such as batch sizes, capacities, multiple sourcing and time-varying bill of materials, EIS provides targets for safety stocks, reorder points, and average inventory values that directly drive inventory replenishment and other planning processes, as shown in Figure 6.14.

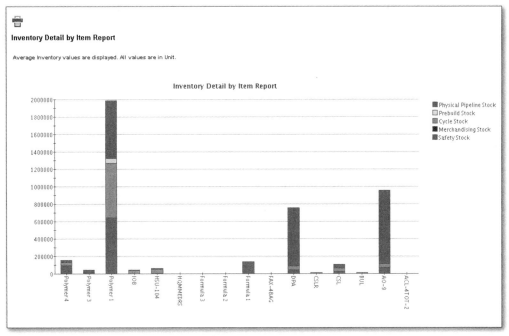

Figure 6.14 SAP EIS Inventory Recommendations

By appropriately characterizing the uncertainty in the supply chain, correctly capturing the relationship between service goals and inventory investment, and finding the right balance between costs and revenues, the application can help "fix-the-mix" of service across the supply chain to increase product availability where it counts, while reducing buffers that do not contribute to profitability. EIS facilitates the adoption of these sometimes counterintuitive recommendations with both embedded reports and customizable analytics that support rapid aggregation and disaggregation, filtering and drill-through, as shown in Figure 6.15.

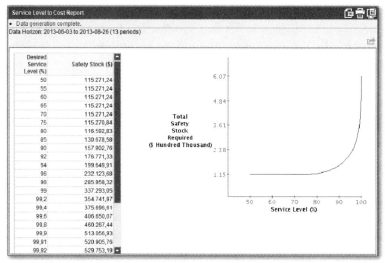

Figure 6.15 SAP EIS Service Level to Cost Report

Alternative scenarios can be compared, as shown in Figure 6.16.

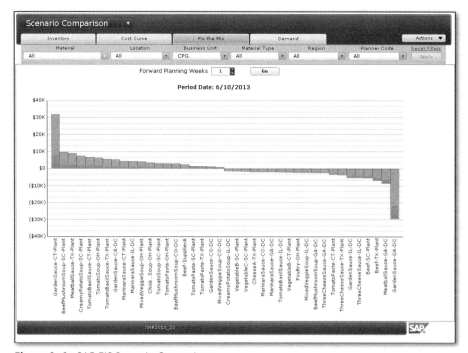

Figure 6.16 SAP EIS Scenario Comparison

EIS captures a supply chain's full complexity and is the ideal platform for what-if analysis and opportunity identification and assessment. It offers alternative scenario creation analysis, which can be used to assess a number of impacts such as forecast accuracy, supplier reliability, and sourcing diversification improvement efforts, as shown in Figure 6.17.

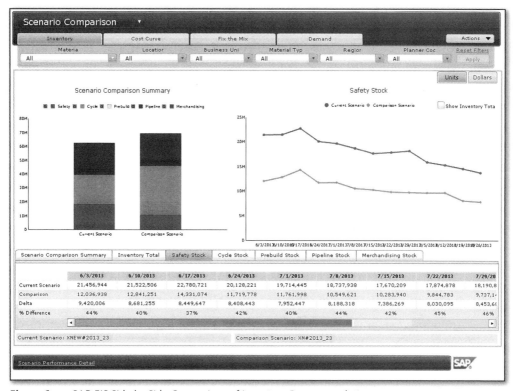

Figure 6.17 SAP EIS Side by Side Comparison of Inventory Recommendations

EIS can also help assess the accuracy of different forecast sources and encourages a dialog between marketing, sales and supply chain planners, as shown in Figure 6.18.

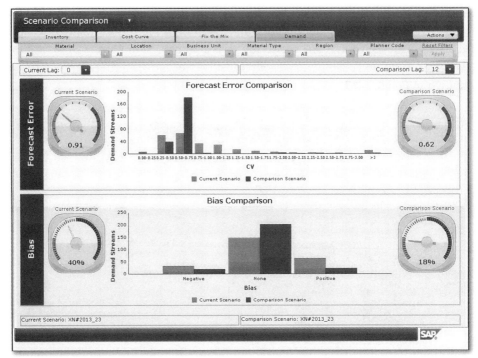

Figure 6.18 SAP EIS Side by Side Comparison of Forecast Error and Bias

6.3.2 Current and Planned Use of Predictive Analysis

SAP Enterprise Inventory and Service-Level Optimization uses a number of predictive analytics algorithms to enable the characterization of uncertainty and the optimization of inventory and service levels:

▶ Inter-quartile range and variance tests are used to detect outliers in analyzing transaction data such as sales, supply delivery lead times, and actual production, to more accurately characterize uncertainty and variability in forecast, lead time and schedule attainment variability.

▶ Moving averages are used for the detection of seasonality and product lifecycle phases to right-size inventory levels over time.

▶ Time-series analysis and distribution fitting are used to characterize demand and compute key forecast error and other risk metrics.

▶ ABC analysis is being evaluated to group demand streams and products into categories based on demand volumes, uncertainty, and other factors to seed the service-level optimization analysis and speed up solution search.

▶ Decision trees, K-Means and K-Nearest Neighbor are being evaluated for use in the development of clusters to facilitate root-cause analysis of large deviations between the results from the different scenarios.

In addition, EIS uses a number of statistical and optimization algorithms for descriptive and predictive analytics to enable the characterization of uncertainty and the optimization of inventory and service levels:

▶ Normal and Gamma Probability Density, Cumulative, Loss, and Inverse Functions are used in the modeling of uncertainty from demand, supply, and production variability and their impact on service and loss demand.

▶ Gradient-guided, bisection search, golden section search, and root-finding algorithms are used in the search for the optimal service-level and inventory targets, as well as in the impact of batch sizes, storage capacities and other replenishment constraints on service.

6.3.3   Benefits

SAP Enterprise Inventory & Service-Level Optimization provides an extensive range of end user benefits, including:

▶ Provide better visibility into the constraints and risks across the entire supply chain by uniting supply chain data from many systems together into a comprehensive model of the supply chain.

▶ Quickly respond to demand or supply issues by sensing when forecast error, bias, actual supply lead times or schedule attainment gets outside of tolerances.

▶ Reduce working capital investment and waste, by eliminating excess via optimizing safety stock and other inventory targets.

▶ Capture more sales by increasing service level goals where it counts with service-level optimization.

▶ Facilitate change management and value realization by having what-if capabilities.

▶ Turn supply chains into competitive advantages with better understanding of opportunities.

6.4 SAP Precision Gaming

SAP Precision Gaming provides real-time analytics cloud services to online and mobile game developers and publishers, and gambling providers, powered by SAP HANA. Fueled by the rapid growth of the Internet and mobile networks, and the resulting ability to directly connect with players, these industries are growing rapidly. Combined global annual revenue from these two industries is projected to exceed $100B by 2017.

SAP Precision Gaming's real-time predictive analytics enable the delivery of personalized, context-relevant real-time offers and messages to individual players, to increase revenue and reduce churn.

SAP Precision Gaming also provides data exploration and visualization tools, plus reports that allow customers to gain important insights into game play and monetization behavior from the terabytes of data collected from a game, thus enabling customers to improve game design and monetization techniques.

6.4.1 Application Description

SAP Precision Gaming is a suite of cloud services provided by SAP to online and mobile game and gambling providers. This description focuses on the real-time predictive analytics services that are designed to identify individual players who are likely to perform a specific future action and then deliver an effective personalized context-relevant message.

Games are played by individuals on a variety of personal computers, game consoles, and mobile devices. Those devices have a bidirectional data connection to SAP Precision Gaming's customers' game engine servers.

A bidirectional real-time data connection is also established between the game server and the SAP Precision Gaming system: see the high level architecture diagram in Figure 6.19.

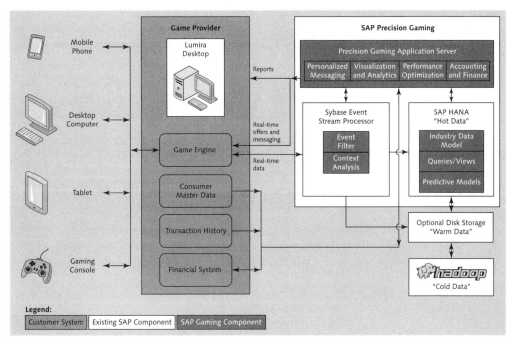

Figure 6.19 SAP Precision Gaming High Level Architecture

The entire game event data stream is delivered to the SAP Precision Gaming system, generally in the form of event logs. Data rates range from a few gigabytes of data per game per day to more than a terabyte per day. Master player data and transaction history is also loaded into the SAP Precision Gaming system, usually as a batch process.

The real-time game event data stream from the game server is ingested by SAP's Event Stream Processor (ESP), which directs the data to the appropriate system component. "Hot data" required by the real-time predictive algorithms is sent to SAP HANA. "Warm data," which is useful for rapid analysis, can be sent to an optional high-performance disk storage system. The remaining "cold data," which is rarely accessed, can be sent to a long-term low-cost disk storage system such as a HADOOP cluster.

ESP also performs context analysis and trigger event detection. When a condition is detected that requires the sophisticated predictive analysis of an individual player, a predictive algorithm is initiated in SAP HANA to determine whether the individual player is likely to perform a specific future action.

If so, then a personalized, context-relevant offer or message is crafted by the SAP Precision Gaming system and delivered back to the game server in real-time for immediate delivery to the individual player.

The ultimate objective of the SAP Precision Gaming system is to identify players likely to perform either specific desirable or undesirable actions, and then deliver an effective personalized, context-relevant message to the individual that increases the probability of performing desirable actions and reduces the probability of undesirable ones.

6.4.2 Current and Planned Use of Predictive Analysis

SAP Precision Gaming predictive algorithms running on SAP HANA constantly analyze all active players, and identify individual players likely to perform specific future actions.

The initial release of SAP Precision Gaming focuses on increasing the number of paying players and reducing churn.

Future releases will include additional predictive algorithms to:

- ▶ Increase revenue per paying player
- ▶ Increase viral messaging to attract new customers to the game
- ▶ Reduce terms of service violations, such as email address harvesting, bot activity, spamming, and gold farming
- ▶ Reduce fraud

6.4.3 Benefits

The initial release of SAP Precision Gaming predictive analytics services focuses on increasing the number of paying players and reducing churn. Its specific benefits are:

- ▶ Increase the conversion rate from free players to paying players. Typically, in the online games industry, less than 2% of players ever make payments.
- ▶ Reduce player churn. Typically, 50% of new players never return to a game after a couple of visits. SAP Precision Gaming's system can reduce churn of new players. With less than 2% of players ever making payments, it is extremely important to identify paying players exhibiting churn predictors and intervene with an appropriate re-engagement message before the player is lost forever.

SAP Precision Gaming also provides data exploration and visualization tools and reports that allow customers to gain important insights into game play and monetization behavior from the terabytes of data collected from a game, thus enabling customers to improve game design and monetization techniques.

6.5   SAP Affinity Insight

SAP Affinity Insight allows retailers to analyze their sales data at the market basket level, with a special focus on identifying quantitative relationships between different products or product groups.

Whilst most reporting tools rely on aggregated information, therefore destroying all information at the individual consumer level, SAP Affinity Insight performs computations at the transaction level, thereby supporting completely new sources of data and new analyses. For example:

▶ Absolute numbers of market baskets that contain products from two selected branches of the product hierarchy.

▶ Average multiplicities of products in market baskets.

▶ Change of such multiplicities during promotion.

▶ Causal relationships between products identified by higher or lower than expected pair sales.

▶ Total market basket sales or profits associated with specific products.

6.5.1   Application Description

The main functionality of SAP Affinity Insight is to calculate metrics, defined as a business relevant quantity or KPI, that can be computed from a set of sales transactions and product hierarchy nodes A and B.

Examples of metrics:

▶ The number of transactions that contain products from both A and B.

▶ The total revenue of those transactions that contain a product A and B.

▶ The share of transactions that contain a product from both A and B, among those transactions that contain a product from at least A or B.

To define the relevant set of sales transactions, the user simply specifies a time range, a set of stores, and additional filters. The tool allows full flexibility in navigating the product and store hierarchies, and selecting arbitrary nodes for analysis, as shown in Figure 6.20.

Figure 6.20   SAP Affinity Insight Navigation Screen

A user can easily compute affinity relationships, for example, between the whole beverages department and one specific brand of potato chips, limited to all stores in France and two specific stores in Belgium. An example is shown in the heatmap in Figure 6.21.

The SAP Affinity Insight system landscape includes two separate machines: one machine running the SAP Business Objects Business Intelligence (BI) platform 4.0, and one the SAP HANA appliance.

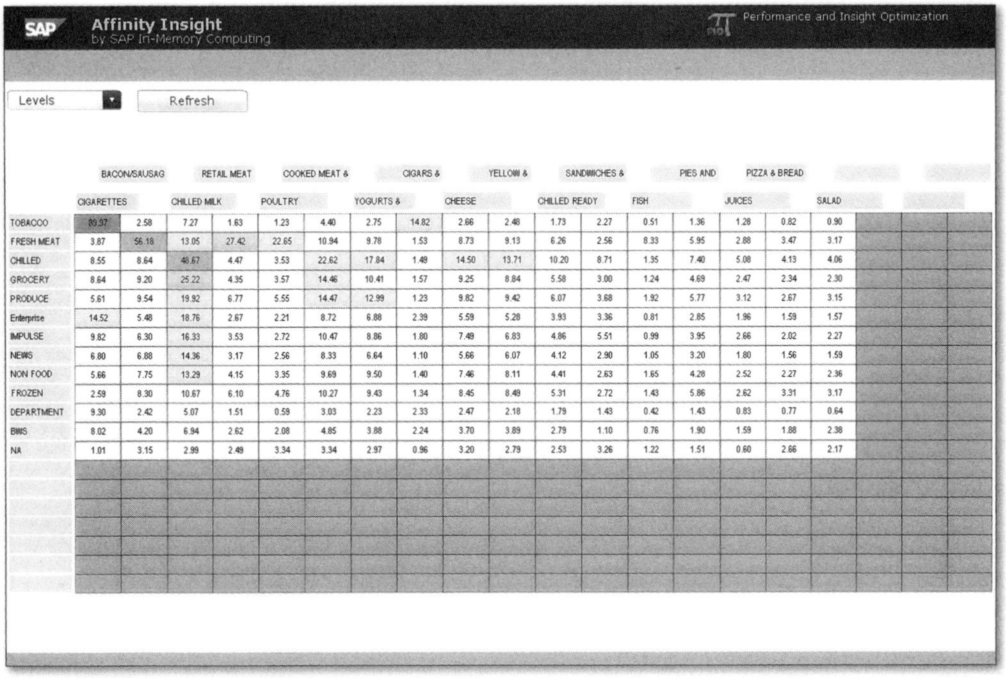

Affinity Insight
by SAP In-Memory Computing

Performance and Insight Optimization

	BACON/SAUSAG CIGARETTES		RETAIL MEAT CHILLED MILK		COOKED MEAT & POULTRY		YOGURTS &	CIGARS &	YELLOW & CHEESE		SANDWICHES & CHILLED READY	FISH	PIES AND		PIZZA & BREAD JUICES		SALAD
TOBACCO	80.37	2.58	7.27	1.63	1.23	4.40	2.75	14.82	2.66	2.48	1.73	2.27	0.51	1.36	1.28	0.82	0.90
FRESH MEAT	3.87	56.18	13.05	27.42	22.65	10.94	9.78	1.53	8.73	9.13	6.26	2.56	8.33	5.95	2.88	3.47	3.17
CHILLED	8.55	8.64	48.67	4.47	3.53	22.62	17.84	1.49	14.50	13.71	10.20	8.71	1.35	7.40	5.08	4.13	4.06
GROCERY	8.64	9.20	25.22	4.35	3.57	14.46	10.41	1.57	9.25	8.84	5.58	3.00	1.24	4.69	2.47	2.34	2.30
PRODUCE	5.61	9.54	19.92	6.77	5.55	14.47	12.99	1.23	9.82	9.42	6.07	3.68	1.92	5.77	3.12	2.67	3.15
Enterprise	14.52	5.48	18.76	2.67	2.21	8.72	6.88	2.39	5.59	5.28	3.93	3.36	0.81	2.85	1.96	1.59	1.57
IMPULSE	9.82	6.30	16.33	3.53	2.72	10.47	8.86	1.80	7.49	6.83	4.86	5.51	0.99	3.95	2.66	2.02	2.27
NEWS	6.80	6.88	14.36	3.17	2.56	8.33	6.64	1.10	5.66	6.07	4.12	2.90	1.05	3.20	1.80	1.56	1.59
NON FOOD	5.66	7.75	13.29	4.15	3.35	9.69	9.50	1.40	7.46	8.11	4.41	2.63	1.65	4.28	2.52	2.27	2.36
FROZEN	2.59	8.30	10.67	6.10	4.76	10.27	9.43	1.34	8.45	8.49	5.31	2.72	1.43	5.86	2.62	3.31	3.17
DEPARTMENT	9.30	2.42	5.07	1.51	0.59	3.03	2.23	2.33	2.47	2.18	1.79	1.43	0.42	1.43	0.83	0.77	0.64
BWS	8.02	4.20	6.94	2.62	2.08	4.85	3.88	2.24	3.70	3.89	2.79	1.10	0.76	1.90	1.59	1.88	2.38
NA	1.01	3.15	2.99	2.49	3.34	3.34	2.97	0.96	3.20	2.79	2.53	3.26	1.22	1.51	0.60	2.66	2.17

Levels ▼   Refresh

Figure 6.21 SAP Affinity Insight Heatmap

For those interested in the technical background and the process, The user logs on to the BusinessObjects Enterprise BI launch pad (see ❶Ⓐ and ❶Ⓑ in Figure 6.22) and then accesses the SAP Affinity Insight dashboard. The SAP BusinessObjects Enterprise (BOE) services manage the authentication and authorization process. The client's web browser then downloads and opens the dashboard designer flash file. The flash file contains variables that are attached to further XML data requests for authentication and authorization checks against the BOE Central Management Server (CMS).The user can enter business rules and parameters in the Dashboard Designer user interface ❷. The Dashboard Designer GUI makes a synchronous XML data connection call to a Java servlet that is deployed on the same Tomcat server as the BOE BI launch pad web application ❸. The Java servlet authenticates the user against the BOE CMS using the CESerializedSession token that it has received from the flash file ❹. The Java servlet connects to the HANA database and performs the requested operation synchronously ❺. This operation can either be an SQL data manipulation statement such as INSERT, DELETE, or UPDATE, followed by an SQL query, or it can be a SQLScript procedure. All computations of metrics are performed by such SQLScript procedures. Finally, the Java servlet returns the results to the dashboard designer GUI synchronously ❻.

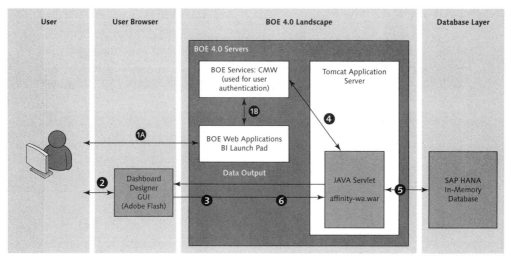

Figure 6.22 SAP Affinity Analysis Technical Architecture

6.5.2 Current and Planned Use of Predictive Analysis

Future ideas under consideration, and, as always, not a specific commitment, are to extend SAP Affinity Insight by adding functionality beyond pure market basket analysis. Some examples of such extensions:

▶ Repeat purchase analysis: Functionality to compute how often certain products or product groups are purchased repeatedly by the same customer. These types of analyses are used, for example, to understand which products attract loyal customers to the stores.

▶ Value driver tree: A tool to quickly visualize how variations in performance in a certain store or product group are caused by underlying factors. For example, the total profit of a certain store is computed as revenues multiplied by margin. Revenues, on the other hand, can be seen as the number of customer transactions multiplied by the average spending per customer, etc. Such analysis can help quickly identify root causes of typical retail business problems.

▶ Key item list: A dashboard that gives an overview of the most and least important products in a retail assortment, where importance is defined as a weighted average of various KPIs. One application of such a tool is to quickly identify products that can be taken out of the assortment.

6.5.3 Benefits

SAP Affinity Insight allows business users to perform market basket analyses directly on point-of-sales data without any need for data transformation or aggregations.

Despite the potentially very large amounts of data, computations in SAP Affinity Insight are usually performed within seconds. This is possible because the calculations are executed directly in the in-memory database SAP HANA. The short response times make it possible to perform analyses in an interactive and explorative fashion. For example, after reviewing computation results, a user might choose to start a new analysis one level deeper in the store or product hierarchy, or compare the results to those from another time frame.

Technically, the frontend of SAP Affinity Insight is a SAP BusinessObjects dashboard and therefore the tool can be fully integrated with an existing reporting cockpit. Users can combine it with existing dashboards or create their own dashboards to extend SAP Affinity Insight.

SAP Affinity Insight helps retailers to make better business decisions by enabling deeper, faster and more flexible market basket analysis. Some examples of typical analyses are:

▶ Identification of product affinities: Finding out which combinations of products are regularly sold together helps plan promotions and optimize the placement of products in the stores.

▶ Computation of associated market baskets: Knowing the total volume of customer transactions that contain certain products shows which products, product groups or brands, attract the most profitable customers to the stores.

▶ Calculation of market basket multiplicities: Understanding how many units customers typically purchase if they buy a specific product, allows retailers to quantify hoarding effects during promotions and thus identify the most effective promotions.

6.6   SAP Demand Signal Management

For leading consumer products and high tech manufacturers, it is becoming more and more important to understand and react to consumer demand. What is needed are demand signals in order to get an insight into the actual situation at the retailer stores and distribution centers. This demand information needs to be compiled from different sources, such as retailer point-of-sale data (POS), as well as from market researchers, whose data can give insight into the buying behavior of consumers. Most of this information can be found only in disparate data sources throughout a company, with little or no linkage or alignment.

Consumer products and high-tech manufacturers mainly use downstream data, for example POS data from retailers such as Wal-Mart, Kroger, Rite Aid or Home Depot. The data is used to measure promotion success and the performance of a new product during a product introduction phase, or the product sales development in certain regions or at certain retailers, and to report on critical out-of-stock situations which can result in lost sales. In addition, it is necessary to understand consumer behavior and its effects on the market share of the manufacturer's own brands, as well as on the market share of competitive brands, and the development of the market as a whole. Therefore, extensive market research data, such as syndicated data, is needed. This data can be bought from market research companies like Nielsen, IRI or GfK. Furthermore, social sentiments as well as weather data can be of interest if combined with the information from other data sources.

All these different data sources need to get collected in one data repository that acts as a single source of truth. This repository takes care of data upload, harmonization of external data with the manufacturer's internal master data (for example, product and location), and enriches the data with value added measures to make the data more useful for downstream consumption. This is the role of SAP Demand Signal Management (DSiM).

6.6.1   Application Description

DSiM, powered by SAP HANA, comprises of a consistent, centralized in-memory database that stores large volumes of data such as internal master and transactional data, shipments, external POS data and market research data, and combines this with the ability to rapidly integrate, cleanse and harmonize data from disparate data sources. Thus, it enables the tracking of performance between trading partners such as manufacturers, distributors and retailers, and supports the analysis of brand and category performance to improve insight into the consumer.

The objectives of DSiM are to enable manufacturers to improve their sales and brand performance, increase promotion effectiveness, optimize the inventory levels throughout the supply and demand chain, and prevent potential lost sales situations by ensuring on-shelf availability of their goods at the retailer stores, as summarized in Figure 6.23. In summary, SAP Demand Signal Management is the enterprise platform for integrating all relevant demand signals, internal and external, into a single source of truth.

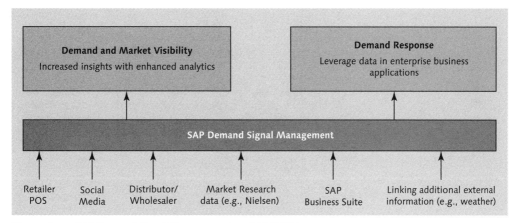

Figure 6.23 SAP Demand Signal Management on SAP HANA

6.6.2 Current and Planned Use of Predictive Analysis

Besides the existing analytics delivered in the DSiM standard solution, it is important for DSiM customers to have predictive capabilities to uncover trends, patterns, and new insights into the demand data. This enables the manufacturer to react to changes in the end-consumer demand, in time or even ahead of time.

DSiM customers and partners can build their company specific predictive analytics on top of DSiM data by leveraging the existing predictive capabilities in SAP HANA, such as the Predictive Analysis Library (PAL), SAP Predictive Analysis (PA), and the SAP HANA Integration for R.

To demonstrate the predictive capability in DSiM, and to investigate the different architectural approaches, the following use cases are presented:

Use Case 1: Retailer Store Clustering Based on Clustering Algorithms

Utilization of clustering algorithms such as K-Means, to group retailer stores based on the enriched KPIs from POS data in order to uncover associations between these KPIs, and to help the manufacturer to identify actions tailored to a store cluster.

For the clustering of stores, enriched DSiM POS KPIs can be used, such as sales revenue, sales quantity, average inventory, promotional information, out-of-shelf count, and out-of-stock count. These KPIs can be retrieved and prepared to the format required by the k-means algorithm using SAP HANA views. The prepared POS data can then be passed to the k-means algorithm in PA or in the PAL. The clustering results can be visualized and shared with business users for further analysis and identification of tailored actions, as shown in Figure 6.24.

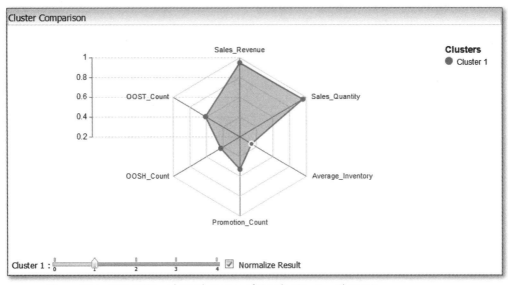

Figure 6.24 SAP DSiM and PA Clustering of Retailer Stores – Cluster 1

For the stores in cluster 1, although sales revenue and quantity are good, the out-of-stock occurrences were high and the average inventory was low. Stores in this cluster could sell more than they currently do, given that the end consumer is not able to buy the products in the store. To react to this, the manufacturer can ask the retailer to increase the inventory for those stores. On the manufacturer's side, the supply chain manager can optimize the replenishment planning and potentially schedule further deliveries to these stores.

Another example is shown in Figure 6.25.

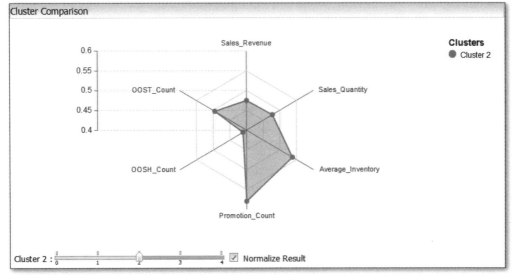

Figure 6.25 DSiM and PA Clustering of Retailer Stores – Cluster 2

For the stores in cluster 2, although the number of trade promotions was very high, the sales revenue and quantity were low. Further analysis of the effectiveness of past promotions in these stores is needed in order to check the root cause. These stores need to be monitored and onsite visits with sales representatives conducted.

Use Case 2: Creation of Missing Market Research Data Based on Extrapolation Algorithms

With DSiM, it is possible to upload retail panel data from different market research institutes and to analyze market share in detail, as well as the overall market development.

These data bases have a very heterogeneous structure, based on different time granularities and different attributes for products. However, the data bases are typically not always available in time for reporting, and the most current delivery of a certain data base has not yet arrived. In this case, SAP HANA predictive capabilities can be used to extrapolate data into future periods of a previous delivery. This temporarily replaces the missing data with extrapolated values, making reporting possible at any time, independent of whether or not data deliveries are provided in time by the market research company. Once the missing data has been uploaded, extrapolated values will be replaced. For example, a time series for sales quantities based on weekly data for about 3 years can be used as input for a PAL predictive algorithm. The PAL algorithm can then interpret seasonality and trend from the time series, in order to predict the extrapolated periods.

Use Case 3: Sales Forecasting Based on Extrapolation Algorithms

This use case concerns the application of data extrapolation algorithms, such as triple exponential smoothing, to the historical POS data to get sales data extrapolated for future time periods, and to check whether or not the sales figures will follow the expected plan.

For this use case, the historical POS sales data can be prepared as a time series using SAP HANA views on the DSiM data model. The time series is then retrieved and passed to the triple exponential smoothing algorithm in PA. In PA, the original and the resulting extrapolated sales revenues can then be visualized, as shown in Figure 6.26. The visualization of the results can then be saved and shared with business users for further actions.

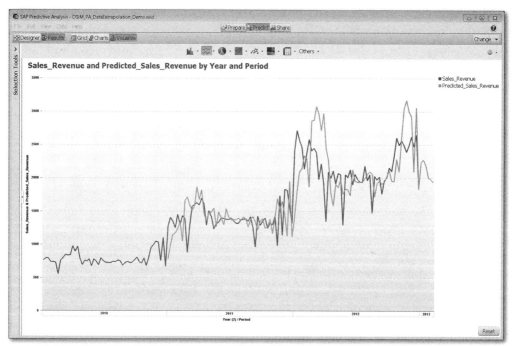

Figure 6.26 Extrapolation of POS Data from DSiM in PA

Using HANA views, a time series of POS sales data can be created for one product category, one region, in weekly time buckets and for a three-year period starting from 2010. To check the trend of the sales for the upcoming weeks, the triple exponential smoothing algorithm was used. The chart in Figure 6.26 shows a continuous sales increase year over year. The prediction shows the sales decreasing at the beginning of 2013.

Additional Use Cases

Additional use cases in which Demand Signal Management may be applicable are as follow:

▶ Reporting and data mining using a combination of social demographics and DSiM demand data to enable more tailored promotions.

▶ Usage of historic weather information to find any correlation between weather data such as temperatures, precipitation and sales, in the respective regions.

▶ Consideration of demand influencing factors, such as weather forecasts, to optimize the sales prediction.

▶ Data mining based on social sentiment information together with POS data in order to improve end consumer insight.

6.6.3 Benefits

Leveraging the out-of-the-box predictive capabilities in SAP HANA and the PAL and PA, helps to identify hidden business opportunities based on DSiM data. This results in:

▶ The ability to predict and analyze huge volumes of demand data, which provides better, earlier visibility of demand changes, which ultimately can lead to increased end consumer satisfaction.

▶ Decrease costs through lower inventory levels that better fit actual demand.

▶ More effective and tailored trade promotions that are possible due to the uncovered associations from the past and a proactive management of marketing campaigns and brand structure.

▶ Decreasing loss of sales due to an early detection of out-of-stock occurrences and the possibility to discover influencing patterns.

6.7 SAP On-Shelf Availability

Poor on-shelf availability is a huge problem affecting the retail industry, especially in its main channels. Even in typical never-out-of-stock assortments such as grocery, drugstore, or DIY, a surprisingly large number of products are repeatedly not available on the store shelves for consumers to purchase. In general, the out-of-stock rates are typically in the range of 5% to 12%.

This leads to a dramatic loss of revenue for retailers and, indirectly, also for the manufacturers of the products. Whereas the loss of revenue can be estimated quite easily from such studies, it is much more difficult to quantify the losses caused by customer dissatisfaction.

Two of the main root causes of poor on-shelf availability have been identified:

1. Wrong order quantities. This is particularly the case if the stores order manually or if the system inventory data is incorrect.
2. Weak in-store processes. The last 50 meters to the shelf are definitely the most problematic part of a product's journey through the retail supply chain. Shelves are replenished too late from back room inventories, shelf tags are missing, consumers are unable to find products on cluttered shelves, or perished products are not replaced by new merchandise.

Measuring on-shelf availability using system inventory data will yield a biased, overly optimistic view of the situation. System inventory figures are often wildly wrong. In addition, they do not distinguish between the inventory in the back room and that on the shelf, and, of course, it is the stock on the shelves that customers see, so this is the only part of the inventory that counts.

6.7.1 Application Description

Instead of analyzing inventory data, which is not a reliable source of information for this purpose, SAP On-Shelf Availability (OSA) assesses the on-shelf availability using the most accurate piece of information available in a retail store, namely the point of sales (POS) transaction data. Not only does this data reveal which product was sold when and in what quantity, but it also provides additional information on prices, discounts, and promotional activities.

OSA aims at improving on-shelf availability in the retail business by supporting tactical root cause analyses of out-of-shelves as well as operational responses to out-of-shelves as they occur.

Tactical root cause analyses may lead to process improvements, such as the optimization of delivery cycles, pack sizes, or shelf layouts, but they may also provide input for better workforce planning, or reveal other organizational weaknesses that degrade on-shelf availability. With the analytical features of OSA, previous out-of-shelf situations in the stores can be detected together with an estimate of their financial impact in terms of lost revenue. This information can be used to determine out-of-shelf hotspots, such as particular categories, specific stores or certain days of the week, in order to derive appropriate tactical responses. Continuous monitoring of the out-of-shelf rate allows the assessing of the effect of the process enhancements. Figure 6.27 shows a screen shot from a SAP BusinessObjects Design Studio report based on the analysis results. It provides an overview at a corporate level of the detected availability issues and shows clusters of out-of-shelf situations in different dimensions such as time, products, suppliers, and stores.

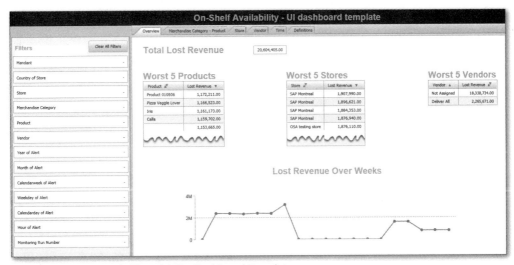

Figure 6.27 SAP On-Shelf Availability Dashboard Template

Operational responses to out-of-shelf situations, on the other hand, are in-store activities that are performed to ensure the availability of the products for the customers. These activities include replenishment of the shelves from the backroom, tidying of shelves and adjustments of the system inventory where it deviates from the actual shelf inventory. To drive these in-store activities, OSA monitors the current on-shelf-availability, issuing near real-time alerts for products that are probably out-of-shelf as soon as the time since the last sales transaction exceeds a critical value. These alerts are augmented by the estimated lost sales and lost revenue, allowing a prioritization of the issues.

Figure 6.28 shows an example mobile application built on top of OSA. This application was delivered to an iPad using the provided OData interfaces. It demonstrates a possible way of leveraging OSA. A list of critical products is issued to the store manager for verification at the shelf where he can either add the product to the list for later replenishment from the back room, or correct the inventory if necessary, or dismiss the alert if it was false.

Figure 6.28 SAP On-Shelf Availability Mobile Application

OSA is a backend component providing statistical modeling as well as analysis and monitoring capabilities. The algorithm itself is implemented as an SAP HANA Application Function Library and runs inside SAP HANA in order to achieve a high performance when processing massive transaction data. OSA is an add-on to the SAP Customer Activity Repository, which provides a common foundation and a harmonized multichannel transaction data model for retail applications.

6.7.2 Current and Planned Use of Predictive Analysis

The principal idea is to automatically identify products that have not sold for an unusually long period of time, in other words, products that are "overdue." The most probable cause for this is an out-of-shelf situation. The challenge is to define what unusually long means for each individual product. For a slow-selling product, an inter-arrival time of several days might be completely acceptable, whereas a fast-selling product can be overdue after no more than a few minutes. A product is also expected to sell more frequently when it is on promotion or sold at a discount. Obviously, a statistical model is required for each product in each store, to describe its expected selling behavior and to detect situations when the product behaves unexpectedly, such as not selling for an unusually long period of time.

From the basic assumption that consumers buy a product at arbitrary points in time, we can derive the principal form of the model. The inter-arrival times t_L of each product, which are the time periods between subsequent sales transactions of the same product in the same store, are expected to be exponentially distributed as

$$t_L \sim Exp(\lambda)$$

The exponential parameter λ is specific for each product and depends on various influencing factors such as the sales price p_i, the discount d_i, the promotion flag x_i, and the transaction time t_i, i being the transaction index.

OSA uses a simple linear expression:

$$\lambda = \lambda(i) = \lambda_0 + \lambda_p p_i + \lambda_d d_i + \lambda_x x_i + \lambda_T t_i$$

The parameters need to be estimated from observed historic data. It is worth noting that λ becomes implicitly time-dependent because of the time dependency of the influencing factors.

The estimation is done by maximizing the log-likelihood of the parameters, given the historical inter-arrival times $t_{L,i}$ using a conjugate gradient algorithm.

$$\ln \pounds(\lambda_0, \lambda_p, \lambda_d, \lambda_x \mid t_{Li}) = \sum_i \ln f(\lambda_0, \lambda_p, \lambda_d, \lambda_x \mid t_{Li}) \rightarrow Max$$

The parameter estimates are stored and used in a later step for comparing the actual inter-arrival times with pre-configured percentiles of the exponential distribution. This reveals unusually long inter-arrival times. The cumulative distribution function for the exponential distribution is

$$F_\lambda(t_L) = 1 - e^{-\lambda tL}$$

which immediately gives the critical inter-arrival time for a given probability q (for example, 99%):

$$\tilde{t}_L = -\frac{1}{\lambda}\ln(1 - q)$$

The term (1-q) can be interpreted as the tolerable false alert rate. Unfortunately, the long tail of the exponential distribution, where intervals that are 4.6 times as long as the mean inter-arrival time will occur 1% of the time, even if there is full shelf availability. This implies that you need to select rather high percentiles, such as 99%, to avoid false alerts. This is not a weakness of the algorithm; it is due to the stochastic nature of the problem.

Retail sales, and thus the inter-arrival times, typically show a strong cyclic intra-week and intra-day pattern. Sales on Saturdays are higher than on Tuesdays, higher in the evening than in the morning. This effect is not covered by the statistical model discussed so far. OSA uses a pre-processing technique to eliminate this influencing factor from the input data before feeding the data into the parameter estimation. This concept is similar to deseasonalizing techniques used in classical time series analysis. The basic idea is a transformation of the real time into a virtual time in which the cyclic intra-week variations are balanced out. The store ticks uniformly in this virtual time. The statistical modeling is then applied to the transformed data. The method has been filed by SAP as a US patent application: Schuetz & Martic, 2012.

6.7.3 Benefits

SAP On-Shelf Availability extracts highly valuable information from the big data acquired at the point-of-sale. It enables retailers to optimize their in-store processes, thereby increasing revenue and profit.

6.8   SAP Product Recommendation Intelligence

The topic of product recommendations is an important part of a consistent and convincing multi-channel offering, given that it can directly influence a company's top and bottom line, and strongly affect customer retention through brand experience. Product recommendations are designed to influence customer's buying behavior and thus change it in a direction desired by the company, which usually means increasing revenue or traffic.

In addition to what the customer already intends to purchase when coming to the respective touch point, be that the web, mobile, store, etc., the recommendations represent the part they potentially would not have bought. This incremental sale needs to be divided into "what they would buy, if they just knew" and "what a marketer wants to push at them to make them buy."

The former is more or less a matter of inferring suggestions based on facts that exist in the data, such as a consumer's past purchasing patterns, their peer group's past purchasing patterns, browsing patterns, etc. The recommendations can be surfaced just by visualizing them and have a good likelihood to be turned into sales. Conversion is increased without even additional marketing dollars.

The latter is more a matter of a marketing department setting up and executing along a given marketing strategy and, based on this, having campaigns, promotions, and certain rule sets that the marketer wants to use to push products to the consumer. These often come with incentives such as discounts or coupons, public advertisements, and other specific marketing activities to generate additional demand through influencing motivation.

6.8.1   Application Description

SAP Product Recommendation Intelligence (PRI) is currently under development; therefore, the following description is of the ideas being considered and not commitments in a plan. At the time of writing, this information is planned as a predictive analysis tool.

Product recommendations will be made in the first iteration for the notion of the awareness purchase. These recommendations will be made context aware in real-time during customer conversation using predictive models. The recommendations are relevant to the consumer and verified against their peer group; specifically, they will be supporting their intent in alignment with their consumer decision stages. The recommendations will be based on consumer's purchase history from all channels as well as pre-structured, business event click stream data, but they can also take other data streams into account. The application will learn from the recommendation history and the consumer's reaction.

Starting the tour from the consumer perspective, it's obvious that the capabilities surface in the interaction at the different touch points of a selling company, be it a retailer, a consumer product goods company, a retail bank, an insurance company etc. So this might very well be a web shop that offers alternatives or up-sells in certain screen areas, as shown in Figure 6.29.

Figure 6.29 Website Recommendations

Product recommendations could equally be used in any other channel from mobile to a customer interaction center or call center, or supporting store assistants in their service effort for the consumer.

Based on the different places where it's being used and the likely intent at that place, different models are to be prepared so that they apply differently, based on the consumer's intent. There will be multiple models, and the most appropriate one will be used in specific situations. Such a model is then eventually built up in a way that it is comparable to ensemble learning in which multiple algorithms or tasks kick off in parallel and their combined result will eventually be used and refined in subsequent steps, as shown in Figure 6.30.

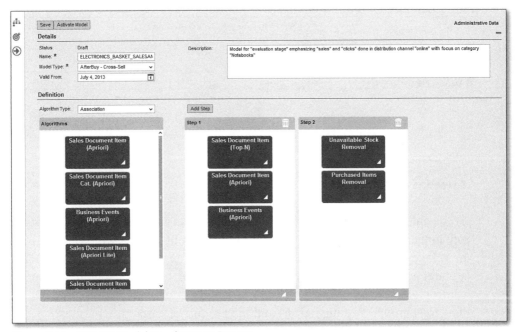

Figure 6.30 SAP PRI Model Development Process

Algorithms or tasks being used in such a step can then again be based on collaborative filtering, which builds a model of user preferences gathered from past behavior such as purchase or browsing histories and explicit numerical preference ratings, and then uses that model to predict items or ratings for items, that a given user may be interested in. They may be based on content-based filtering, which uses a set of numeric and categorical attributes of an item to recommend additional items with similar properties. This eventually yields a hybrid recommender system.

6.8.2 Current and Planned Use of Predictive Analysis

One example of an algorithm is the use of the Apriori algorithm as part of the PAL. This is a classic association analysis to which a data source, such as past purchases, is input. The respective parameters for the Apriori algorithm are set in such a way that they ultimately fulfill, in combination with the other algorithms and steps of the specific model, the intent of the consumer, as shown in Figure 6.31.

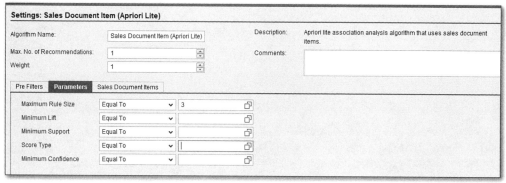

Figure 6.31 SAP PRI Apriori Dialogue Parameters

To be able to adjust the model to the environment, it is also necessary that the key influencing context aspects, such as who the consumer is, which target group he is in, and what product or category the consumer is looking at, are taken into account and also thus determine when a certain part of the model is executed to contribute to the overall result Figure 6.32 shows, for example, the pre-filter for the target group of young Italians and the product of pasta.

Finally, it is critical to be able to determine the subset of the data relevant to this specific model, for example, for a certain model the purchases from the web channels will have a higher importance than those of the brick-and-mortar channel, which will be displayed in the format shown in Figure 6.33.

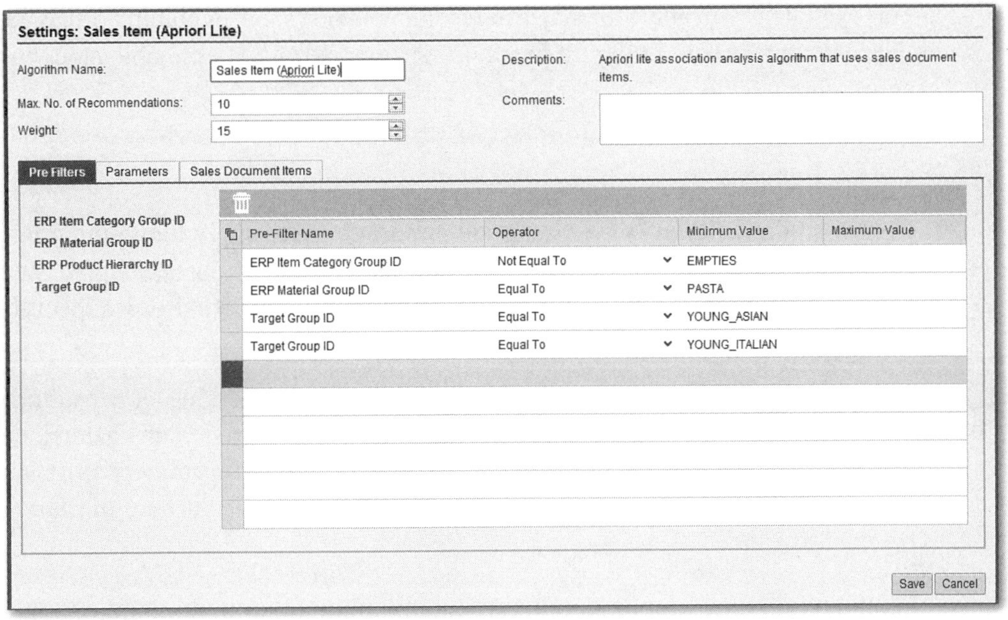

Figure 6.32 SAP PRI Apriori Dialogue Pre-Filters

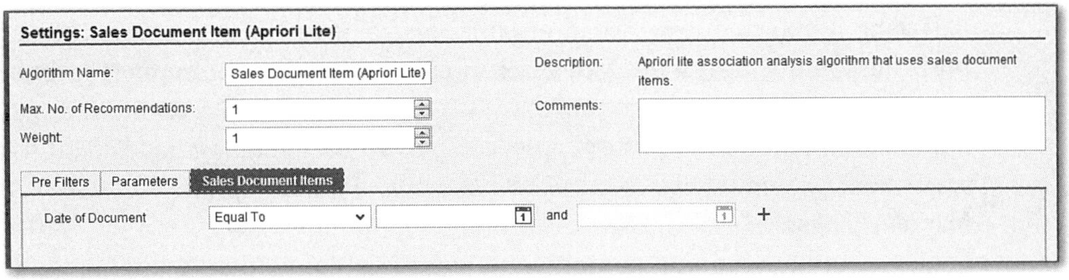

Figure 6.33 SAP PRI Sales Document Items

The current version focuses on leveraging algorithms from the association analysis space on a variety of data sources. It also allows more query type of algorithms to be combined with this data. The plan is to provide algorithms around product attribute affinity.

This eventually will allow for a hybrid recommender system combining collaborative and content based filtering possibilities supported in an ensemble modeling approach.

6.8.3   Benefits

Recommendation engines are now common in web-based applications, providing a wide range of benefits, from delivering relevant content, engaging shoppers and converting them to loyal customers, with consequent increased order quantity and value.

Product sales will be increased by understanding your customers' needs in real-time across all channels. Being able to let customers experience true omni-channel, no matter which channel they prefer, will drive brand value and customers' trust and thus eventually increase customer loyalty, which will secure current and future revenue streams.

6.9   SAP Credit Insight

Balancing profits and losses is an essential part of credit management. The key problems are that businesses face a lack of credit intelligence to support revenue growth and improve operating margin. It is difficult to obtain a centralized real-time snapshot of credit exposure across complex global operations, and credit risk assessment procedures are costly and inflexible, especially given economy and market changes.

SAP Credit Insight (CI) is a proactive and intelligent credit management application that enables smarter and faster credit decisions with the power of prediction and in-memory computing.

6.9.1   Application Description

CI enables real-time global credit exposure by supporting multiple ERP systems. It enables credit strategy optimization and translates it into a series of implementable actions. CI proactively monitors credit risk and provides early warning. It provides up-to-date credit profiling including comprehensive qualitative and quantitative data points. The solution is summarized in Figure 6.34 and shows the different user personas and their respective responsibilities.

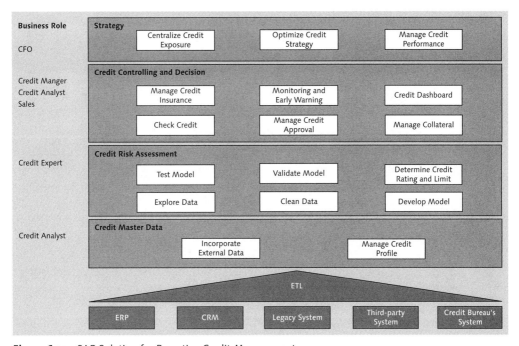

Figure 6.34 SAP Solution for Proactive Credit Management

6.9.2 Current and Planned Use of Predictive Analysis

The CI architecture replicates SAP and non-SAP data to SAP HANA with SAP SLT/ SAP BO Data Services. It deploys side-by-side application on SAP HANA with a one-click installer. The credit decision is written back to SAP ERP, such as credit limit, release a blocked order, or the optimal credit strategy.

The web client for the back-office user is powered by SAP UI5 technology, and a iPad application is available for sales and credit executives. CI provides an improved accuracy of risk prediction with sophisticated statistical models, judgmental models and hybrid models.

6.9.3   Benefits

The main benefits to be derived from SAP Credit Insight are:

▶ Increased revenue and margin with optimal trade sale strategy.

▶ Reduced days sales outstanding (DSO) and bad debt losses, by proactively controlling credit risk.

▶ Improved effectiveness and efficiency of credit management.

6.10   SAP Convergent Pricing Simulation

SAP Convergent Pricing Simulation (CPS) is a cross-industry mass pricing simulation solution that simulates the effect of pricing changes on actual historical data.

With CPS, customers can configure any kind of pricing rule to use for a pricing simulation. These pricing rules are then executed against actual historical events and contracts that are stored in SAP HANA. This allows customers to quickly simulate and simultaneously test one or more pricing schemes, using massive amounts of actual historical records for maximum accuracy, and to quickly analyze and compare the results of various simulations side-by-side.

6.10.1   Application Description

SAP Convergent Pricing Simulation (CPS) leverages SAP's cross-industry pricing and real-time charging solution, SAP Convergent Charging (CG), for pricing configuration and modeling to use with CPS. CG supports configuring any kind of pricing logic to apply to a transactional event, or to be created on a periodic or one-time basis. GC provides business users with tools to configure decision tree rules, which represents the pricing rule to be applied, as shown in Figure 6.35.

Once a pricing rule is configured in CG, it can be exported and compiled into an L-script version of the pricing rule that can be executed directly in SAP HANA. Other mechanisms are provided to replicate historical usage data and contract data, from CG into SAP HANA, all for the purpose of executing a pricing simulation.

SAP Convergent Pricing Simulation (CPS) provides various application control tools that allow users to control the end-to-end process for pricing simulations. Some of the key features provided include starting new simulation models, opening existing models or configuring pricing tariffs to use in a simulation, as shown in Figure 6.36.

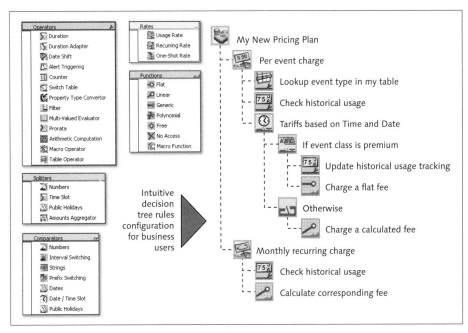

Figure 6.35 SAP Convergent Charging Screenshot

Figure 6.36 SAP Convergent Pricing Simulation Launch Page

A key feature is the analysis of historical or actual data by running simulations and thereby compare and contrast them, based on the results of the pricing simulation, see Figure 6.37.

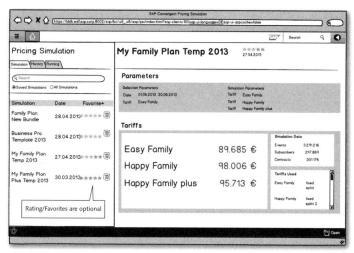

Figure 6.37 SAP Convergent Pricing Simulation

Another key feature is the ability for users to explore and compare various attributes used in a simulation and receive recommendations based simulation results, as shown in Figure 6.38.

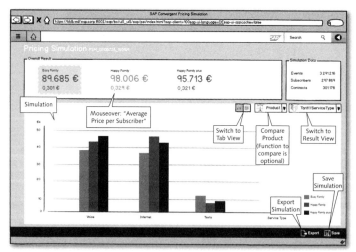

Figure 6.38 SAP Convergent Pricing Simulation Results Graph

6.10.2 Current and Planned Use of Predictive Analysis

Predictive analytics is a logical extension of core pricing simulation functionality. As customers leverage core pricing simulation on SAP HANA to simulate the effect of a price change using historical data, customers also want to better predict the effect a price change can have, not just on projected revenue and costs, but on other aspects of business performance, such as market share and growth strategies, customer sentiment and potential attrition, and the success of loyalty programs and sales strategies. Coupling SAP HANA's in-database predictive algorithms with pricing simulation provides our customers with a unique platform to identify and exploit hidden revenue opportunities, and to make highly informed business decisions that eventually lead to increasingly positive customer sentiment and business growth.

6.10.3 Benefits

The benefits of SAP Convergent Pricing Simulation include:

▶ Identify new business opportunities by analyzing and testing innovative pricing strategies on historical data.

▶ Leverage real, dynamic business data for simulations, hence increasing the accuracy of results and business projections.

▶ Predict trends and tendencies using historical data to test various what-if pricing scenarios.

▶ Make informed decisions in response to changing business conditions by quickly adapting pricing strategies to dynamically changing business conditions.

▶ Boost customer satisfaction and retention by quickly finding innovative solutions to typical causes of attrition.

6.11 Summary

In this chapter we have described ten business applications that SAP has developed that incorporate predictive analysis. From a low base several years ago, this is a remarkable growth and recognition of the importance of predictive analysis and the adage that management is about the future, not the past.

In the next chapter and subsequent ones, we delve into the algorithms used in predictive analysis.

This chapter describes SAP Predictive Analysis in detail, building on the introduction given in Chapter 2. We look at data preparation, applying algorithms, and the deployment of models in PA. This chapter will provide you with a strong understanding of PA functionality.

7   SAP Predictive Analysis

SAP Predictive Analysis (PA) is the user interface for data scientists, data analysts and business users, to define predictive analyses based on the algorithms in the SAP HANA Predictive Analysis Library (PAL), the R Integration for SAP HANA, the R integration for PA, and a group of native algorithms available in PA. PA is fully integrated with SAP Lumira, for initial data access, exploration and visualization, and the sharing of the results of the analysis. In this chapter, we look at the SAP Predictive Analysis product and show how easy it is to get started using PA. We explore the stages of how to access and view the input data, perform any required data preparation, and then apply the algorithms to analyze the data. Our first step into PA is the welcome screen.

7.1   Getting Started in PA

After starting PA, the Welcome screen is displayed, as shown in Figure 7.1.

Immediately, a simple five-step Getting Started guide is displayed, comprising the following steps:

1. Connecting to a data source. Select a data source.
2. Prepare your data. Explore the input data.
3. Analyze your data. Click on the PREDICT VIEW.
4. Visualize the analysis results. Click on RESULTS.
5. Save the analysis: an optional step.

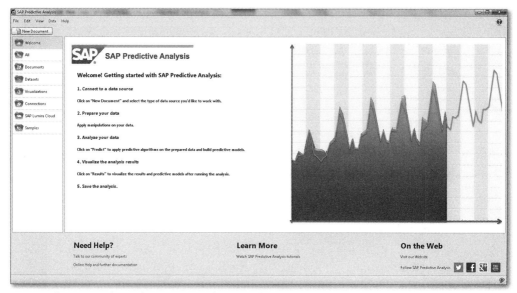

Figure 7.1 The Welcome Screen of SAP Predictive Analysis

In sections 7.2 through 7.6, we look at each of these steps in detail, but let's first very briefly explore the user-friendly click-through process for these five steps with accompanying screenshots. We will discuss each of these steps in further detail but the click through process is intended to give you a big picture overview of the process itself.

1. Connecting to a data source. Select a data source. See Figure 7.2.

Figure 7.2 Connecting to a Data Source

2. Prepare your data by selecting the PREPARE radio button. Explore the input data. See Figure 7.3.

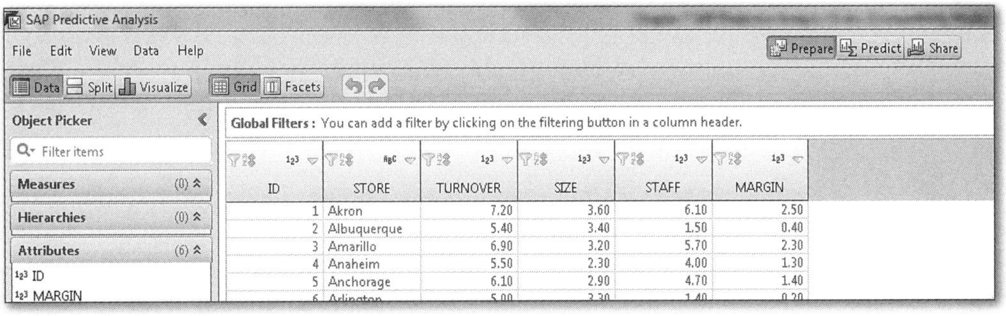

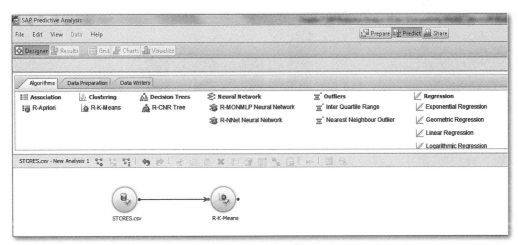

Figure 7.3 The Prepare View in PA for Data Exploration and Preparation

3. Analyze your data. Click on the PREDICT View. See Figure 7.4.

Figure 7.4 The Predict View including the Algorithms and Analysis Process

4. Visualize the analysis results by selecting the VISUALIZE button. Click on RESULTS. See Figures 7.5 and 7.6.

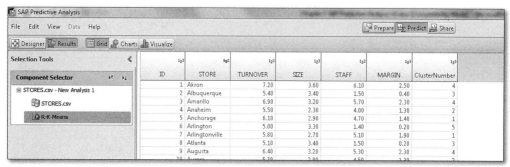

Figure 7.5 The Results of the Analysis in Grid Format

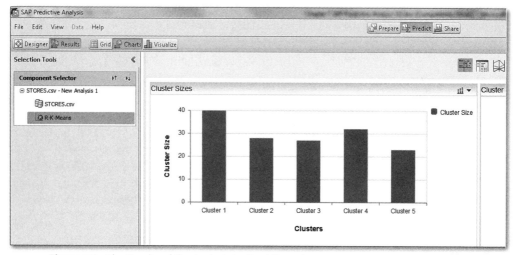

Figure 7.6 The Results of the Analysis in Chart Format

5. Save the analysis. An optional step. See Figure 7.7.

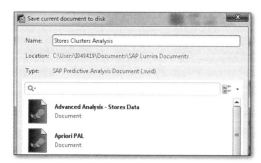

Figure 7.7 Save the Analysis

It is really that simple by design! The user experience and interface reflect the modern design of PA as a predictive analysis tool.

The Welcome screen of PA also contains a collection of SAMPLES to help the new user see various examples to learn the product, and which are shown in Figure 7.8.

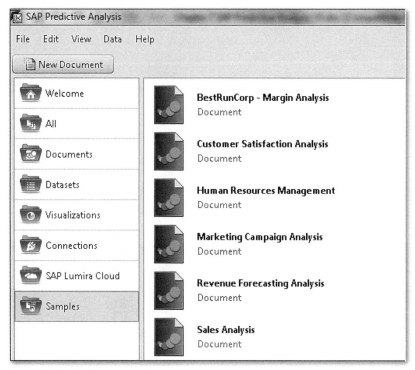

Figure 7.8 The Samples in PA

As an example, if you select the CUSTOMER SATISFACTION ANALYSIS sample, then the PREPARE View is opened, as shown in Figure 7.9, with the data initially displayed in a line chart.

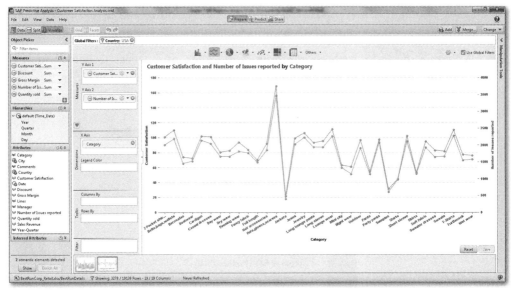

Figure 7.9 The Customer Satisfaction Analysis Sample in the Prepare View

Selecting the PREDICT View opens the sample analysis, as shown in Figure 7.10.

Figure 7.10 The Customer Satisfaction Analysis Sample in the Predict View

The Welcome screen also includes links to the SAP Predictive Analysis Community, Online Help, Product Tutorial Videos, and the product website.

We now look at each of the five steps in the Getting Started guide in more detail.

7.2   Accessing and Viewing the Data Source

After selecting the NEW DOCUMENT button on the PA Welcome screen, the SELECT A SOURCE dialogue opens, as shown in Figure 7.11.

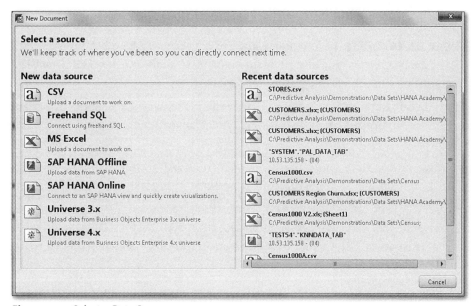

Figure 7.11   Select a Data Source

The various data sources supported in PA are shown under the NEW DATA SOURCE column, while recently acquired data sources are listed for convenience and fast access. There is an important distinction between SAP HANA Online as a data source, and the rest. With SAP HANA Online, you can acquire data from SAP HANA tables, views, analysis views, and perform in-database predictive analysis using the PAL algorithms and the R Integration for SAP HANA. All the other data sources are non in-database SAP HANA, and therefore exclude the PAL algorithms and the R Integration for SAP HANA, as the analysis is not in SAP HANA. PA uses the distinction of in-database and in-process.

The seven different data sources are:

1. **CSV file**: Here you can acquire data from a comma-separated value data file and perform in-process analysis using native PA algorithms and the R integration for PA.

2. **Free hand SQL**: Here you can create your own data provider by manually entering the SQL for a target data source and perform in-process analysis using native PA algorithms and the R integration for PA.

3. **SAP HANA Offline**: Here you can acquire data from SAP HANA tables, views, and analysis views, and also perform in-process analysis using native PA algorithms and the R integration for PA.

4. **SAP HANA Online**: Here you can acquire data from SAP HANA tables, views, and analysis views, and also perform in-database analysis using SAP HANA PAL algorithms and the R Integration for SAP HANA.

5. **MS Excel**: Here you can acquire data from a Microsoft Excel spreadsheet and perform in-process analysis using native PA algorithms and the R integration for PA.

6. **Universe 3.x**: Here you can acquire data from SAP BusinessObjects universes that exist on the XI 3.x platform and perform in-process analysis using native PA algorithms and the R integration for PA.

7. **Universe 4.x**: Here you can acquire data from SAP BusinessObjects universes that exist on the BI 4.x platform and perform in-process analysis using native PA algorithms and the R integration for PA.

When you select SAP HANA Online, a dialogue appears prompting you for the SAP HANA connection information and table selection, for the input data, as shown in Figure 7.12.

After selecting an SAP HANA table and acquiring the data, PA takes you to the PREPARE View, from which you can select the PREDICT View where all the in-database PAL algorithms are listed for use in an in-database analysis, as shown in Figure 7.13, along with the data source component in the analysis editor or workspace. In addition to the PAL algorithms, the R Integration for SAP HANA is supported for specific algorithms, for example Apriori, K-Means, CNR Tree and Multiple Linear Regression. The Data Preparation and Data Writer components are also executed in-database in SAP HANA.

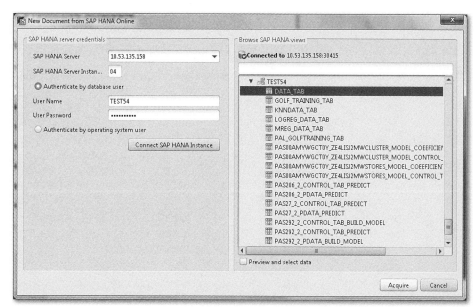

Figure 7.12 SAP HANA Online Data Source Dialogue

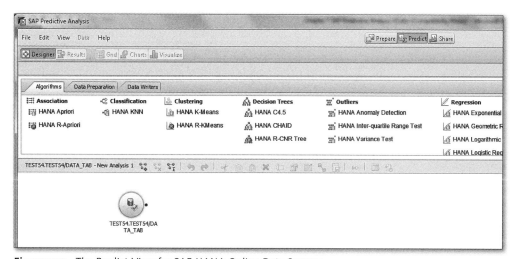

Figure 7.13 The Predict View for SAP HANA Online Data Sources

For data sources other than SAP HANA Online, such as a CSV file, the prompt for the data source is as shown in Figure 7.14.

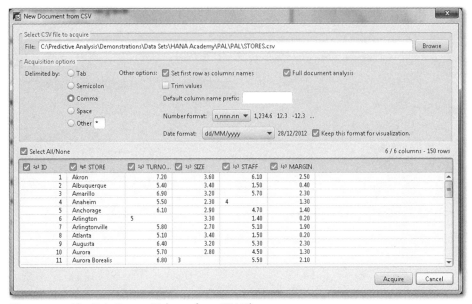

Figure 7.14 The Data Source Dialogue for a CSV File

Upon acquiring the data, PA takes you to the PREPARE View, from which you can select the PREDICT View, where all the native PA algorithms and PA supported R algorithms are listed for use in an in-process analysis, as shown in Figure 7.15, along with the data source component in the analysis workspace.

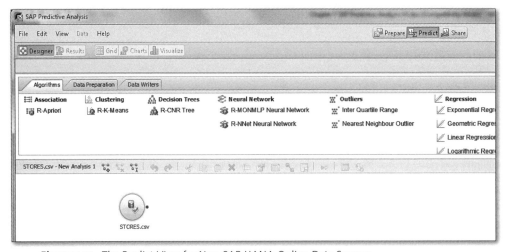

Figure 7.15 The Predict View for Non-SAP HANA Online Data Sources

In the PREPARE View of PA, you can combine the data from two different data sets. You have two options for combining two data sets. The MERGE functionality matches a key column from both data sets to create a combined table; the UNION option adds the selected columns of the source data set to the target data set, as long as the matching columns are of the same data type. Figure 7.16 shows the merging of two data sets in the PREPARE View of PA.

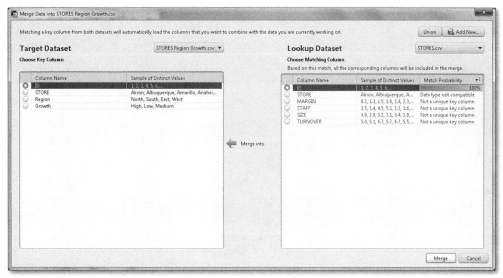

Figure 7.16   Merge Data Sets in the PA Prepare View

Once you have acquired the input data for analysis, you are ready to do an initial data exploration and preparation, prior to applying any algorithms.

7.3   Preparing Data for Analysis

PA is divided into three main views – PREPARE, PREDICT and SHARE. After acquiring the input data, PA moves to the PREPARE View, where you can review the data in a grid format, as shown in Figure 7.17. Columns can be sorted, filtered, renamed, merged, created as a geographical hierarchy for geo maps, created as a time hierarchy, reformatted, and converted to a different data type.

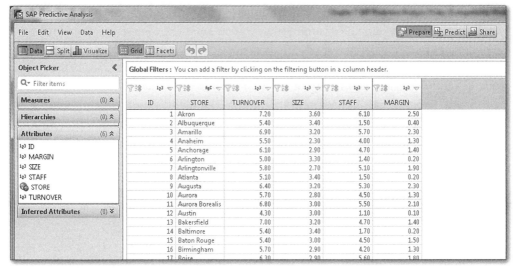

Figure 7.17 The PA Prepare View Grid Display

The data can also be displayed in the FACETS View, as shown in Figure 7.18. Here the data is shown by distinct value, equivalent to a horizontal bar chart, but by value. This is useful when there are not too many distinct values. The data manipulations available in the GRID View are also available in the FACETS View.

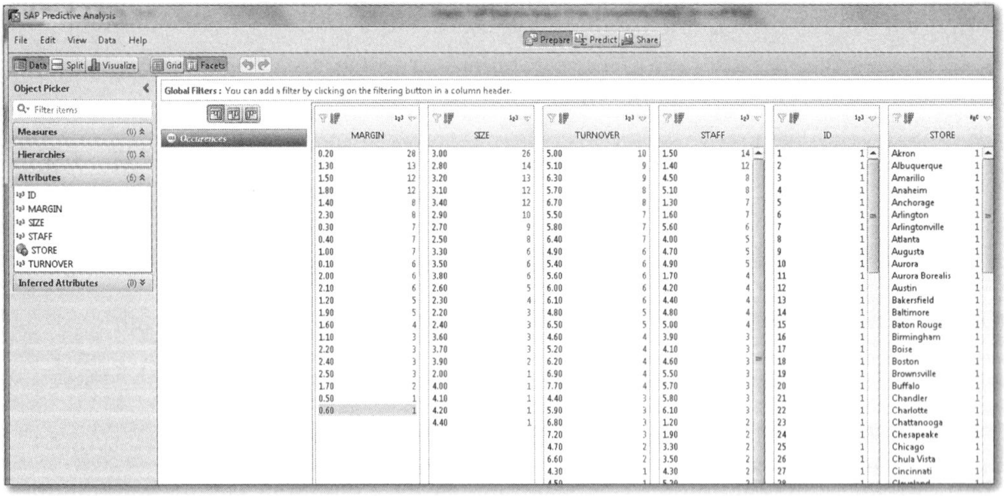

Figure 7.18 The PA Prepare View Facets Display

A major feature within the PREPARE View is the VISUALIZE View and the extensive chart library, as shown in Figure 7.19.

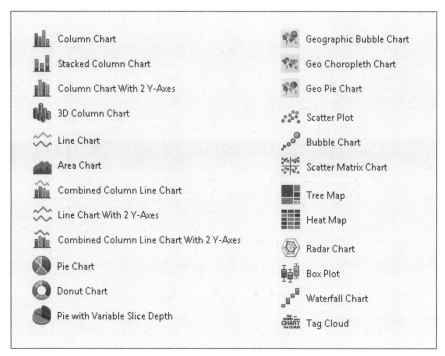

Figure 7.19   Chart Types Available in PA Prepare Visualize View

We have shown many examples of visualizations in earlier chapters of this book. However, just as an example, we show in Figure 7.20 a geographic bubble chart, having first converted the STORE column to a geographical hierarchy in the GRID View. Note the drill-up and drill-down functionality in the chart.

Having now accessed the data and explored the data using the many data visualizations that are available in PA, you are ready to perform any further data preparation and apply predictive analysis algorithms in the PREDICT View of PA.

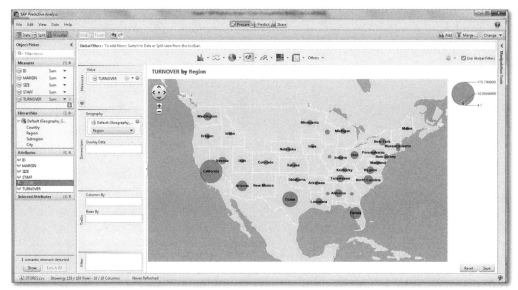

Figure 7.20 A Geographic Bubble Plot of the Stores Turnover Data

7.4   Applying Algorithms to Analyze the Data

The PREDICT View in PA lists all the components that can be added to create an analysis, and they are grouped by tabs into ALGORITHMS, DATA PREPARATION, and DATA WRITERS. The actual components that are available depend on whether you are building an in-database analysis using SAP HANA algorithms or, alternatively, an in-process analysis, as shown previously in Figures 7.13 and 7.15 respectively. The actual construction of the analyses is the same for either method.

To build an analysis, you simply select a component and then drag the desired component on to the analysis editor or workspace, which will then be automatically connected to the component with current focus. Alternatively, you can double click the desired next component and it is then automatically connected to the component with focus. Each component contains input and output anchors, or connection points, which are used to connect components through connectors. A data source component just has the output connection point. When you connect components together, data is transmitted from predecessor components to their successor components.

The structure of a component is shown in Figure 7.21, with options to rename, run, delete, and configure its properties. Also shown are the various states a component can be in, for example, NOT CONFIGURED applies when you drag a component on to the analysis editor or workspace and it therefore needs to be configured before running the analysis. CONFIGURED means that all the mandatory properties of the component are configured, and SUCCESS is displayed after the successful execution of the analysis. FAILURE is shown when the component causes the execution of the analysis to fail.

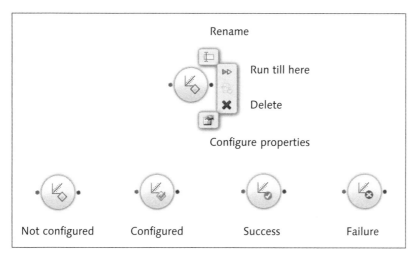

Figure 7.21 Component Options and States in PA

In the next two subsections, we build an analysis of the Stores data in PA: first, as an in-database analysis with the data sourced from an SAP HANA table and the algorithms based on the PAL, and, second, as an in-process analysis with the data sourced from a CSV file and the algorithms based on the R integration in PA.

7.4.1 In-Database Analysis using an SAP HANA Table and the PAL

You first select the data in SAP HANA, as was shown in Figure 7.12, and then open the PREDICT View in PA, as was shown in Figure 7.13. Importantly, the data does not leave SAP HANA. The whole analysis is in-database. Our analysis aims to segment or cluster the retail stores data into similar groups based on their sales turnover, profit margins, staff numbers and store size. To do this, you select the HANA K-Means algorithm and drag and connect the component in the analysis editor or workspace, as shown in Figure 7.22.

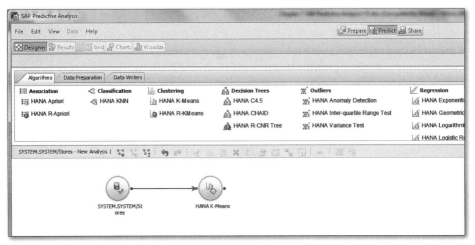

Figure 7.22 SAP HANA In-Database Cluster Analysis using PA

Next you configure the properties of the HANA K-Means component, as shown in Figure 7.23, where the primary properties are displayed. You select the variables to be used in the analysis, e.g., TURNOVER, SIZE, STAFF and MARGIN and the number of clusters–the value of K, which in our example is set to 5.

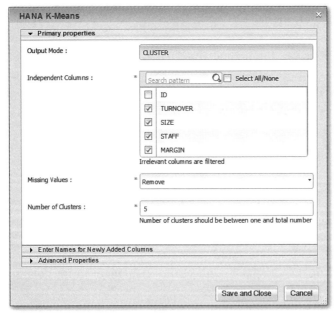

Figure 7.23 The Primary Properties of the HANA K-Means Component in PA

Selecting the ADVANCED PROPERTIES in the dialogue displays the rest of the control parameters for the PAL K-Means algorithm, as shown in Figure 7.24, which are clearly defined for the business analyst, as opposed to writing in SQLScript. The asterisk indicates a mandatory input field. The default values for the advanced properties are displayed, and can be changed, for example, the maximum number of iterations of the algorithm might be changed from 100 to a smaller number if the data volumes are very large and processing time is important.

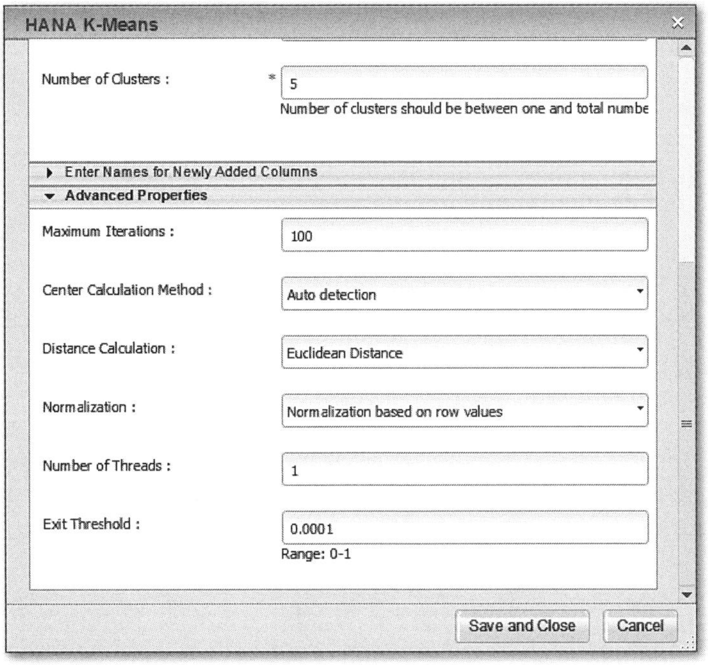

Figure 7.24 The Advanced Properties of the HANA K-Means Component

The analysis is now ready to be run, as we show in Section 7.5.

7.4.2 In-Process Analysis using a CSV File and R Integration in PA

For the in-process analysis, you first access the data from a CSV file, as was shown in Figure 7.14, and then open the PREDICT View, as shown in Figure 7.15. As before, our analysis aims to cluster or group the retail stores. You select the R K-Means algorithm and drag and connect the component in the analysis editor or workspace, as shown in Figure 7.25.

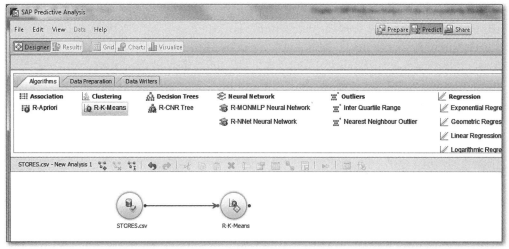

Figure 7.25 An In-Process Analysis of a CSV file using R K-Means

Next you configure the properties of the R K-Means component, as shown in
Figure 7.26 where the primary properties are displayed. You select the variables
for the analysis and the value of K, which is the number of clusters to be created
from the analysis.

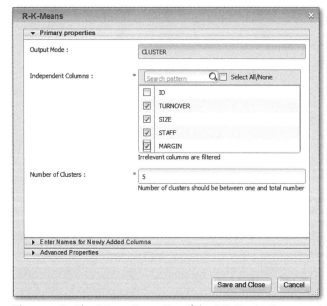

Figure 7.26 The Primary Properties of the R K-Means Component in PA

Selecting the ADVANCED PROPERTIES in the dialogue displays the rest of the control parameters for the R K-Means algorithm, as shown in Figure 7.27, again simply defined for the business analyst, as opposed to writing R language script. The values displayed are the default values for the analysis, which can be changed by the user, or left as they are.

R-K-Means ☒

▸ Enter Names for Newly Added Columns
▾ Advanced Properties

Maximum Iterations :   100

Number of Initial Sets :   1

Algorithm :   Hartigan-Wong ▾

Save and Close   Cancel

Figure 7.27 The Advanced Properties of the HANA K-Means Component in PA

The analysis is now ready to be run, as we show in the next section.

The analyses that you have built so far have been very simple, comprising just two components; however, by way of illustration, a more advanced and more realistic analysis is shown in Figure 7.28.

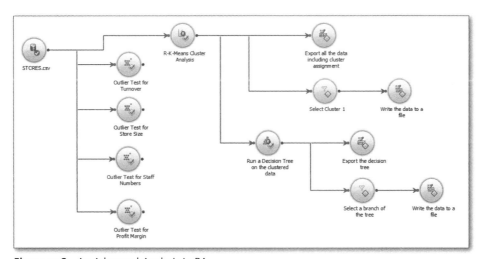

Figure 7.28 An Advanced Analysis in PA

The diagram in Figure 7.28 starts with the STORES.csv data source and then runs the Inter-Quartile Range Test on each variable to check for outliers prior to running a cluster analysis on the data. The cluster analysis is then run, after which the source data and its assigned cluster number is written to a database table, while the specific results for cluster 1, are written to a file. The data from the cluster analysis is then analyzed using a decision tree whereby the target or dependent variable is the previously derived cluster number and the independent variables are the store turnover, margin, staff and size, from which you can obtain rules describing why the clusters were formed. Finally, you export all the results, plus a filtered subset. Our decision tree model could have been saved and then applied to new data to predict a new stores cluster assignment. We show this in Section 7.6. When models are saved, PA also offers the option to export the model to another application using the Predictive Modeling Markup Language (PMML) standard, which we also show in Section 7.6.

A recent and major addition to PA has been the ability to define and run any R algorithm from the PA analysis editor. PA provides a GUI to add R script as a new component in PA, based on either the R integration for PA or the R Integration for SAP HANA and then run the scripts. In addition, the capability to add your own custom algorithm, written in C++ or JAVA, is available. Figure 7.29 shows part of the wizard for creating your own custom R script components, which are then available for inclusion in an analysis.

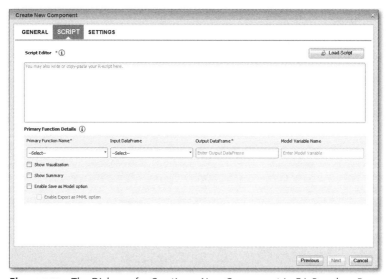

Figure 7.29 The Dialogue for Creating a New Component in PA Based on R

This integration provides SAP Predictive Analysis access to the thousands of algorithms from the R libraries. An expert user can create the new components, which a business user can then easily embed into their own analyses. It is a very powerful addition to the capabilities of PA.

Having defined the analysis, you are ready to run it and view the results.

7.5 Running the Model and Viewing the Results

Running an analysis is the same for in-database and in-process, so we focus on the in-process example that we have developed so far, because that is the easier one for you to replicate, as it is simply based on a CSV file.

The analysis shown in Figure 7.25 can be run either using the "Run till here" option of the R K-Means component, as was shown in Figure 7.21, or can be invoked from the RUN ANALYSIS icon on the ANALYSIS EDITOR toolbar. Upon successful completion of the analysis, you can switch to the PREDICT RESULTS View for tabular or grid output, plus specific charts for the algorithms used and the general ad hoc chart viewer for user defined visualizations. Figure 7.30 shows the RESULTS view for the first few records of our cluster analysis, with the input data listed along with a new column, showing for each record, its assigned cluster number.

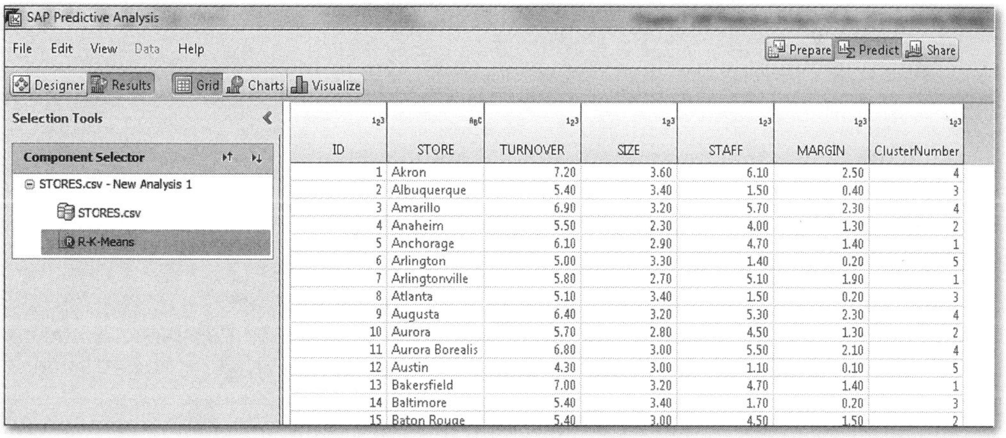

ID	STORE	TURNOVER	SIZE	STAFF	MARGIN	ClusterNumber
1	Akron	7.20	3.60	6.10	2.50	4
2	Albuquerque	5.40	3.40	1.50	0.40	3
3	Amarillo	6.90	3.20	5.70	2.30	4
4	Anaheim	5.50	2.30	4.00	1.30	2
5	Anchorage	6.10	2.90	4.70	1.40	1
6	Arlington	5.00	3.30	1.40	0.20	5
7	Arlingtonville	5.80	2.70	5.10	1.90	1
8	Atlanta	5.10	3.40	1.50	0.20	3
9	Augusta	6.40	3.20	5.30	2.30	4
10	Aurora	5.70	2.80	4.50	1.30	2
11	Aurora Borealis	6.80	3.00	5.50	2.10	4
12	Austin	4.30	3.00	1.10	0.10	5
13	Bakersfield	7.00	3.20	4.70	1.40	1
14	Baltimore	5.40	3.40	1.70	0.20	3
15	Baton Rouge	5.40	3.00	4.50	1.50	2

Figure 7.30 The Predict Results Grid View for the R K-Means Algorithm in PA

If you select the CHARTS option, then for the K-Means algorithm, you see the CLUSTER CHART, as shown in Figure 7.31, which provides four different visualizations of the results of the cluster analysis for exploration by the user. The vertical bar chart shows the size of each cluster for easy comparison, and which can be changed to a horizontal bar chart or pie chart. Then a cluster density and distance chart with a color coded scale of dark to light for dense to sparse clusters, and the distance between the cluster centers is shown with the thicker the line, the closer the clusters. Small-sized clusters that are close to other clusters may be considered for combining; alternatively, small-sized clusters that are far apart from other clusters may be considered as outliers. The two charts at the bottom allow the user to compare clusters by variable to see what differentiates each cluster.

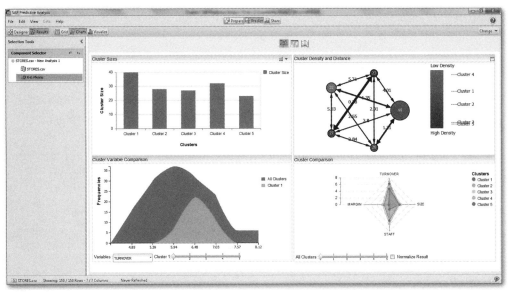

Figure 7.31 The Cluster Chart in PA

For each algorithm, an algorithm summary is given, which for the R K-Means algorithm is the output from R, as shown in Figure 7.32, and includes the cluster center coordinates; the within cluster sum of squares, which is the squared sum of the distances between individual records in the cluster and the cluster center for all records in the cluster; and, finally, the size of each cluster.

A third chart is available from the CHARTS option, namely the CLUSTER PARALLEL COORDINATES CHART, where each record is plotted as a horizontal line connected by its value on the vertical axis of each displayed variable, and then color coded by its cluster number, as shown in Figure 7.33.

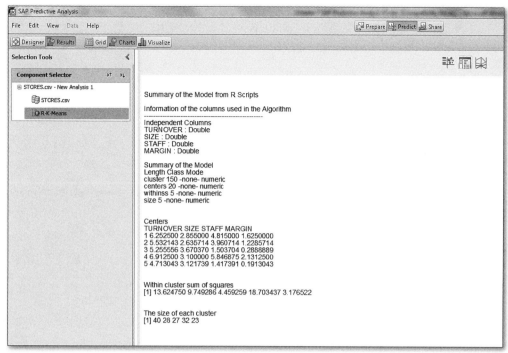

Figure 7.32 The R K-Means Algorithm Summary Output in PA

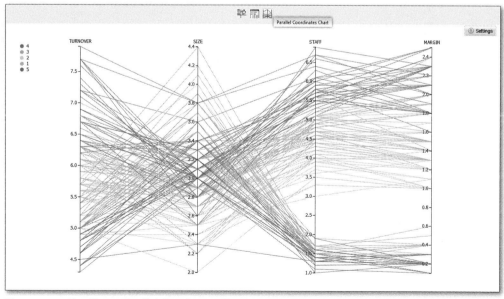

Figure 7.33 The Cluster Parallel Coordinates Chart in PA

The five color-coded clusters show that there are perhaps three clusters in the data, perhaps only two. In practice, you would run the analysis again for K = 3 and K = 2 and examine the output.

As with many of the visualizations in PA, you can drill down into the data to examine it in more detail, as shown in Figure 7.34, where we look at the specific records in cluster numbers 3 and 5.

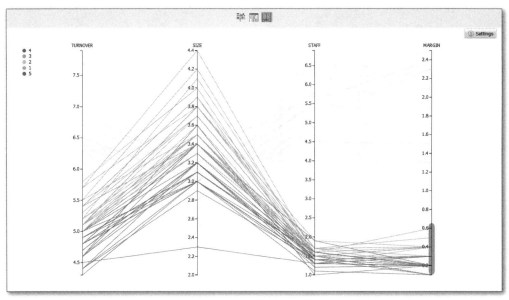

Figure 7.34 Drill Down into the Cluster Parallel Coordinates Chart in PA

Each algorithm has a default visualization, which we show in the specific chapters later in the book.

Finally, you can choose the VISUALIZE option for ad hoc user defined chart creation. In Figure 7.35 we have created a trellis chart showing each variable by cluster group for comparison.

Following on from building and running the analysis, you now want to use the model to predict new data, either within PA or in an external application.

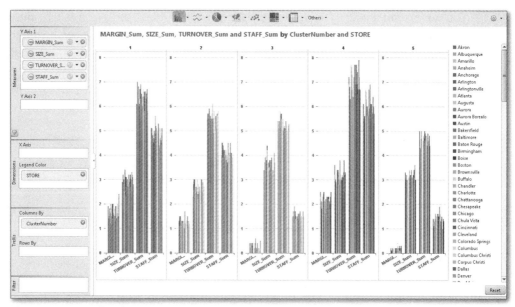

Figure 7.35 A Trellis Chart in the Visualize Results View of PA

7.6 Deploying the Model in a Business Application

PA offers several options for deploying models:

▸ Scoring models in PA and exporting the results.

▸ Exporting the model as PMML.

▸ Sharing the analysis in the SHARE VIEW in PA.

▸ Exporting and importing analyses between PA users.

▸ Exporting an SAP HANA PAL model from PA as a stored procedure.

One of the main options is to use Predictive Analysis to predict new data or score the model.

When you have built a model and then want to make predictions using that model, based on new input data, PA provides the functionality to save the built model. The saved model can then be fed new data from which the target or dependent variable can be predicted. This is also called scoring models, taken from the phrase of scoring a customer's credit worthiness or their propensity to churn.

You can extend the analysis shown in Figure 7.25 by adding the decision tree algorithm R-CNR Tree to derive the rules that describe why records have been assigned to specific clusters. The independent or input variables are the retail store turnover, margin, staff number, and shop size, and the target or dependent variable is the cluster number. This is shown in Figure 7.36, along with the selection to save the model, with a model name and description. The screenshot has been truncated slightly to show the relevant parts in one figure.

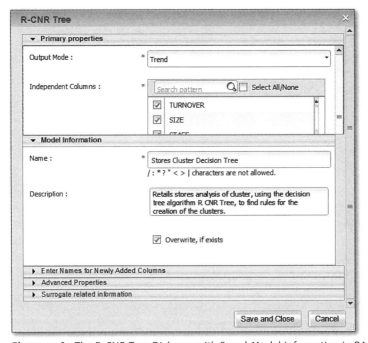

Figure 7.36 The R-CNR Tree Dialogue with Saved Model Information in PA

After you run the analysis, the saved model is shown in a new tab, alongside the ALGORITHMS, DATA PREPARATION and DATA WRITERS tabs, as shown in Figure 7.37.

Now you can build a new analysis using the saved model to predict new data, as shown in Figure 7.38. In the PREPARE View, you can add the new data set and then use the saved model to predict. Alternatively, you can export the saved model from the current analysis and then create a new analysis with the new data for scoring, and import the saved model. Either way, you create the analysis, as shown in Figure 7.38.

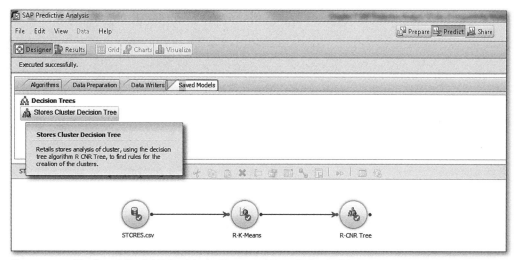

Figure 7.37 The Saved Model Tab with the Name and Description in PA

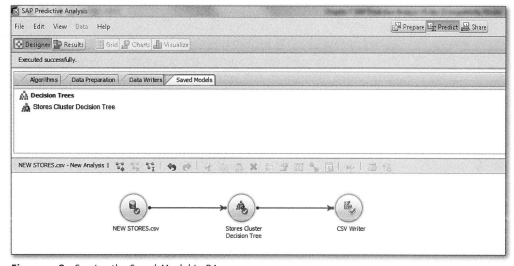

Figure 7.38 Scoring the Saved Model in PA

You can then run the analysis for the new predictions, with the output as shown in Figure 7.39. These new predictions can be exported to a file for use in another application. This applies to all output from models built in PA.

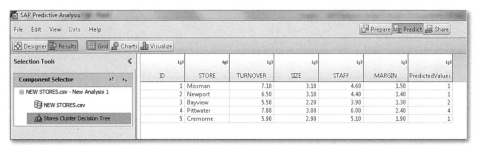

Figure 7.39 The Predicted Cluster Numbers for the New Stores

In this section we described how to export the predictions of a model. In the next section we show how you can export the actual model.

7.6.1 Exporting the Model as PMML

A saved model in PA can be exported using the Predictive Modeling Markup Language (PMML), the industry standard for sharing models between applications. By right-clicking on the saved model component in the PA analysis editor, the option Export as PMML appears, from which you can specify a file to contain the XML. Figure 7.40 shows part of the PMML generated for the saved decision tree model. Another application can read the PMML, which describes the created model, and then use it to make predictions.

Figure 7.40 The PMML Output for the Decision Tree Model in PA

When developing analyses, it is important to be able to share that analysis with other users. We show how you can do this in PA in the next section.

7.6.2   Sharing the Analysis in the Share View in PA

Using the SHARE View in PA, you can do the following with your data, chart, or both:

▶ Share your chart.

▶ Export your data set to a file.

▶ Publish your data set to SAP HANA as an analytic view.

▶ Publish your data set and charts to StreamWork.

▶ Publish your data set to a BusinessObjects information space to be accessed in SAP BusinessObjects Explorer.

▶ Publish your data set to the SAP Lumira cloud.

An example of sharing the CUSTOMERS.xlsx data and associated visualizations is shown in Figure 7.41.

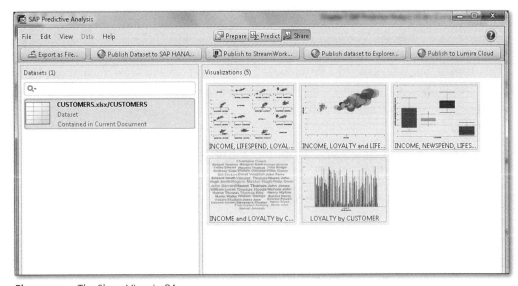

Figure 7.41   The Share View in PA

Finally, in terms of model deployment, in the next section we describe how to export and import analyses between PA users.

7.6.3 Exporting and Importing Analyses between PA Users

You can export a model created in a SVID document into a .spar file and use it in another SVID document by importing it. This is achieved by selecting the model and choosing EXPORT MODEL from the PA tool bar in the PREDICT View, then providing a name for the .spar file, and choosing SAVE.

You can reuse a model created in a SVID document in another SVID document by importing it from a .spar file. This is achieved by selecting IMPORT MODEL from the PA tool bar in the PREDICT View and choosing a valid .spar file, and then the OPEN option. The model is imported and displayed in the SAVED MODELS tab.

SVID is the acronym for SAP Visual Intelligence Document (Visual Intelligence being the previous name of Lumira), which stores the data set and visualizations that are created by the user. If you had saved the model, it would also get stored in the SVID. This can be shared with other users or to the SAP Lumira cloud, and can be used by them directly opening it in SAP Lumira or PA.

SPAR is the acronym for SAP Predictive Analysis Archive file and it is the proprietary format of exporting PA created models. This is mainly for model transportation today, but it is planned to also cover analysis and custom created components as well in this format. An example use case is where one user creates the model and another user wishes to use it.

7.6.4 Exporting an SAP HANA PAL Model from PA as a Stored Procedure

You can export a saved SAP HANA PAL model created in PA and use it as a stored procedure in SAP HANA. After creating an in-database SAP HANA model in PA and saving it, you can export it by completing the prompts shown in the dialogue in Figure 7.42.

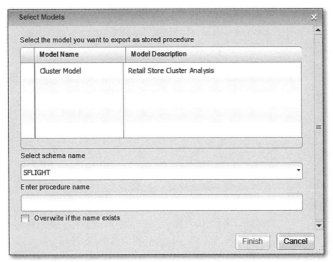

Figure 7.42 The Select Models Dialogue for Model Export in PA

The exported procedure and the associated objects of the procedure, tables, and types, appear under the selected schema in SAP HANA.

Further Sources of Information

In this chapter we have provided an introduction to PA. There are many resources available for further reading and review. For example, SAP Predictive Analysis has a comprehensive help system and reference manual, available from *http://help.sap.com/pa*.

The SAP HANA Academy provides many excellent how-to videos, including PA, see *http://www.saphana.com/community/implement/hana-academy#predictive-analysis*.

The SAP Community Network (SCN) has a very active community on SAP Predictive Analysis, see *http://scn.sap.com/community/predictive-analysis*.

Finally, just Google the words "SAP Predictive Analysis" for a wealth of material, including several YouTube presentations.

7.7   Summary

In this chapter we described in detail the SAP Predictive Analysis product, and showed how easy it is to get started using PA. We then went through the stages of how to access and view the input data, perform any required data preparation, and apply the algorithms to analyze the data. After running the analysis, we showed the various visualizations available for the results of the analysis. Finally, we described various methods of deploying the model. We concluded the chapter with a list of further sources of information regarding SAP Predictive Analysis.

In the next part, Predictive Analysis Categories, we will build upon our previous discussions and look at specific analysis categories, the algorithms, and worked examples. In the next chapter we start our detailed discussion and worked examples of predictive analysis algorithms, beginning with the group of algorithms for outlier detection.

PART III
Predictive Analysis Categories

This chapter describes the outlier detection algorithms in the PAL and PA. They are an important preliminary step in predictive analysis and have major application in the field of fraud detection.

8   Outlier Analysis

Outlier analysis is a very important topic in predictive analysis for two key reasons. First, outliers may exist because of errors in the data that need correcting or removing before beginning any model building. Second, outliers may occur naturally in the data as they are genuinely different from other values and therefore model building has to take into account these variations.

8.1   Introduction to Outlier Analysis

Some algorithms are significantly affected by outliers; some are not. For example, the mean is affected by outliers, whereas the median is not. A simple example is shown in Figure 8.1 using linear regression, where the effect of a single outlier significantly changes the line of best fit and model quality, and therefore also any prediction – both the value and the confidence of the prediction.

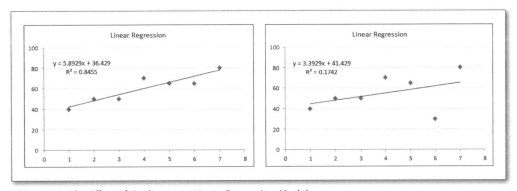

Figure 8.1   The Effect of Outliers on a Linear Regression Model

Outliers can sometimes be detected visually, for example, in scatter plots, as shown in Figure 8.1., and for multidimensional data in scatter plot matrices or lattice plots, as shown in Figure 8.2, which was created in SAP Predictive Analysis.

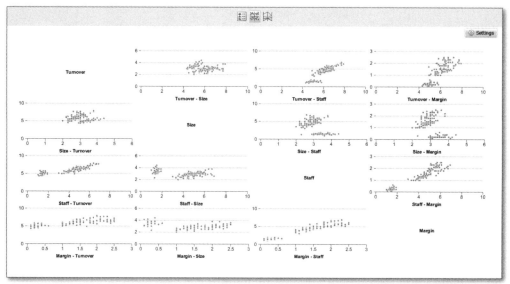

Figure 8.2 A Scatter Plot Matrix for Outlier Detection

Bubble plots and parallel co-ordinate plots can also be used for visual outlier detection; however, the most common visualization is a box plot, as shown in Figure 8.3. This chart is specifically designed to summarize numeric data, with the box representing data between the upper and lower quartiles, the "fences" around the box representing a factor times the inter-quartile range, and the dots outside the fences representing the outliers.

To a certain degree, outliers can be detected in data visualizations; however, for very large and multidimensional data sets, this is limited because of the data volume and the difficulty of visualizations to represent the large amounts of data. Hence the need for outlier detection algorithms to automatically search and find unusual values.

In this chapter, we start with the Inter-Quartile Range test in the PAL, which is in fact the basis of the box plot, and then the very simple, but still very useful, Variance test. Then the chapter describes the more subtle algorithms of the Nearest Neighbor Outlier test and Anomaly Detection using cluster analysis. These two algorithms look for local outliers in the data rather than overall outliers. Looking toward the practical application and use of outlier analysis, we review the applications of this type of analysis, its strengths and weaknesses, and finally the business case.

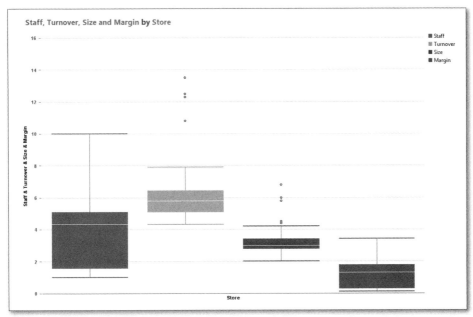

Figure 8.3 A Box Plot for Outlier Detection

8.2 Applications of Outlier Analysis

The two main applications of outlier analysis reflect the two main reasons for doing such analysis. The first application is as a pre-cursor to building a model to try to identify any errors in the data that may be subsequently corrected or to identify any unusual values that are in fact valid and that need to be accounted for in a model. Such outliers may influence the type of algorithm used in the analysis, as some algorithms are more sensitive to outliers than others. Second, outlier or anomaly detection is a key component of fraud analysis, which involves looking for the unusual. It is applicable in a variety of domains, such as production process control, fault detection, intrusion detection, fraud detection, system monitoring, and event detection.

The SAP Fraud Management module uses outlier detection methods as shown in Figure 8.4 and Figure 8.5.

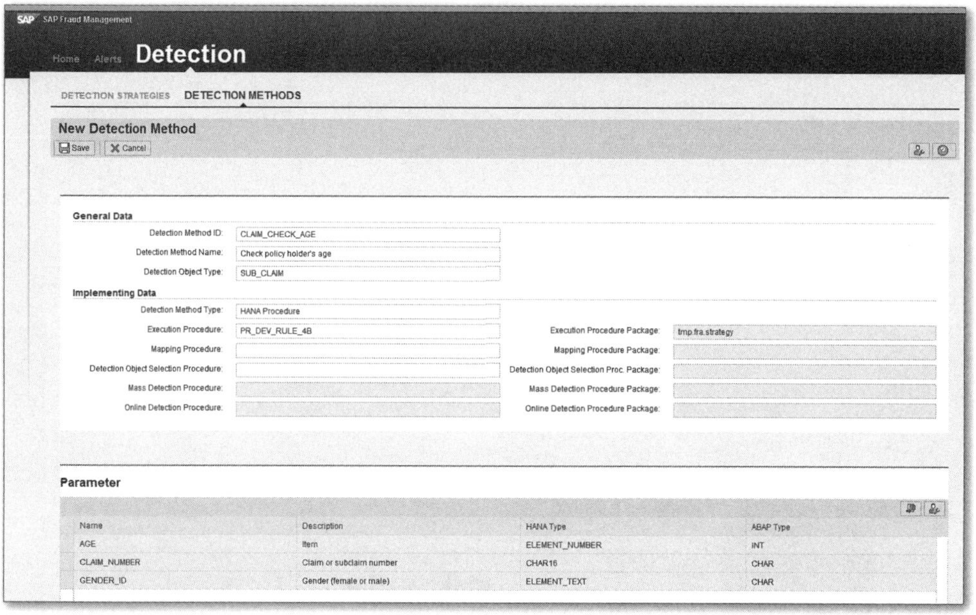

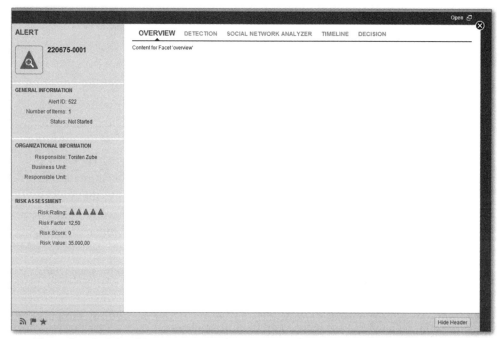

Figure 8.4 SAP Fraud Management Outlier Detection Methods

Figure 8.5 SAP Fraud Management Outlier Detection Alerts

8.3   The Inter-Quartile Range Test

The Inter-Quartile Range test, also known as the Tukey test, named after its author, John Tukey, is a simple yet robust test for identifying numeric outliers. It is the calculation behind the construction of box plots, which are created using the test to help identify outliers.

Given a time series X_1 to X_j, calculate the upper and lower quartiles, 75th and 25th percentiles, denoted as UQ and LQ, calculate the mid spread as MID = UQ – LQ. An outlier is then defined to be any observation where

$$X_i < LQ - N * MID \qquad or \qquad X_i > UQ + N * MID$$

The value of N is usually set to 1.5; however, for large time series, say more than 36 data points, it is recommended to use a value of 2. The concept of very significant and significant outliers could be introduced by using values of N = 3 and N = 2 respectively.

8.3.1   The Inter-Quartile Range Test in the PAL

In the Predictive Analysis Library, the algorithm name is Inter-Quartile Range Test (IQR) and the associated function name is IQRTEST.

The Input Table comprises two columns, the first containing the record ID and the second containing the data to be tested, as shown in Table 8.1.

Table	Column	Data Type	Description
Data	1st column	Integer, varchar, or char	ID
	2nd column	Integer or double	Data to be tested

Table 8.1   The Input Table Definition for IQR

The Parameter Table, Table 8.2, simply specifies the parameter N, the multiplier to be used in the IQR test. The default is 1.5.

Name	Data Type	Description
MULTIPLIER	Double	The multiplier used in the IQR test. The default is 1.5.

Table 8.2   The Parameter Table Definition for IQR

The Output Tables are defined as shown in Table 8.3. The first table contains the values of the lower quartile (Q1) and the upper quartile (Q3). The second table displays a 0 for each record ID if its value is in the range between the lower and upper quartiles; else it displays a 1, in other words, an outlier.

Table	Column	Data Type	Description
IQR Values	1st column	Double	Q1 the lower quartile value
	2nd column	Double	Q3 the upper quartile value
Test Result	1st column	Integer	ID
	2nd column	Integer or double	Test result: 0: shows that a value is within the range 1: shows that a value is outside of the range

Table 8.3 The Output Table Definitions for IQR

8.3.2 An Example of the IQR Test in the PAL

This example is based on the data shown in Figure 8.6., which follows the definition of Table 8.1.

SELECT * FROM TESTDT_TAB		
	ID	VAL
1	P10	10
2	P11	11
3	P12	10
4	P13	9
5	P14	10
6	P15	22
7	P16	11
8	P17	12
9	P18	10
10	P19	9
11	P20	1
12	P21	11
13	P22	12
14	P23	20
15	P24	12

Figure 8.6 Data for the IQR Test in Table TESTDT_TAB

In SAP HANA Studio and using the DATA PREVIEW, we can plot the data as shown in Figure 8.7.

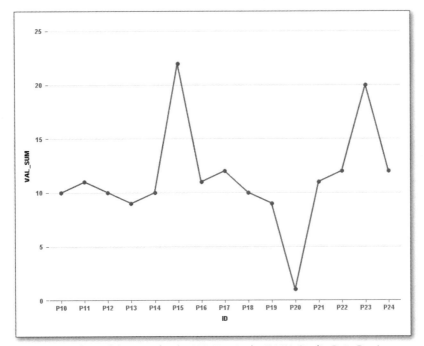

Figure 8.7 Chart of the Data for the IQR Test in the HANA Studio Data Preview

The main elements of the SQLScript are as follows, with the full code available in the file SAP_HANA_PAL_IQRTEST_Example_SQLScript on the SAP PRESS website:

```
-- The procedure generator
call SYSTEM.afl_wrapper_generator ('palIQR','AFLPAL','IQRTEST',PDATA);

-- The Control Table parameters

INSERT INTO #CONTROL_TAB VALUES ('MULTIPLIER',null,2.0,null);

-- Assume the data shown in Figure 8.6 has been stored in the table
TESTDT_TAB

-- Calling the procedure

CALL palIQR(TESTDT_TAB, "#CONTROL_TAB", IQR_TAB, RESULTS_TAB) with
overview;
```

```
SELECT * FROM IQR_TAB;
SELECT * FROM RESULTS_TAB;
```
Listing 8.1 The PAL SQLScript for the IQR Test

After running the SQLScript in SAP HANA Studio, the IQR_TAB Output Table is as shown in Figure 8.8, with Q1 being the lower quartile and Q3 being the upper quartile.

SELECT * FROM IQR_TAB		
	Q1	Q3
1	10	12

Figure 8.8 The Table Output from the IQR Test showing the Quartiles

The RESULTS_TAB Output Table is as shown in Figure 8.9. As defined in Table 8.3, the 1 in the TEST column indicates an outlier. The algorithm has automatically identified the outliers, which we suspected when looking at the chart in Figure 8.7. Of course, visual searching for outliers does not scale and is by definition subjective.

SELECT * FROM RESULTS_TAB		
	ID	TEST
1	P10	0
2	P11	0
3	P12	0
4	P13	0
5	P14	0
6	P15	1
7	P16	0
8	P17	0
9	P18	0
10	P19	0
11	P20	1
12	P21	0
13	P22	0
14	P23	1
15	P24	0

Figure 8.9 The Table Output from the IQR Test showing the Outliers

However, SQLScript is not for everyone, not even every data scientist. This is where SAP Predictive Analysis (PA) comes in, not only for the ease of defining such analysis, but also for the visualization of the results.

8.3.3 An Example of the Inter-Quartile Range Test in PA

In Chapter 7, we discussed PA in detail. In this example, we will complete the same analysis using PA, shown in Figure 8.10, with the data sourced from the same table in SAP HANA and using the PAL IQRTEST algorithm.

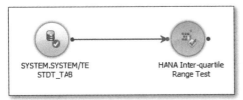

SYSTEM.SYSTEM/TE
STDT_TAB

HANA Inter-quartile
Range Test

Figure 8.10 The IQR Test in PA using the HANA PAL IQRTEST Algorithm

The HANA Inter-Quartile Range Test component dialogue in PA is shown in Figure 8.11 with prompts for the parameter values of the algorithm. Note here the option to SHOW OUTLIERS with the OUTPUT MODE dropdown box providing the alternative to HIDE OUTLIERS.

HANA Inter-quartile Range Test	✕
▼ Primary Properties	
Output Mode :	* Show Outliers ▾
Independent Column :	* VAL ▾
	Non-numerical columns are filtered
Missing Values :	* Remove ▾
Fence Coefficient :	* 2.0
	Range: (1.5 - 3.0)
▶ Enter Names for Newly Added Columns	
	Save and Close Cancel

Figure 8.11 The HANA Inter-Quartile Range Test Component Dialogue in PA

After running the process in PA, we can view the results in tabular form, as shown in Figure 8.12.

ID (Private Attr...	VAL (Private A...	Outliers Detect...
P10	10.00	0
P11	11.00	0
P12	10.00	0
P13	9.00	0
P14	10.00	0
P15	22.00	1
P16	11.00	0
P17	12.00	0
P18	10.00	0
P19	9.00	0
P20	1.00	1
P21	11.00	0
P22	12.00	0
P23	20.00	1
P24	12.00	0

Figure 8.12 The IQR TEST Analysis Results Table in PA

The Inter-Quartile Range test is a very popular test; however, it can be computationally expensive for very large data volumes. Consequently, the even simpler but more efficient Variance test is sometimes preferred.

8.4 The Variance Test

The Variance test is one of the simplest algorithms in the PAL and is very similar in structure to the Inter-Quartile Range test. Given a series of data values X_1 to X_j, calculate the mean and standard deviation (S.D). An outlier is then defined to be any observation where

$X_i < Mean - N * S.D$

$X_i > Mean + N * S.D$

The value of N is usually set to 2; however, for large time series, say more than 36 points, it is recommended to use a value of 3. The concept of significant and very significant outliers could be introduced by using values of N = 2 and N = 3 respectively. The Inter-Quartile Range test is more robust and better than the more common Variance test, as the outliers themselves do not necessarily contribute to the statistic, although it is more computationally expensive.

In the Predictive Analysis Library, the algorithm name is VARIANCE TEST and the function name is VARIANCETEST.

The Input Table has the same structure as that of the IQR test as shown in Table 8.1. We will also use the same data for comparison of the two algorithms.

The Parameter table is shown in Table 8.4 and parallels the IQR test with the SIGMA_NUM equating to the multiplier parameter.

Name	Data Type	Description
SIGMA_NUM	Double	Multiplier for sigma
THREAD_NUMBER	Integer	Number of threads

Table 8.4 The Parameter Table for the Variance Test

The Output table is comprised of two tables, as shown in Table 8.5. The first table contains the values of the mean and the standard deviation. The second table displays a 0 for each record ID if its value is within the range; else it displays a 1, in other words, an outlier.

Table	Column	Data Type	Description
Test Values	1st column	Double	The mean value
	2nd column	Double	The standard deviation
Test Result	1st column	Integer	ID
	2nd column	Integer or double	Test result: 0: shows that a value is within the range 1: shows that a value is outside of the range

Table 8.5 The Output Table Definitions for the Variance Test

8.4.1 An Example of the Variance Test in the PAL

This example is based on the same data that was used in the IQR test as shown in Figure 8.6. and visualized in Figure 8.7. The main elements of the SQLScript are as follows with the full code available in the fileSAP_HANA_PAL_VARIANCE-TEST_Example_SQLScript on the SAP PRESS website.

```
-- The procedure generator
call SYSTEM.afl_wrapper_generator( 'palVarianceTest','AFLPAL','VARIANCE
TEST',PDATA);

-- The Control Table parameters
```

```
INSERT INTO #CONTROL_TAB VALUES ('SIGMA_NUM',null,2.0,null);

-- Assume the data shown in Figure 8.6 has been stored in the table
DATA_TAB

-- Calling the procedure

CALL palVarianceTest(DATA_TAB, "#CONTROL_TAB", RESULT_TAB, TEST_TAB)
with overview;

SELECT * FROM RESULT_TAB;
SELECT * FROM TEST_TAB;
```

Listing 8.2 The PAL SQLScript for the Variance Test

The RESULT_TAB Output Table is as shown in Figure 8.13 with the values for the mean and standard deviation

SELECT * FROM RESULT_TAB		
	MEAN	SD
1	11.3333...	4.7459...

Figure 8.13 The Table Output from the IQR Test showing the Mean and Standard Deviation

The TEST_TAB Output Table is as shown in Figure 8.14. As defined in Table 8.5, the 1 in the TEST column indicates an outlier.

SELECT * FROM TEST_TAB		
	ID	Test
1	P10	0
2	P11	0
3	P12	0
4	P13	0
5	P14	0
6	P15	1
7	P16	0
8	P17	0
9	P18	0
10	P19	0
11	P20	1
12	P21	0
13	P22	0
14	P23	0
15	P24	0

Figure 8.14 The Table Output from the Variance Test showing the Outliers

The Variance test has found two outliers, ID P15 and P20. In comparison, the IQR Test found three outliers (see Figure 8.9), ID P15, P20 and P23. Neither one is correct or incorrect. The next step is to investigate the data to determine whether they are errors or true variations in the data.

The IQR test and the Variance test look for overall outliers across the entire numeric variable. However, also of interest is whether there are local outliers within the range of a variable's data values. For such analysis, we can use the K Nearest Neighbor Outlier algorithm.

8.5   K Nearest Neighbor Outlier

SAP Predictive Analysis includes the K Nearest Neighbor Outlier algorithm, which is based on the concept of looking for local outliers within a region or neighborhood of the data, with the region being defined as the K nearest objects or records. All the inter-object distances are calculated and, for each record, the average of the K nearest other records is determined. The records with the largest of these average distances are then highlighted as potential outliers. A worked example is shown in Figure 8.15, which we will run in PA.

K Nearest Neighbour Outlier Test															
			Example												
Number of neighbors to be used (K)			K=3												
Number of outliers to be detected (N)			N=2												
		Euclidean Distances													
Row	Column	Row 1	Row 2	Row 3	Row 4	Row 5	Row 6	Row 7	Row 8	Row 9	Row 10	Min	Next	Next	Average	
Row 10	16.9		7.1	16.0	0.2	22.9	16.1	1.4	15.0	0.7	15.2	0.2	0.7	1.4	0.77	
Row 11	24.0	7.1		8.9	6.9	15.8	9.0	8.5	7.9	7.8	8.1	6.9	7.1	7.8	7.27	Largest 1
Row 12	32.9	16.0	8.9		15.8	6.9	0.1	17.4	1.0	16.7	0.8	0.1	0.8	1.0	0.63	
Row 13	17.1	0.2	6.9	15.8		22.7	15.9	1.6	14.8	0.9	15.0	0.2	0.9	1.6	0.90	
Row 14	39.8	22.9	15.8	6.9	22.7		6.8	24.3	7.9	23.6	7.7	6.8	6.9	7.7	7.13	Largest 2
Row 15	33.0	16.1	9.0	0.1	17.4	6.8		17.5	1.1	16.8	0.9	0.1	0.9	1.1	0.70	
Row 16	15.5	1.4	8.5	17.4	1.6	24.3	17.5		16.4	0.7	16.6	0.7	1.4	1.6	1.23	
Row 17	31.9	15.0	7.9	1.0	14.8	7.9	1.1	16.4		15.7	0.2	0.2	1.0	1.1	0.77	
Row 18	16.2	0.7	7.8	16.7	0.9	23.6	16.8	0.7	15.7		15.9	0.7	0.7	0.9	0.77	
Row 19	32.1	15.2	8.1	0.8	15.0	7.7	0.9	16.6	0.2	15.9		0.2	0.8	0.9	0.63	

Figure 8.15   A Worked Example of the K Nearest Neighbor Outlier Algorithm

In this example, K = 3; therefore, we find the average of the three nearest distances to each record and highlight the two largest averages, which are Row 11 and Row 14, as shown in Figure 8.15. We had set N = 2, being the number of outliers we wanted to highlight. If we review the data in a chart, as shown in Figure 8.16, we can see how Row 11 and Row 14 are local outliers. Rows 10, 13, 16 and 18 form

235

a close group, and Rows 12, 15, 17and 19 form another close group. Row 11 is an outlier to the first group, and Row 14 is an outlier to the second group. Unlike outliers of all the data, local outliers are harder to identify. Of course, as with any outlier, the identification is the easier part; the harder part is determining the cause.

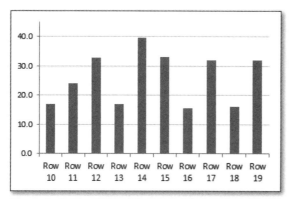

Figure 8.16 The Chart of the Data in the Worked Example

The analysis in SAP Predictive Analysis is shown in Figure 8.17, with the same data sourced from a CSV file and the Nearest Neighbor Outlier algorithm connected.

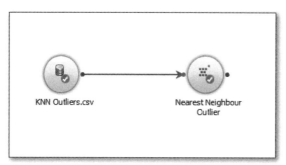

Figure 8.17 The Nearest Neighbor Outlier Analysis in PA

The dialogue in PA for the algorithm component is shown in Figure 8.18 where we choose to SHOW OUTLIERS in the Output Mode dropdown, as opposed to REMOVE OUTLIERS, and we have set K, the NEIGHBORHOOD COUNT prompt, to 3, and N, the NUMBER OF OUTLIERS, to 2.

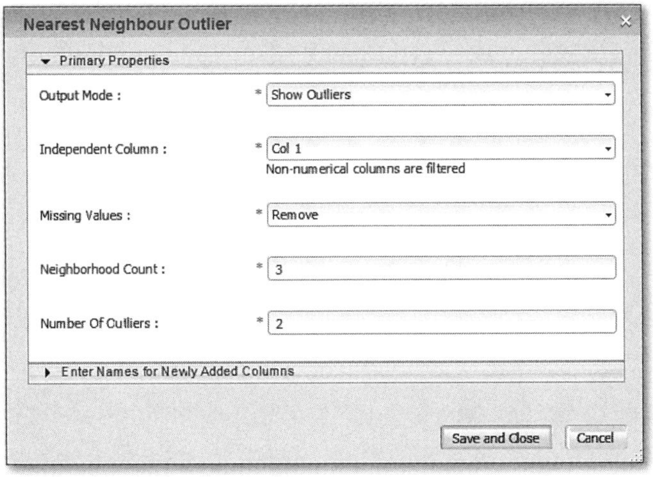

Figure 8.18   The Nearest Neighbor Outlier Analysis Dialogue in PA

After running the analysis, the results are given in the RESULTS tab, as shown in Figure 8.19, and outliers are detected for Row 11 and Row 14, just as we had calculated in the spreadsheet in Figure 8.15.

Row	Col 1	Outliers Detect...
Row 10	16.90	0
Row 11	24.00	1
Row 12	32.90	0
Row 13	17.10	0
Row 14	39.80	1
Row 15	33.00	0
Row 16	15.50	0
Row 17	31.90	0
Row 18	16.20	0
Row 19	32.10	0

Figure 8.19   The Nearest Neighbor Outlier Analysis Results in PA

If you examine the data carefully in Figure 8.15, you will notice that if we had set N = 3, then Row 16 would have also been highlighted as an outlier, when clearly, as shown in the chart in Figure 8.16, it is not. This is a weakness of the algorithm: by setting the value of N, the number of outliers, it will find that number, whether they are mathematically outliers or not. The solution is to run the IQR test on the Average Distance column and let that algorithm determine the number of outliers, based on the K Nearest Neighborhood.

Finally, there is another approach to looking for local outliers: first performing a cluster analysis and then looking for data values that are far away from the cluster centers.

8.6   Anomaly Detection using Cluster Analysis

An algorithm similar to the K Nearest Neighbor is available from the PAL and is called ANOMALY DETECTION, with the function name of ANOMALYDETECTION. It is very comparable in concept to K Nearest Neighbor as described in the previous section but gives more control over the calculation and, importantly, is not fixed to clusters of the same size. It is based on the K-Means algorithm and looks for objects far from the K cluster centers. Figure 8.20 shows the example data set that we will use, displayed in HANA Studio Data Preview. You can see the local outlier highlighted as ID 7.

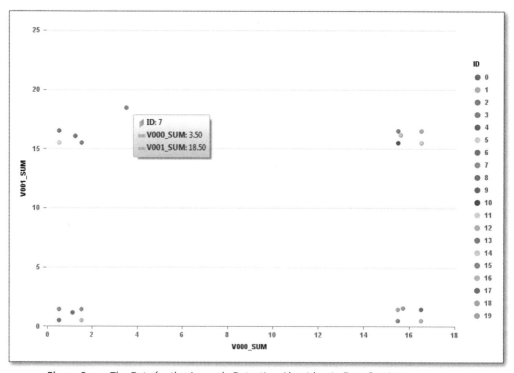

Figure 8.20 The Data for the Anomaly Detection Algorithm in Data Preview

The Input table for anomaly detection is the same as for K-Means cluster analysis, given that it is based on that algorithm and therefore uses the same input data structure. This is shown in the Cluster Analysis Chapter 10, Table 10.4. The Parameter table is also the same, as shown in Chapter 10, Table 10.5, and described there, but with the addition of the two parameters shown in Table 8.6.

Name	Data Type	Description
OUTLIER_PERCENTAGE	Double	Indicates the proportion of anomalies to be detected in the input data.
OUTLIER_DEFINE	Integer	Specifies how data points should be defined as outliers: ▶ 1 = max distance between the point and the center it belongs to ▶ 2 = max sum distance from the point to all centers

Table 8.6 The Additional Parameters for the Anomaly Detection Algorithm

The Output table simply displays the records identified as outliers by the algorithm. It is defined as shown in Table 8.7.

Table	Column	Data Type	Description	Constraint
Result	1st column	Integer or string	ID	
	Other columns	Integer or double	Coordinates of outliers	It must have the same type as the input data table.

Table 8.7 The Output Table for the Anomaly Detection Algorithm

8.6.1 An Example of the Anomaly Detection Algorithm in the PAL

This example is based on the data shown in Figure 8.21 and presented in a chart, as shown in Figure 8.20.

SELECT * FROM PAL_AD_DATA_TAB

	ID	V000	V001
1	0	0.5	0.5
2	1	1.5	0.5
3	2	1.5	1.5
4	3	0.5	1.5
5	4	1.1	1.2
6	5	0.5	15.5
7	6	1.5	15.5
8	7	3.5	18.5
9	8	0.5	16.5
10	9	1.2	16.1
11	10	15.5	15.5
12	11	16.5	15.5
13	12	16.5	16.5
14	13	15.5	16.5
15	14	15.6	16.2
16	15	15.5	0.5
17	16	16.5	0.5
18	17	16.5	1.5
19	18	15.5	1.5
20	19	15.7	1.6

Figure 8.21 The Data for the Anomaly Detection Algorithm

The main elements of the SQLScript are as follows, with the full code available in the fileSAP_HANA_PAL_ANOMALYDETECTION_Example_SQLScript on the SAP PRESS website.

```
-- The procedure generator
call SYSTEM.afl_wrapper_generator ('PAL_ANOMALY_DETECTION', 'AFLPAL',
'ANOMALYDETECTION', PDATA);

-- The Control Table parameters

INSERT INTO PAL_CONTROL_TAB VALUES ('GROUP_NUMBER',4,null,null);
INSERT INTO PAL_CONTROL_TAB VALUES ('INIT_TYPE',4,null,null);
INSERT INTO PAL_CONTROL_TAB VALUES ('DISTANCE_LEVEL',2,null,null);
INSERT INTO PAL_CONTROL_TAB VALUES ('MAX_ITERATION',100,null,null);
INSERT INTO PAL_CONTROL_TAB VALUES ('OUTLIER_DEFINE',1,null,null);
INSERT INTO PAL_CONTROL_TAB VALUES ('OUTLIER_
PERCENTAGE',null,0.05,null);
INSERT INTO PAL_CONTROL_TAB VALUES ('NORMALIZATION',0,null,null);
INSERT INTO PAL_CONTROL_TAB VALUES ('THREAD_NUMBER',2,null,null);

-- Assume the data shown in Figure 8.21 has been stored in the table
PAL_AD_DATA_TAB

-- Calling the procedure
```

```
CALL PAL_ANOMALY_DETECTION(PAL_AD_DATA_TAB, PAL_CONTROL_TAB, PAL_AD_
RESULT_TAB) with overview;
SELECT * FROM PAL_AD_RESULT_TAB;
```

Listing 8.3 The PAL SQLScript for the Anomaly Detection Algorithm

The PAL_AD_RESULT_TAB Output Table is as shown in Figure 8.22 with the ID and its co-ordinates. This matches our expectations from the chart in Figure 8.20.

SELECT * FROM PAL_AD_RESULT_TAB			
	ID	V000	V001
1	7	3.5	18.5

Figure 8.22 The Table Output from the Anomaly Detection Algorithm

8.6.2 An Example of Anomaly Detection in PA

The same analysis using PA is shown in Figure 8.23 with the data sourced from the same table in SAP HANA and using the PAL ANOMALYDETECTION algorithm.

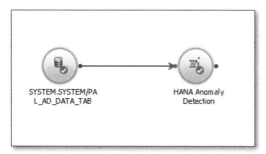

SYSTEM.SYSTEM/PA
L_AD_DATA_TAB

HANA Anomaly
Detection

Figure 8.23 Anomaly Detection in PA using the HANA PAL ANOMALYDETECTION Algorithm

After selecting the HANA Anomaly Detection component in PA, the dialogue opens as shown in Figure 8.24, with prompts for the parameter values of the algorithm.

The advanced properties of the component dialogue are shown in Figure 8.25, which completes all the parameter settings for the algorithm. It is recommended that you leave the default values for the parameters as shown, other than perhaps change the Maximum Iterations value if processing times are proving lengthy. The Normalization prompt might also be changed from False to True if the variables in the analysis all have very difference scales, whereas you want them to have equal input to the analysis.

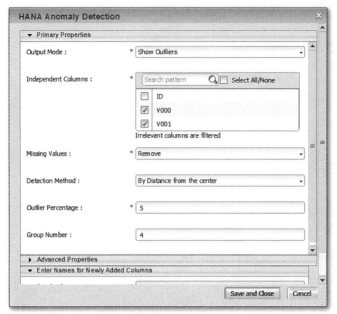

Figure 8.24 The HANA Anomaly Detection Component Dialogue in PA

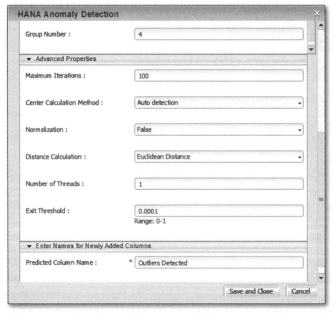

Figure 8.25 The Advanced Properties of the HANA Anomaly Detection Component Dialogue in PA

After running the process in PA, we can view the results in tabular form, as shown in Figure 8.26.

ID (Private Attr...	V000 (Private ...	V001 (Private ...	Outliers Detect...
0	0.50	0.50	0
1	1.50	0.50	0
2	1.50	1.50	0
3	0.50	1.50	0
4	1.10	1.20	0
5	0.50	15.50	0
6	1.50	15.50	0
7	3.50	18.50	1
8	0.50	16.50	0
9	1.20	16.10	0
10	15.50	15.50	0
11	16.50	15.50	0
12	16.50	16.50	0
13	15.50	16.50	0
14	15.60	16.20	0
15	15.50	0.50	0
16	16.50	0.50	0
17	16.50	1.50	0
18	15.50	1.50	0
19	15.70	1.60	0

Figure 8.26 The Anomaly Detection Analysis Results Table in PA

As you can see from Figure 8.26, the record ID 7 is identified as an outlier, by the value 1 in the OUTLIERS DETECTED column.

8.7   The Business Case for Outlier Analysis

The business case for outlier analysis is very compelling, starting with its use in the initial analysis of data and looking for any outliers that may affect subsequent analysis and bias any predictions. However, its main business benefit comes from its application to fraud detection, where huge sums of money are involved. The amounts are staggering. Some statistics are below:

▶ The total cost in the US of insurance fraud (non-health) is estimated to be more than $40 billion per year. (Source: Federal Bureau of Investigation, US)

▶ According to the Association of British Insurers, the sector is detecting more than 2,500 fraudulent claims worth £18 million every week. (Source: Experian Fraud Report 2012)

- The United States Government Accountability Office (GOA) estimates $125.4 billion in improper payments.

- The UK National Fraud Authority (NFA) estimates public sector fraud at £38.4 billion.

With such vast sums of money involved, deriving even very small percentage improvements as a result of applying predictive analysis, will deliver substantial savings.

The kinds of business questions that arise are:

- How can we identify fraud before damage occurs?

- How can we improve the fraud investigation efficiency?

- How can we keep track of changing fraud behaviors?

- How can we reduce the false positive signals?

- What is the best approach to automate the fraud detection process and predict the likelihood of fraud?

- How do we manage to check all transactions for fraud but ensure no business impact?

Answering these questions is, of course, not simple. If it were, it would probably have already been acted upon. Furthermore, it is one thing to identify outliers or unusual values; the challenge is to determine whether they are fraudulent.

Fraud detection is an excellent example of where predictive analysis and business acumen can synergistically combine. The output of predictive analysis is usually augmented by business rules that encapsulate business logic, for example, if credit card spend is in location A, then investigate; if insurance claim repeats x times, then investigate. This is a good example of how the implementation of the findings of predictive analysis is in reality generally translated into business processes.

8.8 Strengths and Weaknesses of Outlier Analysis

The main strength of outlier analysis comes from its importance to predictive analysis. It is an essential first step in any analysis to examine the quality of the data, before applying any algorithms. The Inter-Quartile Range test is a simple and popular test for outlier detection and as mentioned earlier, is the basis of the very useful box plot. It is also a robust test in that the outliers do not themselves affect the statistics of the test, as opposed to the Variance test, where outliers clearly affect the limits given that they are measured in terms of standard deviations. That is the weakness of the Variance test, but, again, its simplicity makes it popular. K Nearest Neighbors looks for local outliers, as opposed to global outliers, which is very useful as these are often harder to find because they are not so obvious. The weakness of the test is that the value of K may affect the solution, but this can be minimized by exploring the solution using several values of K. The other weakness is that by specifying the number of outliers, you ensure that you get that number, and some may not really be outliers. This weakness can be obviated by applying the IQR test to the results as suggested earlier in this chapter. Anomaly Detection using Cluster Analysis gives greater flexibility in finding local outliers, but, again, it may be influenced by the choice of the cluster number. As always, sensitivity analysis can be used to test the robustness of the model solution to the settings of the model parameters. Overall, the strengths of outlier analysis outweigh the weaknesses, given the importance of the topic, and to a certain extent, the weaknesses can be minimized.

The algorithms described in this chapter use numeric distance measures to try to identify outliers and consequently apply to numeric data. Clearly, non-numeric data can have outliers. To try to identify them, other methods, such as classification and association analysis, and of course text analysis, may be used. These methods are described in the chapters on those topics.

A final comment: the methods described in this chapter look for outliers in existing data. There is a subtle difference between outliers in existing data and unexpected predicted values compared to actual values, in that the former may be discovered using the methods described in this chapter, while the latter will come from a predictive model where the actual data is very different from the predicted. This is also a form of outlier, so, in general, predictive algorithms can also be used for outlier detection.

8.9   Summary

In this chapter we have reviewed several methods of outlier analysis, which is an important precursor to building predictive models. It is also an important application of predictive analysis in the field of fraud management where a core component is looking for the unusual. The algorithms ranged from the simple statistical tests for global outliers, namely the Inter-Quartile Range Test and the Variance Test, to the more advanced K Nearest Neighbor algorithm and anomaly detection using cluster analysis, both of which can be used to find local outliers.

In the next chapter we begin our review of predictive analysis algorithms, specifically, algorithms for association analysis.

Association analysis is one of the most common techniques of predictive analysis and given that it usually involves very large data volumes, it is an ideal application for SAP HANA.

9 Association Analysis

Association analysis, as the name suggests, is a form of analysis that looks for associations between objects. It is also called affinity analysis, and a specific subset of this analysis is called market basket analysis. The latter name is the most common area of application of association analysis, specifically looking at what products are bought together in a shopping basket. Using the information gathered from market basket analysis, we can, for example, recommend product placement in a store, suggest additional product purchases to a customer, and, conversely, identify unusual combinations as potentially part of a fraud management application.

The output of association analysis is usually in the form of rules such as "if item A is purchased, then so is item B." We evaluate the quality or usefulness of these rules by calculating the number of baskets that support the rule where the combination exists, divided by the total number of baskets. This measure or statistic is referred to as the rule support. We then calculate how good the rule is at predicting the "right-hand side" of the rule, item B in our example, given the "left-hand side" of the rule, item A in our example. This measure or statistic is the number of baskets in which A and B exists, divided by the number of baskets with A in them, expressed as a percentage. It is referred to as rule confidence. Finally, we calculate a measure called lift, which is defined as the confidence of the combination of the items divided by the support of the result. Lift is the ratio of how often when A is bought is B also bought, divided by how often B is bought on its own. It measures how much better the rule is compared to just guessing the "right-hand side" of the rule. If it is greater than 1, then B is more often bought with A; if it is less than 1, then B is more often bought on its own, in which case the rule is not very good.

To help explain these three measures, we will show their calculation in a worked example in this chapter.

The calculations are very simple, however, in practice the challenge of association analysis is usually the very large volumes of transaction data and therefore processing performance. You can address this challenge by restricting the number of rules that are extracted, as shown later in this chapter. Interpreting the results is not always as simple as it might seem, with rules producing either trivial associations or apparent nonsensical associations.

Before we look at the rules in more detail, we review the many different applications of association analysis.

9.1 Applications of Association Analysis

We use association analysis and see it in our everyday lives, sometimes knowingly, sometimes unwittingly. Perhaps the best known application is the 'Frequently Bought Together' and 'Customers Who Bought This Item Also Bought...' sections of the Amazon web site. Then there is the Apple iTunes Genius Application comprising a recommendations engine based on association analysis. Netflix provides predictions of movies that a user might like to watch based on his previous ratings of movies and watching habits, compared to the behavior of other users.

Finally, an example from SAP and the new SAP Product Recommendation Intelligence solution is shown in Figure 9.1. From a high-level concept perspective, it is like the Amazon type "who bought X also bought Y," but in addition, through the Business Suite integration, it leverages all the data relevant to knowing your customers and products better as well as benefiting from the speed of SAP HANA to provide smart recommendations based on predictive analytics.

Clearly, the analysis of shopping baskets is the major application of association analysis; however, in general, the analysis is of a collection of items in some container. Other examples include the analysis of telecom services purchased by subscribers, financial policies held by households, telephone calling patterns, visitor paths through a website, and social network associations.

Figure 9.1 SAP Product Recommendation Intelligence

At SAPPHIRE 2013, there was an application for attendees recommending sessions based on similar attendee profiles and the sessions that they attended, as shown in Figure 9.2 and Figure 9.3.

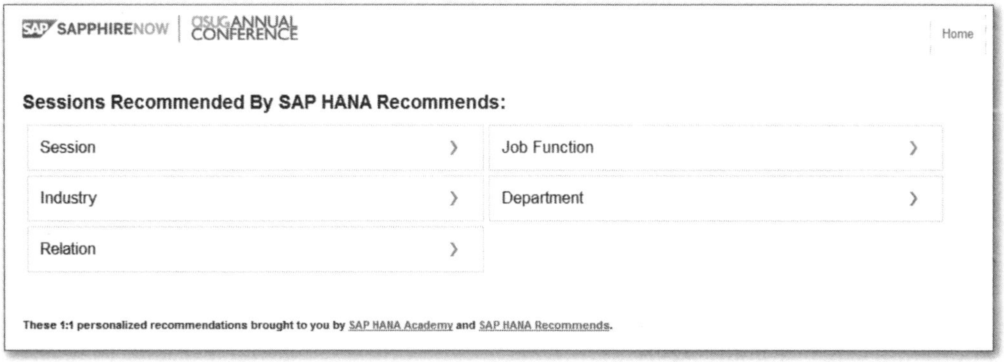

Figure 9.2 The Opening Screen for Session Recommendations at SAPPHIRE 2013

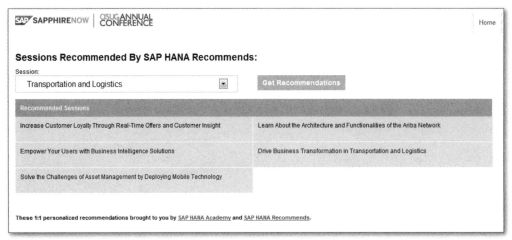

Figure 9.3 Recommended Sessions Based on the Attendees Interest in Transportation and Logistics

There are the converse applications where rare combinations may be of interest, for example, in fraud detection, where the identification of fraudulent medical insurance claims in which common rules are broken may be claims worth investigating.

Then there are examples of differential analysis, where we might compare the results between different stores, between customers in different demographic groups, between different days of the week, or different seasons of the year.

9.2 Apriori Association Analysis

Apriori is a classic algorithm for finding associations in market basket data, for example, sales transaction data. It produces association rules in the general form of "If A Then B and C." It measures the value of these rules using the three statistics, namely support, confidence, and lift. These are simple statistics that are best explained in a worked example.

Consider the data shown in Figure 9.4. There are 30 transactions and 17 baskets, in transaction format, sometimes called till-roll format, as shown by the color highlighting in the figure.

ID	Customer	Item
1	14660358	Product 1
2	14660358	Product 2
3	14660953	Product 2
4	14660953	Product 3
5	14660953	Product 7
6	14662026	Product 1
7	14662026	Product 3
8	14720402	Product 4
9	14736726	Product 5
10	14771185	Product 6
11	14771185	Product 2
12	14771185	Product 4
13	14823951	Product 5
14	14823952	Product 2
15	14877343	Product 1
16	15084229	Product 2
17	15084229	Product 3
18	15084229	Product 4
19	15108022	Product 1
20	15181110	Product 4
21	15181110	Product 5
22	15181110	Product 6
23	15210991	Product 5
24	15210991	Product 6
25	15210991	Product 7
26	15216017	Product 6
27	15240287	Product 2
28	15305591	Product 1
29	15405431	Product 5
30	15405431	Product 6

Figure 9.4 Example Data for the Apriori Algorithm

Support is defined as the number of baskets that support the rule, that is, where the combination exists, divided by the total number of baskets, expressed as a percentage. Support is bidirectional, e.g., If 5 then 6; If 6 then 5; both have the same Rule Support percentage. The calculation is shown in Table 9.1.

Rule	Number of Baskets Supporting the Rule	Total Number of Baskets	Rule Support Percentage
If 5 then 6	3	17	17.6471%
If 2 then 3	2	17	11.7647%

Table 9.1 Apriori Rule Support Calculation

Rule	Number of Baskets Supporting the Rule	Total Number of Baskets	Rule Support Percentage
If 2 then 4	2	17	11.7647%
If 4 then 6	2	17	11.7647%
If 1 then 2	1	17	5.8824%
Etc...	...	...	...
If 2 and 3 then 7	1	17	5.8824%
If 6 and 2 then 4	1	17	5.8824%
If 2 and 3 then 4	1	17	5.8824%
If 4 and 5 then 6	1	17	5.8824%
Etc...	...	...	...

Table 9.1 Apriori Rule Support Calculation (Cont.)

Confidence is defined for If Product A (Pa) then Product B (Pb) as -

The number of baskets in which Pa and Pb both exist, divided by the number of baskets with Pa in them, then expressed as a percentage. See Table 9.2.

Rule If Pa then Pb	No. of Baskets Supporting the Rule	Total Number of Baskets with Pa	Confidence
If 5 then 6	3	5	60%
If 2 then 3	2	6	33%
If 2 then 4	2	6	33%
If 4 then 6	2	4	50%
If 1 then 2	1	5	20%
Etc.	...	...	...

Table 9.2 Apriori Rule Confidence Calculation for If A then B

Conversely, for If Product B then Product A is defined as – The number of baskets in which Pb and Pa both exist, divided by the number of baskets with Pb in them, expressed as a percentage.

Note that confidence is not bidirectional: If Pa then Pb does not necessarily equal If Pb then Pa. For example, in Table 9.2, the rule If 2 then 3 has a confidence of 33%, whereas in Table 9.3, you can see that the rule If 3 then 2 has a confidence of 66%.

Rule If Pa then Pb	No. of Baskets Supporting the Rule	Total Number of Baskets with Pa	Confidence
If 6 then 5	3	5	60%
If 3 then 2	2	3	66%
If 4 then 2	2	4	50%
If 6 then 4	2	5	40%
If 2 then 1	1	6	16%
Etc.	...	...	...

Table 9.3 Apriori Rule Confidence Calculation for If B then A

Both support and confidence are used to test a rule's validity; however, there are times when both of these measures may be high yet still produce a rule that is not useful. For example, assume that the combination of Product A and Product B has a support of 40%: in other words, 40% of the baskets support this rule, and maybe a confidence of 80%: in other words, in 80% of the baskets when customers buy Product A, they also buy Product B. This at first appears to be an excellent rule; it has both very high confidence and support. However, what if customers in general buy Product B 95% of the time anyway? In that case, Product B customers are actually less likely to buy Product A than customers in general.

Thus, we have a third measure of the accuracy of association analysis–lift or improvement, which is defined as the ratio of how often when Product A is bought Product B is also bought, divided by how often Product B is bought on its own. If it's > 1, then Product B is more often bought with Product A; if it's <1, then Product B is more often bought on its own, so the rule is not very good. This can be shown to be equal to the confidence of the combination of items divided by the support of the result. In the example above, 80% / 95% = 0.8421. These calculations are shown in Table 9.4 and Table 9.5.

Rule If Pa then Pb	Confidence	Support Pb (result)	Lift
If 5 then 6	60%	29.41% (5/17)	2.040
If 2 then 3	33%	17.65% (3/17)	1.888
If 2 then 4	33%	23.53% (4/17)	1.417
If 4 then 6	50%	29.41% (5/17)	1.700
If 1 then 2	20%	35.29% (6/17)	0.566
Etc.	...	...	...

Table 9.4 Apriori Rule Lift Calculation for If A then B

Rule If Pb then Pa	Confidence	Support Pa (result)	Lift
If 6 then 5	60%	29.41% (5/17)	2.040
If 3 then 2	66%	23.81% (6/17)	1.888
Etc,	...	...	...

Table 9.5 Apriori Rule Lift Calculation for If A then B

Now we have three measures to judge the usefulness of the rules extracted from the data. If you want to see the most popular rules, use support. If you want to see the most popular and of those, the most useful rules, use confidence. If you want to see overall the most useful rules, use lift.

To jump ahead a little, Figure 9.5 shows the output of the SAP HANA PAL APRIORI algorithm using this worked example. The calculations in the Tables 9.1 to 9.5, are confirmed in the output from SAP HANA.

We now perform this analysis in the PAL.

SELECT * FROM PAL_RESULT_TAB				
	PRERULE	POSTRULE	SUPPORT	CONFI...	LIFT
1	Product1	Product2	0.05882...	0.1999...	0.5666...
2	Product2	Product1	0.05882...	0.1666...	0.5666...
3	Product1	Product3	0.05882...	0.1999...	1.1333...
4	Product3	Product1	0.05882...	0.3333...	1.1333...
5	Product2	Product3	0.11764...	0.3333...	1.8888...
6	Product3	Product2	0.11764...	0.6666...	1.8888...
7	Product2	Product7	0.05882...	0.1666...	1.4166...
8	Product7	Product2	0.05882...	0.5	1.4166...
9	Product2	Product4	0.11764...	0.3333...	1.4166...
10	Product4	Product2	0.11764...	0.5	1.4166...
11	Product2	Product6	0.05882...	0.1666...	0.5666...
12	Product6	Product2	0.05882...	0.1999...	0.5666...
13	Product3	Product7	0.05882...	0.3333...	2.8333...
14	Product7	Product3	0.05882...	0.5	2.8333...
15	Product3	Product4	0.05882...	0.3333...	1.4166...
16	Product4	Product3	0.05882...	0.25	1.4166...
17	Product7	Product5	0.05882...	0.5	1.6999...
18	Product5	Product7	0.05882...	0.1999...	1.6999...
19	Product7	Product6	0.05882...	0.5	1.6999...
20	Product6	Product7	0.05882...	0.1999...	1.6999...

Figure 9.5 Apriori Algorithm Output in SAP HANA PAL

9.3   Apriori Association Analysis in the PAL

In the Predictive Analysis Library, the algorithm name for association analysis is Apriori and the associated function name is APRIORIRULE.

The Input table comprises two columns, the first containing the Transaction ID (Basket ID or Container ID) and the second containing the Item ID, e.g., product name, as shown in Table 9.6.

Table	Column	Data Type	Description
Data set/ Historical Data	1st column	Integer, varchar, or char	Transaction ID
	Item column	Integer, varchar, or char	Item ID

Table 9.6 The Input Table Definition for Apriori

The Parameter table specifies five parameters as shown in Table 9.7. Note that a support and confidence value of 0.01 represents 1%. In practice support is generally a very low percentage, as there are thousands, if not millions, of transactions. For the MAXITEMLENGTH, as an example, the rule If A then B and C will have a value of 3.

Name	Data Type	Description
MIN_SUPPORT	Double	The minimum support value expressed as a percentage.
MIN_CONFIDENCE	Double	The minimum confidence value expressed as a percentage.
MAXITEMLENGTH	Integer	The total length of leading items and dependent items in the output. The default is 10.
PMML_EXPORT	Integer	0. Does not export the Apriori model in PMML. (The default) 1. Exports the Apriori model in PMML in a single row. 2: Exports the Apriori model in PMML in several rows, each row containing a maximum of 5000 characters.
THREAD_NUMBER	Integer	The number of threads.

Table 9.7   The Parameter Table Definition for Apriori

The output comprises two tables, as shown in Table 9.8. The first table contains the association rules, with the leading items or pre-rule or left-hand side, shown in the first column and the dependent items or post-rule or right-hand side shown in the second column. For some applications, you may want to combine the pre-rule and post-rule item columns to construct the total rule. The table then displays the support, confidence, and lift values. The second table, as shown in Table 9.8 shows the PMML definition of the Apriori model, which is essentially the rules and their statistics.

Table	Column	Data Type	Description
Result	1st column	Varchar or char	Leading items
	2nd column	Varchar or char	Dependent items
	3rd column	Double	Support value
	4th column	Double	Confidence value
	5th column	Double	Lift value

Table 9.8   The Output Table Definitions for Apriori

Table	Column	Data Type	Description
PMML Result	1st column	Integer	ID
	2nd column	CLOB or varchar	The Apriori model in PMML format

Table 9.8 The Output Table Definitions for Apriori (Cont.)

9.4 An Example of Apriori Association Analysis in the PAL

This example is based on the data shown in Figure 9.4, shown here in SAP HANA table PAL_TRANS_TAB, in Figure 9.6.

	SELECT * FROM PAL_TRANS_TAB	
	CUSTOMER	ITEM
1	14,660,358	Product1
2	14,660,358	Product2
3	14,660,953	Product2
4	14,660,953	Product3
5	14,660,953	Product7
6	14,662,026	Product1
7	14,662,026	Product3
8	14,720,402	Product4
9	14,736,726	Product5
10	14,771,185	Product6
11	14,771,185	Product2
12	14,771,185	Product4
13	14,823,951	Product5
14	14,823,952	Product2
15	14,877,343	Product1
16	15,084,229	Product2
17	15,084,229	Product3
18	15,084,229	Product4
19	15,108,022	Product1
20	15,181,110	Product4
21	15,181,110	Product5
22	15,181,110	Product6
23	15,210,991	Product5
24	15,210,991	Product6
25	15,210,991	Product7
26	15,216,017	Product6
27	15,240,287	Product2
28	15,305,591	Product1
29	15,405,431	Product5
30	15,405,431	Product6

Figure 9.6 Example Data for the Apriori Association Analysis

The main elements of the SQLScript are as follows, with the full code available in the file SAP_HANA_PAL_Apriori_Example_SQLScript on the SAP PRESS website.

```
-- The procedure generator
CALL "SYSTEM".afl_wrapper_generator('PAL_APRIORI_RULE', 'AFLPAL',
'APRIORIRULE', PDATA);

-- The Control Table parameters

INSERT INTO PAL_CONTROL_TAB VALUES ('MIN_SUPPORT',null,0.01,null);
INSERT INTO PAL_CONTROL_TAB VALUES ('MIN_CONFIDENCE',null,0.01,null);
INSERT INTO PAL_CONTROL_TAB VALUES ('PMML_EXPORT',2,null,null);
INSERT INTO PAL_CONTROL_TAB VALUES ('THREAD_NUMBER',2,null,null);

-- Assume the data shown in Figure 9.4 has been stored in the table
PAL_TRANS_TAB

-- Calling the procedure

CALL PAL_APRIORI_RULE(PAL_TRANS_TAB, PAL_CONTROL_TAB, PAL_RESULT_TAB,
PAL_PMMLMODEL_TAB) with overview;

SELECT * FROM PAL_RESULT_TAB;
SELECT * FROM PAL_PMMLMODEL_TAB;
```

Listing 9.1 The PAL SQLScript for Apriori

After running the PAL SQLScript for Apriori, you will see the PAL_RESULT_TAB Output Table is as shown in Figure 9.5.

In the Parameter table, we set the PMML Export parameter to 2; thus, the PMML is produced as shown in Figure 9.7 and Figure 9.8. For the Apriori algorithm, the PMML could be quite lengthy, so you should set the parameter to 2.

	ID	PMMLMODEL
		SELECT * FROM PAL_PMMLMODEL_TAB
1	1	\<PMML version="4.0" xmlns="http://www.dmg.org/PMML-4_0" xmlns:xsi="http://www.....
2	2	" lift="1.41667" antecedent="2" consequent="5" /> \<AssociationRule id="10" support="0.1...
3	3	id="55" support="0.0588235" confidence="1" lift="3.4" antecedent="18" consequent="7" ...

Figure 9.7 Apriori Algorithm PMML Output

```
<PMML version="4.0" xmlns="http://www.dmg.org/PMML-4_0"
xmlns:xsi="http://www.w3.org/2001/XMLSchema-instance" >
<Header copyright="SAP" >
<Application name="PAL" version="1.0" />
</Header>
<DataDictionary numberOfFields="2" >
<DataField name="CUSTOMER" optype="continuous" dataType="integer" />
<DataField name="ITEM" optype="categorical" dataType="string" />
</DataDictionary>
<AssociationModel modelName="Instance for association"
functionName="associationRules" algorithmName="Apriori"
minimumSupport="0.01"
minimumConfidence="0.01"
numberOfTransactions="17"
numberOfItems="7"
numberOfItemsets="25"
numberOfRules="56" >
<MiningSchema>
<MiningField name="CUSTOMER" usageType="group"/>
<MiningField name="ITEM" usageType="active"/>
</MiningSchema>
<!-- 7 items in input transactions -->
<Item id="1" value="Product1"/>
<Item id="2" value="Product2"/>
<Item id="3" value="Product3"/>
<Item id="4" value="Product7"/>
<Item id="5" value="Product4"/>
<Item id="6" value="Product5"/>
<Item id="7" value="Product6"/>
<!-- 25 frequent itemsets -->
<!-- 7 frequent itemsets with 1 item/items -->
<Itemset id="1" numberOfItems="1" support="0.294118"/>
```

Figure 9.8 Apriori Algorithm PMML Output in Detail

We can use the PMML to transfer the model rules to a business application, such as a Recommendation Engine. The PMML is just the Predictive Modeling Markup Language in XML, which can be read and interpreted by other applications, as with any XML.

The Output Table, as shown in Figure 9.5, presents the PRERULE and POSTRULE in two fields. You may wish to join these two fields into one rule. The SQLScript in Listing 9.2 shows how to do that, with the result shown in Figure 9.9.

```
DROP VIEW TMP_RESULT_V;
CREATE VIEW TMP_RESULT_V  AS SELECT  CONCAT(PRERULE, ' => ') AS
PRERULE, POSTRULE, SUPPORT,  CONFIDENCE,  LIFT  FROM PAL_RESULT_TAB;
DROP VIEW RESULT_V;
CREATE VIEW RESULT_V AS SELECT CONCAT(PRERULE, POSTRULE) AS RULES ,
SUPPORT,  CONFIDENCE,  LIFT  FROM TMP_RESULT_V;
SELECT * FROM RESULT_V;
```

Listing 9.2 The SQLScript to Merge PRERULE and POSTRULE

SELECT * FROM RESULT_V				
	RULES	SUPPO...	CONFI...	LIFT
1	Product1 => Product2	0.0588...	0.1999...	0.5666...
2	Product2 => Product1	0.0588...	0.1666...	0.5666...
3	Product1 => Product3	0.0588...	0.1999...	1.1333...
4	Product3 => Product1	0.0588...	0.3333...	1.1333...
5	Product2 => Product3	0.1176...	0.3333...	1.8888...
6	Product3 => Product2	0.1176...	0.6666...	1.8888...
7	Product2 => Product7	0.0588...	0.1666...	1.4166...

Figure 9.9 The Output from Merging the PRERULE and POSTRULE Fields

However, SQLScript is not for everyone, not even every data scientist. This is where SAP Predictive Analysis (PA) comes in, not only for the ease of defining such analysis but also for the visualization of the results.

9.5   An Example of Apriori in SAP Predictive Analysis

The same analysis using PA is shown in Figure 9.10, with the data sourced from the same table in SAP HANA and using the PAL Apriori algorithm.

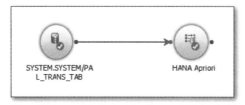

SYSTEM.SYSTEM/PA
L_TRANS_TAB

HANA Apriori

Figure 9.10 Association Analysis in PA using the HANA PAL Apriori Algorithm

For users without access to the PAL, the same analysis can be performed using the interface to R provided by PA, as shown in Figure 9.11, with the same data but this time sourced from an Excel spreadsheet.

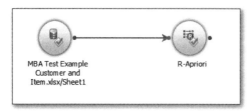

MBA Test Example
Customer and
Item.xlsx/Sheet1

R-Apriori

Figure 9.11 Association Analysis in PA using the R Apriori Algorithm

The HANA Apriori component dialogue in PA is shown in Figure 9.12, with prompts for the parameter values of the algorithm. In our example we set the SUPPORT and CONFIDENCE percents to be 1%. Note here the option to run the algorithm Apriori Lite in the APRIORI TYPE field. We discuss this algorithm in Section 9.6.

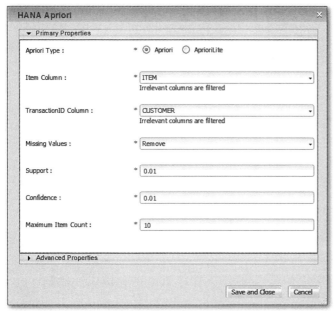

Figure 9.12 Association Analysis Dialogue in SAP Predictive Analysis using the HANA PAL Apriori Algorithm

After running the analysis process in PA, we can view the results in tabular form as shown in Figure 9.13.

Rules	Support	Confidence	Lift
{Product 7} => {Product 3}	0.06	0.50	2.83
{Product 3} => {Product 7}	0.06	0.33	2.83
{Product 7} => {Product 5}	0.06	0.50	1.70
{Product 5} => {Product 7}	0.06	0.20	1.70
{Product 7} => {Product 6}	0.06	0.50	1.70
{Product 6} => {Product 7}	0.06	0.20	1.70
{Product 7} => {Product 2}	0.06	0.50	1.42
{Product 2} => {Product 7}	0.06	0.17	1.42
{Product 1} => {Product 3}	0.06	0.20	1.13
{Product 3} => {Product 1}	0.06	0.33	1.13

Figure 9.13 The Association Analysis Results Table in SAP Predictive Analysis using the HANA PAL Apriori Algorithm

The chart in PA supporting association analysis uses a tag cloud after concatenating the pre-rule and post-rule columns to give the full rule in one column. This is shown in Figure 9.14 along with the slider controls to enable the user to focus in on values of support, confidence, and lift. These columns in the table can be sorted, with the lift shown in sort descending being probably the most useful. The rules with the highest lift are shown with the largest text, and then the more solid the color, the higher the rule confidence.

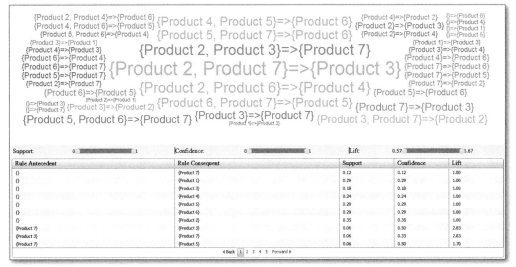

Figure 9.14 The Association Analysis Chart in PA using the HANA PAL Apriori Algorithm

9.6   Apriori Lite Association Analysis

As we mentioned in Section 9.5, when we were setting the parameters for the Apriori algorithm, there is another option: Apriori Lite. This algorithm is a specific instance of the Apriori algorithm in that it looks for only single item pre-rule and post-rule rules. It is therefore more efficient than the generic Apriori algorithm and is applicable when only one-to-one rules are sought. In addition, Apriori Lite also offers sampling within the algorithm. Let's look at the input and parameter tables for the Apriori Lite algorithm and its association analysis.

In the Predictive Analysis Library, the function name is LITEAPRIORIRULE. The Input Table has the same structure as that of the Apriori algorithm, as shown in Table 9.6 because we are analyzing the same data.

The Parameter Table has the same structure as that of the Apriori algorithm, as shown in Table 9.7, except that the MAXITEMLENGTH does not exist, as it is simply 2 for Apriori Lite given we have one pre-rule and one post-rule. There are two extra parameters, as shown in Table 9.9.

Name	Data Type	Description
OPTIMIZATION_TYPE	Integer or double	To use the entire data, set to 0. To sample the source input data, specify a double value as the sampling percentage.
IS_RECALCULATE	Integer	If you use the sampling data, this parameter indicates whether to calculate the precise result using all the data. The setting '0' represents not to recalculate the precise result but just use the sample.

Table 9.9 The Two Additional Parameters for Apriori Lite

Regarding OPTIMIZATION TYPE, then for the entire data use:

'OPTIMIZATION_TYPE', 0, null, null

To just use a sample of the data, then use the following, with the example showing a sample size of 70%:

'OPTIMIZATION_TYPE', 1, 0.7, null

Regarding IS_RECALCULATE, if you choose sampling then leave the support, confidence, and lift calculations as is for the sample use:

'IS_RECALCULATE', 0, null, null

To recalculate the support, confidence, and lift for the rules produced from the sample but using the entire data use:

'IS_RECALCULATE', 1, null, null

As always, this is best understood with examples.

9.6.1 Example 1: Use All the Data to Calculate the Single Items Pre-Rule and Post-Rule

In this examples, we will use the existing data to calculate the single items involved pre-rule and post-rule. The algorithm parameter setting is shown in Listing 9.3.

```
INSERT INTO PAL_CONTROL_TAB VALUES ('OPTIMIZATION_TYPE', 0, null,
null);
```
Listing 9.3 The SQLScript Control Parameter for Apriori Lite – Example 1

The output becomes as shown in Figure 9.15 with single pre- and post-rule items in the PRERULE and POSTRULE columns.

SELECT * FROM PAL_RESULT_TAB

	PRERULE	POSTRULE	SUPP...	CONFI...	LIFT
1	Product1	Product2	0.0588...	0.1999...	0.5666...
2	Product2	Product1	0.0588...	0.1666...	0.5666...
3	Product1	Product3	0.0588...	0.1999...	1.1333...
4	Product3	Product1	0.0588...	0.3333...	1.1333...
5	Product2	Product3	0.1176...	0.3333...	1.8888...
6	Product3	Product2	0.1176...	0.6666...	1.8888...
7	Product2	Product7	0.0588...	0.1666...	1.4166...
8	Product7	Product2	0.0588...	0.5	1.4166...
9	Product2	Product4	0.1176...	0.3333...	1.4166...
10	Product4	Product2	0.1176...	0.5	1.4166...

Figure 9.15 Apriori Lite Algorithm Output using all the Data

9.6.2 Example 2: 70% Sample Single Items Pre-Rule and Post-Rule

In this example, we take a sample of 70% to calculate the single items pre-rule and post-rule, and calculate the support, confidence, and lift on the sample data. The algorithm parameter settings are shown in Listing 9.4.

```
INSERT INTO PAL_CONTROL_TAB VALUES ('OPTIMIZATION_TYPE',1, 0.7, null);
INSERT INTO PAL_CONTROL_TAB VALUES ('IS_RECALCULATE',0, null, null);
```
Listing 9.4 The SQLScript Control Parameters for Apriori Lite – Example 2

The output becomes as shown in Figure 9.16.

SELECT * FROM PAL_RESULT_TAB					
	PRERULE	POSTRULE	SUPPO...	CONFI...	LIFT
1	Product1	Product3	0.0909...	0.25	1.375
2	Product3	Product1	0.0909...	0.5	1.375
3	Product2	Product3	0.0909...	0.3333...	1.8333...
4	Product3	Product2	0.0909...	0.5	1.8333...
5	Product2	Product4	0.1818...	0.6666...	1.8333...
6	Product4	Product2	0.1818...	0.5	1.8333...
7	Product2	Product6	0.0909...	0.3333...	0.9166...
8	Product6	Product2	0.0909...	0.25	0.9166...
9	Product3	Product4	0.0909...	0.5	1.375
10	Product4	Product3	0.0909...	0.25	1.375

Figure 9.16 Apriori Lite Algorithm Output using a Sample and No Re-calculate

9.6.3 Example 3: Using All the Available Data to Sample and Calculate Single Items

In this example, we take a sample to calculate the single items pre-rule and post-rule, and calculate the support, confidence, and lift on rules discovered in the sample but using the entire data.

The algorithm parameter settings are shown in Listing 9.5.

```
INSERT INTO PAL_CONTROL_TAB VALUES ('OPTIMIZATION_TYPE',1, 0.7, null);
INSERT INTO PAL_CONTROL_TAB VALUES ('IS_RECALCULATE',1, null, null);
```

Listing 9.5 The SQLScript Control Parameter for Apriori Lite – Example 3

The output becomes as shown in Figure 9.17.

SELECT * FROM PAL_RESULT_TAB					
	PRERULE	POSTRULE	SUPPO...	CONFI...	LIFT
1	Product1	Product3	0.0588...	0.1999...	1.1333...
2	Product3	Product1	0.0588...	0.3333...	1.1333...
3	Product2	Product3	0.1176...	0.3333...	1.8888...
4	Product3	Product2	0.1176...	0.6666...	1.8888...
5	Product2	Product4	0.1176...	0.3333...	1.4166...
6	Product4	Product2	0.1176...	0.5	1.4166...
7	Product3	Product4	0.0588...	0.3333...	1.4166...
8	Product4	Product3	0.0588...	0.25	1.4166...
9	Product7	Product5	0.0588...	0.5	1.6999...
10	Product5	Product7	0.0588...	0.1999...	1.6999...

Figure 9.17 Apriori Lite Algorithm Output using a Sample and Re-calculate

9.7 Strengths and Weaknesses of Association Analysis

The main strength of association analysis is that it produces clear results. Furthermore, the calculations are simple and therefore easy to understand, which increases the chance that management will implement the results. The rules provided are actionable for many applications and in particular for suggesting product cross-selling and up-selling opportunities. These are major advantages in predictive analysis, where often the algorithms are very complex and consequently hard to explain, which leaves doubt in the mind of those being asked to implement their findings in business processes.

One of the main weaknesses of the Apriori algorithm is that it requires exponentially more computations as the data size grows. This why SAP offers Apriori Lite to support one-to-one rules and also sampling, although care must be taken, as in all cases of sampling, to ensure that the sample is representative of the total data set.

Some of the results may be trivial and therefore of no value. Conversely, some of the results may be inexplicable; however, this latter problem applies to much of predictive analysis – mathematical relationships may be found but is the relationship mathematical or casual? Another weakness is that the algorithm will discount rare items, given that it is essentially looking for common ones.

Despite the weaknesses, they are far outweighed by the strengths. Also, although data volumes may be huge, in practice they often break down into segments as users usually look for relationships within product hierarchies or by location, such as retail stores, and consequently at smaller data volumes.

9.8 Business Case for Association Analysis

The potential number of business cases for association analysis is overwhelming. Every B2C website now includes recommendation engines, which are fundamentally based on association analysis with recommendations for what else you might be interested in buying. We use these recommendations in our daily lives. From shopping on the Amazon website, to music recommendations, film recommendations, and television programs, and so on. Association analysis, or market basket analysis as it was called initially, is used for store product placement, last minute check-out items, sales bundles, etc. In fact, one of the earliest examples of data mining in the practice is of market basket analysis in retail stores.

Association analysis isn't just restricted to basket analysis. It can be applied to any container of things, such as household purchases, social groups, and attending conference sessions, as we saw in the earlier examples.

Interestingly, just as we look for the common associations, it is sometimes useful to find the uncommon ones, as they may be an indication of fraud.

This topic will continue to develop as the Internet continues to expand its reach and application.

9.9   Summary

In this chapter we started with a look at some of the applications of association analysis and highlighted probably the best known, that of Amazon recommendations. We also noted how SAP is itself using the PAL Apriori algorithm in their B2C Product Recommendations solution. Then we discussed the Apriori association algorithm using a worked example to help in the explanation of the algorithm measures, namely support, confidence, and lift. Where processing times are high and only simple one-to-one association rules are required, then the PAL offers Apriori Lite. Finally, for both Apriori and Apriori Lite, the output can be usefully displayed in a tag cloud chart, where the important rules are highlighted.

In the next chapter we turn our attention to cluster analysis, which comprises an equally popular group of algorithms as that of association analysis.

This chapter describes the major topic of cluster analysis using the Predictive Analysis Library, R and SAP Predictive Analysis.

10   Cluster Analysis

In this chapter we look at cluster analysis, also referred to as segmentation analysis, which is one of the most well-known applications of predictive analysis. We start with one of the simplest of all the algorithms in the SAP HANA Predictive Analysis Library (PAL), namely ABC Classification, in which the records in a data set are grouped by a selected variable into the top A%, then the next B% and finally the last C%, to make up 100% of the data. Then we turn our attention to the popular statistical analysis algorithm, K-Means cluster analysis, and, for comparison, the machine learning cluster algorithm, Self Organizing Maps, both of which are available in the PAL.

10.1   Introduction to Cluster Analysis

Cluster analysis is concerned with organizing data into groups with similar characteristics. Ideally the data within a group is closely matched, while the groups themselves are very dissimilar. Put another way, the inter-cluster object distances are small within the cluster–they are compact; the intra-cluster distances between the clusters are large–they are disparate.

We group data all the time. People are grouped by county of origin, race, social class, age; animals and plants into biological classifications; organizations into public, private, profitable, size, function etc. We have been grouping data since the days of early man who, for example, needed to distinguish between edible and poisonous food, dangerous and innocuous animals. Aristotle's system for classifying animals divided them into those having red blood and those who do not, which corresponds closely to today's distinction between vertebrates and invertebrates. The blooded animals included five genera: mammals, birds, reptiles and amphibians, fishes, and whales; the bloodless animals were classified as cephalopods, crustaceans, insects, shelled animals, and zoophytes or plant-animals. Theophrastus, a pupil of Aristotle, wrote the first systemization of the botanical world whereby plants were classified according to their modes of generation, their localities, their sizes, and according to their practical uses such as foods, juices, and medicines. This system was superseded only by the 18th century when in 1737 Linnaeus published *Genera Plantarum*, which provides this excellent quotation on cluster analysis:

> *All the real knowledge which we possess depends on methods by which we distinguish the similar from the dissimilar. The greater number of natural distinctions this method comprehends the clearer becomes our idea of things.*

In his seminal book *Cluster Analysis*, Professor Brian S. Everitt states:

> *In the widest sense, a classification scheme may represent simply a convenient method for organizing a large set of data so that the retrieval of information may be made more efficiently.*

This is at the heart of why we do cluster analysis. Just as Theophrastus and Linnaeus wanted to better understand the biological and botanical world by grouping or segmenting, so today when we are faced with the vast volumes of data, we may be able to get a better understanding of it by breaking it down into groups or clusters.

Cluster analysis is often a preliminary step in the predictive analysis process. The derived clusters or segments are then specifically analyzed by predictive models to look for patterns within the clusters.

10.2 Applications of Cluster Analysis

Market segmentation is one of the major applications of cluster analysis. Instead of marketing generically to everyone, it is generally agreed that it is more beneficial to focus on specific segments with, for example, targeted product offers. There is a whole industry devoted to market segmentation.

Segmentation has been used to find groups of similar customers for selecting test markets for promotional offers, to try to understand the key attributes of the segments, and to track the movement of customers from different segments over time to try to understand the dynamics of customer behavior.

We have seen how cluster analysis can be used to refine predictive analysis when dealing with large and complex data sets. A parallel example of this would be where we have thousands of products or hundreds of stores, and we want to develop strategies to manage these products and stores. We don't want a thousand or even a hundred strategies, so we need to group the products and stores and devise a manageable number of strategies where each strategy applies to groups of products or stores. An unusual example of cluster analysis was that of the US Army, which wanted to reduce the number of different uniform sizes and so analyzed many measurements of body size and derived a system whereby individuals were allocated to specific sizes/clusters.

Cluster analysis is probably the most widely used class of predictive analysis methods with applications in a whole host of areas, such as criminal pattern analysis, medical research, social services, psychiatry, education, archaeology, astronomy, and taxonomy. It is indeed ubiquitous.

The Predictive Analysis Library (PAL) supports three cluster analysis algorithms: ABC Analysis, K-Means and Self Organizing Maps. ABC Analysis creates three user defined clusters; K-Means creates K clusters whose membership is driven by the data; Self Organizing Maps use a map, usually an m*n matrix, to map the input data to coordinates on the map that become clusters when multiple records are mapped to specific coordinates. We can think of a spectrum of methods from very simple to complex; from three clusters, to K clusters, to M*N clusters; from user driven to data driven. Each method has merits, and just because a method is simple does not mean that it has no value. Sometimes in predictive analysis, we get distracted by algorithm complexity and forget the basics such as data quality and model usefulness; the latter is often positively correlated to model understanding.

Before we continue, it is worth having a brief word on terminology. Cluster analysis using the above algorithms is sometimes referred to as undirected data mining, in that there is no target or dependent variable that we are trying to predict. As such, it is debatable what is a good cluster analysis as we are not comparing actual with predicted. We will discuss cluster quality measures later in this chapter. Undirected data mining leads to the amusing corollary and conundrum that if you don't know what you are looking for, how will you know when you have found it?

10.3 ABC Analysis

ABC Analysis clusters data based on its contribution to a total, for example, to find the top 10% of customers based on their spending, or the top 20% of products based on their contribution to overall profit. The data is first sorted in descending numeric order and then partitioned into the first A%, the second B% and the final C%, with the sum of A+B+C equal to 100%. The A cluster may be considered the most important or the Gold segment, the B cluster the next most important or the Silver segment, and finally the C cluster is the least important or the Bronze segment.

An example is shown in Figure 10.1, where A is 20%, B is 30% and C is 50%. From this we can see that:

▶ 20% of the total, the A segment, is accounted for by 5 items out of 70, or 7.1% of all the items.

▶ The next 30% of the total, the B segment, is accounted for by 9 items, or 12.9% of all the items.

▶ The next 50% of the total, the C segment, is accounted for by 56 items, or 80% of all the items.

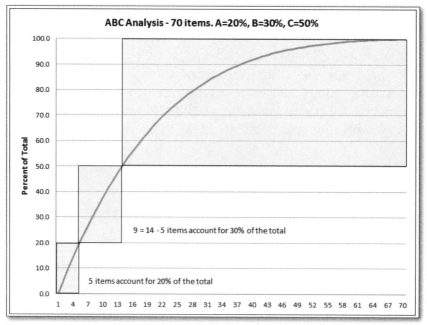

Figure 10.1 An Example of ABC Analysis

Now that we have an understanding of ABC analysis, let's look at the analysis in PAL and PA.

10.3.1 ABC Analysis in the PAL

In the Predictive Analysis Library, the algorithm name is ABC ANALYSIS and the associated function name is ABC.

The Input table comprises two columns, the first containing the item or record names, and the second containing the numeric values to be used in the analysis, as shown in Table 10.1.

Table	Column	Data Type	Description
Data	1st column	Varchar/Char	Item name
	2nd column	Double	Value

Table 10.1 The Input Table Definition for ABC Analysis

The Parameter table specifies four parameters–the values of A, B and C, and the Number of Threads, as shown in Table 10.2.

Name	Data Type	Description
PERCENT_A	Double	Interval for A class
PERCENT_B	Double	Interval for B class
PERCENT_C	Double	Interval for C class
THREAD_NUMBER	Integer	Number of threads

Table 10.2 The Parameter Table Definition for ABC Analysis

The values of A, B and C must add up to 100%. The PAL will check this. Percentages are entered for example as 0.5 for 50%; 0.15 for 15%, etc.

The Output table comprises two columns, the first column containing the assignment of A, B or C to the item or records, and the second column containing the item name, as shown in Table 10.3.

Table	Column	Data Type	Description
Result	1st column	Varchar/Char	ABC class
	2nd column	Varchar/Char	Items

Table 10.3 The Output Table Definition for ABC Analysis

10.3.2   An Example of ABC Analysis in the PAL

We've discussed how to utilize the PAL in previous chapters. Let's look how the PAL can be used for ABC Analysis. Here's a simple example. Assume a data input table as shown in Figure 10.2.

SELECT * FROM TESTABCTAB		
	ITEM	VALUE
1	item1	15.4
2	item2	50.4
3	item3	55.4
4	item4	40.9
5	item5	30.4
6	item6	25.6
7	item7	18.4
8	item8	10.5
9	item9	46.5
10	item10	10.4

Figure 10.2   The Input Data for the ABC Analysis

The main elements of the SQLScript are as follows, with the control parameters set as A=25%, B=30% and C=45%. The full code is available in the file SAP_HANA_PAL_ABC_Example_SQLScript on the SAP PRESS website.

```
-- The procedure generator

call SYSTEM.afl_wrapper_generator ('PAL_ABC','AFLPAL','ABC',PDATA);

-- The Control Table parameters

INSERT INTO #CONTROL_TBL VALUES ('PERCENT_A',null,0.25,null);
INSERT INTO #CONTROL_TBL VALUES ('PERCENT_B',null,0.30,null);
INSERT INTO #CONTROL_TBL VALUES ('PERCENT_C',null,0.45,null);
INSERT INTO #CONTROL_TBL VALUES ('THREAD_NUMBER',1,null,null);

-- Assume the data has been stored in table TESTABCTAB as shown in
Figure 10.2

-- Calling the procedure

CALL PAL_ABC(TESTABCTAB, "#CONTROL_TBL", RESULT_TBL) with overview;

SELECT * FROM RESULT_TBL;
```

Listing 10.1 The PAL SQLScript for ABC Analysis

Then the Output Table becomes as shown in Figure 10.3.

SELECT * FROM RESULT_TBL		
	ABC	ITEM
1	A	item3
2	A	item2
3	B	item9
4	B	item4
5	B	item5
6	C	item6
7	C	item7
8	C	item1
9	C	item8
10	C	item10

Figure 10.3 The Results of the ABC Analysis

The column marked ITEM, shows that items 3 and 2 comprise the top 25% of the total value, the A group; while items 9, 4 and 5 comprise the next 30% of the total value, the B group, and the rest the C group.

As you can see, ABC Analysis is very simple, but that does not mean it is not useful. ABC Analysis is a very popular method among marketing analysts, for supply chain analytics and inventory control, and management information in general.

With ABC Analysis, the number of clusters or groups is fixed at three. The K-Means algorithm allows you to choose the number of clusters–it's the value of K.

10.4 K-Means Cluster Analysis

The K-Means algorithm groups the records or observations into K clusters in which each record belongs to the cluster with the nearest mean. It is one of the best known predictive analysis algorithms and very popular for cluster analysis.

10.4.1 A Visualization of K-Means

The algorithm starts by choosing K initial cluster centers or means. In the example in Figure 10.4, K=3 and we have randomly generated the three starting cluster centers, shown in the diargram as circles. This is referred to as seeding the algorithm and is an important topic that we cover in Section 10.8 as the choice can affect performance and even the algorithm's solution.

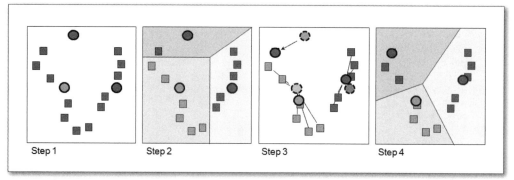

Figure 10.4 A Visualization of the Steps of the K-Means Algorithm

As shown in Figure 10.4, the next step, (Step 2), the content of the K clusters is defined by assigning every record or observation to its nearest center. The measure of "nearest" is also a topic for discussion as there are several inter-object distance measures and, as such, they can affect the assignment. In the next step (Step 3) of Figure 10.4, the centers of each of the K clusters are recalculated and become the new means. In Step 4, the cluster membership is updated. Steps 3 and 4 are then repeated until the cluster means do not change, or, in other words, the solution converges or reaches a threshold value for exiting the iterations.

K-Means is a simple and seemingly logical algorithm, which is why it is very popular. Management is more likely to implement the results of an analysis that they understand. Here's another simple example, this time calculated in Excel.

10.4.2 A Simple Example of K-Means in Excel

In this example, there are 14 values in the data set, and the data in Figure 10.5 suggests we set K=3. This is of course a key question–how do you decide what value to use for K? For up to three dimensions in the data, you can plot the data and examine it for possible clusters. For more than three dimensions, you can use the Parallel Co-Ordinate Plot available in SAP Predictive Analysis. We will show an example of that later in the chapter. Determining the best value for K is a topic in its own right and more of that later in Section 10.4.5. The difficulty is that cluster analysis is undirected data mining, so the concept of best is less precise.

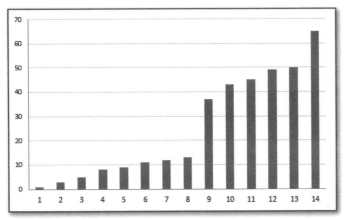

Figure 10.5 A Plot of the Data for the Simple Example of K-Means

The example in Figure 10.6, created and presented in Excel, starts with three initial cluster centers evenly spaced across the data set, located on record 4, value 8; record 9, value 37; and record 14, value 65.

In iteration 1, the 14 data values are then assigned to the nearest cluster center and grouped. The cluster centers or centroids are then updated and are as shown: 5.2, 12 and 48.17.

In iteration 2, the 14 data values are then assigned to the updated cluster center and grouped. The cluster centers or centroids are then updated and are as shown: 4.25, 11.25 and 48.17.

In iteration 3, the 14 data values are then assigned to the updated cluster center and grouped. The cluster centers or centroids are then updated and are as shown: 3, 10.6 and 48.17.

Finally, in iteration 4, the 14 data values are assigned to the same cluster center as in iteration 3, so the iterations finish and the final clustering is given. The final clustering is:

- ▶ Cluster 1 comprises records 1 to 3; values 1, 2 and 3
- ▶ Cluster 2 comprises records 4 to 8; values 8, 9, 11, 12 and 13
- ▶ Cluster 3 comprises records 9 to 14; values 37, 43, 45, 49, 50 and 65

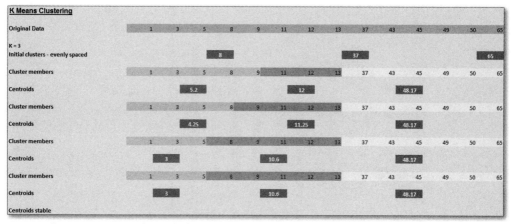

Figure 10.6 A Simple Worked Example of K-Means in Excel

10.4.3 K-Means in the PAL

In the Predictive Analysis Library, the algorithm name is K-Means and the associated function name is KMEANS.

The Input table comprises an initial ID column, then columns containing the variables to use for the cluster analysis, as shown in Table 10.4. Note the variables to be used for the cluster analysis must be numeric. K-Means clusters numeric objects using inter-object distance measures, and thus requires numeric data to calculate the distance. How we handle non-numeric data in cluster analysis is a topic for discussion later in this chapter.

Table	Column	Column Data Type	Description	Constraint
Data	1st column	Integer or string	ID	This must be the first column
	Other columns	Integer or double	Attribute data	

Table 10.4 The Input Table Definition for K-Means

The Parameter table is shown in Table 10.5.

Name	Data Type	Description
GROUP_NUMBER	Integer	The value of K, the number of clusters.
DISTANCE_LEVEL	Integer	Computes the distance between the item and cluster center. ▸ 1 = Manhattan distance ▸ 2 = Euclidean distance ▸ 3 = Minkowski distance
MAX_ITERATION	Integer	The maximum number of iterations.
INIT_TYPE	Integer	Center initialization method: ▸ 1 = First K ▸ 2 = Random with replacement ▸ 3 = Random without replacement ▸ 4 = SAP's patent for selecting the initial centers (US 6,882,998 B1)
NORMALIZATION	Integer	Normalization method: ▸ 0 = No ▸ 1 = Yes. For each point X (x1,x2,...,xn), the normalized value will be X'($|x1|/S,|x2|/S,...,|xn|/S$), where S = $|x1|+|x2|+...|xn|$. ▸ 2 = For each column C, get the minimum and maximum value of C, and then C[i] = (C[i]-min)/(max-min).
EXIT_THRESHOLD	Double	The threshold (actual value) for exiting the iterations.
THREAD_NUMBER	Integer	The number of threads.

Table 10.5 The Parameter Table Definition for K-Means

The value of K is simply the number of groups, clusters, or segments we wish to derive from the data set. Three inter-object distance measurements are offered:

1. Manhattan distance: This is the distance between two points on a grid based on a horizontal and/or vertical path, in other words, along the grid lines. It is also referred to as the city block distance.

2. Euclidean distance: This is the most common distance measure between two points. It is the unique shortest path.

3. Minkowski distance: This is a generalization of both the Euclidean distance and the Manhattan distance.

The maximum number of iterations provides some control over the processing of the algorithm and also protection from potentially very lengthy processes.

Four initialization or seeding methods are provided:

1. The first K records are used as the initial cluster centers. This method needs to be treated with caution, in case the data is ordered.

2. Random with replacement. The records for the initial centers for the K clusters are selected randomly.

3. Random without replacement.

4. This method uses the SAP Patent US 6,882,998 "Apparatus and method for selecting cluster points for a clustering analysis." This is a form of Max-Min approach whereby the initial center is chosen as near to the minimum point and then subsequent centers chosen, which are further away from the already selected centers. This is the recommended method, as it separates the initial cluster centers as much as it can.

There are three methods of normalizing the data:

1. The data stays as is. The default.

2. For each point X $(x1,x2,...,xn)$, the normalized value will be $X'(|x1|/S,|x2|/S,...,|xn|/S)$, where $S = |x1|+|x2|+...|xn|$. In other words for each value, its absolute value is divided by the total of all the absolute values in the variable or data column.

3. For each variable C, find the minimum and maximum values of C, and then $C[i] = (C[i]-min)/(max-min)$. In other words, rescale the data between 0 and 1, where the minimum value of C becomes 0, and the maximum becomes 1.

The threshold value when reached, signals the end of the iterative procedure. The default value is 0.00001.

We usually normalize or standardize data in cluster analysis to ensure that each variable has equal weight in the calculation; otherwise, very large numbers will dominate very small numbers in the cluster analysis.

The output from K-Means consists of two tables, as shown in Table 10.6. The first is a table of the results of the analysis, which shows for each record or item in the data set the assigned cluster number, plus the distance from that item to its cluster center. This is the Results row in Table 10.6. The second table lists the co-ordinates of each cluster center, identified in Table 10.6 as the Center Points row.

The distances of each item from its cluster centers can be used to measure the compactness of the clusters and also to identify unusual values or outliers. This is used in the PAL functions ANOMALYDETECTION and VALIDATEKMEANS.

Table	Column	Data Type	Description
Results	1st column	Integer or string	Record ID
	2nd column	Integer or double	The cluster number assigned to the record ID
	3rd column	Integer or double	The distance between the cluster center and each point in the cluster
Center Points	1st column	Integer	The cluster center ID
	Other columns	Double	The cluster center coordinates

Table 10.6   The Output Tables Definition for K-Means

10.4.4 An Example of K-Means in the PAL

Here is a simple example, based on the input table as shown in Figure 10.7.

SELECT * FROM PAL_KMEANS_DATA_TAB			
	ID	V000	V001
1	0	0.5	0.5
2	1	1.5	0.5
3	2	1.5	1.5
4	3	0.5	1.5
5	4	1.1	1.2
6	5	0.5	15.5
7	6	1.5	15.5
8	7	1.5	16.5
9	8	0.5	16.5
10	9	1.2	16.1
11	10	15.5	15.5
12	11	16.5	15.5
13	12	16.5	16.5
14	13	15.5	16.5
15	14	15.6	16.2
16	15	15.5	0.5
17	16	16.5	0.5
18	17	16.5	1.5
19	18	15.5	1.5
20	19	15.7	1.6

Figure 10.7 The Input Data for the K-Means Example

We can view the data in SAP HANA Studio Data Preview as shown in Figure 10.8, which shows that there are clearly four clusters in the data.

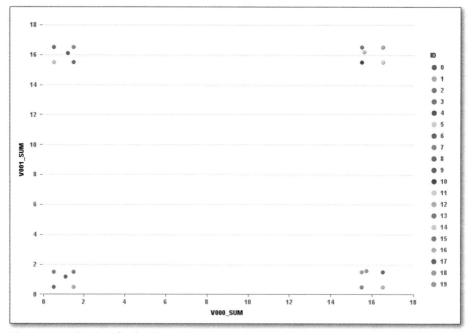

Figure 10.8 The Data for the Cluster Analysis in a Scatter Chart

The SQLScript is as follows, with the parameters settings as:

```
-- The procedure generator

call SYSTEM.afl_wrapper_generator ('PAL_KMEANS','AFLPAL', 'KMEANS',
PDATA);

-- The Control Table parameters

INSERT INTO PAL_CONTROL_TAB VALUES ('GROUP_NUMBER',4,null,null);
INSERT INTO PAL_CONTROL_TAB VALUES ('INIT_TYPE',4,null,null);
INSERT INTO PAL_CONTROL_TAB VALUES ('DISTANCE_LEVEL',2,null,null);
INSERT INTO PAL_CONTROL_TAB VALUES ('MAX_ITERATION',100,null,null);
INSERT INTO PAL_CONTROL_TAB VALUES ('EXIT_
THRESHOLD',null,0.000001,null);
INSERT INTO PAL_CONTROL_TAB VALUES ('NORMALIZATION',0,null,null);
INSERT INTO PAL_CONTROL_TAB VALUES ('THREAD_NUMBER',2,null,null);


-- Assume the data has been stored in table PAL_KMEANS_DATA_TAB as
shown in Figure 10.7

-- Calling the procedure

CALL _SYS_AFL.PAL_KMEANS(PAL_KMEANS_DATA_TAB, PAL_CONTROL_TAB, PAL_
KMEANS_RESASSIGN_TAB, PAL_KMEANS_CENTERS_TAB) with overview;

SELECT * FROM PAL_KMEANS_CENTERS_TAB;
SELECT * FROM PAL_KMEANS_RESASSIGN_TAB;
```

Listing 10.2 The PAL SQLScript for K-Means

The full code is available in the file SAP_HANA_PAL_KMEANS_Example_SQLScript on the SAP PRESS website.

The results of running the SQLScript are shown in Figure 10.9 and Figure 10.10, which show the assignment of each record to a specific cluster and the data points for each cluster center.

SELECT * FROM PAL_KMEANS_RESASSIGN_TAB			
	ID	CENTER_ASSIGN	DISTANCE
1	0	1	0.749666...
2	1	1	0.722495...
3	2	1	0.664830...
4	3	1	0.694262...
5	4	1	0.178885...
6	5	3	0.749666...
7	6	3	0.694262...
8	7	3	0.664830...
9	8	3	0.722495...
10	9	3	0.178885...
11	10	0	0.684105...
12	11	0	0.792464...
13	12	0	0.740270...
14	13	0	0.622896...
15	14	0	0.357770...
16	15	2	0.760263...
17	16	2	0.835463...
18	17	2	0.676756...
19	18	2	0.581377...
20	19	2	0.536656...

Figure 10.9 The Record Cluster Assignment Number and the Distance to its Centroid

SELECT * FROM PAL_KMEANS_CENTERS_TAB			
	CENTER_ID	V000	V001
1	0	15.919...	16.04
2	1	1.02	1.04
3	2	15.940...	1.119...
4	3	1.04	16.02

Figure 10.10 The Cluster Center Co-ordinates from the K-Means Analysis

We can define and run the same analysis in SAP Predictive Analysis (PA), not only for the ease of defining such analysis but also for the visualization of the results. Here is the same analysis using PA with the data sourced from K_MEANS_DATA_TAB and connected to the SAP HANA PAL K-Means algorithm, as shown in Figure 10.11.

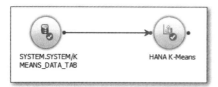

SYSTEM.SYSTEM/K
MEANS_DATA_TAB   HANA K-Means

Figure 10.11 The Cluster Analysis in SAP Predictive Analysis using HANA K-Means

The HANA K-Means component dialogue is shown in Figure 10.12 and Figure 10.13 with prompts for the parameter values of the algorithm. Figure 10.12 shows the prompts for the primary properties of the dialogue, for example, the independent variables for the cluster analysis and the input value of K, the number of clusters.

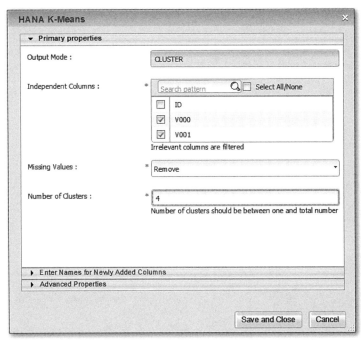

Figure 10.12 The PA HANA K-Means Dialogue Primary Properties

Figure 10.13 shows the advanced properties of the K-Means dialogue, for example, the maximum number of iterations, the distance calculation method, normalization, etc. as defined in Table 10.5.

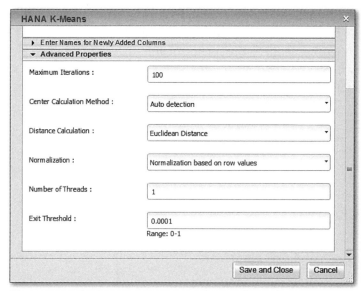

Figure 10.13 The PA HANA K-Means Dialogue Advanced Properties

For users without access to the PAL, the same analysis can be performed using the interface to R provided by PA, as shown in Figure 10.14.

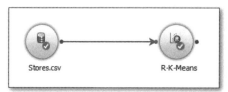

Figure 10.14 The Cluster Analysis in PA using HANA R-K-Means

We have changed the data source to provide a better example to show the PA Cluster Viewer as the previous data set is two-dimensional with equal cluster sizes. In this example, we use the Stores.csv data for more variety and a visualization to illustrate all the features of the cluster viewer. After running the process, we can view the results in tabular form as shown in Figure 10.15, with the CLUSTER NUMBER assigned to each record, and also in the cluster viewer as shown in Figure 10.16.

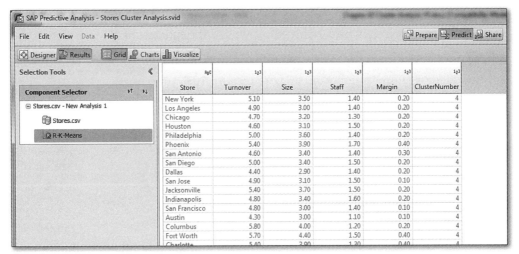

Figure 10.15 The Cluster Analysis Results in PA

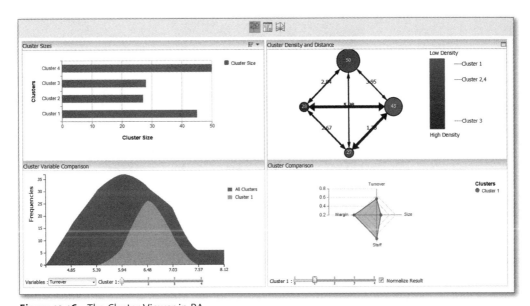

Figure 10.16 The Cluster Viewer in PA

The cluster viewer, in Figure 10.16 is comprised of four charts. First, a horizontal bar chart showing the size of each cluster for easy comparison. Then a cluster density and distance chart with a color coded scale of dark to light, for dense to sparse clusters, and the distance between the cluster centers is shown with the thicker the line, the closer the clusters. The two charts at the bottom allow the user to compare clusters by variable to see what differentiates them.

We can also view the results in a parallel co-ordinate plot with the records color coded by cluster number, as shown in Figure 10.17.

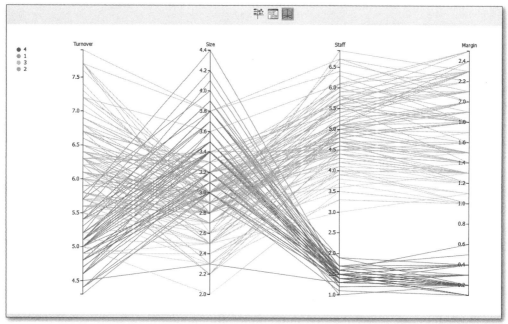

Figure 10.17   The Parallel Co-ordinate Plot Color Coded by Cluster

10.4.5 Choosing the Value of K

Clearly, a key question for the K-Means algorithm is how to decide what value of K to use. For some applications, you may already know the value you want to use, for example, as in the US Army uniform size application, or if you are deciding on product or store groupings for strategic planning, there may a maximum number of strategies that you consider are manageable. However, in most cases, the value of k will not be pre-set before the analysis.

One suggestion is to use the SQRT(N/2), where N is the number of records in the dataset; however, this results in large values of K, for example, for a million records, K would be 707.

Perhaps data visualization can help. For example, the Stores data can be plotted in a bubble plot, see Figure 10.18 , or plotted in a parallel co-ordinate plot, see Figure 10.19, which suggests K be set to 2 or 3.

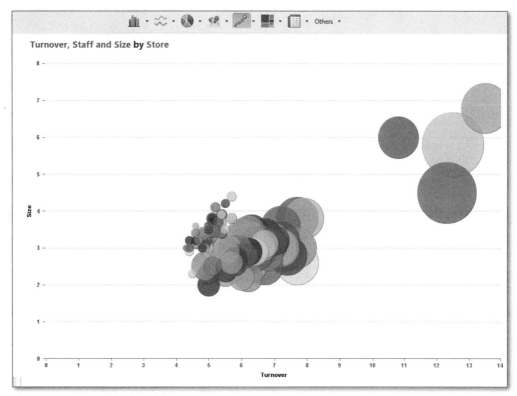

Figure 10.18   A Bubble Plot of the Input Data

A more quantitative approach to determining the value of K is to try to use measures of cluster quality, although, as we said earlier in this chapter, cluster analysis is sometimes referred to as undirected data mining, in that there is no target or dependent variable that we are trying to predict, and as such, it is debatable what is a good cluster analysis since we are not comparing actual values with predicted. A popular measure of cluster quality is the silhouette.

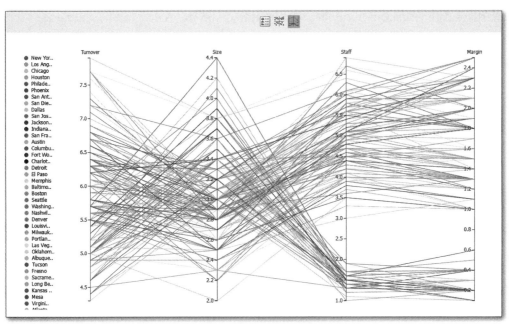

Figure 10.19   A Parallel Co-ordinate Plot of the Input Data

10.5   Silhouette

The silhouette is a measure of the quality of the cluster analysis. We would expect good clusters to be where cluster members are close to each other yet far from members of other clusters. The silhouette calculates the average for all the records in the dataset of (b–a) / max (a,b), where a is the average distance of the record to all other records within the same cluster (referred to as cohesion) and b is the average distance of the record to all the other records in the nearest cluster center that it does not belong to (referred to as separation). A silhouette coefficient of 1 will occur when all records are located directly on their cluster centers, while a value of –1 will occur when all records are located on the cluster centers of some other cluster. A value of 0 shows on average that records are equidistant between their own cluster center and the nearest other cluster. A general guide is that a value less than 0.2 represents a poor clustering, while a value above 0.5 is good.

10.6   An Example of the Silhouette in the PAL

In the Predictive Analysis Library, the function name is VALIDATEKMEANS.

The Input table is comprised of two tables. The first table is the input table for the cluster analysis–in our example, PAL_KMEANS_DATA_TAB. The second table is the table of the cluster number assignment to each record.

Table	Column	Column Data Type	Description
Data	1st column	Integer or string	Record ID
	Other columns	Integer or double	Attribute data
Type Data/ Class Data	1st column	Integer	Record ID
	2nd column	Integer	Cluster number assigned

Table 10.7   The Input Table Definition for Validate K-Means

In our example, these two tables are shown side by side in Figure 10.20.

SELECT * FROM PAL_KMEANS_DATA_TAB					SELECT * FROM V_KMEANS_TYPE_ASSIGN		
	ID	V000	V001			ID	TYPE_ASSIGN
1	0	0.5	0.5		1	0	1
2	1	1.5	0.5		2	1	1
3	2	1.5	1.5		3	2	1
4	3	0.5	1.5		4	3	1
5	4	1.1	1.2		5	4	1
6	5	0.5	15.5		6	5	3
7	6	1.5	15.5		7	6	3
8	7	1.5	16.5		8	7	3
9	8	0.5	16.5		9	8	3
10	9	1.2	16.1		10	9	3
11	10	15.5	15.5		11	10	0
12	11	16.5	15.5		12	11	0
13	12	16.5	16.5		13	12	0
14	13	15.5	16.5		14	13	0
15	14	15.6	16.2		15	14	0
16	15	15.5	0.5		16	15	2
17	16	16.5	0.5		17	16	2
18	17	16.5	1.5		18	17	2
19	18	15.5	1.5		19	18	2
20	19	15.7	1.6		20	19	2

Figure 10.20   The Input Data and Cluster Assignment Tables

The Parameter table is shown in Table 10.8.

In our example, the number of variables is 2, V000 and V001.

Name	Data Type	Description
VARIABLE_NUM	Integer	The number of variables
THREAD_NUMBER	Integer	The number of threads

Table 10.8 The Parameter Table Definition for Validate K-Means

The output from Validate K-Means is shown in Table 10.9.

Table	Column	Data Type	Description
Results	1st column	Varchar or char	Name
	2nd column	Double	The Silhouette value

Table 10.9 The Output Tables Definition for Validate K-Means

10.7 An Example of Validate K-Means in the PAL

The SQLScript is as follows:

```
-- The procedure generator

call SYSTEM.afl_wrapper_generator ('palValidateKMeans','AFLPAL','VALIDA
TEKMEANS',PDATA);

-- The Control Table parameters
INSERT INTO #CONTROL_TAB VALUES ('VARIABLE_NUM',2,null, null);
INSERT INTO #CONTROL_TAB VALUES ('THREAD_NUMBER',1,null, null);

-- Calling the procedure

CALL palValidateKMeans(PAL_KMEANS_DATA_TAB, V_KMEANS_TYPE_ASSIGN,
"#CONTROL_TAB", KMEANS_SVALUE_TAB) with overview;

SELECT * FROM KMEANS_SVALUE_TAB;
```

Listing 10.3 The PAL SQLScript for Validate K-Means

The full code available in the file SAP_HANA_PAL_VALIDATEKMEANS_Example_ SQLScript on the SAP PRESS website.

In our worked example, the silhouette value is 0.9459, as shown in Figure 10.21. This is a very high value; however, it is to be expected given that we have created a data set specifically for the example and clearly K = 4 as we saw in Figure 10.8.

SELECT * FROM KMEANS_SVALUE_TAB		
	NAME	S
1	Silhouette	0.9459...

Figure 10.21 The Output Table from Validate K-Means showing the Silhouette Value

Now we can run the SQLScript for various values of K and then see which value of K gives the highest silhouette value. In our example, K = 2 to 8, as shown in Figure 10.22.

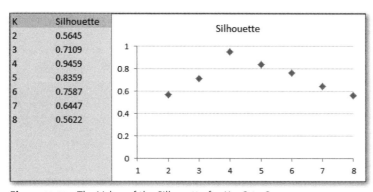

Figure 10.22 The Value of the Silhouette for K = 2 to 8

The maximum silhouette value is when K = 4. A word of caution, though: as the value of K approaches the number of records (N), the silhouette will increase and, finally, when K = N it be equal to 1. For K greater than 9, the value starts to increase as shown in Figure 10.23.

K	Silhouette
9	0.5812
10	0.6219
11	0.6652
12	0.6819

Figure 10.23 The Silhouette Value for K = 9 to 12

Another important topic in cluster analysis is how to choose the initial cluster centres, as that choice can affect the final results of the cluster analysis.

10.8 Choosing the Initial Cluster Centers

For the K-Means algorithm, we need to decide the starting values of the cluster centers, sometimes referred to as the seeding strategy. In Figure 10.6 we saw that using an evenly spaced approach leads to the final clusters of:

- ▶ Cluster 1 = 1,3,5
- ▶ Cluster 2 = 8,9,11,12,13
- ▶ Cluster 3 = 37,43,45,49,50,65

However, if we start with the first K records as the K initial centers, then, from Figure 10.24, we see that again the final clusters are:

- ▶ Cluster 1 = 1,3,5
- ▶ Cluster 2 = 8,9,11,12,13
- ▶ Cluster 3 = 37,43,45,49,50,65

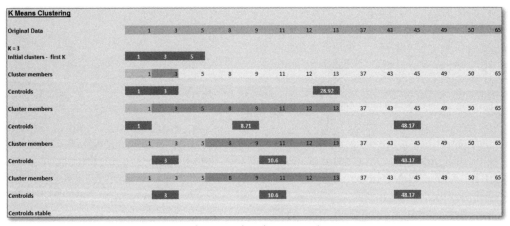

Figure 10.24   The First K Records are used as the First K Cluster Centers

However, if we start with a minimum and maximum approach to determining the values of the K initial centers, then from Figure 10.25, we see that now the final clusters are:

▸ Cluster 1 = 1,3,5, 8,9,11,12,13

▸ Cluster 2 = 37,43,45,49,50

▸ Cluster 3 = 65

K Means Clustering

	1	3	5	8	9	11	12	13	37	43	45	49	50	65
Original Data	1	3	5	8	9	11	12	13	37	43	45	49	50	65
K = 3														
Initial clusters - using a maximin algorithm														
Cluster 1 - first record	1													
Cluster 1 - distances		2	4	7	8	10	11	12	36	42	44	48	50	64
Select the largest														65
Cluster 2 - distances		63	61	58	57	55	54	53	29	23	21	17	15	
Minimum of C1 and C2 distances		2	4	7	8	10	11	12	29	23	21	17	15	
Select the largest									37					
Initial clusters - using a maximin algorithm	1								37					65
Cluster members	1	3	5	8	9	11	12	13	37	43	45	49	50	65
Centroids			7.75								44.8			65
Cluster members	1	3	5	8	9	11	12	13	37	43	45	49	50	65
Centroids			7.75								44.8			65
Centroids stable														

Figure 10.25 A Minimum-Maximum Approach to Determining the First K Cluster Centers

The solution to this problem is to run different seeding strategies and see how robust the solution is, in other words: does the solution change or is it constant? If it changes, you need to investigate the construction of the clusters to try to understand the reasons for the differences.

In our worked example, we show all four initialization methods using INIT_TYPE 1,2,3 and 4 and find that all give the same result. The cluster center ID varies, but the clusters are the same in content, as shown in Figure 10.26.

CENTER_ID	V000	V001
0	1.02	1.04
1	15.94...	1.119...
2	15.91...	16.04
3	1.04	16.02

CENTER_ID	V000	V001
0	15.91...	16.04
1	1.04	16.02
2	1.02	1.04
3	15.94...	1.119...

CENTER_ID	V000	V001
0	15.91...	16.04
1	1.04	16.02
2	1.02	1.04
3	15.94...	1.119...

CENTER_ID	V000	V001
0	15.91...	16.04
1	1.02	1.04
2	15.94...	1.119...
3	1.04	16.02

ID	CENTER_ASSIGN	DISTA...
0	0	0.7496...
1	0	0.7224...
2	0	0.6648...
3	0	0.6942...
4	0	0.1788...
5	3	0.7496...
6	3	0.6942...
7	3	0.6648...
8	3	0.7224...
9	3	0.1788...
10	2	0.6841...
11	2	0.7924...
12	2	0.7402...
13	2	0.6228...
14	2	0.3577...
15	1	0.7602...
16	1	0.8354...
17	1	0.6767...
18	1	0.5813...
19	1	0.5366...

ID	CENTER_ASSIGN	DISTA...
0	2	0.7496...
1	2	0.7224...
2	2	0.6648...
3	2	0.6942...
4	2	0.1788...
5	1	0.7496...
6	1	0.6942...
7	1	0.6648...
8	1	0.7224...
9	1	0.1788...
10	0	0.6841...
11	0	0.7924...
12	0	0.7402...
13	0	0.6228...
14	0	0.3577...
15	3	0.7602...
16	3	0.8354...
17	3	0.6767...
18	3	0.5813...
19	3	0.5366...

ID	CENTER_ASSIGN	DISTA...
0	2	0.7496...
1	2	0.7224...
2	2	0.6648...
3	2	0.6942...
4	2	0.1788...
5	1	0.7496...
6	1	0.6942...
7	1	0.6648...
8	1	0.7224...
9	1	0.1788...
10	0	0.6841...
11	0	0.7924...
12	0	0.7402...
13	0	0.6228...
14	0	0.3577...
15	3	0.7602...
16	3	0.8354...
17	3	0.6767...
18	3	0.5813...
19	3	0.5366...

ID	CENTER_ASSIGN	DISTA...
0	1	0.7496...
1	1	0.7224...
2	1	0.6648...
3	1	0.6942...
4	1	0.1788...
5	3	0.7496...
6	3	0.6942...
7	3	0.6648...
8	3	0.7224...
9	3	0.1788...
10	0	0.6841...
11	0	0.7924...
12	0	0.7402...
13	0	0.6228...
14	0	0.3577...
15	2	0.7602...
16	2	0.8354...
17	2	0.6767...
18	2	0.5813...
19	2	0.5366...

Figure 10.26   Cluster Analysis using Initialization Methods 1,2,3 and 4

So far, we have used numeric variables in our cluster analysis. However, we often have categorical data in our analysis and we need to consider how to handle them.

10.9   Categorical Data and Numeric Cluster Analysis

To cluster data using inter-object distance measures, we need numeric data. However, for categorical data, such measures are not directly available, for example, what is the distance between an apple and a banana?

One approach is as shown below in Figure 10.27 whereby we convert each category into a new variable with binary values 0 or 1. Given the 0/1 new variables, it is sometimes recommended to rescale them by multiplying by the SQRT(0.5) to reduce their influence, as the 0/1 is a strong contrast and will therefore strongly affect the clustering.

	Column1	Fruit			Column1	Fruit	Apples	Bananas
1	Record 1	Apple		1	Record 1	Apple	1	0
2	Record 2	Banana		2	Record 2	Banana	0	1
3	Record 3	Apple		3	Record 3	Apple	1	0
4	Record 4	Apple		4	Record 4	Apple	1	0
5	Record 5	Banana		5	Record 5	Banana	0	1
6	Record 6	Banana		6	Record 6	Banana	0	1
7	Record 7	Apple		7	Record 7	Apple	1	0
8	Record 8	Apple		8	Record 8	Apple	1	0
9	Record 9	Banana		9	Record 9	Banana	0	1
10	Record 10	Apple		10	Record 10	Apple	1	0

Figure 10.27   Transposing Categorical Data to Numeric

If there are many categorical variables and within each variable there are many categories, then the number of variables in the revised/transposed data will be large. Perhaps some categories can be merged. Perhaps non-distance-based clustering algorithms need to be considered. In some circumstances, we can use decision trees and association analysis for clustering.

We can analyze why individual records/observations are assigned to particular clusters by using classification methods, for example, decision trees, where the cluster assigned number is the dependent or target variable and the other variables are the independent or input variables. More information on this topic is offered—in Chapter 13. The decision tree in Figure 10.28 shows an analysis of the Stores.csv data set into 3 clusters and the rules derived therefrom, e.g., Cluster 3 comprises all records with staff numbers less than 2.45, etc.

A final method of cluster analysis that we will review is a very flexible method, but also, very mathematical–Kohonen Self-Organizing Maps.

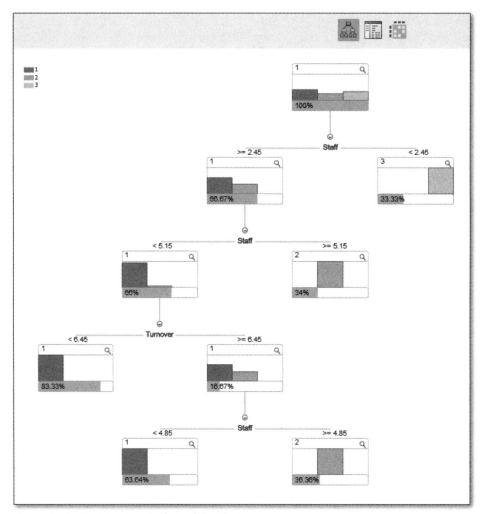

Figure 10.28 Decision Tree Analysis of the Clusters

10.10 Self-Organizing Maps

Self-Organizing Maps or SOMs are a type of neural network that can be used to cluster a dataset into distinct groups. They were invented by Professor Teuvo Kohonen, of the Academy of Finland, and are therefore sometimes known as Kohonen SOMs. They provide a way of representing multi-dimensional data in much lower dimensional space, usually of one or two dimensions in a vector or matrix, known as a map. When the network is trained, records in a data set that are similar should appear close together on the output map, while records that are different will appear far apart. The number of records or observations captured by each cell or unit in the map will show the more populated units, which will indicate groupings of the records or segments, and which may give a sense of the appropriate number of clusters in the dataset. Unlike K-Means cluster analysis, the value of 'K' is not predetermined.

In the example shown in Figure 10.29, the network is created from a 2D lattice of "nodes"–the map, each of which is fully connected to the input layer. Figure 10.29 shows a small SOM network of 3 * 3 nodes connected to the input layer of a two dimensional vector, that is, a two-variable dataset.

Each node has a specific topological position, an x, y coordinate in the lattice or map, and contains a vector of weights of the same dimension as the input vectors. In our example, we have 2 dimensions/variables in the input vector/dataset, so each node will have a corresponding weight vector W, of 2 dimensions: W1, W2. The lines connecting the nodes in Figure 10.29 are only there to represent adjacency and do not signify a connection.

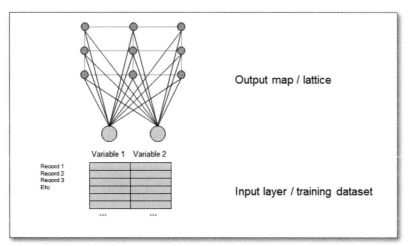

Output map / lattice

Variable 1   Variable 2

Record 1
Record 2
Record 3
Etc.

Input layer / training dataset

Figure 10.29   A 3*3 SOM Connected to a 2-Variable Dataset

Training of the SOM occurs in several steps and over many iterations:

1. Each node in the map has its weights initialized. The PAL sets them as random values between -0.05 and 0.05.

2. A vector is chosen, starting with the first, from the set of training data and presented to the map.

3. Every node is examined to calculate which one's weights are most similar or closest to the input vector using a distance measure such as the Euclidean distance. The "winning" node is known as the Best Matching Unit (BMU).

4. The radius of the neighborhood of the BMU is now calculated. This is a value that starts large, typically set to the radius of the lattice but diminishes with each iteration. Any nodes found within this radius are deemed to be inside the BMU's neighborhood.

5. Each neighboring node's (the nodes found in step 4) weights are adjusted to make them more like the input vector. The closer a node is to the BMU, the more its weights get altered.

6. We then repeat steps 2 to 5 for the next vector in the data set and then for N iterations or until the weights do not change.

Figure 10.30 shows an example of the size of a typical neighborhood close to the commencement of training. A unique feature of the Kohonen SOM learning algorithm is that the area of the neighborhood shrinks over time, which is accomplished by making the radius of the neighborhood shrink using a decay function. Over time, the neighborhood will shrink to the size of just one node, the BMU.

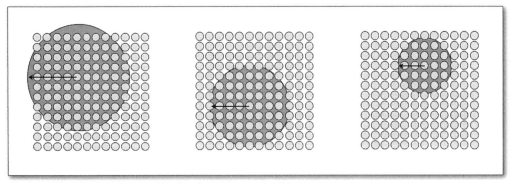

Figure 10.30   The Neighborhood Size During the SOM Iterations

If a node is found to be within the neighborhood, then its weight vector is adjusted as follows; otherwise, it is left alone.

$W(t+1) = W(t) + \lambda(t) * (V(t) - W(t))$

where t represents the iteration and λ is a small variable called the learning rate, which decreases with each iteration. In other words, the new adjusted weight for the node is equal to the old weight (W), plus a fraction of the difference (λ) between the old weight and the input vector (V).

$$\lambda(t) = \lambda_0 \; exp \; (-t / \lambda)$$

where λ_0, denotes the width of the lattice at iteration t = 0 and the Greek letter lambda, λ, denotes a constant. In the PAL λ_0 is set to 0.5.

Not only does the learning rate have to decay over time, but the effect of learning should be proportional to the distance a node is from the BMU. At the edges of the BMUs neighborhood, the learning process should have barely any effect at all. The amount of learning should fade over distance similar to the Gaussian decay shown below:

$$\lambda(t) = exp \; (-dist^2 / 2\lambda^2(t))$$

As the process goes through the iterations, then records from the training data set are allocated to cells on the map, with similar records grouped together, as shown in Figure 10.31.

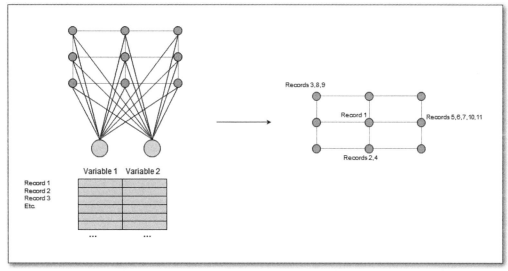

Figure 10.31 The Assignment of the Data Set Records to the Map, Showing the Clusters

10.10.1 Self-Organizing Maps in the PAL

In the Predictive Analysis Library, the algorithm name is Self-Organizing Maps and the associated function name is SELFORGMAP.

The Input table comprises an initial ID column, then columns containing the variables to use for the cluster analysis, as shown in Table 10.10. Note the variables to be used for the cluster analysis must be numeric. SOMs cluster numeric objects using the inter object distance, and thus the input variables need to be numeric.

Table	Column	Column Data Type	Description	Constraint
Data	1st column	Integer or string	Record ID	This must be the first column
	Other columns	Integer or double	Attribute data	

Table 10.10   The Input Table Definition for Self-Organizing Maps

The Parameter table is shown in Table 10.11.

Name	Data Type	Description
SIZE OF MAP	Integer	The self-organizing map is made up of n × n unit cells. This parameter defines the value n.
MAX_ITERATION	Integer	The maximum number of iterations.
NORMALIZATION	Integer	Normalization method: ▶ 0 = No ▶ 1 = Transform to new range (0.0, 1.0) ▶ 2 = Z-score normalization
THREAD_NUMBER	Integer	Number of threads.

Table 10.11   The Parameter Table Definition for Self-Organizing Maps

There are three methods of normalizing the data:

1. The parameter is set to 0. The data stays as is, the default setting.

2. The parameter is set to 1. For each variable X (x1,x2,...,xn), find the minimum and maximum value of X, and then *X[i] = (X[i]-min)/(max-min)*. In other words, rescale the data between 0 and 1, where the minimum value of X becomes 0 and the maximum becomes 1.

3. The parameter is set to 2. For each variable X (x1,x2,...,xn), the normalized values are based on the mean and standard deviation of X. A value, x1, of X is normalized to X' by computing *X' = (xi – Mean(X)) / S.D.(X)*.

The output from Self-Organizing Maps consists of two tables, as shown in Table 10.12. The first table, SOM Map row, shows the final weights used for each of the map cell IDs, and the number of records or tuples that were assigned to that map cell ID. This number therefore represents the cluster sizes. The second table, the SOM Assign row, shows the Cell ID assigned to each record; hence, the membership of the clusters.

Table	Column	Data Type	Description
SOM Map	1st column	Integer	Unit cell ID.
	Other columns except the last one	Double	The weight vectors used to simulate the original tuples.
	Last column	Integer	The number of original tuples that every unit cell contains.
SOM Assign	1st column	Integer or string	The ID of the original records or tuples
	2th column	Integer	The ID of the unit cells

Table 10.12   The Output Tables Definition for Self-Organizing Maps

10.10.2 An Example of Self-Organizing Maps in the PAL

In this example, we use the dataset shown in Figure 10.32, which is the same as was used in the example of K-Means and therefore will provide an interesting basis for comparison of the two cluster analysis algorithms.

SELECT * FROM PAL_SOM_DATA_TAB

	TRANS_ID	V000	V001
1	0	0.5	0.5
2	1	1.5	0.5
3	2	1.5	1.5
4	3	0.5	1.5
5	4	1.1	1.2
6	5	0.5	15.5
7	6	1.5	15.5
8	7	1.5	16.5
9	8	0.5	16.5
10	9	1.2	16.1
11	10	15.5	15.5
12	11	16.5	15.5
13	12	16.5	16.5
14	13	15.5	16.5
15	14	15.6	16.2
16	15	15.5	0.5
17	16	16.5	0.5
18	17	16.5	1.5
19	18	15.5	1.5
20	19	15.7	1.6

Figure 10.32 The Input Data for the Self-Organizing Maps Example

The SQLScript is as follows:

```
-- PAL set-up

call SYSTEM.afl_wrapper_generator('PAL_SELF_ORG_MAP', 'AFLPAL',
'SELFORGMAP', PDATA);

-- Preparing application data for calling procedure

INSERT INTO PAL_CONTROL_TAB VALUES ('MAX_ITERATION',200, null, null);
INSERT INTO PAL_CONTROL_TAB VALUES ('SIZE_OF_MAP',4,null, null);
INSERT INTO PAL_CONTROL_TAB VALUES ('NORMALIZATION',0,null, null);
INSERT INTO PAL_CONTROL_TAB VALUES ('THREAD_NUMBER',2, null, null);


-- Assume the data has been stored in table PAL_SOM_DATA_TAB as shown
in Figure 10.32

-- Calling the procedure
```

```
CALL PAL_SELF_ORG_MAP(PAL_SOM_DATA_TAB, PAL_CONTROL_TAB, PAL_SOM_MAP_
TAB, PAL_SOM_RESASSIGN_TAB) with overview;

select * from PAL_SOM_MAP_TAB;
select * from PAL_SOM_RESASSIGN_TAB;
```

Listing 10.4 The PAL SQLScript for SOMs

The full code available in the file SAP_HANA_PAL_ SELFORGMAP_Example_ SQLScript on the SAP PRESS website.

The Output tables become as shown in Figure 10.33 and Figure 10.34.

The first output table, Figure 10.33, shows the final weights used for each of the map cell IDs, in the example 4 * 4 = 16, and the number of records or tuples that were assigned to that map cell ID. This number represents the cluster sizes.

	CELL_ID	WEIGHT000	WEIGHT001	NUMS_TUPLE
1	0	16.499999151751773	16.00839673881344	2
2	1	15.87449064834603	16.220823235634093	0
3	2	15.55083693758167	16.347440277276707	2
4	3	11.961966889331434	16.280210672232258	0
5	4	15.984327592622952	8.967948470240426	0
6	5	15.50067935565064	15.509402344555694	1
7	6	6.437540708503749	15.965872117849178	0
8	7	1.040908648507586	16.02522794605194	5
9	8	16.008442653033853	0.5001074647763601	2
10	9	16.491960083987586	1.4986494734867206	1
11	10	15.965763322198018	2.9566297962809753	0
12	11	1.0471160493848806	13.779880847347483	0
13	12	15.756356953749638	1.4279779217221233	0
14	13	15.601722922995062	1.5508368481187114	2
15	14	8.894511278253121	1.3762977512973933	0
16	15	1.0204207745254232	1.0457158200341077	5

select * from PAL_SOM_MAP_TAB

Figure 10.33 The Cell ID Weights and Number of Tuples or Records Assigned to that Cell

The second output table, shown in Figure 10.34, shows the Cell ID assigned to each record; hence, the membership of the clusters, e.g., Cell ID 15 has 5 records (Trans ID 0,1,2,3,4); Cell ID 7 has 5 records (Trans ID 5,6,7,8,9); Cell ID 5 just one record (Trans ID 10); etc.

select * from PAL_SOM_RESASSIGN_TAB		
	TRANS_ID	CELL_ID
1	0	15
2	1	15
3	2	15
4	3	15
5	4	15
6	5	7
7	6	7
8	7	7
9	8	7
10	9	7
11	10	5
12	11	0
13	12	0
14	13	2
15	14	2
16	15	8
17	16	8
18	17	9
19	18	13
20	19	13

Figure 10.34 The Record ID and its Assigned Cell ID

We can present the results in a visualization, as shown in Figure 10.35, where we can see the clustering of the data, for example, cell 7 has five records, cell 8 has two records, and so on.

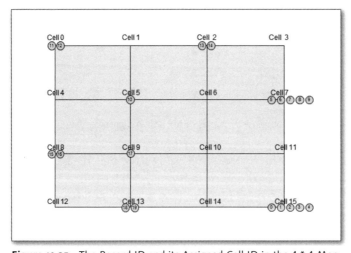

Figure 10.35 The Record ID and its Assigned Cell ID in the 4 * 4 Map

The data set that we used was the same as the one that we used for the K-Means example and was constructed to contain four clusters. If we now re-run the worked example in the SOM, but for a 3*3 grid, then the results are as shown in Figure 10.36 and Figure 10.37. It's a smaller grid, so the records are more grouped. If you look at the weights and the data set, you can see how the records are allocated. Five records to Cell ID 0, with weights 1.02 and 1.04; five records to Cell ID 2, with weights 1.04 and 16.02; five records to Cell ID 6, with weights 15.93 and 1.12; and finally, five records to Cell ID 8, with weights 15.91 and 16.04.

select * from PAL_SOM_MAP_TAB				
	CELL_ID	WEIGHT000	WEIGHT001	NUMS_TUPLE
1	0	1.0204207745254232	1.0457158200341077	5
2	1	1.0490993592706914	14.622442794434678	0
3	2	1.0409086485075865	16.02522794605194	5
4	3	14.573005002510401	1.3640946777909486	0
5	4	14.538532191990315	16.208360801537054	0
6	5	14.53853219393622	16.20836080612193	0
7	6	15.93846927859678	1.1276673159627537	5
8	7	15.850600421771365	2.8891061386936623	0
9	8	15.91798140461461	16.045715820034136	5

Figure 10.36 The Cell ID and its Assigned Number of Records or Tuples in the 3 * 3 Map

select * from PAL_SOM_RESASSIGN_TAB		
	TRANS_ID	CELL_ID
1	0	0
2	1	0
3	2	0
4	3	0
5	4	0
6	5	2
7	6	2
8	7	2
9	8	2
10	9	2
11	10	8
12	11	8
13	12	8
14	13	8
15	14	8
16	15	6
17	16	6
18	17	6
19	18	6
20	19	6

Figure 10.37 The Record ID and its Assigned Cell ID in the 3 * 3 Map

We can show the results in a visualization, as shown in Figure 10.38.

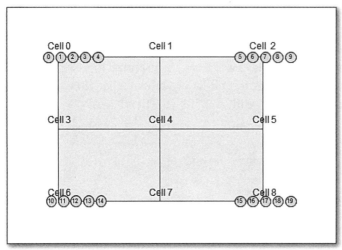

Figure 10.38   A Visualization of the Assigned Cell ID in the 3* 3 Map

There are clearly four clusters. In fact, the same number as when we used K-Means with K=4. However, with the K-Means algorithm we had to predetermine the value of K prior to running the algorithm. With Kohonen SOMs we let the data suggest the value of K.

When we ran the data through a SOM of 16 cells, remember that we only had 20 records so the proportion of records to cells is close to one to one. The four clusters can be seen in the map as shown in Figure 10.39. A SOM can have more cells than there are variables, which will create a sparse SOM with empty regions between the classified objects. Alternatively, a SOM with very few cells can be used, which will force objects to share cells thereby making groups or clusters.

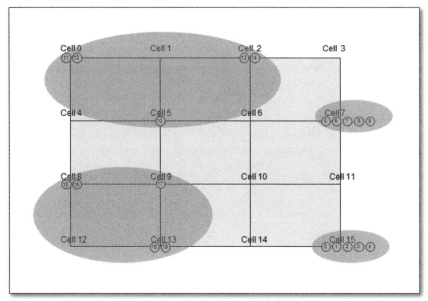

Figure 10.39 The Four Clusters in the 4 * 4 Map

10.11 The Business Case for Cluster Analysis

The business case for cluster analysis is more related to its value in breaking down large amounts of data into more manageable groups and potentially a better understanding of the data, rather than analyzing all the data to make predictions. One of the best specific use cases is market segmentation, given the generally agreed proposition that focused marketing is more effective than a generic approach.

It is one of the most popular methods of predictive analysis and its application is indeed ubiquitous, reaching far beyond the realms of predictive analysis to such areas as sociology, medical research, archaeology, astronomy, taxonomy – the list is practically endless.

The main challenge, however, is in trying to understand the reasons for the creation of the clusters, which is where classification models can be deployed. The benefits of cluster analysis are then indirectly the benefits of classification analysis.

Although there are no direct financial benefits attributed to cluster analysis, its value is reflected in its popularity and extensive range of application.

10.12   Strengths and Weaknesses of Cluster Analysis

The major strength of cluster analysis is that the concept is easy to understand. We are not trying to predict new data, which is always uncertain; we are just trying to cluster existing data. Each cluster analysis algorithm has individual strengths and weaknesses.

ABC Classification is very simple, very practical and therefore very popular. It is, of course, constrained to 3 groupings, and maybe a user wants more groups, and maybe not necessarily adding to 100%, for example: find the top 5%, second 10% and third 20%.

K-Means is easy to understand and to apply. K-Means cluster detection is undirected and it is data driven. The user just has to decide the value of K. This is a strength, but it is also a potential weakness, as K-Means is clearly driven by the choice of K, which may be a bad choice. There is no optimal value of K in that we are not maximizing or minimizing some function. K-Means can be sensitive to the initial choice of cluster centers and the results may vary dependent on the choice of distance measure. These choices can be changed to see whether they impact the solution. This is referred to as using sensitivity analysis, testing the robustness of the solution, and it is an important step in any analysis. It can sometimes be difficult to interpret or understand the results, but that applies to many algorithms. Finally, the input data has to be numeric. Non-numeric data can be transposed to numeric and other approaches to cluster analysis can be considered, such as using decision trees and association analysis to find groups in the data. Overall, it is a very popular algorithm.

Self-Organizing Maps have as their main strength that the number of clusters is not predetermined, although it is constrained to the size of the map. SOMs enable the user to explore the solution space in a more unconstrained manner compared to that of K-Means. SOMs have been applied in many areas: image browsing systems, medical diagnosis, interpreting seismic activity, speech recognition, data compression, and even vampire clustering! The algorithm can be sensitive to the parameter selections, but, again, sensitivity analysis can be used to explore the robustness of the solution. The results may be difficult to interpret. The main weakness of SOMs is that the algorithm is not easy to understand and is therefore less popular than the K-Means algorithm.

10.13 Summary

In this chapter we have looked at cluster analysis and the three algorithms available in the PAL, namely, ABC Analysis, K-Means and SOMs, plus K-Means in R. We have shown various user interfaces to the algorithms using SAP HANA Studio and SAP Predictive Analysis. For each algorithm, we have provided a worked example and discussed the results. We looked at issues such as choosing the value of K, dealing with non-numeric data, and measuring the quality of the cluster analysis using the silhouette calculation. Finally, we reviewed the strengths and weaknesses of cluster analysis, with the former outweighing the latter. Plus, there are approaches to minimizing the weaknesses. Overall, cluster analysis is a very popular technique in predictive analysis.

In the next chapter we begin our introduction to classification analysis: the major group of algorithms in predictive analysis.

This chapter provides a brief introduction to classification analysis, which is concerned with predicting a variable based on the values of other variables. In Part IV, we go into greater detail on this type of analysis and the algorithms used.

11 Classification Analysis

Classification analysis is a rather unobvious name for the group of algorithms used in the traditional application of predicting a variable based on the values of other variables. The name comes from the objective of such analysis, which is to classify new data based on a trained model. For example, to classify new data regarding customer attributes into those likely to churn versus those likely to stay; to classify a new loan application as accept or reject; to classify a financial transaction as suspicious or not. It is the major group of algorithms in predictive analysis given the relevance of such analysis to a very extensive range of applications.

11.1 Introduction to Classification Analysis

Probably the best known algorithm for classification analysis is regression, and specifically bi-variate linear regression, which simply means two variables, where we use one variable to predict another, based on a model of the relationship between the two variables. Statisticians refer to the former as the independent variable and the latter the dependent variable, as it "depends" on the other variable. Data miners refer to the independent variables as the input variables, and the dependent variable as the output variable, and sometimes it is also called the target variable. Whatever name we choose to use, we are trying to predict one variable based on the values of one or more other variables.

The type or attributes of the data will vary, with some being integer, some continuous numeric, some categorical, and some Boolean. To a certain degree, the data types determine the algorithms that can be used, for example, linear and non-linear regression are suitable for continuous numeric variables; logistic regression is suitable when the dependent variable is Boolean; decision trees are used when the data is categorical. Different classification algorithms also produce different types of outputs. For example, regression models produce mathematical expressions of the relationships between the variables and, from them, numeric predictions; whereas decision trees can produce model rules, for example, if income is high and debts are low, then approve a loan. The choice of the appropriate classification algorithm is therefore in part driven by the type of data being modeled and the form of output required. It is also driven by other considerations such as ease of understanding. Decision makers are more likely to use a model that they can understand than one that is a complete mystery. Chapter 4, "Which Algorithm When?", elaborates on the selection of the correct algorithm that meets your needs.

In this introduction to classification analysis, we cover the topics of Regression Analysis, Decision Trees and Nearest Neighbor algorithms. The first is by far the most well-known, given its relevance to so many applications. It is a major methodology of statistical analysis, first appearing in the early 1800's and developed into many different models such as multiple linear regression, non-linear regression, polynomial regression, logistic regression–all of which are available in the PAL. An interesting side note: apparently, before 1970, it sometimes took up to 24 hours to receive the result from one regression! How times have changed! Now we can't even wait for a few seconds. Decision Trees are another major method in predictive analysis. As was seen in Chapter 1, Figure 1.12, according to the most recent Rexer Analytics Survey, they are the second most popular group of algorithms, just after regression. They get their name from the decision tree that is produced by the analysis where each leaf, or end point of the tree, represents a value of the target variable, based on the values of the input variables represented by the path from the root to the leaf–the decisions made in navigating that path. This is best understood in the examples in Section 11.4. Finally, we conclude this chapter with the Nearest Neighbor classification analysis. This is beautifully simple–a record is predicted or classified based on the values of other records that are very similar.

11.2   Applications of Classification Analysis

Classification analysis has so many applications that it is impossible to list them all. Given the very generic nature of this class of analyses, the list is practically infinite. Just think of how many applications that there are in business where we want to predict something from other things—sales analysis, pricing models, cost analysis, root cause analysis, churn analysis, credit scoring, mailshot campaign targeting, preventive maintenance, workforce planning, and so on. Then there are the fields of biological classification, drug development and analysis, character recognition, and document classification.

In a recent survey of predictive applications in SAP, we listed applications of classification analysis by industry, as shown in Figure 11.1, with color coding showing a subjective view of the value, with the darker the color indicating higher value. For those applications that are darker in coding, Classification Analysis is more applicable.

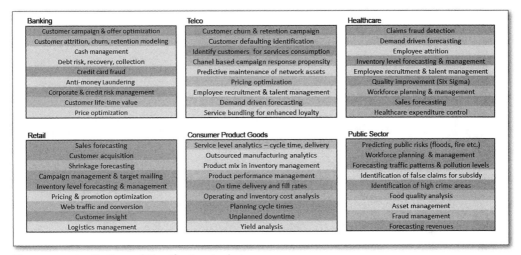

Figure 11.1 Applications of Classification Analysis

Even the list shown in Figure 11.1 is just a sample of the many applications of classification analysis.

We start our introduction to classification analysis with a discussion of regression analysis.

11.3 An Introduction to Regression Analysis

As with most algorithms, the best way to start to understand how they work is to go through a simple example. Assume that we have the data as shown in Figure 11.2, in tabular and graphical form.

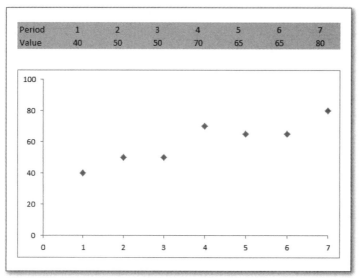

Period	1	2	3	4	5	6	7
Value	40	50	50	70	65	65	80

Figure 11.2 A Simple Data Set for Bi-Variate Linear Regression Analysis

We want to fit a straight line through this data that minimizes the sum of the squared differences between the observed values and the fitted values, sometimes referred to as the residual sum of squares. We square the difference so that positive and negative values do not cancel each other out. This is referred to as the method of least squares. Hence we now have Bi-Variate Linear Least Squares Regression. Statisticians use the word regression to refer to regressing one variable on another. The line of best fit is shown in Figure 11.3.

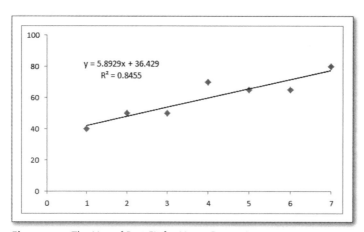

Figure 11.3 The Line of Best Fit for Linear Regression

The regression line is given by the equation *Y = 5.8929 * X + 36.429*, which is derived by solving what are called the normal equations to find the values for the slope of the line, 5.8929, and what is called the intercept, 36.429, that minimizes the residual sum of squares. From this equation or model, we can predict values of Y for various values of X, for example, for X = 8, Y = 83.5722.

The quality of the model is given by the statistic R squared, which has the property of the nearer to 1, the better the model. In our example, it is 0.8455, so we have a good model from which we can make predictions. We can derive confidence intervals for our forecast. It is important with any prediction to say how confident we are with that prediction. Statisticians refer to 95% and 99% confidence intervals, which are very high and consequently can produce very wide confidence intervals. In life, we are rarely that confident of the future. Out of interest, the 95% confidence interval for X = 8, is 83.57 plus 20.06 for the upper limit, and minus 20.06 for the lower limit.

Those are the basics of linear regression. Now there is much more on the topic of model quality, for example, the analysis of the residuals, the analysis of the variance between explained and unexplained model variation, statistical tests of the significance of individual independent variables and the overall model fit. As well as bi-variate linear regression, there is multi-variate and non-linear regression analysis. Perhaps a non-linear curve such as exponential or geometric would be a better fit. There's polynomial regression, where the nth degree polynomial curves may be fitted, for example cubic, quadratic curves. Then there are regression models for when the data is not numeric, but, for example, Boolean, in which case we might use logistic regression. All these topics are discussed in detail in Chapter 12.

A second major group of predictive analysis algorithms for classification problems are decision trees.

11.4   An Introduction to Decision Trees

Again, the best way to start to understand how an algorithm works is to go through a simple example. In Figure 11.4, we show a decision tree to help decide whether to play or not to play a game of golf, based on whether it is windy or not, the outlook is rain or sunny or overcast, and the humidity is high or low. The variables windy, outlook, and humidity are the independent variables or input variables, and the variable play or not is the target or dependent variable, sometimes also called the class variable, as we are trying to decide which class to choose.

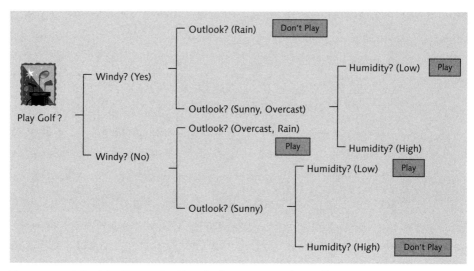

Figure 11.4 A Decision Tree to Decide Whether or Not to Play Golf

From the decision tree shown in Figure 11.4, we can derive the rules:

▶ Don't play if the outlook is rain and its windy.

▶ Don't play if humidity is high, the outlook is sunny, and it's not windy.

▶ Otherwise, go play!

Before we see how the data is used to construct the decision tree, here are two more examples, shown in Figure 11.5 and Figure 11.6.

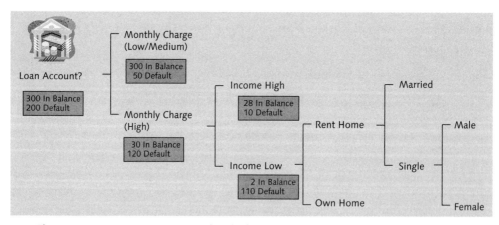

Figure 11.5 A Decision Tree to Decide Whether or Not to Give a Loan

From the decision tree shown in Figure 11.5, we may derive the rule:

▶ Don't make loans to single males who rent their homes, have low income, and have a high monthly charge.

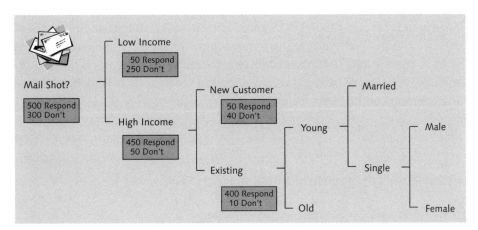

Figure 11.6 A Decision Tree to Decide Whether or Not to Send a Mail

From the decision tree shown in Figure 11.6, we may derive the rule:

▶ Young, single, females who are existing customers with a high income are most likely to respond to our mail campaign.

Let's return to the golf example and look at the data used to build the decision tree. It is shown in Figure 11.7.

Scenario	Outlook	Temp.	Humidity	Windy?	Class
1	Sunny	75	70	Yes	Play
2	Sunny	80	90	Yes	Don't Play
3	Sunny	85	85	No	Don't Play
4	Sunny	72	95	No	Don't Play
5	Sunny	69	70	No	Play
6	Overcast	72	90	Yes	Play
7	Overcast	83	78	No	Play
8	Overcast	64	65	Yes	Play
9	Overcast	81	75	No	Play
10	Rain	71	80	Yes	Don't Play
11	Rain	65	70	Yes	Don't Play
12	Rain	75	80	No	Play
13	Rain	68	80	No	Play
14	Rain	70	96	No	Play

Figure 11.7 The Data for the Decision Tree Play Golf

We have two categorical input variables, Outlook and Windy, and two numeric input variables, Temperature and Humidity. The Scenario number is just a record ID, and the Class variable is the output or target variable that we wish to predict. Where a numeric variable has many different values, then the decision tree can become quite complex in dealing with each value, so sometimes such data is grouped or binned in order to give simpler or cleaner decision trees. In our example, we define 'bins' or "groups." We have defined several bins for temperature and humidity. The rules above can be user created or system created as there is a binning function in the PAL. In the bullet list below, you can see that we have defined 3 bins for temperature and 2 bins for humidity:

▶ 1 < =70, 2 >70 and < =80, 3 >80 for Temp.

▶ 1 < =75, 2 >75 for Humidity.

As a result, the data becomes as shown in Figure 11.8.

Scenario	Outlook	Temp.	Humidity	Windy?	Class
1	Sunny	2	1	Yes	Play
2	Sunny	2	2	Yes	Don't Play
3	Sunny	3	2	No	Don't Play
4	Sunny	2	2	No	Don't Play
5	Sunny	1	1	No	Play
6	Overcast	2	2	Yes	Play
7	Overcast	3	2	No	Play
8	Overcast	1	1	Yes	Play
9	Overcast	3	1	No	Play
10	Rain	2	2	Yes	Don't Play
11	Rain	1	1	Yes	Don't Play
12	Rain	2	2	No	Play
13	Rain	1	2	No	Play
14	Rain	1	2	No	Play

Figure 11.8 The Data for the Decision Tree Play Golf using Bins for Temperature and Humidity

To build the decision tree, we recursively split the data to maximize diversity at each split. Put another way, which independent variable makes the best "splitter" – the best job of separating the records into groups. Looking at Figure 11.8 we can see that the variable Outlook with the value Overcast is always Play; Rain and whether it is Windy or not clearly splits the outcome between Play and Don't Play; Sunny with Humidity 1 or 2 clearly splits the outcome between Play and Don't Play. Of course, this is a small data set and the outcomes are reasonably clear; in practice, it's the opposite. Also guessing from looking at the data is very subjective; hence, there a range of tests for diversity that lead to various decision tree algorithms. One measure of diversity is the Chi-Squared Test; hence, the CHAID decision tree algorithm, which stands for CHi-squared Automatic Interaction Detection. Another measure is Entropy, which is used in the C 4.5 decision tree algorithm. Both of these algorithms are available in the PAL and are discussed in depth in Chapter 13.

The final algorithm in our introduction to classification analysis is the Nearest Neighbor algorithm, which has a different approach to predicting compared to regression analysis and decision trees: it simply looks at the most similar records to the one to be predicted, and uses those similar, or nearest neighbors as the basis for the prediction.

11.5   An Introduction to Nearest Neighbors

The Nearest Neighbor algorithm is a method for predicting data based on its similarity to other values in the training dataset. The number of 'other' values to consider for comparison is input, usually denoted as K, and the average value or most popular class of the closest cases, becomes the prediction.

The algorithm is commonly called K Nearest Neighbor and it is one of the simplest of all predictive algorithms. If $K = 1$, then the record to be predicted is simply the value or class of its nearest neighbor, in other words, the closest record based on a numeric distance measure. For values of $K > 1$, then it is the average of the numeric predictions or the most popular of the categorical predictions. As always, a diagram helps with understanding – see Figure 11.9.

The chart in Figure 11.9 is based on the data shown in Figure 11.10. There are 24 records, with values for X1 and X2, the input variables, and a resultant value of Y, the target variable. In mathematical terms Y is a function of X1 and X2. Given new values for X1 and X2, we want to predict if $Y = 1$ or $Y = 0$.

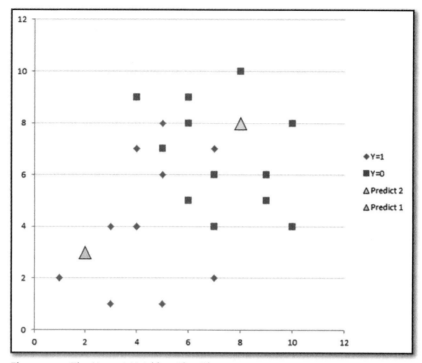

Figure 11.9 The Nearest Neighbor Algorithm

ID	X1	X2	Y	ID	X1	X2	Y
1	3	1	1	13	9	5	0
2	1	2	1	14	6	9	0
3	1	2	1	15	6	5	0
4	4	7	1	16	9	6	0
5	4	4	1	17	7	4	0
6	4	4	1	18	5	7	0
7	7	2	1	19	6	8	0
8	3	4	1	20	8	10	0
9	7	7	1	21	4	9	0
10	5	1	1	22	10	8	0
11	5	8	1	23	7	6	0
12	5	6	1	24	10	4	0

Figure 11.10 The Data for the Nearest Neighbor Algorithm Example

If the value to be predicted as shown by the green triangle in Figure 11.9 is (X1=2, X2=3), then if K=5, the 5 nearest values are the blue stars and therefore the prediction is Y = 1.

If the value to be predicted as shown by the yellow triangle in Figure 11.9 is (X1=8, X2=8), then if K=5, the 5 nearest values are the 4 red squares and 1 blue star, therefore the prediction is Y = 0.

The algorithm is very simple, which is a major benefit; however, it has its weaknesses, as in fact does every algorithm. We explore the strengths and weaknesses of each algorithm class in the coming chapters. Figure 11.11 shows how a new case would be classified using different values of K. When K = 3, the new case is placed in category 1 because a majority of the nearest neighbors belong to category 1. However, when K = 6, the new case is placed in category 0 because the majority of the nearest neighbors belong to category 0.

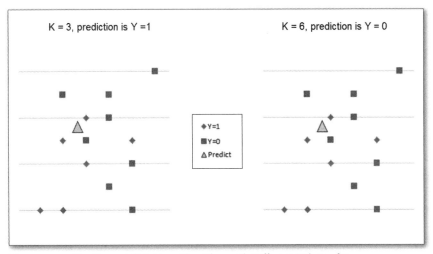

Figure 11.11   The Nearest Neighbor Algorithm with Different Values of K

Care needs to be taken when choosing the value of K. However, as always, some simple what-if or sensitivity analysis can be used to explore how robust the solution is by trying various values of K and seeing how the prediction changes. This approach applies to any application of predictive analysis whereby we should review our model assumptions in terms of the model parameters and see their impact on the solution. If the solution varies widely, then we need to go back and review our assumptions. In the end, we may not have a model from which we can predict with confidence, and that is at times, the reality.

11.6   Summary

In this chapter we began our introduction to classification algorithms, which form the largest group of predictive analysis algorithms. Regression models comprise a major subset of this group, given their extensive application, while decision tree models are also very popular because of the potentially useful output of rules from the models. We ended with the Nearest Neighbor classification algorithm, which, in contrast to the other algorithms, is very simple and yet valuable. This topic is covered in detail in Part IV.

PART IV
Classification Analysis

This chapter describes the major topic of regression analysis using the SAP HANA Predictive Analysis Library, the integration of R, and SAP Predictive Analysis.

12   Classification Analysis—Regression

Within classification analysis, regression models are the best known because they are included in almost all introductory textbooks on statistics. This chapter starts by describing the most simple of regression models, namely bi-variate linear regression, as a foundation for the understanding of the other regression models supported in the SAP HANA Predictive Analysis Library (PAL), the integration of R, and SAP Predictive Analysis. We then review bi-variate non-linear regression models, then multi-variate regressions models, and finally polynomial regression and logistic regression.

In Section 11.3, we introduced the topic of regression analysis with a simple example. We now develop that example and show how we can perform the analysis in the PAL and in PA.

12.1   Bi-Variate Linear Regression

Regression analysis provides an objective method of fitting a curve to a set of observations. Least squares regression finds the curve of "best fit" using the criteria of minimizing the sum of squares of observed values compared to the fitted values from the regression analysis.

In linear least squares regression of two variables, referred to as bi-variate linear regression, the objective is to fit the line $Y = a + b * X$, where Y is referred to as the dependent variable and X is the independent variable, and we refer to the regressing of Y on X. The value of Y depends of the value of X, and the parameters, a and b.

These two parameters are calculated so that they minimize the squared difference between Y actual and Y fitted, or the residual sum of squares, as it is called.

In Chapter 11 we used the data shown in Figure 11.2, which for convenience is redrawn here in Figure 12.1.

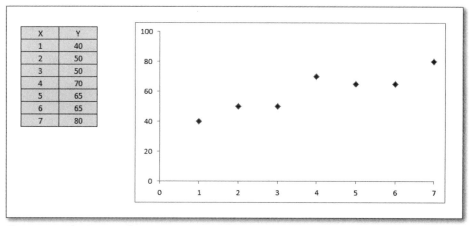

Figure 12.1 The Data Set for Bi-Variate Linear Regression Analysis

In bi-variate linear regression, we can derive the values of a and b very simply if we first transform X by calculating $x_i = X_i - Mean$ of X, after which the least squares values of a and b are:

$$a = \bar{Y}$$

$$b = \frac{\sum x_i Y_i}{\sum x_i^2}$$

and thus $\hat{Y} = a + b(X_i - \bar{X})$

where the line above the Y and X denotes the mean of Y and X, and the caret symbol above the Y denotes the fitted values of Y. To translate back to the original frame of reference, then a is transformed back as $a - b * Mean$ of X.

This calculation is shown in Figure 12.2 and the derived regression line of Y = 36.429 + 5.8929 * X.

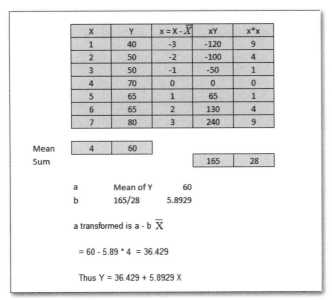

X	Y	x = X - $\overline{X}$	xY	x*x
1	40	-3	-120	9
2	50	-2	-100	4
3	50	-1	-50	1
4	70	0	0	0
5	65	1	65	1
6	65	2	130	4
7	80	3	240	9

Mean 4   60

Sum   165   28

a   Mean of Y   60
b   165/28   5.8929

a transformed is a - b $\overline{X}$

= 60 - 5.89 * 4 = 36.429

Thus Y = 36.429 + 5.8929 X

Figure 12.2   Worked Example of Bi-Variate Linear Regression

The regression equation and fitted line are shown along with the actual data values in Figure 12.3.

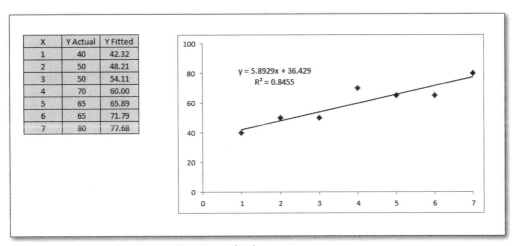

X	Y Actual	Y Fitted
1	40	42.32
2	50	48.21
3	50	54.11
4	70	60.00
5	65	65.89
6	65	71.79
7	80	77.68

$y = 5.8929x + 36.429$
$R^2 = 0.8455$

Figure 12.3   The Fitted Regression Equation and Values

The objective of least squares regression is to minimize the residual sum of squares, that is, the difference between the actual values and the fitted values.

$(Y_i - \hat{Y}_i)^2$

The total sum of squares is defined as: $\sum (Y_i - \bar{Y})^2$. This represents the choice of $\bar{Y}$ to represent the fit of the data. That is, for any value of X we always use the mean of Y to fit the data, or alternatively Y does not vary with X.

This total sum of squares comprises the regression sums of squares, defined as:

$$\sum (\hat{Y}_i - \bar{Y})^2$$

This is known as the Explained Sum of Squares.

Plus the residual sum of squares, defined as observed less fitted:

$$\sum (Y_i - \hat{Y}_i)^2$$

This is known as the Unexplained Sum of Squares.

In our example, these calculations are shown in Figure 12.4.

X	$(Y_i - \bar{Y})^2$ Total	$(\hat{Y} - \bar{Y})^2$ Explained	$(Y_i - \hat{Y}_i)^2$ Unexplained
1	400	312.53	5.39
2	100	138.90	3.19
3	100	34.73	16.87
4	100	0.00	100.00
5	25	34.73	0.80
6	25	138.90	46.05
7	400	312.53	5.39
Total Sum of Squares	1150	972.32	177.68
Degrees Freedom	6	1	5
		972.32	35.54

Figure 12.4 Explained and Unexplained Sum of Squares

In Figure 12.4 we can see that the total sum of squares is 1150, which we can interpret as: if we use the mean of Y to predict X, then the sum of the squared errors or variance between the actual and fitted line is 1150.

Of this total, our regression line has "explained" 972.32 of this total, being the sum of the squared variance between our fitted values of Y and the mean of Y. The remainder is the unexplained variance or residual sum of squares.

As with any model, we want to know how good it is and how confident can we be when using it to make predictions. The calculations shown in Figure 12.4 are an analysis of variance of the regression model, known by the acronym ANOVA. The more of the total variance that our model explains, the better the model.

In regression analysis, there are two key measures of model quality, R Squared and the F Statistic, both of which are based on the explained and unexplained sum of squares.

R Squared or the Coefficient of Determination, is the proportion of the total variation in Y explained by fitting the regression

$$R^2 = \frac{\text{Explained Variation of } Y}{\text{Total Variation of } Y} = \frac{\sum(\hat{Y}_i - \bar{Y})^2}{\sum(Y_i - \bar{Y})^2} = \frac{972.32}{1150} = 0.8455$$

The closer this value is to 1, the better the model.

The F Value is defined as:

Variance explained by regression divided by

Unexplained variance

This is:

Explained Sum of Squares/1 divided by

Unexplained / (N–2)

N is the number of data points or observations, and for bi-variate regression, we divide the variances by 1, and by N-2, which are referred to as the degrees of freedom. In statistics, the number of degrees of freedom is the number of values in the final calculation of a statistic that are free to vary.

In our example, the F Value is 972.32/35.54, which equals 27.36.

F_{01} and F_{05} are the values of the F distribution for 99% and 95% limits for 1 degree of freedom in the numerator and N-2 degrees of freedom in the denominator, which allows us to test the null hypothesis H_0 of b = 0, that is, no slope or linear relationship between Y and X. If the calculated F Value exceeds F_{05} or F_{01}, then we reject the hypothesis of b = 0, in favor of the alternative hypothesis that b is not equal to zero and consequently that there is a relationship between Y and X at the appropriate confidence level.

From the F tables, the F Value at the 99% level is 16.26, and at the 95% level it is 6.61. In our example, the F Value = 27.36; thus, we reject H_0 at the 99% level. In other words, there is strong statistical evidence to suggest a linear relationship between Y and X.

Let's now look at this example in the PAL.

12.1.1 Bi-Variate Linear Regression in the PAL

In the SAP HANA Predictive Analysis Library, the algorithm name is Multiple Linear Regression and the associated function name is LRREGRESSION. We started this chapter looking at Bi-Variate Linear Regression, which is a subset of multiple linear regression, but of two variables only.

The Input Table comprises three columns, the first containing an ID, the second containing the values for Y, and the third containing the values for X, as shown in Table 12.1.

Table	Column	Data Type	Description
Data	1st column	Integer or varchar	Record ID
	2nd column	Integer or double	Y values
	3rd column	Integer or double	X values

Table 12.1 The Input Table Definition for Bi-Variate Linear Regression

The Parameter Table specifies five parameters, as shown in Table 12.2.

Name	Data Type	Description
VARIABLE_NUM	Integer	Optional. Specifies the number of independent variables (Xi).
ADJUSTED_R2	Integer	▶ 0 (default): Does not output adjusted R squared ▶ 1: Outputs adjusted R squared

Table 12.2 The Parameter Table Definition for Bi-Variate Linear Regression

Name	Data Type	Description
PMML_EXPORT	Integer	▸ 0 (default): Does not export the linear regression model in PMML. ▸ 1: Exports linear regression model in PMML in a single row. ▸ 2: Exports linear regression model in PMML in several rows, each row containing a maximum of 5000 characters.
ALG	Integer	Optional. Specifies decomposition method: ▸ 0 (default): Doolittle decomposition ▸ 2: Singular value decomposition
THREAD_ NUMBER	Integer	Number of threads

Table 12.2 The Parameter Table Definition for Bi-Variate Linear Regression (Cont.)

Solving equations to find the regression coefficients involves matrix inversion, which can in some circumstances be unstable. The ALG (algorithm) parameter provides the option of using another internal matrix calculation method for finding the model parameters if problems exist.

The Output table comprises the result in terms of the model parameters, the second table contains the fitted data, the third table contains the significance statistics of the model, and the fourth table contains the PMML output, as defined in Table 12.3.

Table	Column	Data Type	Description
Result	1st column	Integer	Record ID
	2nd column	Integer or double	Parameter values, a and b.
Fitted Data	1st column	Integer or varchar	Record ID
Significance	1st column	Varchar	Name
	2nd column	Double	Value
PMML Result	1st column	Integer	Record ID
	2nd column	CLOB or varchar	Regression model in PMML format

Table 12.3 The Output Table Definitions for Bi-Variate Linear Regression

We now run the bi-variate linear regression algorithm using the data shown in Figure 12.1.

12.1.2   An Example of Bi-Variate Linear Regression in the PAL

Here's a simple example, with the Input Table as shown in Figure 12.5.

We have replaced Y and X by the variables Yield and Fertilizer to give it more of a business context.

SELECT * FROM DATA_TAB			
	ID	Yield	Fertilizer
1	1	40	1
2	2	50	2
3	3	50	3
4	4	70	4
5	5	65	5
6	6	65	6
7	7	80	7

Figure 12.5   The Input Data for Bi-Variate Linear Regression

The main elements of the SQLScript are as shown in Listing 12.1. The full code is available in the file SAP_HANA_PAL_LRREGRESSION_Example_SQLScript on the SAP PRESS website.

```
-- The procedure generator

call SYSTEM.afl_wrapper_generator ('palLR','AFLPAL','LRREGRESSION',PDA
TA);

-- The Control Table parameters

INSERT INTO #CONTROL_TAB VALUES ('ADJUSTED_R2',1,null,null);
INSERT INTO #CONTROL_TAB VALUES ('PMML_EXPORT',1,null,null);
INSERT INTO #CONTROL_TAB VALUES ('THREAD_NUMBER',8,null,null);

-- Assume the data has been stored in table DATA_TAB as shown in Figure
12.5

-- Calling the procedure

CALL palLR(DATA_TAB, "#CONTROL_TAB", RESULTS_TAB, FITTED_TAB,
SIGNIFICANCE_TAB, PAL_PMMLMODEL_TAB) with overview;
```

```
SELECT * FROM RESULTS_TAB;
SELECT * FROM FITTED_TAB;
SELECT * FROM SIGNIFICANCE_TAB;
SELECT * FROM PAL_PMMLMODEL_TAB;
```

Listing 12.1 The PAL SQLScript for Bi-Variate Linear Regression

After running the SQLScript in SAP HANA Studio, the Results table becomes as shown in Figure 12.6, and lists the model parameters. Our regression line is Yield = 36.4285 + 5.89285 * Fertilizer. This is the same equation as was shown in Figure 12.3.

SELECT * FROM RESULTS_TAB		
	ID	Ai
1	0	36.4285...
2	1	5.89285...

Figure 12.6 The Model Parameters for Bi-Variate Linear Regression Example

The fitted data is output and shown in Figure 12.7.

SELECT * FROM FITTED_TAB		
	ID	Fitted
1	1	42.3214...
2	2	48.2142...
3	3	54.1071...
4	4	60
5	5	65.8928...
6	6	71.7857...
7	7	77.6785...

Figure 12.7 The Model Fitted Values

The model goodness of fit statistics are shown in Figure 12.8. The R Squared value of 0.84549 is the same as our calculation in Section 12.1.1, along with the F value of 27.36.

SELECT * FROM SIGNIFICANCE_TAB		
	NAME	VALUE
1	R2	0.8454968944099378
2	F	27.361809045226135
3	Adjusted R2	0.8145962732919254

Figure 12.8 The Goodness of Fit Statistics

This is a high value of R2 as it has a maximum value of 1. R Squared can take on any value between 0 and 1, with a value closer to 1 indicating that a greater proportion of the variance in the data is accounted for by the model. For example, an R Squared value of 0.8 means that the model fit explains 80% of the total variation in the data about the average. There is no hard and fast rule on what value constitutes good because it depends on the amount of data being used in the analysis, the sample size in statistical terms, and the number of regressors or independent variables. This is where the F statistic is more useful.

In pure statistical terms the significance of the curve fit is given by the F statistic. In our example, there are N = 7 observations and K = 1 regressors (Fertilizer). The F Value at the 99% confidence level for K,N-K-1 degrees of freedom is 16.26, the level 99% being very significant. The F Value at the 95% confidence level for K,N-K-1 degrees of freedom is 6.61, with 95% being described as significant by statisticians. So an F value greater than 16.26 is very significant indeed. Our model has a value of 27.3618.

In conclusion, we have a very good model and can use it to make predictions with a high degree of confidence.

The Adjusted R2, also known as the Goodness of Fit statistic, is related to R Squared and is a better statistic in that is does not necessarily increase as the sample size and the number of independent variables increase. It is defined as:

1 – (Residual Variation of Y/(N – K))/(Total Variation of Y/(N – 1))

where *N* is the number of data points or sample size and *K* is the number of regressors (one in bi-variate linear regression).

Finally, we chose to output the PMML from the regression analysis and this is shown in Figure 12.9. Note in the XML the model parameters of 36.4286 and 5.8929, and the R Squared value of 0.8455. This output could be used as the input to an external application for scoring or predicting new values.

Having built the model, we now wish to predict values using the model.

12.1.3 Predicting or Scoring the Model in the PAL

To make predictions we use the PAL function FORECASTWITHLR. Our model is Yield = 36.42857 + 5.89286 * Fertilizer. In our example, we wish to predict Yield from new values for Fertilizer of 8 and 9.

```
<PMML version="4.0" xmlns="http://www.dmg.org/PMML-4_0"
xmlns:xsi="http://www.w3.org/2001/XMLSchema-instance" >
<Header copyright="SAP" >
<Application name="PAL" version="1.0" />
</Header>
<DataDictionary numberOfFields="2" >
<DataField name="Yield" optype="continuous" dataType="double" />
<DataField name="Fertilizer" optype="continuous" dataType="double" />
</DataDictionary>
<RegressionModel modelName="Instance for regression"
functionName="regression" algorithmName="LinearRegression"
targetFieldName="Yield" >
<MiningSchema>
<MiningField name="Yield" usageType="predicted"/>
<MiningField name="Fertilizer" />
</MiningSchema>
<ModelExplanation>
<PredictiveModelQuality targetField="Yield" dataUsage="training" r-
squared="0.845497" >
</PredictiveModelQuality>
</ModelExplanation>
<RegressionTable intercept="36.4286">
<NumericPredictor name="Fertilizer" exponent="1" coefficient="5.89286"/>
</RegressionTable>
</RegressionModel>
</PMML>
```

Figure 12.9 The PMML Output from Bi-Variate Linear Regression

There are two Input tables. The first table, Predictive Data, is comprised of two columns, the first column containing the item or record names, and the second column containing the numeric values to be used in the prediction, as shown in Table 12.4. The second table, Coefficients, is comprised of the model coefficients to be used for the predictions. This could simply be the output results table from the function LRREGRESSION.

Table	Column	Data Type	Description
Predictive Data	1st column	Integer or varchar	Record ID
	2nd column	Integer or double	X values
Coefficients	1st column	Integer	Record ID (start from 0)
	2nd column	Integer, double, varchar, or CLOB	Values a and b, or the PMML model. Varchar and CLOB types are only valid for PMML model.

Table 12.4 The Input Table Definition for FORECASTWITHLR

The Parameter table specifies two parameters, as shown in Table 12.5.

Name	Data Type	Description
MODEL_FORMAT	Integer	0 (default): coefficients in a table 1: coefficients in PMML format
THREAD_NUMBER	Integer	Number of threads

Table 12.5 The Parameter Table Definition for FORECASTWITHLR

The Output table comprises two columns, the first column containing an ID, and the second column containing the predicted values of Y, as shown in Table 12.6.

Table	Column	Data Type	Description
Fitted result	1st column	Integer or varchar	Record ID
	2nd column	Integer or double	Predicted values of Y

Table 12.6 The Output Table Definition for FORECASTWITHLR

Continuing with our example to predict the variable Yield given values for Fertilizer of 8 and 9, the main elements of the SQLScript are as shown in Listing 12.2. The model coefficients could have been read from the table where they were saved when the model was built. The full code is available in the file SAP_HANA_PAL_FORE-CASTWITHLR_Example_SQLScript on the SAP PRESS website.

```
-- The procedure generator

call SYSTEM.afl_wrapper_generator
('palForecastWithLR','AFLPAL','FORECASTWITHLR',PDATA);
-- The values to Predict, the Control Table parameters, and the model
coefficients

INSERT INTO PREDICTDATA_TAB VALUES (1,8);
INSERT INTO PREDICTDATA_TAB VALUES (2,9);

INSERT INTO #CONTROL_TAB VALUES ('THREAD_NUMBER',2,null,null);

INSERT INTO COEEFICIENT_TAB VALUES (0,36.42857);
INSERT INTO COEEFICIENT_TAB VALUES (1,5.892857);

-- Calling the procedure
```

```
CALL palForecastWithLR(PREDICTDATA_TAB, COEEFICIENT_TAB, "#CONTROL_
TAB", FITTED_TAB) with overview;

SELECT * FROM FITTED_TAB;
```
Listing 12.2 The PAL SQLScript for Bi-Variate Linear Regression

The Fitted Table becomes as shown in Figure 12.10, and shows the predictions of Yield for values of Fertilizer of 8 and 9.

SELECT * FROM FITTED_TAB		
	ID	Fitted
1	1	83.5714...
2	2	89.4642...

Figure 12.10 The Predicted Values of Yield

The same example can also be run in SAP Predictive Analysis either as an in-database analysis in SAP HANA and using the PAL algorithm, or as an in-process analysis with the data sourced from a non-SAP HANA data source such as a CSV file, and using the R integration in PA or the PA native predictive analysis algorithm for bi-variate linear regression.

12.1.4 Bi-Variate Linear Regression in PA

In this example, we use the same data that we used in the PAL example but this time stored in a CSV file and, as a variation from our other examples, use the Linear Regression algorithm native to PA, thus obviating the need for either the PAL, the R Integration for SAP HANA, or the R integration in PA.

The analysis is shown in Figure 12.11.

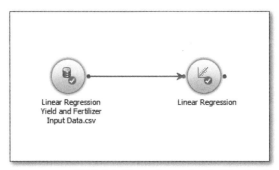

Linear Regression
Yield and Fertilizer
Input Data.csv

Linear Regression

Figure 12.11 Bi-Variate Linear Regression in PA using the PA Native Algorithm

After we select the linear regression component in PA, the dialogue for the PA native linear regression component is opened, as shown in Figure 12.12, where we also save the model, with a name and description, for subsequent use when we wish to make predictions from the model.

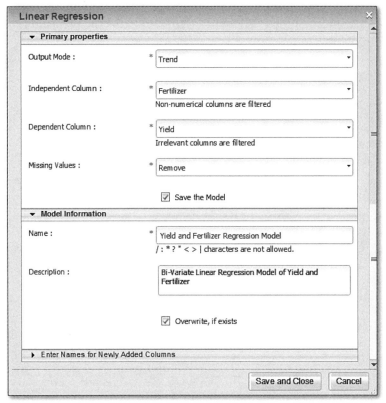

Figure 12.12 The PA Native Linear Regression Component Dialogue

After running the analysis, we can switch to the RESULTS View to see the fitted values of the model, as shown in Figure 12.13. Note that we entered the name Fitted Values for the newly added columns, using that prompt in the dialogue, but we have not shown it in the figure.

Fertilizer	Yield	Fitted Values
1	40	42.32
2	50	48.21
3	50	54.11
4	70	60.00
5	65	65.89
6	65	71.79
7	80	77.68

Figure 12.13 The Fitted Values from the Regression Analysis in PA

If we view the RESULTS, CHARTS, ALGORITHM SUMMARY in PA, it confirms the calculations earlier in this chapter, and is as shown in Figure 12.14.

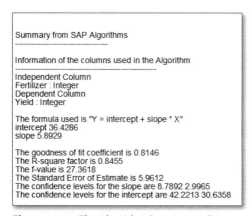

```
Summary from SAP Algorithms
----------------------------------

Information of the columns used in the Algorithm
-----------------------------------------------------
Independent Column
Fertilizer : Integer
Dependent Column
Yield : Integer

The formula used is "Y = intercept + slope * X"
intercept 36.4286
slope 5.8929

The goodness of fit coefficient is 0.8146
The R-square factor is 0.8455
The f-value is 27.3618
The Standard Error of Estimate is 5.9612
The confidence levels for the slope are 8.7892 2.9965
The confidence levels for the intercept are 42.2213 30.6358
```

Figure 12.14 The Algorithm Summary in PA

The saved model now appears in the SAVED MODELS TAB in the PREDICT VIEW in PA, as shown in Figure 12.15.

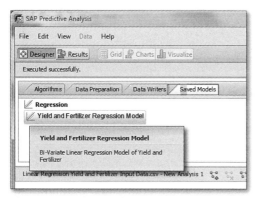

Figure 12.15 The Saved Models Tab in PA

Now we have a saved predictive model for the bi-variate linear regression analysis, which we can use to make predictions.

12.1.5 Predicting or Scoring the Model in the PA

First, we go back to the PREPARE View and select ADD, and the CSV file named Linear Regression Yield and Fertilizer Predict Data. We then connect the saved model to the data to be predicted, as shown in Figure 12.16.

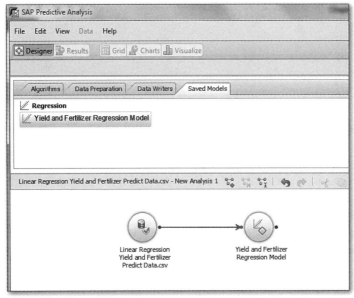

Figure 12.16 Using the Saved Model to Make Predictions

After we run the analysis we can view the predicted values, as shown in Figure 12.17.

Fertilizer	Yield	Fitted Values
1	40	42.32
2	50	48.21
3	50	54.11
4	70	60.00
5	65	65.89
6	65	71.79
7	80	77.68
8		83.57
9		89.46

Figure 12.17 The Actual, Fitted and Predicted Data

We can visualize this data in the PA, Predictive, Results, Visualize View, as shown in Figure 12.18.

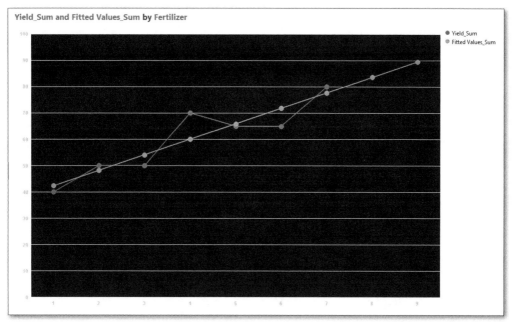

Figure 12.18 A Plot of Actual, Fitted and Predicted Yield

Having built the model and used it to make predictions, we may want to export the model to another business application, to predict new data.

12.1.6 PMML and Exporting the Model

The Predictive Modeling Markup Language (PMML) is a standard for sharing predictive models between applications. As we saw in Figure 12.9, we can save PMML output from PAL algorithms in SAP HANA tables, which can then be accessed by other applications. In the case of Linear Regression in the PAL, the model parameters are also saved in a table in SAP HANA as shown in Figure 12.6, which again can be accessed by other applications.

In SAP Predictive Analysis, a saved model can be exported in PMML as shown in Figure 12.19.

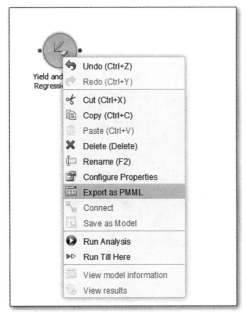

Figure 12.19 Exporting Saved Models in PA

The generated PMML is shown in Figure 12.20.

```
<?xml version="1.0" encoding="UTF-8" standalone="yes"?><PMML
xmlns="http://www.dmg.org/PMML-4_0" version="4.0"><Header
copyright="Copyright" description="desc"><Application name="PAS"
version="1.0"/><Timestamp>Wed Aug 14 17:57:47 BST
2013</Timestamp></Header><DataDictionary numberOfFields="2"><DataField
name="Fertilizer" optype="continuous" dataType="integer"/><DataField
name="Yield" optype="continuous"
dataType="integer"/></DataDictionary><RegressionModel
modelName="LinearRegression" functionName="regression"
algorithmName="LinearRegression" modelType="linearRegression"
normalizationMethod="none"><MiningSchema><MiningField name="Fertilizer"
usageType="active" optype="continuous"/><MiningField name="Yield"
usageType="predicted" optype="continuous"/></MiningSchema><Targets><Target
field="Yield" optype="continuous"/></Targets><RegressionTable
intercept="36.42857142857143"><NumericPredictor name="Yield"
coefficient="5.892857142857143"/></RegressionTable><Output><OutputField
name="PredictedValues" optype="continuous" dataType="double"
feature="predictedValue"/></Output></RegressionModel></PMML>
```

Figure 12.20 The PMML Exported from PA for Linear Regression

The PMML in Figure 12.20 shows the model type as linear regression, and the model parameters for the intercept a of 36.42857, and the coefficient b of 5.892857. The XML containing this PMML can be accessed by other applications.

So far we have looked at bi-variate linear regression as a simple introduction to regression analysis. We now expand on that model by looking at several bi-variate non-linear regression models.

12.2 Bi-Variate Geometric, Exponential, and Logarithmic Regression

The bi-variate geometric, exponential, and logarithmic curves have the attractive properties that they can be easily transformed into linear form, and therefore be analyzed using the simple bi-variate linear regression model, but applied to data that shows non-linear behavior.

They can be defined in the PAL, in the R Integration for SAP HANA, in the R integration in PA, and also using PA native algorithms.

We discuss each algorithm and, for illustrative purposes, define the geometric regression model in the PAL, the exponential regression model in PA using the R integration in PA, and finally the logarithmic regression again in PA but this time using the PA native algorithm.

12.2.1 Bi-Variate Geometric Regression in the PAL

Bi-Variate Geometric Regression is performed by transforming the geometric curve into a linear form, from which the linear least squares equations may be used to determine the model parameters. The Geometric or Power curve is defined as $Y = a * X^b$, which can be transformed into a linear form as $\log(Y) = \log a + b * \log(X)$.

The PAL therefore internally transforms Y and X to $\log(Y)$ and $\log(X)$ respectively, calculates the parameters a and b using the linear least squares equations, and then takes the anti-log of a to give the untransformed value of a, along with b, which needs no transformation.

Examples of the bi-variate geometric curve, given different values of b, are shown in Figure 12.21.

The PAL procedure is GEOREGRESSION. The definitions of the Input table, Parameter table and Output tables are all the same as for LRREGRESSION as was shown in Table 12.1, Table 12.2, and Table 12.3.

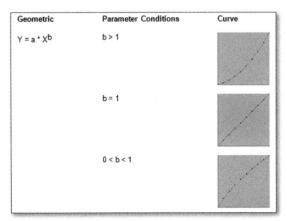

Figure 12.21 Examples of the Bi-Variate Geometric Curve

12.2.2 An Example of Bi-Variate Geometric Regression in the PAL

Here's a simple example, with the data in tabular and graphical format as shown in Figure 12.22. A non-linear curve looks like it will give a better fit to the data than a linear one.

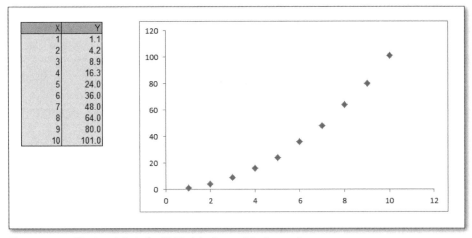

Figure 12.22 The Input Data for Bi-Variate Geometric Regression

The main elements of the SQLScript are as shown in Listing 12.3. The full code is available in the file SAP_HANA_PAL_GEOREGRESSION_Example_SQLScript on the SAP PRESS website.

```
-- The procedure generator

call SYSTEM.afl_wrapper_generator ('palGeoR','AFLPAL','GEOREGRESSION',P
DATA);

-- The Control Table parameters

INSERT INTO #CONTROL_TAB VALUES ('PMML_EXPORT',1,null,null);
INSERT INTO #CONTROL_TAB VALUES ('THREAD_NUMBER',8,null,null);

-- Assume the data has been stored in table DATA_TAB as shown in Figure
12.22

-- Calling the procedure

CALL palGeoR(DATA_TAB, "#CONTROL_TAB", RESULTS_TAB, FITTED_TAB,
SIGNIFICANCE_TAB, PAL_PMMLMODEL_TAB) with overview;
SELECT * FROM RESULTS_TAB;
SELECT * FROM FITTED_TAB;
SELECT * FROM SIGNIFICANCE_TAB;
SELECT * FROM PAL_PMMLMODEL_TAB;
```

Listing 12.3 The PAL SQLScript for Bi-Variate Geometric Regression

After running the SQLScript in SAP HANA Studio, the Results Table becomes as shown in Figure 12.23, and shows the model parameters. Our regression line is Y = 1.0722 * X $^{1.9596}$, also sometimes written as Y = 1.0722 * X Power(1.9596).

SELECT * FROM RESULTS_TAB		
	ID	Ai
1	0	1.0722...
2	1	1.9596...

Figure 12.23 The Model Parameters for the Bi-Variate Geometric Regression

The fitted data is output and shown in Figure 12.24.

SELECT * FROM FITTED_TAB		
	ID	Fitted
1	1	1.0722...
2	2	4.1705...
3	3	9.2313...
4	4	16.221...
5	5	25.119...
6	6	35.906...
7	7	48.569...
8	8	63.097...
9	9	79.478...
10	10	97.705...

Figure 12.24   The Geometric Regression Model Fitted Values

The model goodness of fit statistics are shown in Figure 12.25. The R Squared value of 0.9997 and the F value of 26,378 represent almost a perfect fit of the data, which is to be expected, given that we are using a contrived data set. Figure 12.22 shows that the data clearly follows a geometric curve. Of course, in reality, we are very unlikely to get such perfect fits.

Out of interest, a linear regression on this data gives an F value of 195.6575, so, in comparison, the geometric curve is a much better fit.

SELECT * FROM SIGNIFICANCE_TAB		
	NAME	VALUE
1	R2	0.999696...
2	F	26,378.3...

Figure 12.25   The Goodness of Fit Statistics

Finally, we chose to output the PMML from the geometric regression analysis and that is shown in part in Figure 12.26. Note in the XML the model parameters of 1.07222 and 1.95963, and the R Squared value of 0.999697. This output could be used as the input to an external model for scoring or predicting new data.

Having built the model, we now wish to predict values using the model.

```
<RegressionModel modelName="Instance for regression"
functionName="regression" algorithmName="GeoRegression"
targetFieldName="Y" >
<MiningSchema>
<MiningField name="Y" usageType="predicted"/>
<MiningField name="X1" />
</MiningSchema>
<ModelExplanation>
<PredictiveModelQuality targetField="Y" dataUsage="training" r-
squared="0.999697" >
</PredictiveModelQuality>
</ModelExplanation>
<RegressionTable intercept="1.07222">
<NumericPredictor name="X1" exponent="1" coefficient="1.95963"/>
</RegressionTable>
</RegressionModel>
</PMML>
```

Figure 12.26   The PMML Output from Bi-Variate Geometric Regression

12.2.3   Using the Bi-Variate Geometric Regression Model to Predict

To make predictions we use the PAL function FORECASTWITHGEOR. Our model is $Y = 1.0722 * X^{1.9596}$. In our example, we wish to predict Y from new values of $X = 11$ and 12. We basically extrapolate the data, which is a common use case for bi-variate linear and non-linear regression in time series analysis. The Input table, Parameter table and Output tables are the same as in Bi-Variate Linear Regression as was defined in Table 12.4, Table 12.5, and Table 12.6.

The main elements of the SQLScript are as shown in Listing 12.4. The model coefficients could have been read from the table where they were saved when the model was built. The full code is available in the file SAP_HANA_PAL_FORECASTWITH-GEOR_Example_SQLScript on the SAP PRESS website.

```
-- The procedure generator

call SYSTEM.afl_wrapper_generator
('palForecastWithGeoR','AFLPAL','FORECASTWITHGEOR',PDATA);

-- The values to Predict, the Control Table parameters, and the model
coefficients

INSERT INTO PREDICTDATA_TAB VALUES (1,11);
INSERT INTO PREDICTDATA_TAB VALUES (2,12);

INSERT INTO #CONTROL_TAB VALUES ('THREAD_NUMBER',2,null,null);
```

```
INSERT INTO COEEFICIENT_TAB VALUES (0,1.0722);
INSERT INTO COEEFICIENT_TAB VALUES (1,1.9596);

-- Calling the procedure

CALL palForecastWithGeor(PREDICTDATA_TAB, COEEFICIENT_TAB, "#CONTROL_
TAB", FITTED_TAB) with overview;

SELECT * FROM FITTED_TAB;
```

Listing 12.4 The PAL SQLScript for Bi-Variate Geometric Regression

The Fitted Table becomes as shown in Figure 12.27, and shows the predictions of Y for values of X of 11 and 12.

SELECT * FROM FITTED_TAB		
	ID	Fitted
1	1	117.76...
2	2	139.66...

Figure 12.27   The Predicted Values using Bi-Variate Geometric Regression

The predicted values are saved in an SAP HANA table and could therefore be used by another application.

12.2.4   Bi-Variate Exponential Regression in PA using R

Bi-Variate Exponential Regression is performed by transforming the exponential curve into a linear form, from which the linear least squares equations may be used to determine the model parameters. The exponential curve, $Y = a * \exp^{bx}$ or simply $Y = a * e^{bx}$, is transformed to linear as $\log Y = \log a + b * X$.

For this example we use PA and the R integration in PA. R transforms the exponential curve to linear by simply taking logs of Y, calculating the linear line of best fit and then taking the anti-log of a, to derive the transformed value of a, with b as given. Examples of the bi-variate exponential curve, given different values of b, are shown in Figure 12.28.

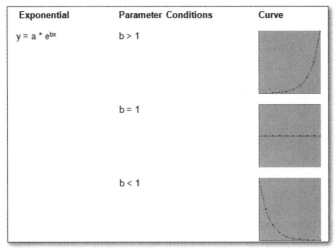

Figure 12.28   Examples of the Bi-Variate Exponential Curve

Here is a simple example, with the data in tabular and graphical format as shown in Figure 12.29. A non-linear curve looks like it will give a better fit to the data than a linear one.

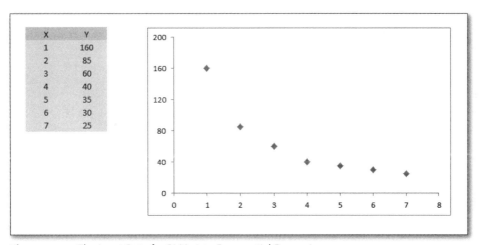

Figure 12.29   The Input Data for Bi-Variate Exponential Regression

In this example we input the data using a CSV file and use the exponential regression component in the R integration in PA. The analysis is shown in Figure 12.30.

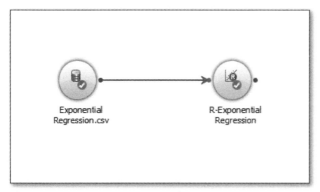

Figure 12.30 Bi-Variate Exponential Regression in PA using R

The dialogue for the PA R Exponential Regression component matches that of the PA R Linear Regression component as was shown in Figure 12.12 where we also saved the model, with a name and description, for subsequent use when we wish to make predictions from the model.

After running the analysis, as we discussed in Chapter 7, we can switch to the RESULTS VIEW to see the fitted values of the model, as shown in Figure 12.31. Note that we entered the name Fitted Values for the newly added columns.

X	Y	Fitted Values
1	160	121.85
2	85	90.95
3	60	67.88
4	40	50.66
5	35	37.81
6	30	28.22
7	25	21.07

Figure 12.31 The Fitted Values from the Exponential Regression Analysis

We can plot this data in PA using the VISUALIZE option, as shown in Figure 12.32.

The algorithm summary from R is shown in Figure 12.33, from which we can see that the bi-variate exponential regression model is

$$Y = 163.2567 * e^{-0.2925X}$$

The model quality statistics are also shown with very significant values for R2, Adjusted R2, and the F Value.

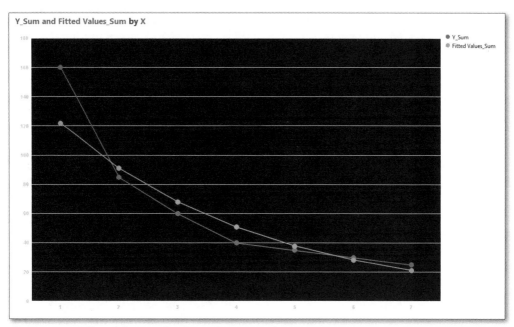

Figure 12.32 A Plot of the Actual and Fitted Exponential Regression in PA

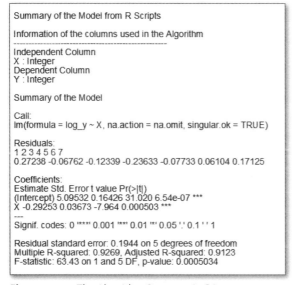

Figure 12.33 The Algorithm Summary in PA

As with bi-variate linear regression in Section 12.1.6, we can use the saved model to make predictions, which we can visualize and export either to a file or table, or via PMML.

12.2.5 Bi-Variate Logarithmic Regression using the PA Native Algorithm

Bi-Variate Natural Logarithmic Regression is performed by transforming the natural log curve into a linear form, from which the linear least squares equations may be used to determine the model parameters. The Natural Log curve is given by the equation $y = a + b \log(x)$, so we simply take logs of the X variable, and determine the parameters a and b as in linear least squares regression analysis. Examples of the bi-variate logarithmic curve, given different values of b, are shown in Figure 12.34.

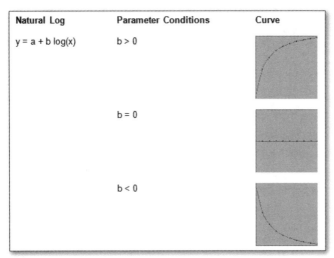

Figure 12.34 Examples of the Bi-Variate Logarithmic Curve

Here is a simple example, with the data in tabular and graphical format as shown in Figure 12.35. A non-linear curve looks like it will give a better fit to the data than a linear one.

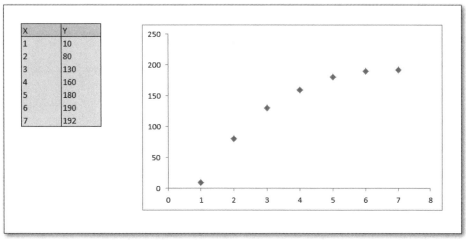

Figure 12.35   Data for Bi-Variate Logarithmic Regression

In this example we input the data using a CSV file and then use the Logarithmic Regression component native to PA. The analysis is shown in Figure 12.36.

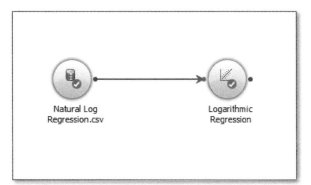

Figure 12.36   Bi-Variate Logarithmic Regression using the Native PA Algorithm

The dialogue for the PA Logarithmic Regression component matches that of the PA R Linear Regression component as was shown in Figure 12.12 where we also saved the model, with a name and description, for subsequent use when we wish to make predictions from the model.

After running the analysis we can switch to the RESULTS VIEW to see the fitted values of the model, as shown in Figure 12.37. Note that we entered the name Fitted Values for the newly added columns.

X	Y	Fitted Values
1	10	14.86
2	80	82.99
3	130	122.85
4	160	151.13
5	180	173.06
6	190	190.98
7	192	206.13

Figure 12.37   The Fitted Values from the Logarithmic Regression Analysis

We can plot this data in PA using the VISUALIZE option, as shown in Figure 12.38.

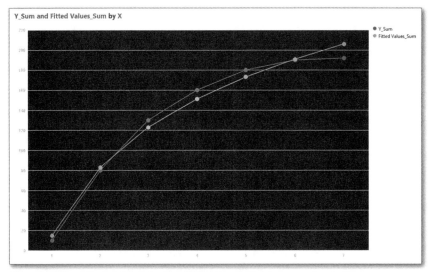

Figure 12.38   A Plot of the Actual and Fitted Logarithmic Regression in PA

The algorithm summary from PA is shown in Figure 12.39 and thus the logarithmic regression model is Y = 14.862 + 98.294 * Log(X).

The model quality statistics are very significant, which we would expect given the plot of the actual and fitted data shown in Figure 12.38.

As with bi-variate linear regression in section 12.1.6, we can use the saved model to make predictions, which we can visualize and export the predicted data to a file or table, and the model via PMML.

So far our regression analysis has been bi-variate, concerned with only two variables, a dependent variable and single independent variable. However, we can extend the bi-variate model to multi-variate whereby we have multiple independent variables.

356

The PAL and R integrations support Multiple Linear Regression and Multiple Exponential Regression, which we discuss next.

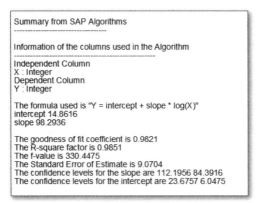

```
Summary from SAP Algorithms
-------------------------------

Information of the columns used in the Algorithm
-----------------------------------------------------
Independent Column
X : Integer
Dependent Column
Y : Integer

The formula used is "Y = intercept + slope * log(X)"
intercept 14.8616
slope 98.2936

The goodness of fit coefficient is 0.9821
The R-square factor is 0.9851
The f-value is 330.4475
The Standard Error of Estimate is 9.0704
The confidence levels for the slope are 112.1956 84.3916
The confidence levels for the intercept are 23.6757 6.0475
```

Figure 12.39 The Algorithm Summary in PA

12.3 Multiple Linear Regression

The general form of the model is $Y = \beta_0 + \beta_1 * X_1 + \beta_2 * X_2 + ...\beta_N * X_N$, where the parameters $\beta_0, \beta_1... \beta_N$ are estimated using the principle of least squares. It is a simple extension to the bi-variate linear regression model $Y = \beta_0 + \beta_1 * X_1$, which we discussed at the beginning of this chapter.

12.3.1 An Example of Multiple Linear Regression in the PAL

For this example we extend the bi-variate model in section 12.1.3 to a multi-variate one of Yield = $\beta_0 + \beta_1$ * Fertilizer + β_2 * Rainfall

The data Input table is as shown in Figure 12.40.

SELECT * FROM DATA_TAB				
	ID	Yield	Fertilizer	Rainfall
1	1	40	100	10
2	2	50	200	20
3	3	50	300	10
4	4	70	400	30
5	5	65	500	20
6	6	65	600	20
7	7	80	700	30

Figure 12.40 The Input Data for the Multiple Linear Regression Example

The Input, Parameter and Output tables are as for bi-variate regression analysis as defined in Section 12.1.1.

The main elements of the SQLScript are as shown in Listing 12.5. The code is as for Bi-Variate Linear Regression, other than the input data source. The full code is available in the file SAP_HANA_PAL_LRREGRESSION_Example_MLR_SQLScript on the SAP PRESS website.

```
-- The procedure generator

call SYSTEM.afl_wrapper_generator ('palLR','AFLPAL','LRREGRESSION',PDA
TA);

-- The Control Table parameters

INSERT INTO #CONTROL_TAB VALUES ('ADJUSTED_R2',1,null,null);
INSERT INTO #CONTROL_TAB VALUES ('PMML_EXPORT',1,null,null);
INSERT INTO #CONTROL_TAB VALUES ('THREAD_NUMBER',8,null,null);

-- Assume the data has been stored in table DATA_TAB as shown in Figure
12.40

-- Calling the procedure

CALL palLR(DATA_TAB, "#CONTROL_TAB", RESULTS_TAB, FITTED_TAB,
SIGNIFICANCE_TAB, PAL_PMMLMODEL_TAB) with overview;
SELECT * FROM RESULTS_TAB;
SELECT * FROM FITTED_TAB;
SELECT * FROM SIGNIFICANCE_TAB;
SELECT * FROM PAL_PMMLMODEL_TAB;
```

Listing 12.5 The PAL SQLScript for Multiple Linear Regression

After running the SQLScript, the Results table becomes as shown in Figure 12.41, and lists the model parameters, and therefore our regression line is

Yield = 28.0952 + 0.0381 * Fertilizer + 0.8333 * Rainfall

SELECT * FROM RESULTS_TAB		
	ID	Ai
1	0	28.0952...
2	1	0.03809...
3	2	0.83333...

Figure 12.41 The Model Parameters for Multiple Linear Regression

The fitted data is output and shown in Figure 12.42.

SELECT * FROM FITTED_TAB		
	ID	Fitted
1	1	40.2380...
2	2	52.3809...
3	3	47.8571...
4	4	68.3333...
5	5	63.8095...
6	6	67.6190...
7	7	79.7619...

Figure 12.42 The Model Fitted Values

The model goodness of fit statistics are shown in Figure 12.43.

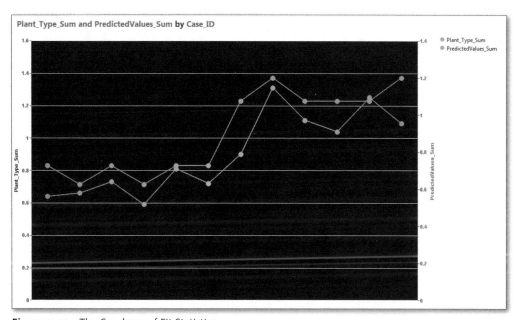

Figure 12.43 The Goodness of Fit Statistics

This is a very high value of R2, given that it has a maximum value of 1. In practice you would expect much lower values. Furthermore, we should now use the Adjusted R2 to compare models as it is a better statistic of model quality in that it does not necessarily increase as the sample size and the number of independent variables increases.

In pure statistical terms the significance of the curve fit is given by the F statistic. In our example, there are N = 7 observations and K = 2 regressors, namely Fertilizer and Rainfall.

The F Value at 99% confidence level for K, N-K-1 degrees of freedom is 18.00 (99% being very significant)

The F Value at 95% confidence level for K, N-K-1 degrees of freedom is 6.94 (95% is described as significant by statisticians)

Therefore an F value greater than 18.00 is very significant indeed. We have a value of 105.33, so we have an extremely good model.

We can compare these model quality measures with those of the bi-variate regression model in Figure 12.8, and note that by introducing the second independent variable, Rainfall, we have improved the model, with the Adjusted R2 value increasing from 0.8146 to 0.9261.

Finally, we chose to output the PMML from the regression analysis and this is shown in Figure 12.44. Note in the XML the model parameters as per our fitted equation Yield = 28.0952 + 0.0381 * Fertilizer + 0.8333 * Rainfall. This output could be used as the input to an external application for scoring or predicting new values.

```xml
<RegressionModel modelName="Instance for regression"
functionName="regression" algorithmName="LinearRegression"
targetFieldName="Yield" >
<MiningSchema>
<MiningField name="Yield" usageType="predicted"/>
<MiningField name="Fertilizer" />
<MiningField name="Rainfall" />
</MiningSchema>
<ModelExplanation>
<PredictiveModelQuality targetField="Yield" dataUsage="training" r-
squared="0.981366" >
</PredictiveModelQuality>
</ModelExplanation>
<RegressionTable intercept="28.0952">
<NumericPredictor name="Fertilizer" exponent="1" coefficient="0.0380952"/>
<NumericPredictor name="Rainfall" exponent="1" coefficient="0.833333"/>
</RegressionTable>
</RegressionModel>
</PMML>
```

Figure 12.44   The PMML Output from Multiple Linear Regression

12.3.2 An Example of Multiple Linear Regression in PA using the PAL

This same analysis can be defined in PA but executed in SAP HANA, as shown in Figure 12.45.

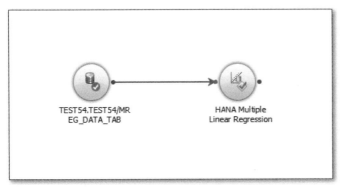

Figure 12.45 Multiple Linear Regression in PA using the PAL

The fitted data is shown in Figure 12.46, and of course, matches the results from the PAL as shown in Figure 12.42.

ID (Private Attr...	Yield (Private ...	Fertilizer (Priva...	Rainfall (Privat...	PredictedValue
1	40.00	100.00	10.00	40.24
2	50.00	200.00	20.00	52.38
3	50.00	300.00	10.00	47.86
4	70.00	400.00	30.00	68.33
5	65.00	500.00	20.00	63.81
6	65.00	600.00	20.00	67.62
7	80.00	700.00	30.00	79.76

Figure 12.46 The Model Fitted Values

12.3.3 Predicting or Scoring the Model in the PAL

To make predictions using our Multiple Linear Regression model we use the PAL function FORECASTWITHLR. Our model is Yield = 28.0952 + 0.0381 * Fertilizer + 0.8333 * Rainfall. We wish to predict Yield from new values for Fertilizer and Rainfall of 800,10; 800,20; 800,30; 900,10; 900,20; 900,30.

The table definitions for prediction are as for the bi-variate example listed in Tables 12.4, 12.5, and 12.6.

The main elements of the SQLScript are as shown in Listing 12.6. The model coefficients could have been read from the table where they were saved when the model was built, as shown in Figure 12.41. The full code is available in the file SAP_HANA_PAL_FORECASTWITHLR_ Example_ MLR_SQLScript on the SAP PRESS website.

```
-- The procedure generator

call SYSTEM.afl_wrapper_generator
('palForecastWithLR','AFLPAL','FORECASTWITHLR',PDATA);
-- The values to Predict, the Control Table parameters, and the model
coefficients

INSERT INTO PREDICTDATA_TAB VALUES (1,800,10);
INSERT INTO PREDICTDATA_TAB VALUES (2,800,20);
INSERT INTO PREDICTDATA_TAB VALUES (3,800,30);
INSERT INTO PREDICTDATA_TAB VALUES (4,900,10);
INSERT INTO PREDICTDATA_TAB VALUES (5,900,20);
INSERT INTO PREDICTDATA_TAB VALUES (6,900,30);

INSERT INTO #CONTROL_TAB VALUES ('THREAD_NUMBER',2,null,null);

INSERT INTO COEEFICIENT_TAB VALUES (0, 28.0952);
INSERT INTO COEEFICIENT_TAB VALUES (1, 0.03809);
INSERT INTO COEEFICIENT_TAB VALUES (2, 0.83333);

-- Calling the procedure

CALL palForecastWithLR(PREDICTDATA_TAB, COEEFICIENT_TAB, "#CONTROL_
TAB", FITTED_TAB) with overview;

SELECT * FROM FITTED_TAB;
```
Listing 12.6 The PAL SQLScript for Multiple Linear Regression

The Fitted table becomes as shown in Figure 12.47, and shows the predictions of Yield for the various values of Fertilizer and Rainfall.

SELECT * FROM FITTED_TAB		
	ID	Fitted
1	1	66.9047...
2	2	75.2380...
3	3	83.5714...
4	4	70.7142...
5	5	79.0476...
6	6	87.3809...

Figure 12.47 Predicted Values from the Multiple Linear Regression Model

The same example can also be run in SAP Predictive Analysis either as an in-database analysis in SAP HANA and using the PAL algorithms, or as an in-process analysis with the data sourced from a non-SAP HANA data source such as a CSV file and using the R integration in PA.

12.4 Multiple Exponential Regression

The general form of the model is $Y = \beta_0 * \exp^{(\beta1 * X1 + \beta2 * X2 + ... + \beta n * XN)}$, where the parameters $\beta_0, \beta_1 ... \beta_N$ are estimated using the principle of least squares. It is a simple extension to the bi-variate exponential regression model

$Y = \beta_0 * \exp^{(\beta1 * X1)}$ which we discussed in section 12.2.4, and which would apply when we have multiple independent variables and non-linear relationships.

To transform to linear we take natural logarithms on both sides of the equation:

$Log\ (Y) = Log(\beta_0 * exp^{(\beta1 * X1 + \beta2 * X2 + ... + \beta n * Xn)})$

Transform it into:

$Log\ (Y) = Log(\beta_0) + \beta_1 * X1 + \beta_2 * X2 + ... + \beta_n * Xn$

12.4.1 An Example of Multiple Exponential Regression in the PAL

For this example we extend the bi-variate model example in section 12.2.4 to a multi-variate one of $Yield = \beta_0 * \exp^{(\beta1 * Fertilizer + \beta2 * Rainfall)}$

We use the same data as we used for Multiple Linear Regression and as shown in Figure 12.40. The Input, Parameter, and Output tables are as for multiple linear regression analysis.

The main elements of the SQLScript are as shown in Listing 12.7. The code is as for Multiple Linear Regression, other than the function called is EXPREGRESSION. The full code is available in the file SAP_HANA_PAL_EXPREGRESSION_Example_ MER_SQLScript on the SAP PRESS website.

```
-- The procedure generator

call SYSTEM.afl_wrapper_generator ('palExpR','AFLPAL','EXPREGRESSION',P
DATA);
-- The Control Table parameters

INSERT INTO #CONTROL_TAB VALUES ('ADJUSTED_R2',1,null,null);
INSERT INTO #CONTROL_TAB VALUES ('PMML_EXPORT',1,null,null);
INSERT INTO #CONTROL_TAB VALUES ('THREAD_NUMBER',8,null,null);

-- Assume the data has been stored in table DATA_TAB as shown in Figure
12.40

-- Calling the procedure

CALL palExpR(DATA_TAB, "#CONTROL_TAB", RESULTS_TAB, FITTED_TAB,
SIGNIFICANCE_TAB, MODEL_TAB) with overview;

SELECT * FROM RESULTS_TAB;
SELECT * FROM FITTED_TAB;
SELECT * FROM SIGNIFICANCE_TAB;
SELECT * FROM PAL_PMMLMODEL_TAB;
```

Listing 12.7 The PAL SQLScript for Multiple Linear Regression

Then the Results table becomes as shown in Figure 12.48, and lists the model parameters, and therefore our regression line is

$$Yield = 33.8421 * exp^{(\,0.00067\,*\,Fertilizer\,+\,0.01391\,*\,Rainfall\,)}$$

SELECT * FROM RESULTS_TAB		
	ID	Ai
1	0	33.8421...
2	1	0.00067...
3	2	0.01391...

Figure 12.48 The Model Parameters for Multiple Exponential Regression

The fitted data is output and shown in Figure 12.49.

SELECT * FROM FITTED_TAB		
	ID	Fitted
1	1	41.6129...
2	2	51.1681...
3	3	47.6371...
4	4	67.3176...
5	5	62.6721...
6	6	67.0552...
7	7	82.4524...

Figure 12.49 The Model Fitted Values

The model goodness of fit statistics are shown in Figure 12.50.

SELECT * FROM SIGNIFICANCE_TAB		
	NAME	VALUE
1	R2	0.9734...
2	F	73.441...
3	Adjusted R2	0.8953...

Figure 12.50 The Goodness of Fit Statistics

Now it is interesting to compare these model quality statistics with the Multiple Linear Regression model shown in Figure 12.43. The F Value and Adjusted R Squared are higher for the linear model compared to the exponential model, so that would be preferred when making predictions.

Finally, we chose to output the PMML from the regression analysis and that is shown in Figure 12.51. This output could be used as the input to an external application for scoring or predicting new values.

```
<RegressionModel modelName="Instance for regression"
functionName="regression" algorithmName="ExpRegression"
targetFieldName="Yield" >
<MiningSchema>
<MiningField name="Yield" usageType="predicted"/>
<MiningField name="Fertilizer" />
<MiningField name="Rainfall" />
</MiningSchema>
<ModelExplanation>
<PredictiveModelQuality targetField="Yield" dataUsage="training" r-
squared="0.97349" >
</PredictiveModelQuality>
</ModelExplanation>
<RegressionTable intercept="33.8422">
<NumericPredictor name="Fertilizer" exponent="1" coefficient="0.000676"/>
<NumericPredictor name="Rainfall" exponent="1" coefficient="0.0139105"/>
</RegressionTable>
</RegressionModel>
</PMML>
```

Figure 12.51 The PMML Output from Multiple Exponential Regression

12.4.2 An Example of Multiple Exponential Regression in PA using the PAL

This same analysis can be defined and run in PA, as shown in Figure 12.52.

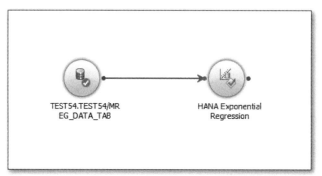

Figure 12.52 Multiple Exponential Regression in PA using the PAL

12.4.3 Predicting or Scoring the Model in the PAL

To make predictions using our Multiple Exponential Regression model we use the PAL function FORECASTWITHEXPR. Our model is $Yield = 33.8421 * exp^{(\,0.00067\, *\, Fertilizer\, +\, 0.01391\, *\, Rainfall\,)}$. We wish to predict Yield from new values for Fertilizer and Rainfall of 800,10; 800,20; 800,30; 900,10; 900,20; 900,30.

The table definitions for prediction are as for the example listed in Tables 12.4, 12.5 and 12.6.

The main elements of the SQLScript are as shown in Listing 12.8. The model coefficients could have been read from the table where they were saved when the model was built, as shown in Figure 12.48. The full code is available in the file SAP_HANA_PAL_FORECASTWITHEXPR_ Example_ MER_SQLScript on the SAP PRESS website.

```
-- The procedure generator

call SYSTEM.afl_wrapper_generator ('palForecastWithExpR','AFLPAL','FORE
CASTWITHEXPR',PDATA);

-- The values to Predict, the Control Table parameters, and the model
coefficients
```

```
INSERT INTO PREDICTDATA_TAB VALUES (1,800,10);
INSERT INTO PREDICTDATA_TAB VALUES (2,800,20);
INSERT INTO PREDICTDATA_TAB VALUES (3,800,30);
INSERT INTO PREDICTDATA_TAB VALUES (4,900,10);
INSERT INTO PREDICTDATA_TAB VALUES (5,900,20);
INSERT INTO PREDICTDATA_TAB VALUES (6,900,30);

INSERT INTO #CONTROL_TAB VALUES ('THREAD_NUMBER',2,null,null);

INSERT INTO COEEFICIENT_TAB VALUES (0,33.8421);
INSERT INTO COEEFICIENT_TAB VALUES (1,0.00067);
INSERT INTO COEEFICIENT_TAB VALUES (2,0.01391);

-- Calling the procedure

CALL palForecastWithExpR(PREDICTDATA_TAB, COEEFICIENT_TAB, "#CONTROL_
TAB", FITTED_TAB) with overview;

SELECT * FROM FITTED_TAB;
```

Listing 12.8 The PAL SQLScript for Multiple Exponential Regression

The Fitted table becomes as shown in Figure 12.53, and shows the predictions of Yield for the various values of Fertilizer and Rainfall.

	ID	Fitted
1	1	66.7939...
2	2	76.7625...
3	3	88.2189...
4	4	71.4653...
5	5	82.1311...
6	6	94.3887...

SELECT * FROM FITTED_TAB

Figure 12.53 Predicted Values from Multiple Exponential Regression Model

Another popular non-linear regression model is polynomial regression, whereby we fit polynomial curves of varying degrees to the data. We do this when we have non-linear relationships in the data and then we use polynomial regression to see how good a model fit that it provides, and compare that with the other regression models.

12.5 Polynomial Regression

The general form of polynomial regression is given by the equation:
$Y = \beta_0 + \beta_1 * X + \beta_2 * X^2 + \beta_3 * X^3 + \ldots + \beta_N * X^N$, where the parameters $\beta_0, \beta_1, \ldots \beta_N$ are estimated using the principle of least squares. The value of N determines the degree of the polynomial. All that is required is to take the independent variable X, raise it to the required degree of the polynomial, and then use multiple linear regression to determine the model parameters $\beta_0, \beta_1, \ldots \beta_N$.

An example is shown in Figure 12.54 of a polynomial regression curve fit of degree 6 to a data set.

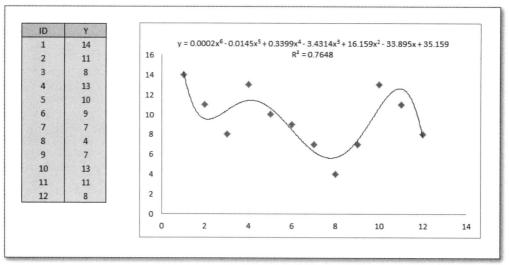

Figure 12.54 Example of Polynomial Regression of Degree 6

The SAP Predictive Analysis Library supports polynomial regression with the function POLYNOMIALREGRESSION. Now that we've looked at the general form, let's look at the Polynomial Regression in the PAL.

12.5.1 An Example of Polynomial Regression in the PAL

The Data Input table is as shown in Figure 12.55, and is shown in a scatter plot in Figure 12.54.

SELECT * FROM DATA_TAB			
	ID	Y	X1
1	0	14	1
2	1	11	2
3	2	8	3
4	3	13	4
5	4	10	5
6	5	9	6
7	6	7	7
8	7	4	8
9	8	7	9
10	9	13	10
11	10	11	11
12	11	8	12

Figure 12.55 The Input Data for the Polynomial Regression Example

The Input, Parameter and Output tables are as for bi-variate regression analysis as defined in Section 12.1.1, with the addition of the control parameter, VARIABLE_NUM, representing the degree of the polynomial curve.

The main elements of the SQLScript are as shown in Listing 12.9. The code is as for Bi-Variate Linear Regression, other than the additional control parameter and the input data source. The full code is available in the file SAP_HANA_PAL_LRRE-GRESSION_Example_PLR_SQLScript on the SAP PRESS website.

```
-- The procedure generator

call SYSTEM.afl_wrapper_generator ('palPolynomialR','AFLPAL','POLYNOMIA
LREGRESSION',PDATA);


-- The Control Table parameters

INSERT INTO #CONTROL_TAB VALUES ('VARIABLE_NUM',3,null,null);
INSERT INTO #CONTROL_TAB VALUES ('ADJUSTED_R2',1,null,null);
INSERT INTO #CONTROL_TAB VALUES ('PMML_EXPORT',1,null,null);
INSERT INTO #CONTROL_TAB VALUES ('THREAD_NUMBER',8,null,null);


-- Assume the data has been stored in table DATA_TAB as shown in Figure
12.55


-- Calling the procedure
```

```
CALL palPolynomialR(DATA_TAB, "#CONTROL_TAB", RESULTS_TAB, FITTED_TAB,
SIGNIFICANCE_TAB, MODEL_TAB) with overview;

SELECT * FROM RESULTS_TAB;
SELECT * FROM FITTED_TAB;
SELECT * FROM SIGNIFICANCE_TAB;
SELECT * FROM PAL_PMMLMODEL_TAB;
```

Listing 12.9 The PAL SQLScript for Polynomial Regression

Then the Results table becomes as shown in Figure 12.56, and lists the model parameters, and therefore our polynomial regression line is:

$$Y = 15.4646 - 2.1670 * X + 0.1818 * X^2 - 0.0032 * X^3$$

SELECT * FROM RESULTS_TAB		
	ID	Ai
1	0	15.4646...
2	1	-2.1669...
3	2	0.18176...
4	3	-0.0032...

Figure 12.56 The Model Parameters for Polynomial Regression

The fitted data is output and shown in Figure 12.57.

SELECT * FROM FITTED_TAB		
	ID	Fitted
1	0	13.476...
2	1	11.831...
3	2	10.512...
4	3	9.4977...
5	4	8.7691...
6	5	8.3069...
7	6	8.0916...
8	7	8.1040...
9	8	8.3244...
10	9	8.7335...
11	10	9.3120...
12	11	10.040...

Figure 12.57 The Model Fitted Values

The model goodness of fit statistics are shown in Figure 12.58.

SELECT * FROM SIGNIFICANCE_TAB		
	NAME	VALUE
1	R2	0.3134...
2	F	1.2172...

SELECT * FROM SIGNIFICANCE_TAB		
	NAME	VALUE
1	R2	0.764767...
2	F	2.709257...

Figure 12.58 The Goodness of Fit Statistics for Polynomials of Degree 3 and 6

The R2 value of 0.3134 is quite low. For the F statistic, in our example there are N = 12 observations and K = 3 regressors (X, X^2, and X^3). The F Value at 95% confidence level for K, N-K-1 degrees of freedom is 4.07, so our F Value of 1.2, being less than 4.07, is therefore not significant. In conclusion, the model is not very good, and we could not use it to make predictions with a high degree of confidence.

If we try a higher degree polynomial and set the control parameter VARIABLE_NUM to 6, in the SQLScript as shown in Listing 12.9, then the R2 value increases to 0.7648 and the F statistic increases to 2.709. The polynomial regression curve fit is shown in Figure 12.54. We could keep increasing the degree of the polynomial and the value of R2 would keep increasing, and if we set the degree of the polynomial to N-1, in our example 11, we would have a perfect fit!

Figure 12.59 shows the polynomial regression curves for values of the polynomial degree of 2 to 6, and we can see how the curve fit improves.

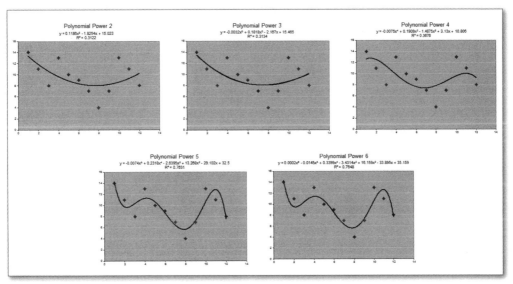

Figure 12.59 Polynomial Regression Curves from 2 to 6 Degrees

The values of R Squared, the F statistic and the F Value at 95% confidence level are shown in Figure 12.60, where we see the value of R Squared steadily increasing; however, the value of the F statistic compared to the F Value at 95% confidence, does decrease.

```
In the PAL –
INSERT INTO #CONTROL_TAB VALUES ('VARIABLE_NUM',N,null,null);
N = 2 to 8
```

Degree of Polynomial	R Squared	F Value	F Value at 95%
2	0.3132	2.0422	4.26
3	0.3134	1.2173	4.07
4	0.3766	1.0171	4.12
5	0.7631	3.8652	4.39
6	0.7648	2.7093	4.95
7	0.8689	3.7869	6.09
8	0.8742	2.6056	8.85

Figure 12.60 R Squared and the F Statistic for Various Polynomial Regressions

Polynomial regression provides an excellent introduction to the subject of model overfitting, defined as where a model provides an excellent fit to the data that it is given, but, for new data, it performs, or fits, very poorly. Overfitting generally occurs when a model is excessively complex, such as having too many parameters relative to the number of observations. Polynomial regression provides a good example of how this can happen.

The standard approach to avoiding overfitting is to split the data into a training data set to train or build the model, and a test data set to test the model on unseen or hold out data. An extension of this is cross-validation where multiple models are run on different samples of the data, which is split into train and test, and the models compared using the model quality measures based on the test data set. In decision tree analysis, the resulting trees are often pruned to more populated leaf nodes, to again avoid model overfitting.

We can make predictions using our Polynomial Regression model the same way as we made predictions for Multiple Linear Regression, using the PAL function FORECASTWITHPOLYNOMIALR.

12.6 Logistic Regression

In predictive analysis we frequently come across applications where we want to predict a binary variable, a 0 or 1, or a categorical variable, a yes or no. Such a dependent variable is also referred to as a dichotomous variable, something that is divided into two parts or classifications. The problem can be extended to predicting more than two categories or integer values.

Examples of such applications:

▶ Churn analysis to predict the probability that a customer may leave.

▶ Mailshot campaign analysis to predict the likelihood of a response.

▶ The success or failure of a medical treatment, dependent on dosage, patient's age, gender, weight and the severity of the condition.

▶ Predict a person's cholesterol level, dependent on gender, age, whether or not they smoke.

There are a huge number of applications in a wide range of fields, including biology, demography, economics, chemistry, and sociology.

As always, an example is the best way to understand an algorithm. We use a subset of the well-known MTCARS data set, which comprises the fuel consumption and various aspects of design and performance for 32 motor vehicles.

12.6.1 Logistic Regression in the PAL

In the SAP HANA Predictive Analysis Library, the algorithm name is Logistic Regression and the associated function name is LOGISTICREGRESSION.

The Input table comprises first of N columns that contain the independent variables, and finally a column for the dependent variable, as shown in Table 12.7.

Table	Column	Data Type	Description
Data	Columns	Integer or double	Variable Xn
	Type column	Integer or varchar	Variable TYPE

Table 12.7 The Input Table Definition for Logistic Regression

The Parameter table specifies nine parameters, as shown in Table 12.8.

Name	Data Type	Description
VARIABLE_NUM	Integer	Specifies the number of independent variables.
METHOD	Integer	▸ 0: The default and recommended, uses the Newton iteration method. ▸ 1: Uses the gradient-decent method.
STEP_SIZE	Double	Step size for convergence. This parameter is used only when METHOD is 1. Default value: 0.0201
EXIT_THRESHOLD	Double	Threshold (actual value) for exiting the iterations. Default value: 0.000001
MAX_ITERATION	Integer	Maximum number of iterations. Default value: 1
CLASS_MAP0	String	The dependent variable, which is mapped to 0.
CLASS_MAP1	String	The dependent variable, which is mapped to 1.
PMML_EXPORT	Integer	▸ 0: The default. Does not export the logistic regression model in PMML. ▸ 1: Exports the model in PMML in a single row. ▸ 2: Exports the model in PMML in several rows, each row containing a maximum of 5000 characters.
THREAD_NUMBER	Integer	Number of threads

Table 12.8 The Parameter Table Definition for Logistic Regression

The Output tables comprise the results of the regression, in terms of the model parameters and the PMML output, as shown in Table 12.9.

Table	Column	Data Type	Description
Result	1st column	Integer	Record ID
	2nd column	Integer or double	Parameter values of the model coefficients
PMML Result	1st column	Integer	Record ID
	2nd column	CLOB or varchar	Logistic regression model in PMML format

Table 12.9 The Output Table Definitions for Logistic Regression

12.6.2 An Example of Logistic Regression in the PAL

The subset of the MTCARS data that we use in our example is shown in Figure 12.61. We wish to predict the type of vehicle (0 or 1) depending on its horsepower and weight.

	Horsepower	Weight	TYPE
1	110	2.62	1
2	110	2.875	1
3	93	2.32	1
4	110	3.215	0
5	175	3.44	0
6	105	3.46	0
7	245	3.57	0
8	62	3.19	0
9	95	3.15	0
10	123	3.44	0
11	123	3.44	0
12	180	4.07	0
13	180	3.73	0
14	180	3.78	0
15	205	5.25	0
16	215	5.424	0
17	230	5.345	0
18	66	2.2	1
19	52	1.615	1
20	65	1.835	1

SELECT * FROM DATA_TAB

Figure 12.61 The First Twenty Input Data Records for Logistic Regression

Linear regression provides a very poor fit for applications where the dependent variable is binary. Using the data from our example we can see in Figure 12.62 that for binary response models, linear regression is really inadequate.

Linear regression is not suitable for other reasons. From a statistical perspective, the method assumes linearity of the relationship between the dependent and independent variables, normality of the error distribution of the difference between actual versus fitted, independence of these errors, and a constant variance of the errors. Statisticians call this homoscedasticity. All these assumptions do not apply when the dependent variable is dichotomous.

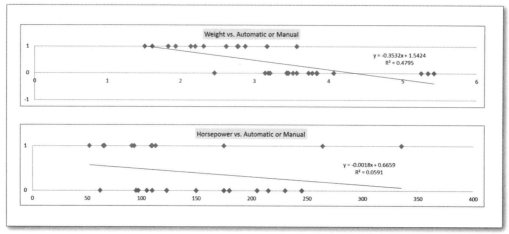

Figure 12.62   Linear Regression Model for a Binary Response Variable

Logistic regression is used for these types of binary dependent variable applications, whereby we estimate the probability that the outcome could be a 0 or 1. We predict the likelihood that Y is equal to 1 or 0, given certain values of X. We refer to predicting probabilities rather than the scores of the dependent variable.

If we plot the car weight versus the cumulative proportion of cars 0 = automatic, 1 = manual, in other words the likelihood or probability, we can see as in Figure 12.63, that we have what is called an s-shaped curve or more technically, a logistic curve or logistic function.

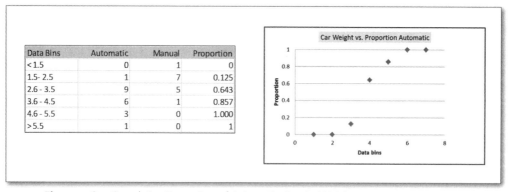

Figure 12.63   Cumulative Proportion of Automatic Cars by Weight

A simple logistic function may be defined by the formula

$p(t) = 1 / (1 + e^{-t})$,

where $p(t)$ is the proportion or probability of the target group or class, usually coded as 1. The benefit of this curve is that the input values can range from minus infinity to plus infinity, while the output ranges from 0 to 1, exactly the range for probability values; hence, its common use as a transfer function.

The curve $p(t) = 1 / (1 + e^{-(\beta 0 + \beta 1 * X1)})$ is a logistic regression equation. To be more general, the logistic regression equation for multiple independent or input variables is $Y = 1 / (1 + e^{-(\beta 0 + \beta 1 * X1 + \beta 2 * X2 + ... \beta n * Xn)})$.

The assumptions of least squared regression do not apply; therefore, we use a different approach with logistic regression, namely maximum likelihood estimation. This is a way of finding the smallest possible deviance between the actual and predicted values, similar to finding the best fitting line but using calculus. Maximum likelihood estimation uses different iterations in which it tries different solutions until it gets the smallest possible deviance or best fit. Once it has found the best solution, it provides a final value for the deviance.

The model we are going to fit is

$Prob(Y=1)$ is $1 / (1 + e^{-(\beta 0 + \beta 1 * Horsepower + \beta 2 * Weight)})$

The main elements of the SQLScript are as shown in Listing 12.10. The full code is available in the file SAP_HANA_PAL_LOGISTICREGRESSION_Example_SQLScript on the SAP PRESS website.

```
-- The procedure generator

call SYSTEM.afl_wrapper_generator ('palLogisticR','AFLPAL','LOGISTICREG
RESSION',PDATA);


-- The Control Table parameters

INSERT INTO #CONTROL_TAB VALUES ('VARIABLE_NUM',2,null,null);
INSERT INTO #CONTROL_TAB VALUES
('METHOD', 0, null, null);
INSERT INTO #CONTROL_TAB VALUES ('EXIT_THRESHOLD',null,0.0001,null);
INSERT INTO #CONTROL_TAB VALUES ('MAX_ITERATION',80,null,null);
INSERT INTO #CONTROL_TAB VALUES ('PMML_EXPORT', 1, null, null);
```

```
INSERT INTO #CONTROL_TAB VALUES ('THREAD_NUMBER',8,null,null);

-- Assume the data has been stored in table DATA_TAB as shown in Figure
12.61

-- Calling the procedure

CALL _SYS_AFL.palLogisticR
(DATA_TAB, "#CONTROL_TAB", RESULTS_TAB,  PAL_PMMLMODEL_TAB) with
overview;

SELECT * FROM RESULTS_TAB;
SELECT * FROM PAL_PMMLMODEL_TAB;
```
Listing 12.10 The PAL SQLScript for Logistic Regression

After running the SQLScript, the Results Table becomes as shown in Figure 12.64, and lists the model parameters. The model is

$$Y = 1 / (1 + e^{-(18.86629 + 0.036255 * Horsepower - 8.084475 * Weight)})$$

To measure the goodness of fit, we can compare actual Y with fitted Y and build what is called a classifier confusion matrix, which we will show after we have calculated the fitted values.

SELECT * FROM RESULTS_TAB		
	ID	Ai
1	0	18.866...
2	1	0.0362...
3	2	-8.0834...

Figure 12.64 The Model Parameters for Logistic Regression

To obtain the fitted values, we use the procedure FORECASTWITHLOGISTICR, and simply pass the actual values of the horsepower and weight for each vehicle, through the fitted model,

The Input and Parameter tables are the same as for predicting multiple linear regression models. The Output table is as shown in Table 12.10.

378

Table	Column	Data Type	Description
Fitted result	1st column	Integer or varchar	Record ID
	2nd column	Integer or double	Predicted values of Y
Fitted Data	1st column	Integer or varchar	Record ID

Table 12.10 The Output Table for Logistic Regression Prediction

The main elements of the SQLScript are as shown in Listing 12.11. The model coefficients could have been read from the table, where they were saved when the model was built, as shown in Figure 12.64. The full code is available in the file SAP_HANA_PAL_ FORECASTWITHLOGISTICR_ Example_ MLR_SQLScript on the SAP PRESS website.

```
-- The procedure generator

call SYSTEM.afl_wrapper_generator ('palForecastWithLogisticR','AFLPAL',
'FORECASTWITHLOGISTICR',PDATA);

-- The values to Predict are as per Figure 12.61
-- The Control Table parameters, and the model coefficients


INSERT INTO #CONTROL_TAB VALUES ('VARIABLE_NUM',2,null,null);
INSERT INTO #CONTROL_TAB VALUES ('THREAD_NUMBER',8,null,null);

INSERT INTO COEEFICIENT_TAB VALUES (0, 18.8662);
INSERT INTO COEEFICIENT_TAB VALUES (1, 0.03625);
INSERT INTO COEEFICIENT_TAB VALUES (2, -8.0834);

-- Calling the procedure

CALL palForecastWithLogisticR(PREDICTDATA_TAB, "#CONTROL_TAB",
COEEFICIENT_TAB, FITTED_TAB) with overview;

SELECT * FROM FITTED_TAB;
```

Listing 12.11 The PAL SQLScript for Logistic Regression Forecast

The Fitted Table becomes as shown in Figure 12.65.

	ID	Fitted	TYPE
		SELECT * FROM FITTED_TAB	
1	0	0.842335...	1
2	1	0.404782...	0
3	2	0.970240...	1
4	3	0.041728...	0
5	4	0.069388...	0
6	5	0.004988...	0
7	6	0.248041...	0
8	7	0.009265...	0
9	8	0.040998...	0
10	9	0.011190...	0
11	10	0.011190...	0
12	11	0.000548...	0
13	12	0.008500...	0
14	13	0.005690...	0
15	14	0.000000...	0
16	15	0.000000...	0
17	16	0.000000...	0
18	17	0.969983...	1
19	18	0.999545...	1
20	19	0.998324...	1

Figure 12.65   Predicted Values from the Logistic Regression Model

The fitted value is the probability of the record being a 1. The TYPE is then determined as for values over 0.5, TYPE = 1, otherwise 0. Now if we compare the predicted Type with the actual, as per Figure 12.61, we can construct what is called the Classifier Confusion Matrix, to see how well the model has classified the data. The matrix is simply a count of where the actual is predicted correctly and, conversely, incorrectly.

We can do this in SQLScript and Figure 12.66 shows the result. Of the 32 records, 13 were automatic and 19 were manual. Of the 13 automatic we predicted 12 correctly and 1 incorrectly, and of the 19 manual we predicted 18 correctly and 1 incorrectly.

There are several measures of the performance of a binary response model. The two main ones are:

▸ Sensitivity, which measures the model's ability to identify positive results

   = True Positives / (True Positives + False Negatives) or TP / (TP + FN)

In our example, this is 0.9231, which is high.

▶ Specificity, which relates to the model's ability to identify negative results
  = True Negatives / (True Negatives + False Positives) or TN / (TN + FP).

In our example, this is 0.9474, which is also high.

We can conclude that we have a good model and that we can use it to predict with
a high level of confidence.

	Fitted	TYPE	Actual					
1	0.8423	1	1		Classifier Confusion Matrix			
2	0.4048	0	1					
3	0.9702	1	1				Fitted	
4	0.0417	0	0				Automatic Manual	Total
5	0.0694	0	0			Automatic	12 1	13
6	0.0050	0	0	Actual		Manual	1 18	19
7	0.2480	0	0			Total	13 19	32
8	0.0093	0	0					
9	0.0410	0	0					
10	0.0112	0	0	Sensitivity	0.9231			
11	0.0112	0	0					
12	0.0005	0	0	Specifity	0.9474			
13	0.0085	0	0					
14	0.0057	0	0					
15	0.0000	0	0					
16	0.0000	0	0					
17	0.0000	0	0					
18	0.9700	1	1					
19	0.9995	1	1					
20	0.9983	1	1					
21	0.9211	1	0					
22	0.0155	0	0					
23	0.0304	0	0					
24	0.0359	0	0					
25	0.0028	0	0					
26	0.9964	1	1					
27	0.9924	1	1					
28	1.0000	1	1					
29	0.9434	1	1					
30	0.9437	1	1					
31	0.8960	1	1					
32	0.5857	1	1					

Figure 12.66 The Classifier Confusion Matrix for MTCARS Example

Other measures include:

▶ Precision = TP / (TP + FP)

▶ Recall = TP / (TP+FN)

▸ Overall Success or Accuracy = (TP + TN) / ALL

▸ Overall Failure = 1 – Overall Success

For dichotomous classification models, we can create a Cumulative Gains Chart and Lift Chart to view the quality of the model and compare multiple models, as shown in Figure 12.67.

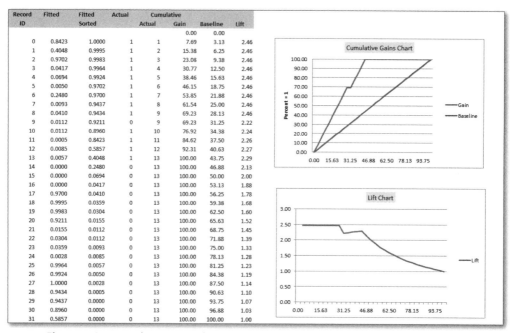

Record ID	Fitted	Fitted Sorted	Actual Actual	Cumulative Gain	Baseline	Lift
				0.00	0.00	
0	0.8423	1.0000	1	1	7.69	3.13	2.46
1	0.4048	0.9995	1	2	15.38	6.25	2.46
2	0.9702	0.9983	1	3	23.08	9.38	2.46
3	0.0417	0.9964	1	4	30.77	12.50	2.46
4	0.0694	0.9924	1	5	38.46	15.63	2.46
5	0.0050	0.9702	1	6	46.15	18.75	2.46
6	0.2480	0.9700	1	7	53.85	21.88	2.46
7	0.0093	0.9437	1	8	61.54	25.00	2.46
8	0.0410	0.9434	1	9	69.23	28.13	2.46
9	0.0112	0.9211	0	9	69.23	31.25	2.22
10	0.0112	0.8960	1	10	76.92	34.38	2.24
11	0.0005	0.8423	1	11	84.62	37.50	2.26
12	0.0085	0.5857	1	12	92.31	40.63	2.27
13	0.0057	0.4048	1	13	100.00	43.75	2.29
14	0.0000	0.2480	0	13	100.00	46.88	2.13
15	0.0000	0.0694	0	13	100.00	50.00	2.00
16	0.0000	0.0417	0	13	100.00	53.13	1.88
17	0.9700	0.0410	0	13	100.00	56.25	1.78
18	0.9995	0.0359	0	13	100.00	59.38	1.68
19	0.9983	0.0304	0	13	100.00	62.50	1.60
20	0.9211	0.0155	0	13	100.00	65.63	1.52
21	0.0155	0.0112	0	13	100.00	68.75	1.45
22	0.0304	0.0112	0	13	100.00	71.88	1.39
23	0.0359	0.0093	0	13	100.00	75.00	1.33
24	0.0028	0.0085	0	13	100.00	78.13	1.28
25	0.9964	0.0057	0	13	100.00	81.25	1.23
26	0.9924	0.0050	0	13	100.00	84.38	1.19
27	1.0000	0.0028	0	13	100.00	87.50	1.14
28	0.9434	0.0005	0	13	100.00	90.63	1.10
29	0.9437	0.0000	0	13	100.00	93.75	1.07
30	0.8960	0.0000	0	13	100.00	96.88	1.03
31	0.5857	0.0000	0	13	100.00	100.00	1.00

Figure 12.67   Cumulative Gains Chart and Lift Chart

In the charts we order the data from our most confident prediction and note the actual prediction. Then we cumulate the data and see how much gain our model gives us, compared to random guessing, which we represent on the chart as the baseline. The better our model, the further away it is from the baseline. The lift is the gain value divided by the baseline value, and we can see in the lift chart that our model starts at 2.5 times better at predicting than the baseline.

We have a very good model; however, in reality, it is likely to be less accurate, and a more realistic gain and lift chart is shown in Figure 12.68, where we have reduced the model's accuracy for illustrative purposes. The red line is the baseline, the top line is the best the model could do, and the ragged line in the middle is the actual performance of the model.

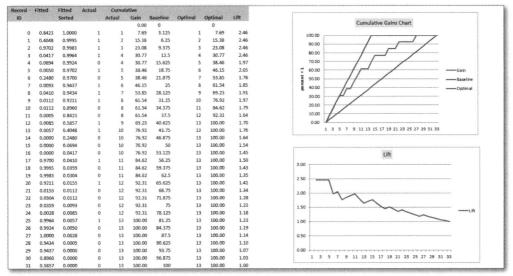

Record ID	Fitted	Fitted Sorted	Actual	Cumulative Actual	Gain	Baseline	Optimal	Optimal	Lift
				0.00	0			0	
0	0.8423	1.0000	1	1	7.69	3.125	1	7.69	2.46
1	0.4048	0.9995	1	2	15.38	6.25	2	15.38	2.46
2	0.9702	0.9983	1	3	23.08	9.375	3	23.08	2.46
3	0.0417	0.9964	1	4	30.77	12.5	4	30.77	2.46
4	0.0694	0.9924	0	4	30.77	15.625	5	38.46	1.97
5	0.0050	0.9702	1	5	38.46	18.75	6	46.15	2.05
6	0.2480	0.9700	0	5	38.46	21.875	7	53.85	1.76
7	0.0093	0.9437	1	6	46.15	25	8	61.54	1.85
8	0.0410	0.9434	1	7	53.85	28.125	9	69.23	1.91
9	0.0112	0.9211	1	8	61.54	31.25	10	76.92	1.97
10	0.0112	0.8960	0	8	61.54	34.375	11	84.62	1.79
11	0.0005	0.8423	0	8	61.54	37.5	12	92.31	1.64
12	0.0085	0.5857	1	9	69.23	40.625	13	100.00	1.70
13	0.0057	0.4048	1	10	76.92	43.75	13	100.00	1.76
14	0.0000	0.2480	0	10	76.92	46.875	13	100.00	1.64
15	0.0000	0.0694	0	10	76.92	50	13	100.00	1.54
16	0.0000	0.0417	0	10	76.92	53.125	13	100.00	1.45
17	0.9700	0.0410	1	11	84.62	56.25	13	100.00	1.50
18	0.9995	0.0359	0	11	84.62	59.375	13	100.00	1.43
19	0.9983	0.0304	0	11	84.62	62.5	13	100.00	1.35
20	0.9211	0.0155	1	12	92.31	65.625	13	100.00	1.41
21	0.0155	0.0112	0	12	92.31	68.75	13	100.00	1.34
22	0.0304	0.0112	0	12	92.31	71.875	13	100.00	1.28
23	0.0359	0.0093	0	12	92.31	75	13	100.00	1.23
24	0.0028	0.0085	0	12	92.31	78.125	13	100.00	1.18
25	0.9964	0.0057	1	13	100.00	81.25	13	100.00	1.23
26	0.9924	0.0050	0	13	100.00	84.375	13	100.00	1.19
27	1.0000	0.0028	0	13	100.00	87.5	13	100.00	1.14
28	0.9434	0.0005	0	13	100.00	90.625	13	100.00	1.10
29	0.9437	0.0000	0	13	100.00	93.75	13	100.00	1.07
30	0.8960	0.0000	0	13	100.00	96.875	13	100.00	1.03
31	0.5857	0.0000	0	13	100.00	100	13	100.00	1.00

Figure 12.68 Adjusted Cumulative Gains Chart and Lift Chart

To predict or score new data, for example, to predict the type of car given horsepower = 120 and weight = 2.8, we continue with the procedure FORECASTWITHLOGISTICR.

Our model is:

$$Y = 1 / (1 + e^{-(18.86629 + 0.036255 * Horsepower - 8.084475 * Weight)}).$$

We run the previous procedure shown in Listing 12.11 with the data input as:

INSERT INTO PREDICTDATA_TAB VALUES (0,120,2.8).

The results are shown in Figure 12.69, where the predicted probability that Type = 1 is 0.64, which is greater than 0.5, so the prediction of the type of car is 1.

SELECT * FROM FITTED_TAB			
	ID	Fitted	TYPE
1	0	0.6418…	1

Figure 12.69 Predicted Car Type using Logistic Regression

12.7 The Business Case for Regression Analysis

The business case for regression analysis is rarely discussed, as it is so relevant and prevalent that it is taken for granted. It is the basis of a huge range of applications. For example, to give just a sample:

- Sales analysis
- Cause and effect analysis
- Churn analysis
- Workforce planning
- Price simulation
- Risk analysis
- Commodity price analysis
- Stock price predictions
- Currency exchange rates
- Medical research
- Social analysis
- Econometrics
- Life sciences
- Astronomy

Along with decision trees, regression analysis is one of the top groups of algorithms used in predictive analysis. Regression is a fundamental tool for statisticians. It is used in every scientific discipline, with application in every industry and line of business. As we have seen in this chapter, it ranges from the simplest of algorithms, which we learn in school mathematics classes, through to the most complex. In the field of predictive analysis, regression analysis has the strongest business case given it is ubiquitous in its application.

12.8 Strengths and Weaknesses of Regression Analysis

The major strength of regression analysis is that it applies to so many business applications. Simple regression models are easy to understand and hence popular.

The great variety of regression models means that they can be applied in a very wide range of applications.

The weaknesses of regression models are that outliers can significantly affect a model. As we have already seen, this applies to many algorithms, and the simplest way to address this weakness is to check for outliers before applying the regression analysis. The overfitting of regression models is another concern. However, again, there are approaches to address this, in particular through the approach of train and test, as we have seen in this and earlier chapters.

The major weakness, although it is really more of a concern, is that although algorithms can find mathematical patterns they may not translate into a cause and effect relationship, particularly with classification models. Of course, this concern applies to all classification models whatever the algorithm. The concern is that analysts should not jump to conclusions. The analysis suggests where to look for relationships, but it does not explain them.

12.9   Summary

In this chapter we have looked at a range of regression analyses, starting with the simple bi-variate linear regression model to help with your understanding. This we extended to bi-variate non-linear regression. From this simple introduction to the topic we moved to the most popular regression model, namely multiple linear regression, and then the variant of multiple exponential regression. We showed how the multiple linear regression model can easily be adapted to support polynomial regression, which also provided a good example of the topic of model overfitting. Finally, we presented logistic regression, a major method for binary classification models.

In the next chapter we discuss the other major group of predictive analysis algorithms for classification analysis, namely decision trees.

This chapter introduces the reader to the very popular predictive analysis topic of decision trees, and specifically the algorithms in the PAL and in the integration of R in PA.

13   Classification Analysis — Decision Trees

According to the KDnuggets poll as shown in Figure 1.13, decision trees are rated as the number one group of algorithms used in predictive analysis. Decision trees are popular because they produce rules that can be easy to understand and are therefore more likely be applied to business processes. This chapter starts with examples of decision trees in order to introduce the subject, and continues with a worked example based upon the CHAID algorithm in the PAL, which is one of the simplest decision tree algorithms. The model output is best viewed in a specific data visualization, namely the decision tree viewer, which we show in PA. After describing the CHAID algorithm, we move to the slightly more complex decision tree algorithms available in the PAL and the R integration in PA, namely C4.5 and CNR Tree.

13.1   Introduction to the Decision Trees Algorithm

A decision tree is a graphical representation of the relationship between a dependent or target variable and one or more independent or input variables. The name comes from the fact that the graphical representation is in the form of a tree-shaped structure that represents a set of decisions. The tree may be binary or multi-branching, depending upon the algorithm used. Each split or branch in the tree represents a decision rule. The end of a branch is referred to as a leaf node and describes all the decisions or rules applied to get to that outcome. Some simple examples will help explain the concept.

We introduced these examples in Chapter 11. In this chapter, we go into more detail. Our first example, shown in Figure 13.1, describes a decision tree for deciding whether or not to play golf, depending on the weather, e.g., is it windy, is the outlook for rain or sunny or overcast, is the humidity high or low? The tree represents a series of decisions or rules, with the final leaf node being the outcome. In the example we derive the rules:

▸ Don't play if the outlook is rain and it's windy.

▸ Don't play if humidity is high, outlook is sunny, and it's not windy.

▸ Otherwise, go play!

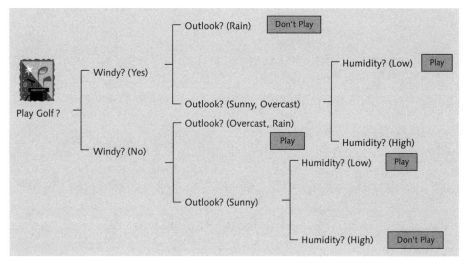

Figure 13.1   A Decision Tree to Decide Whether or Not to Play Golf

In our second example, shown in Figure 13.2, we use a decision tree to decide the attributes of people to whom we might provide a loan. In this example, we have added the number of records at each node in the tree, from which we can derive the probability or strength of the rule.

From Figure 13.2, we might derive the rule: Don't make high monthly loans to single males who rent their homes and have a low income.

This is just an artificial example and not meant to reflect reality, although my bank manager of many years ago seemed to be following it!

We can derive the probability that a person with low income will default on high monthly payments as 110 / (2+110) = 0.98.

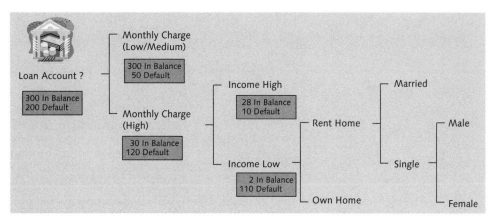

Figure 13.2 A Decision Tree to Determine Whether or Not to Give a Loan

A final example is shown in Figure 13.3, where the decision tree describes the rules to determine who to target in a mail campaign.

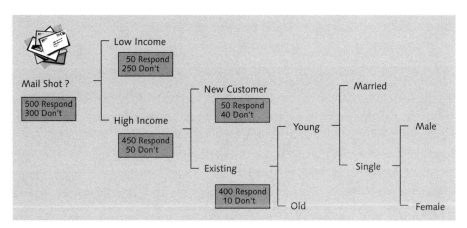

Figure 13.3 A Decision Tree to Determine to Whom to Send a Mail Shot

From the decision tree we might derive the rule: young, single, females who are existing customers with a high income are most likely to respond to our mail shot.

These examples show why decision trees are so popular: they are easy to understand and can be highly productive when deployed in business applications. Of course, in reality the trees may become very complex and consequently perhaps less useful. In this chapter, we discuss how to "prune" decision trees to make them more useful and methods whereby we can reduce the number of branches.

For now, we take the first example, the golf decision tree analysis, and apply our first decision tree algorithm, CHAID analysis, to an example data set.

13.2   CHAID Analysis

CHAID is an acronym for CHi-squared Automatic Interaction Detection. To build the decision tree, we recursively split the data to maximize the diversity of each split. We evaluate each independent variable and compare it to the dependent variable to see which provides the best split, in other words, does the best job of separating the records into groups. A measure of "diversity" is the chi-squared test, hence CHAID analysis. The chi-squared test is a very well-known statistical test and is defined as calculating the following simple equation and looking at its statistical significance:

Chi-Squared = (Observed – Expected) [2] / Expected

In this section we look at a worked example of the algorithm, then run the example in the PAL and PA, using the CHAID function of the PAL.

13.2.1   Worked Example of CHAID Analysis

The data for our worked example is shown in Figure 13.4, with 14 records each with values for the variables Outlook, Temperature, Humidity and Wind, along with the decision that was made as to whether to play golf or not. We wish to use this actual data to derive rules that we can then use to make future decisions as to whether or not to play golf, given the weather conditions.

Scenario	Outlook	Temp.	Humidity	Windy?	Class
1	Sunny	75	70	Yes	Play
2	Sunny	80	90	Yes	Don't Play
3	Sunny	85	85	No	Don't Play
4	Sunny	72	95	No	Don't Play
5	Sunny	69	70	No	Play
6	Overcast	72	90	Yes	Play
7	Overcast	83	78	No	Play
8	Overcast	64	65	Yes	Play
9	Overcast	81	75	No	Play
10	Rain	71	80	Yes	Don't Play
11	Rain	65	70	Yes	Don't Play
12	Rain	75	80	No	Play
13	Rain	68	80	No	Play
14	Rain	70	96	No	Play

Figure 13.4   The Data for the Golf Decision Tree Analysis

In an effort to derive a very simple decision tree using the data shown in Figure 13.4, we group or bin the numeric data in order to try to limit the number of branches in the tree. The fewer the number of distinct values in a variable, the fewer splits in the data to be evaluated and, consequently, the fewer branches in the tree. In our example, we bin the variables as follows, and the revised data is as shown in Figure 13.5. We will discuss the impact of binning later in this chapter. We will apply the following bins to this worked example:

Temp. <= 70 is 1, >=71 and <=80 is 2, >=81 is 3

Humidity <= 75 is 1, > 75 is 2

Scenario	Outlook	Temp.	Humidity	Windy?	Class
1	Sunny	2	1	Yes	Play
2	Sunny	2	2	Yes	Don't Play
3	Sunny	3	2	No	Don't Play
4	Sunny	2	2	No	Don't Play
5	Sunny	1	1	No	Play
6	Overcast	2	2	Yes	Play
7	Overcast	3	2	No	Play
8	Overcast	1	1	Yes	Play
9	Overcast	3	1	No	Play
10	Rain	2	2	Yes	Don't Play
11	Rain	1	1	Yes	Don't Play
12	Rain	2	2	No	Play
13	Rain	1	2	No	Play
14	Rain	1	2	No	Play

Figure 13.5 The Binned Data for the Golf Decision Tree Analysis

Now we apply the chi-squared test for each variable's value compared to the class or target variable value, calculating the observed and expected frequencies and thus the chi-squared statistic, in order to find the most significant split.

Starting with the variable Outlook, we calculate the matrix of observed Play or Don't Play decisions by the three values of Outlook: Sunny, Overcast, and Rain, as shown in Figure 13.6. There are 2 records of Sunny and Play, and 3 records of Sunny and Don't Play; 4 records with Overcast and Play, and none for Overcast and Don't Play; 3 records with Rain and Play, and 2 records for Rain and Don't Play. From the observed values, we can calculate the expected values using the totals by row and column, and then the chi-squared statistic, which for Outlook is 3.5467. It's really quite simple. If you look at the observed values for Outlook, you will note that the 4/0 split for Overcast is the clearest split and contributes most to the chi-squared calculation.

Figure 13.6 The Chi-Squared Statistic for Outlook

We continue the calculation for the other independent variables as shown in Figure 13.7.

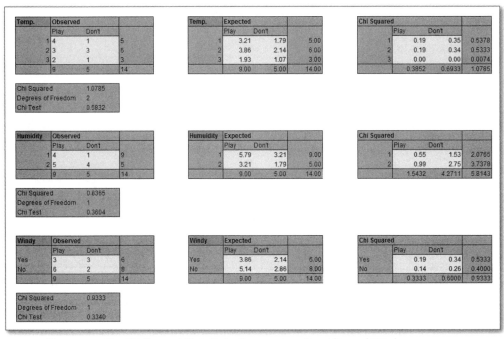

Figure 13.7 The Chi-Squared Statistic for Temperature, Humidity and Windy

We see that the highest value of the chi-squared statistic is for Outlook; hence, this is the first split in our decision tree, as shown in Figure 13.8.

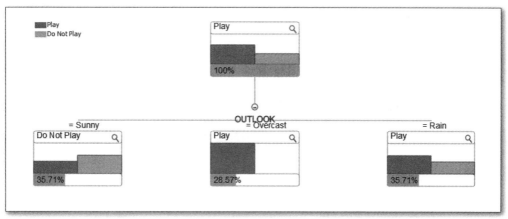

Figure 13.8 The First Split in the Decision Tree Play Golf

The first node represents all the records, plotted as 9 for Play, and 5 for Don't Play. The next level in the tree shows the 4 records for the Overcast Outlook, which are all Play, and then the outcomes for Sunny, which comprise 2 Play and 3 Don't Play, and Rain, which comprise 3 Play and 2 Don't Play. The Outlook Overcast has a single outcome, Play, and is thus a leaf node. We can already derive our first rule that if the Outlook is Overcast, Play golf.

The next split in the tree that we examine is Outlook Sunny. The chi-squared calculations are shown in Figure 13.9 and the best split is Humidity.

Now the decision tree grows to that as shown in Figure 13.10, with the branch of Humidity = 2, Play and Humidity = 1, Don't Play. These are also leaf nodes as all the records are of one class.

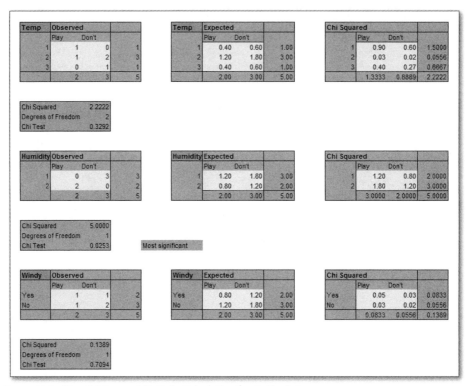

Figure 13.9 The Chi-Squared Statistic Calculation for Outlook Sunny

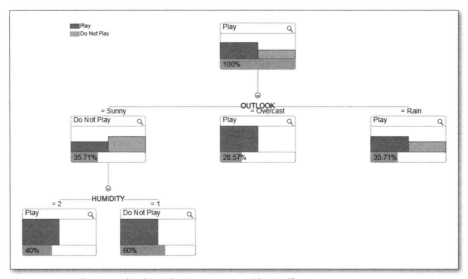

Figure 13.10 The Second Split in the Decision Tree Play Golf

To complete the tree, we analyze Rain, as shown in Figure 13.11, where we see that the most significant split is Windy.

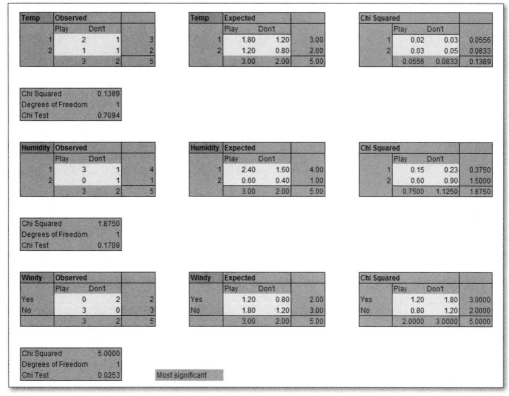

Figure 13.11 The Chi-Squared Statistic Calculation for Outlook Rain

The decision tree is shown in Figure 13.12 and we note that all leaf nodes have a single outcome so the tree is now complete.

The decision tree rules are:

▸ If the Outlook is Sunny and Humid or Rainy and Windy, Do Not Play

▸ Otherwise, Play.

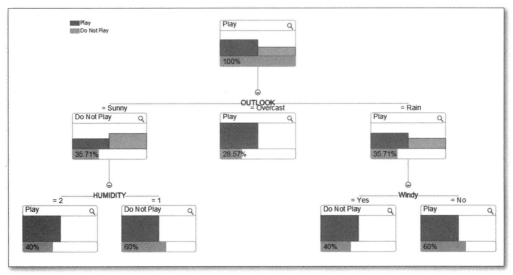

Figure 13.12 The Completed Decision Tree

We now look at performing this analysis in the PAL and also in PA.

13.2.2 CHAID Analysis in the PAL

In the Predictive Analysis Library, the algorithm name is CHAID Decision Tree and the associated function name is CREATEDTWITHCHAID.

The Input table, as shown in Table 13.1 comprises the independent variables and the final column, is the dependent or class variable.

Table	Column	Column Data Type	Description	Constraint
Data	Columns	Varchar, integer, or double	Table used to build the predictive tree model	Discrete value: integer or varchar Continuous value: integer or double

Table 13.1 The Input Table Definition for CHAID Analysis

The Parameter table is shown in Table 13.2.

Name	Data Type	Description
PERCENTAGE	Double	The percentage of the input data to be used to build the tree model. For example, if you set this parameter to 0.7, 70% of the data will be used to train the tree model, and 30% will be used to prune the tree model. Default is 1.
MIN_NUMS_RECORDS	Integer	Specifies the stopping condition. If the number of records in a node is less than the value, the algorithm will stop splitting. Default: 0
MAX_DEPTH	Integer	Specifies the stop condition. If the depth of the tree model is greater than the parameter value, the algorithm will stop splitting. Default: the number of columns in the input table that contain the training data.
IS_SPLIT_MODEL	Integer	Indicates whether the string of the tree JSON model output should be split or not. If the value is not 0, the tree model will be split, and the length of each unit is 5000. Default: 0
CONTINUOUS_COL	Integer or double	Indicates which column contains continuous variables: Integer value specifies the column position. Note that the column index starts from zero. Double value specifies the interval. If this value is not specified, the algorithm will automatically split this continuous value. Default: String or integer is a discrete attribute. Double is continuous attribute
IS_OUTPUT_RULES	Integer	If this parameter is set to 1, the algorithm will extract all the decision rules from the tree model and save them to the result table, which is used to save the PMML model. Default: 0.
PMML_EXPORT	Integer	0: The default. No export of the PMML 1: Exports the PMML tree model in a single row. 2: Exports PMML tree model in several rows, each row containing a maximum of 5000 characters.
THREAD_NUMBER	Integer	The number of threads.

Table 13.2   The Parameter Table Definition for CHAID Analysis

The output from CHAID consists of two tables, as shown in Table 13.3.

Table	Column	Data Type	Description
Tree model in JSON format	1st column	Integer	Record ID
	2nd column	Varchar or CLOB	Tree model saved as a JSON string
Tree model of PMML format	1st column	Integer	Record ID
	2nd column	Varchar or CLOB	Tree model saved as a PMML string

Table 13.3 The Output Tables Definition for K-Means

Using the data shown in Figure 13.5, the SQLScript is as follows with the parameters settings as:

```
-- The procedure generator

call SYSTEM.afl_wrapper_generator ('PAL_CREATEDT_WITH_CHAID', 'AFLPAL',
'CREATEDTWITHCHAID', PDATA);

-- The Control Table parameters

INSERT INTO PAL_CONTROL_TAB VALUES ('PERCENTAGE',null,1.0,null);
INSERT INTO PAL_CONTROL_TAB VALUES ('THREAD_NUMBER',2,null,null);
INSERT INTO PAL_CONTROL_TAB VALUES ('IS_SPLIT_MODEL',0,null,null);
INSERT INTO PAL_CONTROL_TAB VALUES ('MIN_NUMS_RECORDS',1,null,null);
INSERT INTO PAL_CONTROL_TAB VALUES ('PMML_EXPORT', 2, null, null);
INSERT INTO PAL_CONTROL_TAB VALUES ('IS_OUTPUT_RULES', 1, null, null);

-- Assume the data has been stored in table PAL_TRAINING_TAB as shown
in Figure 13.5

-- Calling the procedure

CALL PAL_CREATEDT_WITH_CHAID(PAL_TRAINING_TAB, PAL_CONTROL_TAB, PAL_
JSONMODEL_TAB, PAL_PMMLMODEL_TAB) with overview;

SELECT * FROM PAL_PMMLMODEL_TAB;
```

Listing 13.1 The PAL SQLScript for CHAID Analysis

The full code is available in the file SAP_HANA_PAL_CHAID_Example_SQLScript on the SAP PRESS website.

The Parameter Control table included the setting 'IS_OUTPUT_RULES' as 1, so the decision tree rules are output as shown in Figure 13.13.

SELECT * FROM PAL_PMMLMODEL_TAB		
	ID	PMMLMODEL
1	1	OUTLOOK=Overcast=>Play
2	2	OUTLOOK=Sunny&HUMIDITY=2=>Play
3	3	OUTLOOK=Sunny&HUMIDITY=1=>Do Not Play
4	4	OUTLOOK=Rain&Windy=Yes=>Do Not Play
5	5	OUTLOOK=Rain&Windy=No=>Play

Figure 13.13 The Rules from the Play Golf Decision Tree using CHAID

We can define and run the same analysis in SAP Predictive Analysis (PA), not only for the ease of defining such analysis but also for the visualization of the results.

13.2.3 CHAID Analysis in PA

The same analysis using PA with the data sourced from the SAP HANA table GOLF_TRAINING_TAB, and connected to the SAP HANA PAL CHAID algorithm is shown in Figure 13.14.

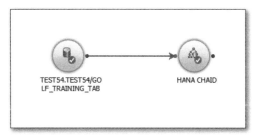

Figure 13.14 The Golf Decision Tree Analysis in PA using the PAL

The HANA CHAID component dialogue is shown in Figure 13.15 with prompts for the parameter values of the algorithm.

In the dialogue, we select the METHOD as CLASSIFICATION as the target variable is categorical, i.e., Play or Don't Play. If the target variable had been numeric, then we would have chosen the alternative of Regression.

Then we select the independent variables: Outlook, Temperature, Humidity, and Windy in the INDEPENDENT COLUMNS dropdown. Finally, we specify the target or dependent variable in the DEPENDENT COLUMN dropdown, namely CLASSLABEL.

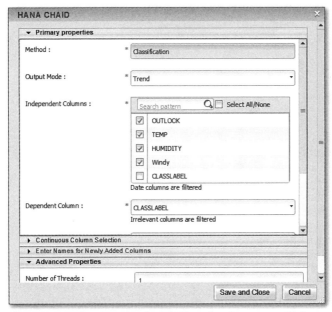

Figure 13.15 The PA HANA CHAID Algorithm Component Dialogue

After running the process, we can view the results in tabular form in PA PREDICT RESULTS view as shown in Figure 13.16.

OUTLOOK (Pri...	TEMP (Private ...	HUMIDITY (Pri...	Windy (Private...	CLASSLABEL (...	PredictedValue
Sunny	2	2	Yes	Play	Play
Sunny	2	1	Yes	Do Not Play	Do Not Play
Sunny	3	1	No	Do Not Play	Do Not Play
Sunny	2	1	No	Do Not Play	Do Not Play
Sunny	1	2	No	Play	Play
Overcast	2	1	Yes	Play	Play
Overcast	3	1	No	Play	Play
Overcast	1	2	Yes	Play	Play
Overcast	3	2	No	Play	Play
Rain	2	1	Yes	Do Not Play	Do Not Play
Rain	1	2	Yes	Do Not Play	Do Not Play
Rain	2	1	No	Play	Play
Rain	1	1	No	Play	Play
Rain	1	1	No	Play	Play

Figure 13.16 The Output from PA PAL CHAID with Predicted Values

The rules from the decision tree model are best displayed in a decision tree viewer, which is supported in PA, and was shown in Figure 13.12. The viewer includes the ability to expand and collapse the tree to navigate through it using the plus and minus signs underneath the nodes. Moreover, the values displayed in each node can be viewed by selecting the magnifying glass icon, as shown in Figure 13.17.

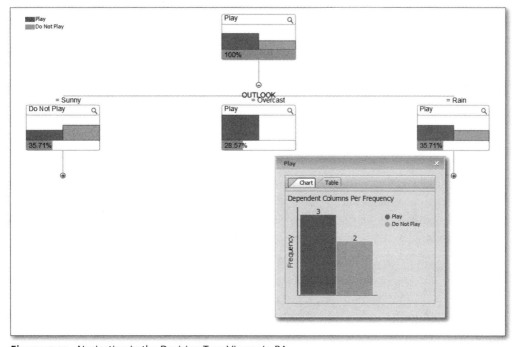

Figure 13.17 Navigation in the Decision Tree Viewer in PA

As with the process of logistic regression, where we were fitting a binary response model, we can construct the classifier confusion matrix, as shown in Figure 13.18, and, with our simple example, we have in fact got a perfect fit.

The more the variation in distinct values within a variable, the more complex the decision tree created by the CHAID algorithm. In the next section, we explore the impact of binning or grouping data.

Figure 13.18 The Classifier Confusion Matrix

13.2.4 Binning of Numeric Variables

In our worked example, we binned the numeric temperature and humidity data in order to produce a simple tree. We didn't have to do this. However, when a variable has many values, then in the CHAID algorithm, it can lead to many branches in the tree and consequently more complex rules.

If we run the data without binning the humidity data and using the values as shown in Figure 13.4, we get a decision tree with 16 nodes as opposed to the previous 8 that we saw in Figure 13.12. The new decision tree is shown in Figure 13.19.

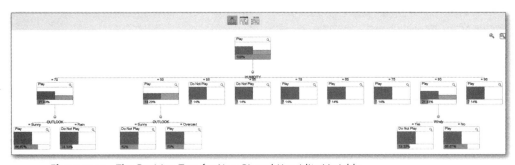

Figure 13.19 The Decision Tree for Non-Binned Humidity Variable

We can use the CONTINUOUS_COL parameter to bin the data within the CHAID algorithm as defined in Table 12.2. For example, for 3 bin boundaries b1, b2 and b3, then the interval is:

$x < b1 => 0$

$b1 <= x < b2 => 1$

$x >= b2 => 2$

In our example, we would use the following, noting that the column index starts from zero. For Temperature b1 = 71 and b2 = 81, and for Humidity we just need to set b1 = 76.

```
INSERT INTO PAL_CONTROL_TAB VALUES ('CONTINUOUS_COL',1,71,null);
INSERT INTO PAL_CONTROL_TAB VALUES ('CONTINUOUS_COL',1,81,null);
INSERT INTO PAL_CONTROL_TAB VALUES ('CONTINUOUS_COL',2,76,null);
```

Listing 13.2 The SQLScript to Bin Continuous Column Data

This listing will not be provided on the SAP PRESS website for download as it is only a slight modification of Listing 13.1.

13.2.5 Predicting using CHAID Analysis in the PAL

To make predictions we use the PAL function PREDICTWITHDT. There are two Input Tables as shown in Table 13.4. The first table comprises the independent variable data to be used for the predictions, and the second table contains the model built using CREATEDTWITHCHAID, as was shown in Listing 13.1.

Table	Column	Data Type	Description
Data to use for prediction	1st column	Integer	Record ID
	Other columns	Varchar, integer, or double	Data to be predicted or classified.
The model to be used	1st column	Integer	Record ID (starting from 0)
	2nd column	Varchar or CLOB	Serialized tree model

Table 13.4 The Input Table Definition for PREDICTWITHDT

The Parameter table specifies two parameters, as shown in Table 13.5.

Name	Data Type	Description
MODEL_FORMAT	Integer	0 (default): De-serializes the tree model from JSON format
		1: De-serializes the tree model from PMML format
THREAD_NUMBER	Integer	Number of threads

Table 13.5 The Parameter Table Definition for PREDICTWITHDT

The Output Table comprises two columns, the first column containing an ID, and the second column containing the predicted values, as shown in Table 13.6.

Table	Column	Data Type	Description
Result	1st column	Integer	Record ID
	2nd column	Varchar	Predicted values

Table 13.6 The Output Table Definition for PREDICTWITHDT

The main elements of the SQLScript are as shown in Listing 13.3, including the data to be used for the prediction. The full code is available in the file SAP_HANA_PAL_PREDICTWITHDT _Example_SQLScript on the SAP PRESS website.

```
-- The procedure generator

call SYSTEM.afl_wrapper_generator ('PAL_PREDICTWITHDT', 'AFLPAL',
'PREDICTWITHDT', PDATA);

-- The values to Predict, the Control Table parameter

INSERT INTO PAL_DATA_TAB VALUES (1,'Overcast',2,2,'No');
INSERT INTO PAL_DATA_TAB VALUES (2,'Sunny',2,1,'Yes');
INSERT INTO PAL_DATA_TAB VALUES (3,'Overcast',2,3,'Yes');
INSERT INTO PAL_DATA_TAB VALUES (4,'Overcast',2,3,'No');
INSERT INTO PAL_DATA_TAB VALUES (5,'Sunny',1,1,'Yes');
INSERT INTO PAL_DATA_TAB VALUES (6,'Rain',2,1,'Yes');
INSERT INTO PAL_DATA_TAB VALUES
```

```
(7,'Rain',1,2,'No');

INSERT INTO PAL_CONTROL_TAB VALUES ('THREAD_NUMBER',2,null,null);

-- Calling the procedure

CALL PAL_PREDICTWITHDT (PAL_DATA_TAB, PAL_CONTROL_TAB, PAL_JSONMODEL_
TAB, PAL_RESULT_TAB) with overview;

SELECT * FROM PAL_RESULT_TAB;
```
Listing 13.3 The PAL SQLScript for CHAID Analysis Prediction

The results become as shown in Figure 13.20, and shows the predictions for the values entered in the SQLScript. The predictions are based on the rules produced by the model as shown in Figure 13.13.

	ID	CLASSLABEL
1	1	Play
2	2	Do Not Play
3	3	Play
4	4	Play
5	5	Do Not Play
6	6	Do Not Play
7	7	Play

Figure 13.20 The Predictions from the Golf Decision Tree

We can also predict the model in PA, by saving it after it has been run, and then presenting the new data to the saved model in order to obtain the predicted values.

Three decision tree algorithms are available in the PAL plus the R integration in PA, and now we look at the second one, namely C4.5.

Just to note: these are various decision tree algorithms; however, their application to business problems is the same. Selecting algorithms was discussed in Chapter 4, and overall you might run the different decision tree algorithms and see which one is best, as discussed in the next section.

13.3 The C4.5 Algorithm

The C4.5 algorithm is used to build decision trees and, from them, rules. In general, decision trees recursively split the data on some criteria that maximizes the usefulness of the split. The CHAID algorithm uses the chi-squared statistic to determine the best splits. The C4.5 works by splitting the data based on the variable that provides the maximum information gain to the model from the split. Information is measured using a concept called entropy. As with the CHAID algorithm, each subset defined by the first split of the data is then split again, and the process repeats until the subsets cannot be split any further or the process is terminated on some stopping criteria. Finally, the lowest level splits are re-examined, and those that do not contribute significantly to the value of the model are removed or pruned. C5.0 is a commercial version available from the author, Professor Ross Quinlan. C4.5 and ID3 are earlier versions of the algorithm. ID3 stands for Iterative Dichotomiser 3. There is an amusing observation in Berry and Linoff's book *Data Mining Techniques*:

> *We have not heard an explanation for the name C4.5, but we can guess that Professor Quinlan's background is mathematics rather than marketing.*

Entropy is a concept from information theory and is a measure of information content, using a scale from 1, which represents complete uncertainty, to 0, which represents complete certainty. Information Theory, developed by Claude Shannon (1948), defines this value of uncertainty as entropy, a probability-based measure used to calculate the amount of uncertainty. The concept is better explained using an example.

A coin has heads on one side, tails on the other, and there is a 50/50 probability of a head or tail coming up when the coin is tossed. The entropy is defined as 1. The outcome is completely uncertain; it could be a head or tail. If the probability is 25/75, then the entropy is a little lower as we are less uncertain. If the coin had heads on both sides, the outcome would be completely certain. The entropy would then be defined as 0.

The goal in decision trees is to get very low entropy, reflecting high certainty, in order to make the most accurate decisions and classifications. In order to calculate the entropy, the following formula is used, which represents the sum of all the events, of the probability of the event times the log to the base 2 of the probability of the event.

$E(S) = Sum \ (-p_i * log_2 p_i)$

The minus sign is used to create a positive value for the entropy as the log of a fraction is negative. The logarithm is used to make more compact and efficient decision trees. The base 2 is used as information is sometimes measured in bits 0 or 1.

Take the two class outcome problem of tossing a coin with the outcome heads or tails. For an unbiased coin, where either outcome is equally likely, e.g., 0.5, then the entropy is calculated as:

$Entropy = -0.5 \ log_2 \ 0.5 - 0.5 \ log_2 \ 0.5 = 1$

For a biased coin, with both sides heads, for example:

$Entropy = -1 \ log_2 \ 1 - 0 \ log_2 \ 0 = -1 * 0 - 0 * log_2 0 = 0$

If the coin had a 75% chance of head and 25% chance of tail then:

$Entropy = -0.75 \ log_2 \ 0.75 - 0.25 \ log_2 \ 0.25 = 0.8113$

The uncertainty or entropy of the decision as to which variable to split on can now be calculated. The entropy will change when the information is narrowed down, in other words, when the dataset is split on a particular piece of information. The branches at that information split that lower the entropy can be calculated. The difference between the initial entropy and the new entropy after following a branch, gives the amount of information gained. Low entropy means less uncertainty, less impurity, less heterogeneity in the data, which is what we want to maximize as we progress with building the decision tree.

In terms of our Play Golf example, at the base of the tree we have 9 records Play, and 5 records Don't Play. The Entropy of (9,5) or E(9,5) is:

$= E(9/14, 5/14)$

$= E(0.64, 0.36)$

$= -(0.64 \ Log2 \ 0.64) - (0.36 \ Log2 \ 0.36)$

$= 0.41 + 0.53$

$= 0.94$

The Entropy (Play Golf, Outlook) is equal to:

= *Prob(Sunny)*E(2,3) + Prob(Overcast)*E(4,0) + Prob(Rain)*E(3,2)= 5/14 * 0.97 + 4/14 * 0 + 5/14 * 0.97*

= *0.69354*

The Information Gain is therefore 0.94 – 0.69354 = 0.24675.

The Split Information is the entropy of the whole attribute or field and is equal to:

= *E(Sunny)+E(Overcast)+E(Rain)*

= *0.53051 + 0.51639 + 0.53051*

= *1.57741.*

The Gain Ratio is Information Gain/Split Information:

= *0.24675 / 1.57741*

= *0.15643*

The information gain ratio biases the decision tree against considering attributes with a large number of distinct values, so it solves a weakness of information gain. Information gain applied to attributes that can take on a large number of distinct values can learn the training set too well. For example, suppose that we are building a decision tree for some data describing a business's customers and one of the input attributes might be the customer's Social Security number. This attribute has a high information gain, because it uniquely identifies each customer, but we do not want to include it in the decision tree. Deciding how to treat customers based on their Social Security numbers is unlikely to generalize to customers we haven't seen before.

The above analysis calculated the Gain Ratio for Play Golf/Outlook. In Figure 13.21 we calculate all the Gain Ratios–Outlook, Temperature, Humidity, and Windy.

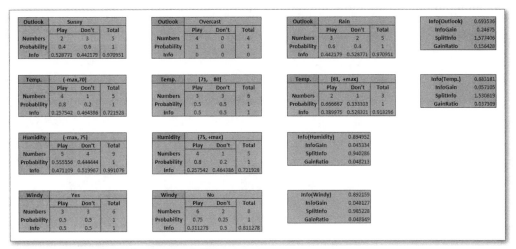

Figure 13.21 Gain Ratios for the Play Golf Data

The maximum Gain Ratio is Outlook, with a value of 0.15643, so that becomes our first split in the decision tree, as shown in Figure 13.22.

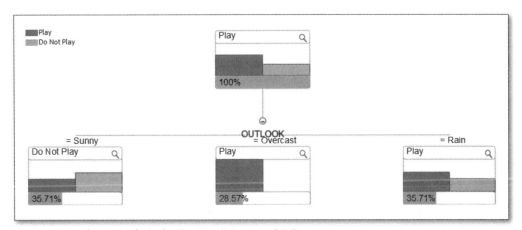

Figure 13.22 The First Split in the Decision Tree using C 4.5

Outlook, Overcast is a leaf node as all records in the node are Play. The entropy is zero, meaning complete certainty.

We repeat the calculations for Outlook/Sunny and Outlook/Rain to find the best splits and eventually derive the complete decision tree shown in Figure 13.23.

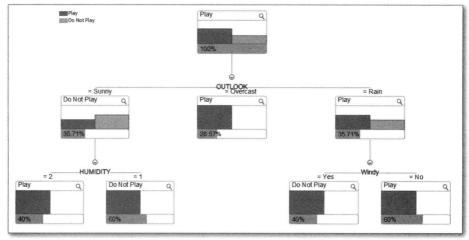

Figure 13.23 The Complete Decision Tree using C 4.5

The decision tree rules are:

▶ If the Outlook is Sunny and Humid; or Rainy and Windy, Do Not Play.

▶ Otherwise, Play.

These are the same rules as we derived using the CHAID algorithm, and we would expect this, given such a simple dataset.

We will now look at performing this analysis in the PAL and also in PA.

13.3.1 C4.5 in the PAL

In the Predictive Analysis Library, the algorithm name is C4.5 Decision Tree and the associated function name is CREATEDT. The Input Table, Parameter Table and Output Tables are the same as for CHAID Analysis, as was shown in Table 13.1, Table 13.2, and Table 13.3.

Using the data in Figure 13.5, the SQLScript is as follows with the parameters settings as:

```
-- The procedure generator

call SYSTEM.afl_wrapper_generator
('PAL_CREATEDT', 'AFLPAL', 'CREATEDT', PDATA);

-- The Control Table parameters

INSERT INTO PAL_CONTROL_TAB VALUES ('PERCENTAGE',null,1.0,null);
INSERT INTO PAL_CONTROL_TAB VALUES ('THREAD_NUMBER',2,null,null);
INSERT INTO PAL_CONTROL_TAB VALUES ('IS_SPLIT_MODEL',1,null,null);
INSERT INTO PAL_CONTROL_TAB VALUES ('MIN_NUMS_RECORDS',1,null,null);
INSERT INTO PAL_CONTROL_TAB VALUES ('PMML_EXPORT', 2, null, null);
INSERT INTO PAL_CONTROL_TAB VALUES ('IS_OUTPUT_RULES',1,null,null);

-- Assume the data has been stored in table PAL_TRAINING_TAB as shown
in Figure 13.5

-- Calling the procedure

CALL PAL_CREATEDT(PAL_TRAINING_TAB, PAL_CONTROL_TAB, PAL_JSONMODEL_TAB,
PAL_PMMLMODEL_TAB) with overview;

SELECT * FROM PAL_PMMLMODEL_TAB;
```
Listing 13.4 The PAL SQLScript for C4.5

The full code is available in the file SAP_HANA_PAL_C45_Example_SQLScript on the SAP PRESS website.

The parameter control table included the setting 'IS_OUTPUT_RULES' as 1, so the decision tree rules are output as shown in Figure 13.24.

	ID	PMMLMODEL
SELECT * FROM PAL_PMMLMODEL_TAB		
1	1	OUTLOOK=Overcast=>Play
2	2	OUTLOOK=Sunny&HUMIDITY=2=>Play
3	3	OUTLOOK=Sunny&HUMIDITY=1=>Do Not Play
4	4	OUTLOOK=Rain&Windy=Yes=>Do Not Play
5	5	OUTLOOK=Rain&Windy=No=>Play

Figure 13.24 The Rules from the Play Golf Decision Tree using C4.5

In practice, the question arises as to which algorithm should be selected, and the answer depends on several things. Which model gives the best fit, (depending of course on how we define that)? As we saw in the Classifier Confusion Matrix, there are several measures of model quality. Which model gives the most comprehensible rules? There is also the option of combining the predictions of models and for a classification variable, use voting for example as the choice of the most popular outcome. This is referred to as ensemble modeling and has been shown to produce more robust models.

We can define and run the same analysis in SAP Predictive Analysis (PA), not only for the ease of defining such analysis but also for the visualization of the results.

13.3.2 C4.5 in PA

Here is the same analysis using PA with the data sourced from the SAP HANA table GOLF_TRAINING_TAB and connected to the SAP HANA PAL C4.5 algorithm, as shown in Figure 13.25.

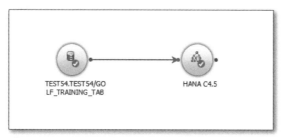

Figure 13.25 The Golf Decision Tree Analysis in PA using the PAL C4.5

The HANA C4.5 component dialogue is shown in Figure 13.26 with prompts for the parameter values of the algorithm.

The values entered into the dialogue are the same as we entered for the CHAID analysis dialogue in PA, where we defined the method as Classification, and then the independent or input variables in the INDEPENDENT COLUMNS and DEPENDENT COLUMN FIELDS, and the target variable.

After running the process, we can view the results in tabular form in PA PREDICT RESULTS, as shown in Figure 13.27.

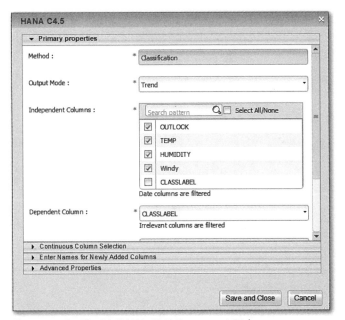

Figure 13.26 The PA HANA C4.5 Component Dialogue

OUTLOOK (Pri...	TEMP (Private ...	HUMIDITY (Pri...	Windy (Private...	CLASSLABEL (...	PredictedValue
Sunny	2	2	Yes	Play	Play
Sunny	2	1	Yes	Do Not Play	Do Not Play
Sunny	3	1	No	Do Not Play	Do Not Play
Sunny	2	1	No	Do Not Play	Do Not Play
Sunny	1	2	No	Play	Play
Overcast	2	1	Yes	Play	Play
Overcast	3	1	No	Play	Play
Overcast	1	2	Yes	Play	Play
Overcast	3	2	No	Play	Play
Rain	2	1	Yes	Do Not Play	Do Not Play
Rain	1	2	Yes	Do Not Play	Do Not Play
Rain	2	1	No	Play	Play
Rain	1	1	No	Play	Play
Rain	1	1	No	Play	Play

Figure 13.27 The Output from PA PAL C4.5 with the Predicted Values

The rules from the decision tree model are best displayed in the decision tree viewer of PA. Given that for this simple example, the decision trees are the same for CHAID and C4.5, as shown in Figure 13.12, along with the Classifier Confusion Matrix, as shown in Figure 13.18, and with our simple example, we have in fact got a perfect fit.

Within PA, we can save the C4.5 model, which was created from the PAL in SAP HANA, by right-clicking on the executed model and choosing SAVE AS MODEL, as shown in Figure 13.28.

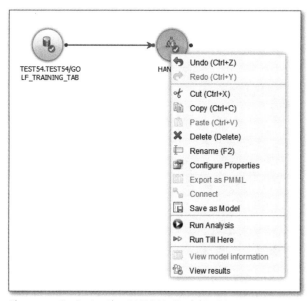

Figure 13.28 Saving the C4.5 PAL Model in PA

The saved model then appears in the SAVED MODELS tab of PA, as shown in Figure 13.29, which you can then drag onto the ANALYSIS EDITOR or workspace and connect to new data for prediction or scoring.

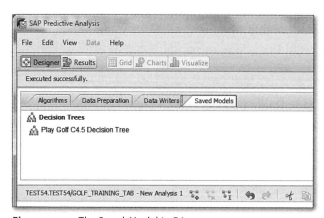

Figure 13.29 The Saved Model in PA

The R integration in PA includes support for the R CNR Tree algorithm, which we can also use to build and analyze data using decision trees.

13.4 CNR Tree—Classification and Regression Trees

CNR Tree or C&RT, sometimes simply referred to as CART, as with the other decision tree algorithms, uses recursive partitioning to split the data into branches with nodes with similar target or dependent field values. The CNR Tree algorithm starts by examining the input fields to find the best split, measured by the reduction in an impurity index that results from the split. The split defines two subgroups, each of which is subsequently split into two more subgroups, and so on, until one of the stopping criteria is met. All splits are binary with only two subgroups. CNR Tree uses classification trees for discrete outcomes and regression trees for continuous outcomes, hence the name of the algorithm. We show an example of both.

For a classification example, we use the data shown in Figure 13.30, where we wish to predict a plant's type depending upon the petal length and petal width. We are looking for the best splits of the data in order to predict the plant type.

CaseID	Plant_Type	Petal_Length	Petal_Width
ID 1	1	8.54	1.70
ID 2	1	2.04	0.80
ID 3	1	5.72	0.80
ID 4	1	1.86	1.30
ID 5	1	7.87	1.50
ID 6	1	9.54	1.60
ID 7	2	5.34	2.60
ID 8	2	2.19	2.60
ID 9	2	7.19	3.10
ID 10	2	4.19	3.20
ID 11	2	5.86	3.50
ID 12	2	4.03	3.20

Figure 13.30 The Example Data Set for CNR Tree Classification

The algorithm first orders the data for each attribute. This is shown in Figure 13.31.

Order the Input Variable - Petal Length				Order the Input Variable - Petal Width		
Case ID	**Plant Type**	**Petal Length**		**Case ID**	**Plant Type**	**Petal Width**
ID 4	1	1.86		ID 2	1	0.80
ID 2	1	2.04		ID 3	1	0.80
ID 8	2	2.19		ID 4	1	1.30
ID 12	2	4.03		ID 5	1	1.50
ID 10	2	4.19		ID 6	1	1.60
ID 7	2	5.34		ID 1	1	1.70
ID 3	1	5.72		ID 7	2	2.60
ID 11	2	5.86		ID 8	2	2.60
ID 9	2	7.19		ID 9	2	3.10
ID 5	1	7.87		ID 10	2	3.20
ID 1	1	8.54		ID 12	2	3.20
ID 6	1	9.54		ID 11	2	3.50

Figure 13.31 The Example Data Ordered by Attribute

Starting with the variable Petal Length, we examine all the potential splits in the variable to see which maximizes the difference between Plant Type 1 and 2, using the chi-squared test of Actual versus Expected, as was used in CHAID Analysis. This is shown for the first three splits in Figure 13.32.

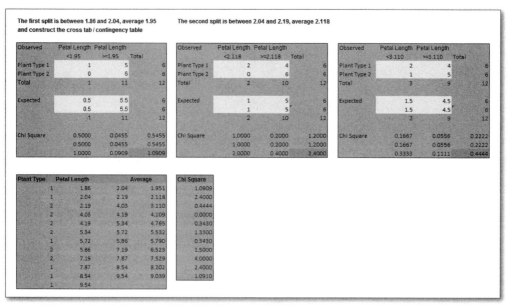

Figure 13.32 Evaluation of the Splits for Petal Length

All eleven splits are evaluated and the most significant for Petal Length is between 7.18 and 7.59 with a chi-squared value of 4.0.

We do the same evaluation for the variable Petal Width, with the results as shown in Figure 13.33.

The first split is between 0.80 and 1.30, average 1.05 and construct the cross tab / contingency table

Observed	Petal Width <1.05	Petal Width >=1.05	Total
Plant Type 1	2	4	6
Plant Type 2	0	6	6
Total	2	10	12
Expected	1	5	6
	1	5	6
	2	10	12
Chi Square	1.0000	0.2000	1.2000
	1.0000	0.2000	1.2000
	2.0000	0.4000	2.4000

The second split is between 1.30 and 1.50, average 1.40

Observed	Petal Width <1.40	Petal Width >=1.40	Total
Plant Type 1	3	3	6
Plant Type 2	0	6	6
Total	3	9	12
Expected	1.5	4.5	6
	1.5	4.5	6
	3	9	12
Chi Square	1.5000	0.5000	2.0000
	1.5000	0.5000	2.0000
	3.0000	1.0000	4.0000

Observed	Petal Width <1.55	Petal Width >=1.55	Total
Plant Type 1	4	2	6
Plant Type 2	0	6	6
Total	4	8	12
Expected	2	4	6
	2	4	6
	4	8	12
Chi Square	2.0000	1.0000	3.0000
	2.0000	1.0000	3.0000
	4.0000	2.0000	6.0000

Plant Type	Petal Width	Average	Chi Square
1	0.80	0.80	
1	0.80 1.30	1.05	2.4000
1	1.30 1.50	1.40	4.0000
1	1.50 1.60	1.55	6.0000
1	1.60 1.70	1.65	8.5714
1	1.70 2.60	2.15	12.0000
2	2.60 2.60	2.60	
2	2.60 3.10	2.85	6.0000
2	3.10 3.20	3.15	4.0000
2	3.20 3.20	3.20	
2	3.20 3.50	3.35	1.0909
2	3.50		

Figure 13.33 Evaluation of the Splits for Petal Width

All eleven splits are evaluated and the most significant for Petal Width is between 1.70 and 2.60, which has an average value of 2.15 with a chi-squared value of 12.0.

Consequently, the first split in our decision tree will be based on the rule:

Plant Type = 1 if Petal Width is < 2.15 Otherwise Plant Type = 2

We can run this analysis in PA using the R CNR Tree algorithm, as shown in Figure 13.34.

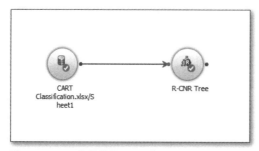

Figure 13.34   R CNR Tree Analysis in PA

The R CNR Tree component dialogue is shown in Figure 13.35. Note, the Method selected is Classification, as we have a binary target variable.

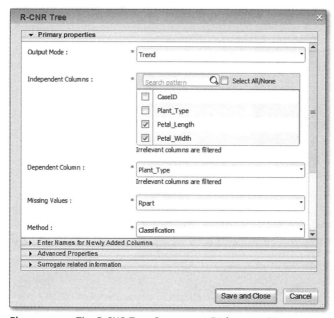

Figure 13.35   The R CNR Tree Component Dialogue in PA

The output from the decision tree can be viewed in the decision tree viewer in PA using the PREDICT RESULTS VISUALIZE option, as shown in Figure 13.36.

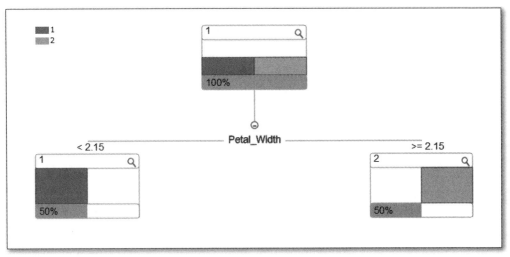

Figure 13.36 The Decision Tree Viewer for the Plant Type Classification

Now, we follow a similar process for the Regression Tree using the example data shown in Figure 13.37.

Case ID	Plant Type	Petal Length	Petal Width
ID 1	0.64	8.54	1.70
ID 2	0.66	2.04	0.80
ID 3	0.73	5.72	0.80
ID 4	0.59	1.86	1.30
ID 5	0.81	7.87	1.50
ID 6	0.72	9.54	1.60
ID 7	0.90	5.34	2.60
ID 8	1.31	2.19	2.60
ID 9	1.11	7.19	3.10
ID 10	1.04	4.19	3.20
ID 11	1.25	5.86	3.50
ID 12	1.09	4.03	3.20

Figure 13.37 The Example Data Set for CNR Tree Regression

The algorithm firstly orders the data for each attribute. This is shown in Figure 13.38.

Starting with the variable Petal Length, we examine all the potential splits in the variable to see which maximizes the difference between Plant Type 1 and 2, using the variance in the data resulting from a split. We want to find the split whereby the variance of the data in each split is minimized, in other words the splits result in compact sub-groups. This is shown for the first three splits in Figure 13.39.

Order the Input Variable - Petal Length

Case ID	Plant Type	Petal Length
ID 4	0.59	1.86
ID 2	0.66	2.04
ID 8	1.31	2.19
ID 12	1.09	4.03
ID 10	1.04	4.19
ID 7	0.90	5.34
ID 3	0.73	5.72
ID 11	1.25	5.86
ID 9	1.11	7.19
ID 5	0.81	7.87
ID 1	0.64	8.54
ID 6	0.72	9.54

Order the Input Variable - Petal Width

Case ID	Plant Type	Petal Width
ID 2	0.66	0.80
ID 3	0.73	0.80
ID 4	0.59	1.30
ID 5	0.81	1.50
ID 6	0.72	1.60
ID 1	0.64	1.70
ID 7	0.90	2.60
ID 8	1.31	2.60
ID 9	1.11	3.10
ID 10	1.04	3.20
ID 12	1.25	3.20
ID 11	1.09	3.50

Figure 13.38 The Example Data Ordered by Attribute

	Branch 1	Branch 2
	0.59	0.66
		1.31
		1.09
		1.04
		0.90
		0.73
		1.25
		1.11
		0.81
		0.64
		0.72
Average	0.5900	0.9327
Variance	0	0.0521
Weighted Ave. Var		0.0478

	Branch 1	Branch 2
	0.59	1.31
	0.66	1.09
		1.04
		0.90
		0.73
		1.25
		1.11
		0.81
		0.64
		0.72
Average	0.6250	0.9600
Variance	0.0012	0.0491
Weighted Ave. Var		0.0412

	Branch 1	Branch 2
	0.59	1.09
	0.66	1.04
	1.31	0.90
		0.73
		1.25
		1.11
		0.81
		0.64
		0.72
Average	0.8533	0.9211
Variance	0.1051	0.0395
Weighted Ave. Var		0.0559

Split		Ave.	Weighted Ave. Variance
1.86	2.04	1.95	0.0478
2.04	2.19	2.12	0.0412
2.19	4.03	3.11	0.0559
4.03	4.19	4.11	0.0567
4.19	5.34	4.77	0.0559
5.34	5.72	5.53	0.0560
5.72	5.86	5.79	0.0567
5.86	7.19	6.52	0.0532
7.19	7.87	7.53	0.0458
7.87	8.54	8.20	0.0467
8.54	9.54	9.04	0.0537
9.54			

Figure 13.39 Evaluation of the Splits for Petal Length

For Petal Length, the first split is between 1.86 and 2.04, with an average of 1.95, which results in two branches, with values as shown. The first branch comprises just the record with value 0.59, and the second branch comprising all the other records. The second split is between 2.04 and 2.19, with two records in one branch, and 10 records in the other branch, and so on. All eleven splits are evaluated and the minimum variance from the splits is 0.0412.

We do the same evaluation for the variable, Petal Width, with the results as shown in Figure 13.40.

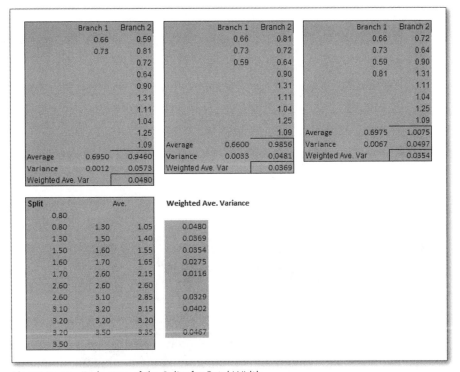

Figure 13.40 Evaluation of the Splits for Petal Width

All eleven splits are evaluated. The most significant for Petal Width is between 1.70 and 2.60, which has an average value of 2.15 with a weighted average variance of 0.0116. This is less than any of the split for Petal Length and consequently, the first split in our decision tree will be based on the rule

- Plant Type = 1 if Petal Width is < 2.15
- Otherwise, Plant Type = 2.

We can run this analysis in PA using the R CNR Tree algorithm, as was shown in Figure 13.34, and the dialogue as was shown in Figure 13.35, other than the method is regression.

The output from the decision tree is viewed in the RESULTS GRID View, as shown in Figure 13.41.

Case_ID	Plant_Type	Petal_Length	Petal_Width	PredictedValues
ID 1	0.64	8.54	1.70	0.69
ID 2	0.66	2.04	0.80	0.69
ID 3	0.73	5.72	0.80	0.69
ID 4	0.59	1.86	1.30	0.69
ID 5	0.81	7.87	1.50	0.69
ID 6	0.72	9.54	1.60	0.69
ID 7	0.90	5.34	2.60	1.12
ID 8	1.31	2.19	2.60	1.12
ID 9	1.11	7.19	3.10	1.12
ID 10	1.04	4.19	3.20	1.12
ID 11	1.25	5.86	3.50	1.12
ID 12	1.09	4.03	3.20	1.12

Figure 13.41 The Grid View for the Plant Type Regression

We can use the PREDICT VISUALIZE option to plot the actual plant type and the predicted, as shown in Figure 13.42.

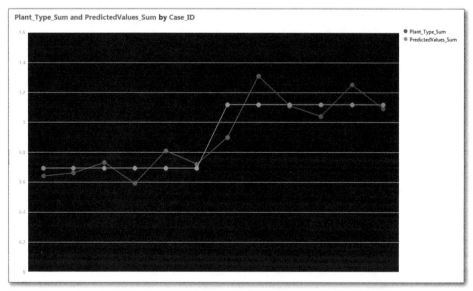

Figure 13.42 Actual and Predicted Plant Type using CNR Tree

When we specified the R-CNR Tree component dialogue we had left the default number of splits at 10 in the advanced properties, which means that the minimum number of observations in a node must be 10 before attempting a split. If we set the value to 5, we will have a deeper decision tree with more nodes and we will get a more accurate prediction, as shown in Figure 13.43.

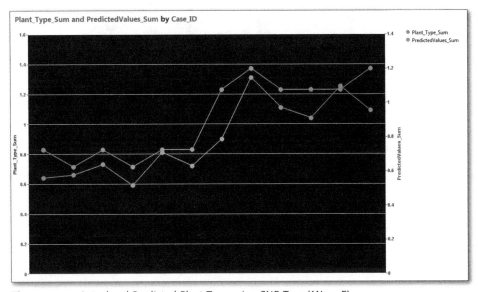

Figure 13.43 Actual and Predicted Plant Type using CNR Tree (Min = 5)

If we set the value to 2, meaning a node can only have 2 records and still be split, we get an almost perfect model fit, as shown in Figure 13.44.

We have a situation parallel to the issue of model overfitting that we saw in regression analysis, where we are effectively adding more variables to the model and getting better model fits but at the possible expense of accurately predicting new data. It provides another example of why, for classification models, it is important to judge model quality using a train and test approach whereby we train the model on one part of the data set, then test it on the other part, which was not used in the training phase.

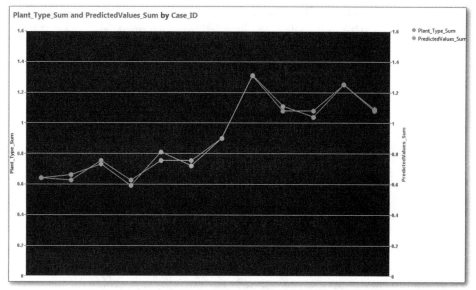

Plant_Type_Sum and PredictedValues_Sum by Case_ID

Figure 13.44 Actual and Predicted Plant Type using CNR Tree (Min = 2)

13.5 Decision Trees and Business Rules

Our examples of decision trees have been very simple in order to help explain how the algorithms work. Of course, in reality, decision trees will be far more complex, and the practical issues become ones of how we address the inherent complexity resulting from the many distinct values that may exist in the input data, which may lead to complexity in the decision tree; how we decide the parameter values for the algorithms; how we manage model overfitting; how we prune the tree; and how we combine the results of several algorithms.

As we have seen in this chapter, decision trees produce rules; however, before we can implement them in business processes, we need to consider the practicality and business context for those mathematically derived rules.

In Figure 13.45, we show a subset of a more realistic example of a decision tree containing many rules. The tree was built using the US Census data set, a well-known data set for data mining. This data is available, along with many other data mining data sets, from the Center for Machine Learning and Intelligent Systems at the University of California, Irvine: *http://archive.ics.uci.edu/ml/datasets.html.*

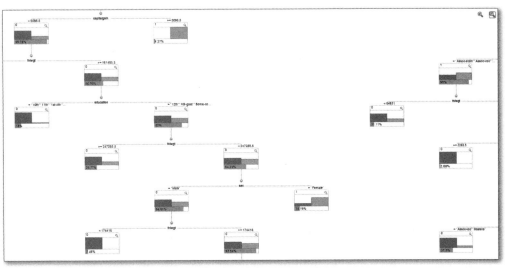

Figure 13.45 A Subset of a Decision Tree for the US Census Data Set

Business Rules Management in SAP HANA is a core component of the extended application services built into SAP HANA, and it enables application developers to easily add business rules to their applications. These rules are designed to be easily maintained by end users without writing code, through a simple intuitive interface that gives users the ability to simulate, look for trends and patterns, and modify physical data based on actions. The rules are defined in decision tables with two examples shown in Figure 13.46.

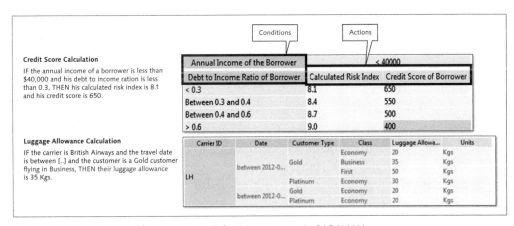

Figure 13.46 Decision Tables in Business Rules Management in SAP HANA

The rules from a decision tree can be exported in a text file or via PMML. They need to be reviewed in terms of their business context and translated into a business rules engine before they can be implemented into a business process.

13.6 Strengths and Weaknesses of Decision Trees

The main strength of decision trees is that they may produce rules that can be implemented in business processes. This is a very important consideration, as predictive analysis is about improving business processes and decision makers are more likely to implement the results of an analysis if those results are clear and understood. Another significant strength of decision trees is that they can handle both continuous numeric variables and categorical variables, whereas many algorithms are restricted to purely numeric data. Decision trees provide a clear indication of variable importance in terms of the initial splits of the data, the length of the branches of the tree, and the probabilities of the leaf node outcomes. Finally, they can perform classification analysis without requiring significant computation, which, for very large data sets with a large number of independent variables, enables the full exploration of the solution in terms of sensitivity analysis and model ensembling.

Their main weakness is that they are clearly sensitive to the initial split, which may not be a significant one, in which case the whole solution may be quite volatile. Added to this weakness is that they generally examine just a single field at a time, a step at a time. However, these weaknesses can be evaluated by using sensitivity analysis and model ensembling, and overall the strengths of decision trees far outweighs their weaknesses, hence their popularity.

13.7 Summary

In this chapter we discussed in detail the important topic of decision tree analysis, one of the most popular groups of algorithms in predictive analysis. We looked at the two decision tree algorithms available in the PAL, namely CHAID Analysis and C4.5, and then the CNR Tree algorithm in the R integration for PA. We covered the important topic of model over fitting, and the need in practice to integrate a business rules engine with the rule output of a decision tree analysis.

In the next chapter we look at our final predictive analysis algorithm for classification, the very simple, but very attractive, K Nearest Neighbor algorithm.

This final chapter on classification analysis presents the K Nearest Neighbor algorithm, one of the simplest algorithms in this category.

14   Classification Analysis—K Nearest Neighbor

The algorithm's name describes it succinctly. To predict a value, look at the actual K records that are most similar to the record to be predicted and use them to make the prediction.

The K Nearest Neighbor (KNN) algorithm is among the simplest of all machine learning algorithms; hence its popularity. An algorithm's simplicity should not be a reason to reject it, as complexity is no guarantee of performance. Furthermore, analyses that are understood by management are more likely to be implemented. The KNN algorithm can be used as a form of benchmark in that if other algorithms cannot significantly improve upon it, then the extra costs and effort are not worth it.

14.1   Introduction

Our objective is to use records containing data regarding a dependent variable or class variable, and a range of independent or input variables, as a basis to predict a dependent or class variable for new data that contains only the independent variables. A record is classified by a majority vote of its neighbors, with the record being assigned to the class most common among its K nearest neighbors. K is a positive integer, typically small. If K = 1, then the record is simply assigned to the class of its nearest neighbor.

The training data are records containing the independent variables, each with a class label. The training phase of the algorithm consists only of storing the records and class labels of the training data. In the classification or prediction phase, K is a user defined constant, and an unlabeled record is classified by assigning the label, which is most frequent among the K training records nearest to that unlabeled record. The Euclidean distance is used as the distance metric. For K > 1, the K nearest records class value for the prediction is either a simple voting scheme for the most popular class or a distance-weighted voting.

A worked example is always the easiest way to understand how an algorithm works.

14.2 Worked Example

We introduced the algorithm in Chapter 11 as part of a general introduction to classification analysis. We will now build on that introduction and explore the algorithm in depth, using both the PAL and PA.

We start by bringing the data that we used in the example in Chapter 11 into a table in SAP HANA, named DATA_TAB, as shown in Figure 14.1. There are 24 records, two independent variables X1 and X2, and a dependent or class variable named TYPE, with a value of 0 or 1. We want to use this actual data, or training data as it is more generally called, as the basis to make predictions of the class variable TYPE, based on the input of new records with just the values of X1 and X2.

SELECT * FROM DATA_TAB				
	ID	TYPE	X1	X2
1	1	1	3	1
2	2	1	1	2
3	3	1	1	2
4	4	1	4	7
5	5	1	4	4
6	6	1	4	4
7	7	1	7	2
8	8	1	3	4
9	9	1	7	7
10	10	1	5	1
11	11	1	5	8
12	12	1	5	6
13	13	0	9	5
14	14	0	6	9
15	15	0	6	5
16	16	0	9	6
17	17	0	7	4
18	18	0	5	7
19	19	0	6	8
20	20	0	8	10
21	21	0	4	9
22	22	0	10	8
23	23	0	7	6
24	24	0	10	4

Figure 14.1 The Data Table for KNN in SAP HANA

The data shown in Figure 14.1 is plotted in Figure 14.2 with the records for TYPE = 1 plotted as blue stars and the records for TYPE = 0 plotted as red squares. The two triangles represent new records with values for X1 and X2 for which we wish to predict the TYPE.

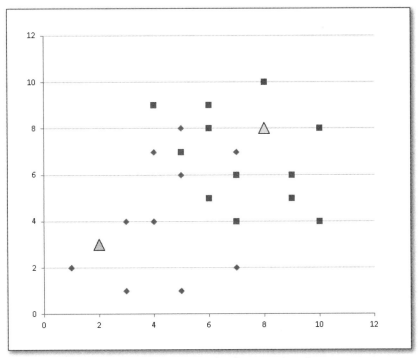

Figure 14.2 Plot of the Data in Figure 14.1 for the KNN Algorithm

The records to be predicted are also brought into a table in SAP HANA, named CLASSDATA_TAB, and shown in Figure 14.3. They are represented by the triangles in the plot in Figure 14.2.

SELECT * FROM CLASSDATA_TAB			
	ID	X1	X2
1	1	8	8
2	2	2	3

Figure 14.3 The Data to be Predicted using the KNN Algorithm

We now look at performing the analysis in the PAL and then in PA.

14.2.1 K Nearest Neighbor Analysis in the PAL

In the Predictive Analysis Library, the algorithm name is KNN and the associated function name is KNN.

KNN has two input tables, one containing the training data and the other containing the class data to be predicted. These are defined as shown in Table 14.1. The dependent variable or class variable can be integer or varchar, whereas the independent or input variables must be numeric, either integer or double, given that we use distance measures to calculate the nearest neighbors.

Table	Column	Column Data Type	Description
Training Data	1st column	Integer or varchar	Record ID
	2nd column	Integer or varchar	Class type or dependent variable
	Other columns	Integer or double	Attribute data or independent variables
Class Data	1st column	Integer or varchar	Record ID
	Other columns	Integer or double	Attribute data or independent variables

Table 14.1 The Input Table Definition for KNN

The Parameter table is shown in Table 14.2.

Name	Data Type	Description
K_NEAREST_NEIGHBORS	Integer	The number of nearest neighbors. In other words the value of K. Default value: 1
ATTRIBUTE_NUM	Integer	The number of attributes or independent variables. Default value: 1

Table 14.2 The Parameter Table Definition for KNN

Name	Data Type	Description
VOTING_TYPE	Integer	Voting type: 0 = majority voting 1 = distance-weighted voting Default value: 1
THREAD_NUMBER	Integer	The number of threads. Default value: 1

Table 14.2 The Parameter Table Definition for KNN (Cont.)

The output from KNN simply consists of the predictions, as defined in Table 14.3.

Table	Column	Data Type	Description
Result	1st column	Integer or varchar	Record ID
	2nd column	Integer or varchar	Class type or dependent variable

Table 14.3 The Output Table Definition for KNN

Using the data shown in Figure 14.1 and Figure 14.3, the SQLScript is as follows along with the parameters settings:

```
-- The procedure generator

call SYSTEM.afl_wrapper_generator ('palKNN','AFLPAL','KNN',PDATA);

-- The Control Table parameters

INSERT INTO #CONTROL_TAB VALUES ('K_NEAREST_NEIGHBOURS',5,null,null);
INSERT INTO #CONTROL_TAB VALUES ('ATTRIBUTE_NUM',2,null,null);
INSERT INTO #CONTROL_TAB VALUES ('VOTING_TYPE',0,null,null);
INSERT INTO #CONTROL_TAB VALUES ('THREAD_NUMBER',8,null,null);
-- Assume the data has been stored in the tables DATA_TAB and
CLASSDATA_TAB as shown in Figures 14.1 and 14.3

-- Calling the procedure

CALL palKNN(DATA_TAB, CLASSDATA_TAB, "#CONTROL_TAB", RESULTS_TAB) with
overview;
```

```
SELECT * FROM RESULTS_TAB;
```
Listing 14.1 The PAL SQLScript for KNN

The full code is available in the file SAP_HANA_PAL_KNN_Example_SQLScript on the SAP PRESS website.

The predicted results are as shown in Figure 14.4. They are as we would have expected, given the plot of the data in Figure 14.2 for this simple example.

SELECT * FROM RESULTS_TAB		
	ID	Type
1	1	0
2	2	1

Figure 14.4 The Predicted Results using KNN in the PAL

Using the same data, we should rerun the analysis for different values of the parameter K_NEAREST_NEIGHBORS to see how it affects the predicted values. In other words, we should use sensitivity analysis to review the robustness of our model and the confidence of our predictions. As we saw in Figure 11.11, the solution can be sensitive to different values of K. In this example, where the data is very clear cut, values of K=5 through to 10 make no difference to the predictions. However, values of K = 1 and 2, result in different predictions for record 1. Specifically, it becomes TYPE = 1. You can see that this will be the result if you again look at the data in Figure 14.1, and the top right triangle representing the point (8,8). As with all analysis, the impact of different values of an algorithm's parameters on the solution should be investigated.

We can define and run the same analysis in SAP Predictive Analysis (PA).

14.2.2 KNN Analysis in PA using the PAL KNN Algorithm

Here is the same analysis using PA. The PAL KNN algorithm has two input tables, one being the model training data set, the other being the data that we wish to predict. Unlike other classification algorithms, KNN does not store a trained model. It uses the training data set in conjunction with the data set to be predicted.

In PA, you need to input these two tables, and you start by inputting the data set to be predicted. Figure 14.5 shows the data to be predicted using the PREPARE view in PA and sourced from the SAP HANA table, PREDICTKNN_DATA_TAB.

ID	X1	X2
1	8.00	8.00
2	2.00	3.00

Figure 14.5 The Data to be Predicted using the KNN Algorithm

Then in the PREDICT View, we connect this data source to the SAP HANA PAL KNN algorithm, as shown in Figure 14.6.

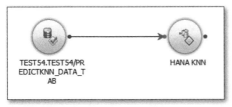

TEST54.TEST54/PR
EDICTKNN_DATA_T
AB

HANA KNN

Figure 14.6 The K Nearest Neighbor Analysis in PA using the PAL

The HANA KNN component dialogue is shown in Figure 14.7 with prompts for the parameter values of the algorithm. We have selected the independent variables as X1 and X2, the value of K as 5, and the majority voting method in the VOTING TYPE dropdown.

HANA KNN   ✕

▾ **Primary properties**

Independent Columns :   *   [Search pattern 🔍] ☐ Select All/None
                              ☐ ID
                              ☑ X1
                              ☑ X2
                              Irrelevant columns are filtered

Neighborhood Count :   *   5

Voting Type :   *   Majority Voting   ▾

Missing Values :   *   Remove   ▾

▸ Training Data Selection
▸ Enter Names for Newly Added Columns
▸ Advanced Properties

                                              [Save and Close] [Cancel]

Figure 14.7 The PA HANA KNN Component Dialogue

The dialogue shown in Figure 14.7 also contains the prompts for the training data set, which for our example are shown in Figure 14.8. Given that the data is stored in an SAP HANA table, you need to specify the SCHEMA NAME and then select the TABLE NAME, with a search capability to assist. We have selected the schema name TEST54 and the table KNN_DATA_TAB.

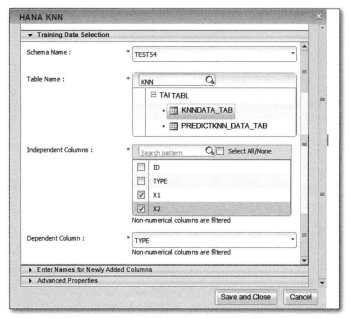

Figure 14.8 The Training Data Selection for KNN in PA

After you have run the analysis and moved to the RESULTS view, the predicted data is as shown in Figure 14.9. The prediction for the record (8,8) is 0, and for the record (2,3) is 1.

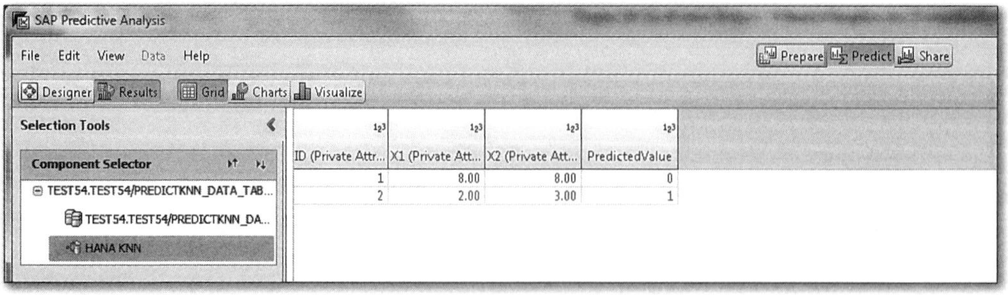

Figure 14.9 The Predicted Data from the KNN Algorithm

PA combines the independent and dependent variables in the GRID View for easier consumption, whereas the PAL shows just the record ID and the prediction in the Results Table.

You could add a simple write component to the analysis to write the predicted results to a table in SAP HANA, as shown in Figure 14.10.

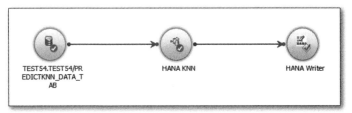

TEST54.TEST54/PR
EDICTKNN_DATA_T
AB

HANA KNN

HANA Writer

Figure 14.10 The PA Analysis for KNN and Storing the Results in SAP HANA

An extension of our analysis could be to run the algorithm using the training data set, KNNDATA_TAB, as the also the predict data set, to see how good the predictions, or fitted values, are of the actual data using different values of K. The results are shown in Figure 14.11, with K = 5.

ID (Private Attr...	TYPE (Private ...	X1 (Private Att...	X2 (Private Att...	PredictedValue
1	1	3.00	1.00	1
2	1	1.00	2.00	1
3	1	1.00	2.00	1
4	1	4.00	7.00	1
5	1	4.00	4.00	1
6	1	4.00	4.00	1
7	1	7.00	2.00	0
8	1	3.00	4.00	1
9	1	7.00	7.00	0
10	1	5.00	1.00	1
11	1	5.00	8.00	0
12	1	5.00	6.00	1
13	0	9.00	5.00	0
14	0	6.00	9.00	0
15	0	6.00	5.00	0
16	0	9.00	6.00	0
17	0	7.00	4.00	0
18	0	5.00	7.00	1
19	0	6.00	8.00	0
20	0	8.00	10.00	0
21	0	4.00	9.00	0
22	0	10.00	8.00	0
23	0	7.00	6.00	0
24	0	10.00	4.00	0

Figure 14.11 KNN Analysis in PA showing the Actual and Predicted Values

The data in Figure 14.11 shows that records 7, 9 and 11 are mis-classified with the actual TYPE being 1, and predicted being 0; record 18 is mis-classified with the actual TYPE being 0, and predicted being 1. With K=5, again we can see the logic of the calculations by reviewing the data as was shown in Figure 14.1. Given that we have a binary target variable, we could construct a Classifier Confusion Matrix, as was shown in Section 12.6.2, from which we have measures of the quality of the model such as specificity and sensitivity.

We could experiment with different values of K, and explore the solution space; however, we should note that with K = 1, we will have a perfect model, as the predicted record is the same as the actual record.

14.2.3 Categorical Target or Class Variable

So far, our examples of the KNN algorithm have been based on an integer value for the target or class variable; however, the variable can also be categorical. Figure 14.12 shows a variation of the data we used in Figure 14.1, where the TYPE variable of value 1 is replaced by the character A, and 0 is replaced by the character B.

	SELECT * FROM DATA_TAB			
	ID	TYPE	X1	X2
1	1	A	3	1
2	2	A	1	2
3	3	A	1	2
4	4	A	4	7
5	5	A	4	4
6	6	A	4	4
7	7	A	7	2
8	8	A	3	4
9	9	A	7	7
10	10	A	5	1
11	11	A	5	8
12	12	A	5	6
13	13	B	9	5
14	14	B	6	9
15	15	B	6	5
16	16	B	9	6
17	17	B	7	4
18	18	B	5	7
19	19	B	6	8
20	20	B	8	10
21	21	B	4	9
22	22	B	10	8
23	23	B	7	6
24	24	B	10	4

Figure 14.12 The Training Data for KNN with a Categorical Target Variable

For this example, we use the same data to be predicted as before, which was shown in Figure 14.3, as it is only the target or class variable that we have changed.

After running the analysis in SAP HANA Studio, we get the Results table as shown in Figure 14.13. We see that the prediction for record ID 1 is B, and for record ID 2 is A.

SELECT * FROM RESULTS_TAB		
	ID	TYPE
1	1	B
2	2	A

Figure 14.13 The Predicted Results from KNN

Given that the KNN algorithm supports both integer and categorical values for the target or class variable, we can apply it to many of the applications that decision tress are used for; therefore, we have an additional type of algorithm to address those applications.

14.3   Strengths and Weaknesses of the KNN Algorithm

The main strength of the KNN algorithm is that it is elegant and logical, and therefore easy to understand. These are good attributes in predictive analysis as complexity does not necessarily equate to value.

The main weakness of the algorithm is that its predictions may be very sensitive to the chosen value of K. However, as with all analyses where the solution may be highly dependent on the algorithm's parameter values, this weakness can be addressed by experimenting with various values and examining the robustness of the solution.

As with many algorithms, outliers can affect the solution. Small values of K will be more sensitive to outliers than larger values of K. The solution is, of course, to examine the data for outliers prior to the analysis.

Overall, the strengths of the algorithm outweigh the weaknesses, and the impact of the latter can be minimized.

14.4 Summary

In this chapter we looked at one of the simplest predictive analysis algorithms, the K Nearest Neighbor algorithm, with an example in both the PAL and PA. We demonstrated how it supports both integer and categorical target variables. The algorithm is a very useful addition to the range of algorithms available for the major field of classification analysis.

In the next part, we will look at the more advanced Predictive analysis, including time series analysis and text analysis. We will conclude the part and book with customer applications. In the next chapter we introduce the very important topic of time series analysis.

PART V
Advanced Predictive Analysis

This chapter describes the major topic of time series analysis using the SAP HANA Predictive Analysis Library, the integration of R, and SAP Predictive Analysis.

15 Time Series Analysis

The chapter begins with an introduction to the many applications of time series analysis, from forecasting daily sales for thousands of inventory items to forecasting a few monthly key performance indicators. In terms of algorithms, we start with the simplest of all the time series analysis methods. These are referred to as naïve methods because of their simplicity, yet they are potentially valuable as benchmarks for what can be done for little cost, in comparison to more sophisticated methods. The chapter then proceeds with an explanation of the three methods of exponential smoothing: Single Exponential Smoothing, Double Exponential Smoothing, and Triple Exponential Smoothing, with worked examples using the SAP HANA Predictive Analysis Library (PAL) and SAP Predictive Analysis (PA). Finally, we also look at how bi-variate regression methods can be used for time series analysis.

15.1 Introduction to Time Series Analysis

A time series is a series of data points, usually at consecutive points in time and at uniform time intervals. Examples of time series are daily stock market prices and volumes, product sales over time, telemetry readings, monthly key performance indicators, daily temperatures, website visits per hour–the list is endless, as are the applications. Time series do not necessarily have to be data points over time. They generally are, but sometimes we just want to analyze a vector of data points with no inherent periodicity. Also, the data is not always at uniform time intervals, for example, we may have sales data for weekdays but not weekends or for public holidays.

Time series analysis is the name given to methods or algorithms for analyzing time series data in order to extract useful patterns. Time series forecasting is the use of a model to predict future values based on the previously observed or actual values.

Time series are very frequently plotted via line charts, as shown in Figure 15.1.

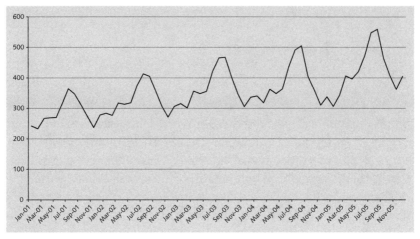

Figure 15.1 Time Series Plot of Airline Passengers 2001 to 2005

The immediate question becomes: Why do I need predictive algorithms to forecast the next few data points? I can see what they are and just draw them, as in Figure 15.2.

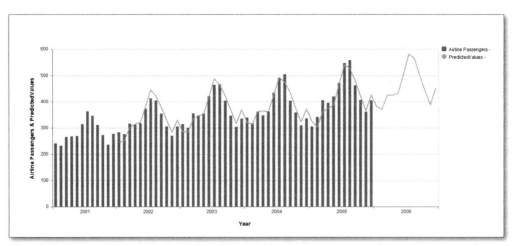

Figure 15.2 Projection of the Time Series using Visual Inspection

We are certainly good at pattern recognition, but we may be biased, for example, be overly optimistic about sales growth. Is the eyeball method, as it is called, regularly repeatable? An amusing alternative name for the eyeball method is BFE Analysis, or Bold Forward Estimating. Do we adapt to errors, or, even more of an issue, do we record and monitor any forecasting errors? The key question, however, is whether the process is scalable. In inventory control and supply chain applications, there may be thousands of product sales data to be projected, and clearly we then need an automated methodology. In fact, many of the time series analysis algorithms available were developed specifically for such applications.

Before we start our review of time series analysis algorithms, it is important to understand the basic patterns of time series data, as they fundamentally determine the appropriate algorithms.

15.2   Time Series Patterns

There are three basic patterns of time series. The first pattern is stationary, which means it is neither increasing nor decreasing, nor is it exhibiting a seasonal pattern. It is essentially a small random walk around a constant value. An example is shown in Figure 15.3. Time series algorithms for forecasting stationary time series focus on projections based on constant values of the actual data such as the average, or where a constant and zero trend line can be fitted.

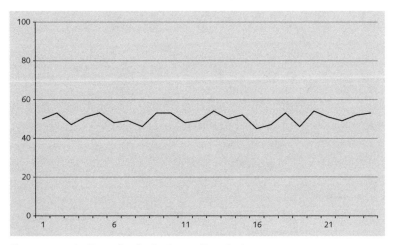

Figure 15.3 An Example of a Stationary Time Series

The second time series data pattern is a trend, with an example shown in Figure 15.4.

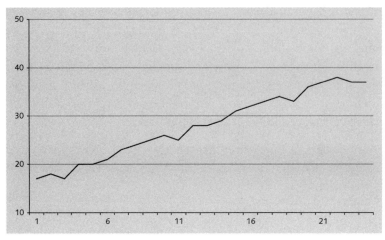

Figure 15.4 An Example of a Time Series with a Trend

Time series algorithms for forecasting time series with trends focus on identifying the trend and rate of change, which could be linear and positively increasing, as in Figure 15.4, or non-linear, increasing, or decreasing.

The third time series data pattern is seasonal, with an example shown in Figure 15.5.

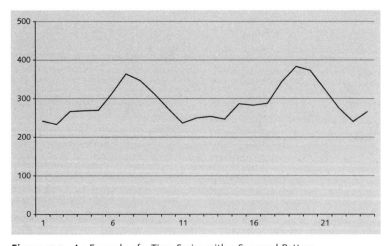

Figure 15.5 An Example of a Time Series with a Seasonal Pattern

Time series algorithms for forecasting time series with seasonality focus on identifying the periodicity of the data and the amplitude of the variation.

The three patterns can, of course, be combined, whereby we have a seasonal pattern with a trend and some randomness within it, as shown in Figure 15.6.

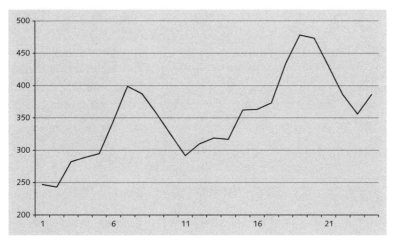

Figure 15.6   An Example of a Time Series with a Seasonal and Trend Pattern

With such time series, our algorithms will look to determine the trend, the seasonality, and any additional random variation.

There are other time series analysis patterns, for example, spikes in the data, step changes, a ramp as a short term trend, and combinations of all of these.

We start our review of time series algorithms with the simplest of all algorithms ever devised, although analogous to the K Nearest Neighbor algorithm with K=1, namely naïve methods. They are called naïve because they are so simple, but that does not mean they have no value. They also form a good basis for the understanding of the other methods of time series analysis described in this chapter.

15.3   Naïve Methods

The very simplest forecasting method is as follows–tomorrow equals today; in other words, the forecast of the next data point is equal to the value of the current data point. It is sometimes referred to as the Naïve 1 forecasting method. In mathematical notation:

$$F_{t+1} = X_t$$

where F is the forecast, X the actual value, and t the period number. When we look at forecasting the weather, it often feels like the best forecast of tomorrow's weather is to assume it will be the same as today.

The Naïve 1 method seems too silly to be sensible, but for data that is behaving randomly, it is a method that can outperform more sophisticated methods. Importantly, it can be used as a basis for comparing other algorithms to see whether they are significantly better to warrant the time and costs involved in more sophisticated analyses.

We can extend the method to: tomorrow equals the average of today and yesterday, known as Naïve 2. Our forecasting equation becomes

$$F_{t+1} = (X_t + X_{t-1}) / 2$$

This can be expanded to taking the average of all the data points, and using that as the forecast, or the median or the trimmed mean, in fact any measure of central tendency of the data. These approaches are fine for stationary time series, but clearly not for time series exhibiting trends or seasonality.

For stationary data, using the average to forecast future values means that all the data points have equal input to the calculation. A possible improvement would be to weight the more recent data points more highly than older data points, on the principle that the older the data points, the less importance they should be given.

This idea leads us to concepts of exponential smoothing.

15.4 Single Exponential Smoothing

Single or Simple Exponential Smoothing is a weighted average of the past. Mathematically it is expressed as

$$F_{t+1} = \alpha X_t + \alpha (1- \alpha) X_{t-1} + \alpha (1- \alpha)^2 X_{t-2} + \ldots + \alpha (1- \alpha)^N X_{t-N}$$

where α, known as alpha, is a smoothing constant between 0 and 1.

For example:

If α is 0.1, then the weights are 0.1, 0.09, 0.081, 0.0729...

If α is 0.5, then the weights are 0.5, 0.25, 0.125, 0.0625...

If α is 0.9, then the weights are 0.9, 0.81, 0.729, 0.6561...

The higher the value of alpha (α), the greater the weight, or importance, that is given to the more recent actual values.

The above equation can be shown to be equal to $F_{t+1} = \alpha X_t + (1-\alpha) F_t$

Now the computation becomes very easy, but we have to start the process with the first forecast, and that is where different starting methods can lead to different forecasts.

15.4.1 Worked Example

A worked example of Single Exponential Smoothing is shown in Figure 15.7.

In the worked example, we use the starting method that $F_2 = X_1$. In other words, the first forecast is equal to the previous periods actual.

		Forecast for Various Values of Alpha				Mean Squared Error		
	Value of alpha	0.1	0.5	0.9		0.1	0.5	0.9
Period	Actual							
1	200.0							
2	135.0	200.0	200.0	200.0		4225.0	4225.0	4225.0
3	195.0	193.5	167.5	141.5		2.3	756.3	2862.3
4	197.5	193.7	181.3	189.7		14.8	264.1	61.6
5	310.0	194.0	189.4	196.7		13447.9	14550.4	12833.5
6	175.0	205.6	249.7	298.7		938.3	5578.2	15294.6
7	155.0	202.6	212.3	187.4		2262.7	3288.3	1047.6
8	130.0	197.8	183.7	158.2		4598.4	2880.7	797.3
9	220.0	191.0	156.8	132.8		839.2	3989.7	7599.7
10	277.5	193.9	188.4	211.3		6984.4	7935.6	4384.8
11	235.0	202.3	233.0	270.9		1070.3	4.2	1287.2
12		205.6	234.0	238.6				
Analysis of Errors					Average	3438.3	4347.2	5039.4

Figure 15.7   A Worked Example of Single Exponential Smoothing

It is easier to review the analysis in a plot of the actual and fitted values of the time series for the different values of the smoothing constant alpha. In our example, we have used 0.1, 0.5, and 0.9. This is shown in Figure 15.8, with the actual data series shown by a solid line and the fitted data shown by a dotted line.

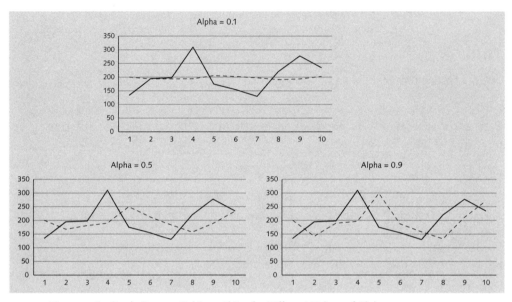

Figure 15.8 Single Exponential Smoothing for Different Values of Alpha

The charts in Figure 15.8 show that for lower values of alpha, the fitted data has a fairly constant value, in fact close to the mean, whereas for high values of alpha, the fitted data reacts much faster to changes in the actual data. If alpha is equal to 1, we then have the Naïve 1 forecasting method.

Figure 15.7 shows that, of the three values of alpha, the best value is 0.1, in that it minimizes the mean sum of squares of the difference between actual and fitted, the usual measure of the performance of time series analysis algorithms.

15.4.2 Single Exponential Smoothing in the PAL

In the Predictive Analysis Library, the algorithm name is Single Exponential Smoothing and the associated function name is SINGLESMOOTH.

The Input table is defined as Table 15.1, and is simply the time series data.

Table	Column	Column Data Type	Description
Data	1st column	Integer	Record ID
	2nd column	Integer or double	The raw data

Table 15.1 The Input Table for Single Exponential Smoothing in the PAL

The Parameter Table is shown in Table 15.2

Name	Data Type	Description
RAW_DATA_COL	Integer	The column number that contains the raw data. Default value: 1 (Note that column numbering starts from 0)
ALPHA	Double	The value of the smoothing constant alpha ($0 < \alpha < 1$). Default value: 0.1
FORECAST_NUM	Integer	The number of values to be forecast. When it is set to 1, the algorithm forecasts one value. Default value: 0
STARTTIME	Integer	Start time of the raw data sequence. Default value: 1

Table 15.2 The Parameter Table Definition for SINGLESMOOTH

The output from SINGLESMOOTH simply consists of the fitted values and the forecasts, as shown in Table 15.3.

Table	Column	Data Type	Description
Result	1st column	Integer	Record ID
	2nd column	Integer or double	Output results – the fitted and forecast values.

Table 15.3 The Output Table Definition for SINGLESMOOTH

The data that we used in our worked example, as shown in Figure 15.7, and the SQLScript is as shown in Listing 15.1 along with the parameters settings:

```
-- The procedure generator

call SYSTEM.afl_wrapper_generator ('SINGLESMOOTH_TEST','AFLPAL','SINGLE
SMOOTH',PDATA);

-- The Control Table parameters

INSERT INTO CONTROL_TAB VALUES ('RAW_DATA_COL',1,null,null);
INSERT INTO CONTROL_TAB VALUES ('ALPHA',null,0.1,null);
INSERT INTO CONTROL_TAB VALUES ('STARTTIME',2002,null,null);
INSERT INTO CONTROL_TAB VALUES ('FORECAST_NUM',1,null,null);

-- Assume the data has been stored in the table SINGLE_TAB as shown in
Figure 15.7

-- Calling the procedure
CALL SINGLESMOOTH_TEST(SINGLE_TAB, CONTROL_TAB, RESULT_TAB) with
overview;
SELECT * FROM RESULTS_TAB;
```
Listing 15.1 The PAL SQLScript for SINGLESMOOTH

The full code is available in the file SAP_HANA_PAL_SINGLESMOOTH_Example_
SQLScript on the SAP PRESS website.

The output results are as shown in Figure 15.9.

	SELECT * FROM RESULT_TAB	
	TIME	OUTPUT
1	2,003	200
2	2,004	193.5
3	2,005	193.65
4	2,006	194.035
5	2,007	205.6315
6	2,008	202.56...
7	2,009	197.81...
8	2,010	191.03...
9	2,011	193.92...
10	2,012	202.28...
11	2,013	205.55...

Figure 15.9 The Output Results from the SINGLESMOOTH PAL Function

Note that the parameter RAW_DATA_COL column numbering starts from 0, so in our worked example, it is column 1 in the control parameter, as the second column contains the raw data.

Also, with the STARTTIME parameter you need to be careful. This number is attached to the first value of the raw data, but when shown in the Result Tab, for Single Exponential Smoothing, the first value shown is 2003 in our example, as there is no Result/Fitted value for 2002.

The predicted value or forecast is 205.55. SINGLESMOOTH only forecasts one period ahead. If you want more periods, just repeat the value, as the method supports only stationary time series.

We can define and run the same analysis in SAP Predictive Analysis (PA).

15.4.3 Single Exponential Smoothing in PA using the PAL

The same analysis using PA is shown in Figure 15.10, with the input data sourced from the SAP HANA table named SINGLE_TAB connected to the algorithm HANA Single Exponential Smoothing. The process is defined in PA, but executed in-database in SAP HANA.

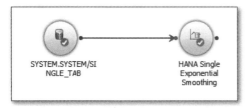

Figure 15.10 SAP HANA In-Database Single Exponential Smoothing in PA

The SAP HANA Single Exponential Smoothing component dialogue is shown in Figure 15.11, with prompts for the parameter values of the algorithm. We have selected the same prompt values that we used in the PAL SQLScript as shown in Listing 15.1, for example the value of the smoothing constant alpha is set to 0.1.

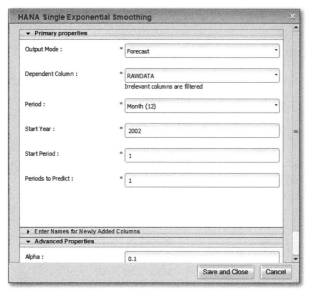

Figure 15.11 The PA Component Dialogue for HANA Single Exponential Smoothing

After you have run the analysis in PA and moved to the RESULTS View, the fitted and predicted data is as shown in Figure 15.12, in the column named PREDICTED-VALUES, which, of course, matches the output from the PAL, as shown in Figure 15.9. The predicted value is 205.56, rounded to two decimal places.

ID (Private Attr...	RAWDATA (Pri...	Month	PredictedValues
1	200.00	1	
2	135.00	2	200.00
3	195.00	3	193.50
4	197.50	4	193.65
5	310.00	5	194.04
6	175.00	6	205.63
7	155.00	7	202.57
8	130.00	8	197.81
9	220.00	9	191.03
10	277.50	10	193.93
11	235.00	11	202.28
		12	205.56

Figure 15.12 The Fitted Data for Months 2 to 11, and Predicted Data for Month 12

As usual, PA also offers excellent default visualizations for every algorithm. For Single Exponential Smoothing, the chart is as shown in Figure 15.13.

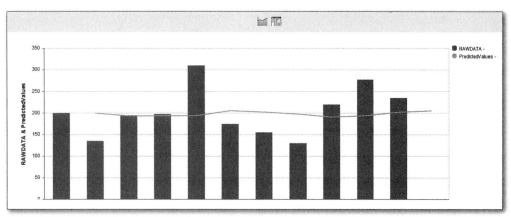

Figure 15.13 PA Visualization for Single Exponential Smoothing

Single Exponential Smoothing is suitable for stationary time series but performs poorly for time series with trends and seasonality. To account for trends in the data, we use Double Exponential Smoothing.

15.5 Double Exponential Smoothing

Single Exponential Smoothing will always lag behind a trend. To address this, we have Double Exponential Smoothing, which comprises a stationary element and a trend element, and applies two smoothing constants, one for the stationary element and the other for the trend.

There are several variations of Double Exponential Smoothing. The specific one that we use in the PAL is Holt's Two-Parameter Model.

Mathematically, it is expressed as:

$S_t = \alpha X_t + (1- \alpha) (S_{t-1} + b_{t-1})$ ... the stationary element

$b_t = \beta (S_t - S_{t-1}) + (1 - \beta) b_{t-1}$ ... the trend element

$F_{t+m} = S_t + b_t * m$ ... where m is the number of periods forecast

The calculations are very easy, but we have to start the process with the first forecast and, as with Single Exponential Smoothing, that is where different starting methods can lead to different forecasts.

In our worked example, we use the method that the first value of $S_1 = X_1$ and the first value for the trend is $b_1 = X_2 - X_1$.

15.5.1 Worked Example

A worked example of Double Exponential Smoothing is shown in Figure 15.14, where we have 24 periods, such as two years of monthly data, of actual data and we wish to predict 6 periods ahead.

Period	Actual	St	Bt	Ft
1	143.0	143.00	9.00	
2	152.0	152.00	9.00	152.00
3	161.0	161.00	9.00	161.00
4	139.0	154.47	7.88	170.00
5	137.0	149.65	6.97	162.35
6	174.0	165.33	7.59	156.62
7	142.0	157.43	6.48	172.92
8	141.0	152.43	5.65	163.91
9	162.0	160.05	5.79	158.08
10	180.0	172.93	6.30	165.84
11	164.0	171.60	5.75	179.24
12	171.0	174.17	5.53	177.36
13	206.0	192.88	6.47	179.70
14	193.0	196.17	6.25	199.35
15	207.0	204.71	6.41	202.41
16	218.0	214.57	6.66	211.12
17	229.0	225.12	6.94	221.23
18	225.0	228.52	6.68	232.06
19	204.0	219.57	5.56	235.21
20	227.0	226.07	5.63	225.13
21	223.0	227.34	5.31	231.69
22	242.0	237.33	5.65	232.65
23	239.0	240.99	5.51	242.98
24	266.0	256.27	6.21	246.49
25				262.48
26				268.69
27				274.90
28				281.11
29				287.32
30				293.53

Figure 15.14 Worked Example of Double Exponential Smoothing

Again, it is easier to review the analysis in a plot of the actual and fitted values of the time series, and the projections. This is shown in Figure 15.15, with the actual data series shown by a solid line and the fitted data shown by a dotted line.

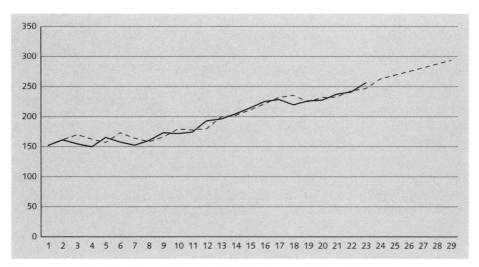

Figure 15.15 Plot of the Worked Example of Double Exponential Smoothing

The chart in Figure 15.15 shows how Double Exponential Smoothing incorporates the trend in the time series.

15.5.2 Double Exponential Smoothing in the PAL

In the Predictive Analysis Library, the algorithm name is Double Exponential Smoothing and the associated function name is DOUBLESMOOTH.

The Input table is the same as that defined for Single Exponential Smoothing in Table 15.1.

The Parameter table is the same as in Table 15.2, with the addition of the beta parameter as shown in Table 15.4.

Name	Data Type	Description
BETA	Double	The value of the smoothing constant beta ($0 < \beta < 1$). Default value: 0.1

Table 15.4 The Beta Parameter Definition for DOUBLESMOOTH

The output table definition for DOUBLESMOOTH is the same as for SINGLES-MOOTH as was shown in Table 15.3.

The data that we used in our worked example, as shown in Figure 15.14, and the SQLScript is as follows in Listing 15.2 along with the parameters settings:

```
-- The procedure generator

call SYSTEM.afl_wrapper_generator ('DOUBLESMOOTH_TEST','AFLPAL','DOUBLE
SMOOTH',PDATA);

-- The Control Table parameters

INSERT INTO CONTROL_TAB VALUES ('RAW_DATA_COL',1,null,null);
INSERT INTO CONTROL_TAB VALUES ('ALPHA',null,0.501,null);
INSERT INTO CONTROL_TAB VALUES ('BETA',null,0.072,null);
INSERT INTO CONTROL_TAB VALUES ('STARTTIME',1,null,null);
INSERT INTO CONTROL_TAB VALUES ('FORECAST_NUM',6,null,null);

-- Assume the data has been stored in the table DOUBLE_TAB as shown in
Figure 15.14

-- Calling the procedure

CALL DOUBLESMOOTH_TEST(DOUBLE_TAB, CONTROL_TAB, RESULT_TAB) with
overview;
SELECT * FROM RESULT_TAB;
```

Listing 15.2 The PAL SQLScript for DOUBLESMOOTH

The full code is available in the file SAP_HANA_PAL_DOUBLESMOOTH_Example_ SQLScript on the SAP PRESS website.

The output results are as shown in Figure 15.16.

SELECT * FROM RESULT_TAB		
	TIME	OUTPUT
1	2	152
2	3	161
3	4	170
4	5	162.35...
5	6	156.61...
6	7	172.92...
7	8	163.90...
8	9	158.08...
9	10	165.83...
10	11	179.23...
11	12	177.35...
12	13	179.69...
13	14	199.35...
14	15	202.41...
15	16	211.12...
16	17	221.22...
17	18	232.06...
18	19	235.20...
19	20	225.13...
20	21	231.69...
21	22	232.65...
22	23	242.98...
23	24	246.49...
24	25	262.47...
25	26	268.68...
26	27	274.89...
27	28	281.10...
28	29	287.31...
29	30	293.52...

Figure 15.16   The Output Results from the DOUBLESMOOTH PAL Function

Again, note that you need to be careful with the variable STARTTIME. This number is attached to the first value of the raw data, but when shown in the RESULT Tab, for Double Exponential Smoothing, the first value shown is 2 in our example, as there is no Result/Fitted value for 1. The 6 forecast periods are therefore TIME for 25, 26, 27, 28, 29 and 30, with the values 262.47, 268.68 etc.

We can define and run the same analysis in PA.

15.5.3   Double Exponential Smoothing in PA using the PAL

The same analysis using PA is shown in Figure 15.17, with the input data sourced from the SAP HANA table named DOUBLE_TAB connected to the algorithm HANA

Double Exponential Smoothing. The process is defined in PA, but executed in-database in SAP HANA.

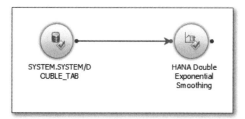

Figure 15.17 SAP HANA In-Database Double Exponential Smoothing in PA

The SAP HANA DOUBLE EXPONENTIAL SMOOTHING component dialogue is shown in Figure 15.18, with prompts for the parameter values of the algorithm. We have selected the same prompt values that we used in the PAL SQLScript as shown in Listing 15.2, for example the value of the smoothing constant alpha is set to 0.501 and for beta the value is set to 0.072.

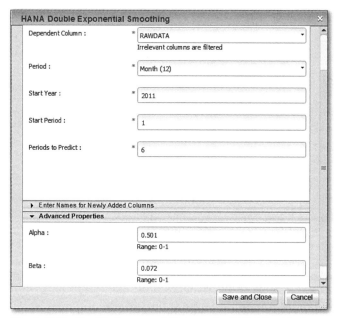

Figure 15.18 The PA Component Dialogue for HANA Double Exponential Smoothing

After you have run the analysis in PA and moved to the RESULTS view, the fitted and predicted data is as shown in Figure 15.19, which, of course, matches the output from the PAL, as shown in Figure 15.16.

ID (Private Attr...	RAWDATA (Pri...	Year	Month	PredictedValues
1	143.00	2011	1	
2	152.00	2011	2	152.00
3	161.00	2011	3	161.00
4	139.00	2011	4	170.00
5	137.00	2011	5	162.35
6	174.00	2011	6	156.62
7	142.00	2011	7	172.92
8	141.00	2011	8	163.91
9	162.00	2011	9	158.08
10	180.00	2011	10	165.84
11	164.00	2011	11	179.24
12	171.00	2011	12	177.36
13	206.00	2012	1	179.70
14	193.00	2012	2	199.35
15	207.00	2012	3	202.41
16	218.00	2012	4	211.12
17	229.00	2012	5	221.23
18	225.00	2012	6	232.06
19	204.00	2012	7	235.21
20	227.00	2012	8	225.13
21	223.00	2012	9	231.69
22	242.00	2012	10	232.65
23	239.00	2012	11	242.98
24	266.00	2012	12	246.49
		2013	1	262.48
		2013	2	268.69
		2013	3	274.90
		2013	4	281.11
		2013	5	287.32
		2013	6	293.53

Figure 15.19 The Fitted and Predicted Data

PA provides the usual excellent default visualizations for every algorithm. For Double Exponential Smoothing, the chart is as shown in Figure 15.20.

Double Exponential Smoothing is suitable for time series exhibiting trends but performs poorly for time series with seasonality. To account for seasonality in the data, we use Triple Exponential Smoothing.

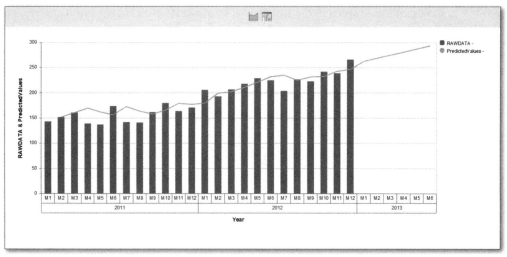

Figure 15.20 PA Visualization for Double Exponential Smoothing

15.6 Triple Exponential Smoothing

Double Exponential Smoothing will always fail to pick up seasonality. To address this, we have Triple Exponential Smoothing. There are several different variations of Triple Exponential Smoothing. The PAL uses what is referred to as Winters Three-Parameter Model, which is defined as

$S_t = \alpha\, X_t\, /\, I_{t\text{-}L} + (1\text{-}\,\alpha)\, (S_{t\text{-}1} + b_{t\text{-}1})$ ... the stationary element

$b_t = \beta\, (S_t - S_{t\text{-}1}) + (1 - \beta)\, b_{t\text{-}1}$ ... the trend element

$I_t = \gamma\, X_t\, /\, S_t + (1 - \gamma)\, I_{\,t\text{-}L}$ ... the seasonality

$F_{t+m} = (S_t + b_t * m) * I_{\,t\text{-}L+m}$ ... where L is the periodicity of the data

The computation is again quite easy, and again we have to start the process with the first forecast, which is where different starting methods can lead to different forecasts. There is no universally accepted method of starting exponential smoothing.

In the worked example, we use the initial value of the stationary element S_t as the average of the first 4 periods, given that we have quarterly data. The initial values of trend b_t are calculated as the difference between each quarter for the first 2 years, averaged to give a trend estimate, again given that we have quarterly data. The initial values of seasonal I_t are calculated as:

Period i = Period i / Average of First Four Periods, again given that we have quarterly data.

15.6.1 Worked Example

A worked example of Triple Exponential Smoothing is shown in Figure 15.21, where we have 6 years of quarterly actual data and we wish to predict 6 periods ahead.

Period	Actual	Single Smoothing	Trend Smoothing	Seasonal Smoothing	Forecast
1	362			0.953	
2	385			1.013	
3	432			1.137	
4	341	380.00	9.75	0.897	
5	382	398.99	10.26	0.953	371.29
6	409	404.68	10.01	1.013	414.64
7	498	433.90	11.06	1.137	471.43
8	387	433.70	10.44	0.897	399.29
9	473	487.08	12.81	0.954	423.22
10	513	505.25	13.10	1.013	506.40
11	582	512.86	12.80	1.137	589.59
12	474	527.89	12.92	0.897	471.57
13	544	565.05	14.25	0.954	515.88
14	582	575.31	14.03	1.013	586.92
15	681	597.11	14.46	1.137	670.26
16	557	619.21	14.88	0.897	548.66
17	628	653.76	15.96	0.955	605.17
18	707	692.87	17.24	1.013	678.47
19	773	685.01	15.86	1.137	807.73
20	592	667.09	14.00	0.897	628.87
21	627	661.07	12.90	0.954	650.26
22	725	708.00	14.77	1.014	683.05
23	854	746.07	16.05	1.137	821.77
24	661	741.57	14.92	0.896	683.41
25					721.98
26					782.25
27					894.38
28					718.27
29					778.94
30					

Alpha	0.822
Beta	0.055
Gamma	0.055

Figure 15.21 Worked Example of Triple Exponential Smoothing

Again, it is easier to review the analysis in a plot of the actual and fitted values of the time series, and the projections. This is shown in Figure 15.22, with the actual data series shown by a solid line and the fitted data shown by a dotted line.

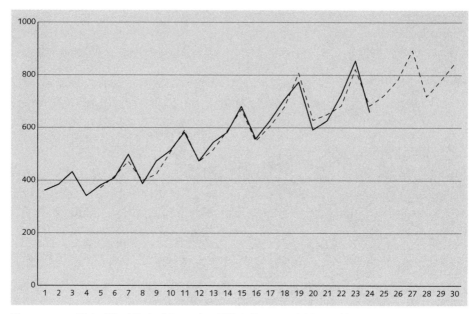

Figure 15.22 Plot of the Worked Example of Triple Exponential Smoothing

The chart in Figure 15.22 shows how Triple Exponential Smoothing incorporates the trend and seasonality in the time series.

15.6.2 Triple Exponential Smoothing in the PAL

In the Predictive Analysis Library, the algorithm name is Triple Exponential Smoothing and the associated function name is TRIPLESMOOTH.

The Input table is the same as that defined for Single Exponential Smoothing in Table 15.1.

The Parameter table is the same as in Table 15.4, with the addition of the gamma parameter and the cycle or periodicity of the data, as shown in Table 15.5.

Name	Data Type	Description
GAMMA	Double	The value of the smoothing constant gamma (0 < Đ < 1). Default value: 0.1

Table 15.5 The Gamma and Cycle Parameter Definition for TRIPLESMOOTH

Name	Data Type	Description
CYCLE	Integer	A cycle of length L (L > 1). For example, quarterly data cycle is 4, monthly data cycle is 12. Default value: 2

Table 15.5 The Gamma and Cycle Parameter Definition for TRIPLESMOOTH (Cont.)

The Output table definition for TRIPLESMOOTH is the same as for SINGLESMOOTH as was shown in Table 15.3.

The data that we used in our worked example, as shown in Figure 15.21, and the SQLScript is as follows in Listing 15.3 along with the parameters settings:

```
-- The procedure generator

call SYSTEM.afl_wrapper_generator ('TRIPLESMOOTH_TEST','AFLPAL','TRIPLE
SMOOTH',PDATA);


-- The Control Table parameters

INSERT INTO CONTROL_TAB VALUES ('RAW_DATA_COL',1,null,null);
INSERT INTO CONTROL_TAB VALUES ('ALPHA',null,0.822,null);
INSERT INTO CONTROL_TAB VALUES ('BETA',null,0.055,null);
INSERT INTO CONTROL_TAB VALUES ('GAMMA',null,0.055,null);
INSERT INTO CONTROL_TAB VALUES ('CYCLE',4,null,null);
INSERT INTO CONTROL_TAB VALUES ('STARTTIME',1,null,null);
INSERT INTO CONTROL_TAB VALUES ('FORECAST_NUM',6,null,null);


-- Assume the data has been stored in the table TRIPLE_TAB as shown in
Figure 15.21


-- Calling the procedure
CALL TRIPLESMOOTH_TEST(TRIPLE_TAB, CONTROL_TAB, RESULT_TAB) with
overview;
SELECT * FROM RESULT_TAB;
```

Listing 15.3 The PAL SQLScript for TRIPLESMOOTH

The full code is available in the file SAP_HANA_PAL_TRIPLESMOOTH_Example_SQLScript on the SAP PRESS website.

The output results are as shown in Figure 15.23.

SELECT * FROM RESULT_TAB		
	TIME	OUTPUT
1	5	371.28...
2	6	414.63...
3	7	471.43...
4	8	399.29...
5	9	423.22...
6	10	506.39...
7	11	589.58...
8	12	471.56...
9	13	515.87...
10	14	586.91...
11	15	670.26...
12	16	548.66...
13	17	605.16...
14	18	678.47...
15	19	807.72...
16	20	628.86...
17	21	650.25...
18	22	683.04...
19	23	821.76...
20	24	683.41...
21	25	721.98...
22	26	782.25...
23	27	894.37...
24	28	718.27...
25	29	778.94...
26	30	842.77...

Figure 15.23 The Output Results from the DOUBLESMOOTH PAL Function

Again, note that you need to be careful with the variable STARTTIME. This number is attached to the first value of the raw data, but when shown in the RESULT Tab, for Triple Exponential Smoothing, the first value shown is 5 in our example, as there is no Result/Fitted values for 1 to 4, given that we have quarterly data. The 6 forecast periods are therefore TIME for 25, 26, 27, 28, 29 and 30, with the values 721.98, 782.25, etc.

We can define and run the same analysis in PA.

15.6.3 Triple Exponential Smoothing in PA using the PAL

The same analysis using PA is shown in Figure 15.24, with the input data sourced from the SAP HANA table named TRIPLE_TAB connected to the algorithm HANA

Triple Exponential Smoothing. The process is defined in PA, but executed in-database in SAP HANA.

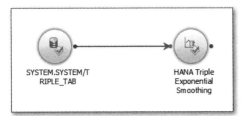

Figure 15.24 SAP HANA In-Database Triple Exponential Smoothing in PA

The SAP HANA TRIPLE EXPONENTIAL SMOOTHING component dialogue is shown in Figure 15.25, with prompts for the parameter values of the algorithm. We have selected the same prompt values that we used in the PAL SQLScript as shown in Listing 15.3, for example the value of the smoothing constant alpha is set to 0.822, and for beta and gamma the values are set to 0.055.

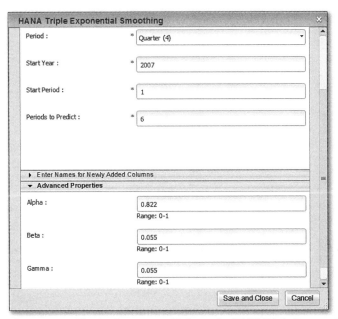

Figure 15.25 The PA Component Dialogue for HANA Triple Exponential Smoothing

After you have run the analysis and moved to the RESULTS view, the fitted and predicted data is as shown in Figure 15.26, which, of course, matches the output from the PAL as shown in Figure 15.23.

ID (Private Attr...	RAWDATA (Pri...	Year	Quarter	PredictedValues
1	362.00	2007	1	
2	385.00	2007	2	
3	432.00	2007	3	
4	341.00	2007	4	
5	382.00	2008	1	371.29
6	409.00	2008	2	414.64
7	498.00	2008	3	471.43
8	387.00	2008	4	399.29
9	473.00	2009	1	423.22
10	513.00	2009	2	506.40
11	582.00	2009	3	589.59
12	474.00	2009	4	471.57
13	544.00	2010	1	515.88
14	582.00	2010	2	586.92
15	681.00	2010	3	670.26
16	557.00	2010	4	548.66
17	628.00	2011	1	605.17
18	707.00	2011	2	678.47
19	773.00	2011	3	807.73
20	592.00	2011	4	628.87
21	627.00	2012	1	650.26
22	725.00	2012	2	683.05
23	854.00	2012	3	821.77
24	661.00	2012	4	683.41
		2013	1	721.98
		2013	2	782.25
		2013	3	894.38
		2013	4	718.27
		2014	1	778.94
		2014	2	842.78

Figure 15.26 The Fitted and Predicted Data

For Triple Exponential Smoothing, the chart in PA is as shown in Figure 15.27.

In addition to using exponential smoothing for time series analysis, we can also use bi-variate regression analysis, where the independent variable is time and the dependent variable the raw data.

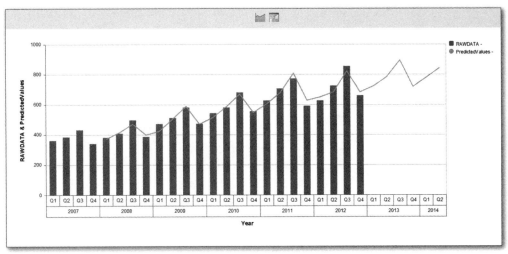

Figure 15.27 PA Visualization for Triple Exponential Smoothing

15.7   Bi-Variate Linear Regression

Regression methods are primarily used for classification analysis, where exploratory methods are used to investigate the relationship between a dependent variable and independent variables, and statistics produced regarding the model quality, confidence intervals for the model parameters, and any predictions. We can, of course, use some regression models for time series analysis where, although we are not building causal models, we wish to take the historical data points and just project them using various regression curves.

As an example, we can take the data that we used for Single Exponential Smoothing, as shown in Figure 15.7, and then using PA, simply fit a bi-variate linear regression model. The actual and fitted values using the PA Predict Results Chart are shown in Figure 15.28.

467

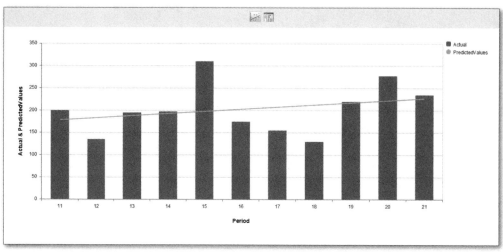

Figure 15.28 Bi-Variate Linear Regression to Predict Stationary Time Series

The model quality statistics are shown in Figure 15.29.

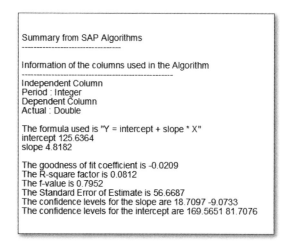

Figure 15.29 Model Quality Statistics

The goodness of fit is poor, with an R Squared of 0.0812; however, when we calculate the Mean Squared Error (MSE), the regression line has a smaller Mean Squared Error than the Single Exponential Smoothing algorithm. The major advantage of exponential smoothing models is that they are very efficient, and thus suitable for very large data volumes and where the actual data is being updated frequently, requiring frequent updates to the forecast.

The bi-variate regression model can also be applied to the data that we used for Double Exponential Smoothing to pick up the trend. Again, we can use PA to perform the regression, with the actual and fitted values using the PA Predict Results Chart as shown in Figure 15.30.

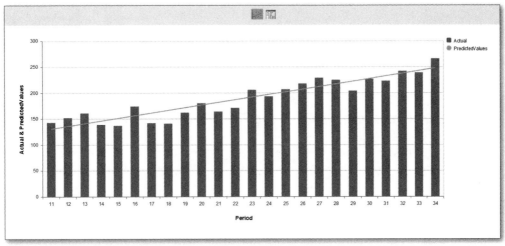

Figure 15.30 Bi-Variate Linear Regression to Predict Trend Time Series

The model quality statistics are shown in Figure 15.31.

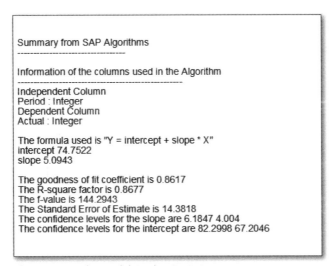

Figure 15.31 The Model Quality Statistics

As shown in Figure 15.31, The R Squared value and F Value are high; therefore, we have a good model upon which to make projections. Again, we can compare the forecast accuracy of the regression model with the exponential smoothing model.

The trend could, of course, be non-linear, and then the bi-variate non-linear regression models could be considered.

Regression models have been used for seasonal data, but they are not really suitable. Algorithms that inherently support seasonality, such as Triple Exponential Smoothing, are in general preferred.

15.8   The Business Case for Time Series Analysis

The business case for time series analysis is very strong because its application is so pervasive. Many business applications gain considerable benefit from providing insights into future data values, from the high data volumes of inventory and control systems, to the forecasting of key performance indicators for a few key indices. Applications of time series analysis occur across all industries, all lines of business, and all geographies. The applications have become so prevalent that the business case is taken for granted, with the focus more on maximizing the quality of the predictions rather than questioning the value of doing it. As with all predictive analyses, of course, the better the predictions, the greater the business value.

15.9   Strengths and Weaknesses of Time Series Analysis

The major strength of time series analysis is that it applies to so many business applications. In terms of the actual algorithms that we looked at, their main strength is that they are easy to understand and computationally efficient. The former increases their chance of adoption by management, while the latter is important when dealing with large volumes of data with a fine level of granularity and the need for frequent updating. The three exponential smoothing algorithms that we showed are as appropriate, good for stationary, trend and seasonal data. Conversely, they are poor if the underlying data pattern does not match the design of the algorithm.

On the weaknesses side, there is the usual issue of outliers affecting performance; however, we can mitigate their impact. An issue that can cause problems is that different starting assumptions can lead to different projections, so care needs to be taken if comparing the same algorithms from different sources. Exponential smoothing can require substantial historical data for seasonal data in order to determine the seasonality indices, when often there is limited historical data available. These methods are poor for non-stationary, trend, and seasonal data patterns, such as spikes or event based time series occurring at irregular intervals.

We have introduced only the very simplest of time series analysis algorithms. There are many very advanced methods to address the weaknesses of the simplest algorithms, and given the importance of the topic it has been the subject of much research.

Many practitioners argue that time series in the real world are more than just data points purely determined by previous data points, and that other factors affect their values as much as previous ones, if not more. For example, it is reasonable to assume ice cream sales are related to the current weather, competitive pricing, promotions, etc. and that these causal factors need to be included in the analysis, and also that they are more important than previous values of sales. In such circumstances, a combination of time series analysis and causal modeling may be used.

15.10 Summary

In this chapter we introduced the important topic of time series analysis and looked at exponential smoothing, specifically Single, Double and Triple Exponential Smoothing, with worked examples in the PAL and PA. We briefly looked at how we can use bi-variate linear and non-linear regression to predict time series. Time series analysis is a huge topic and we have only touched the surface, but hopefully this is enough to introduce you to the topic and the capabilities in the PAL and PA. It is important to add that, with the integration of R in SAP HANA and PA, the wealth of time series algorithms available in R are available to the user of the R Integration for SAP HANA. Furthermore, with the recent addition of custom components in PA, the time series analysis algorithms in R are also available in PA. An example of a recent addition of such a component is the ARIMA time series analysis method, sourced from R, and available in PA.

In the next chapter, we introduce the topics of text analysis and text mining, generally known as unstructured data analysis, in contrast to structured data analysis as described in previous chapters.

In this chapter we introduce the text analysis features of SAP HANA and show how they can be used to add structure to unstructured data, from which we can perform text mining.

16   Text Analysis and Text Mining

Predictive analysis is mainly associated with structured data analysis, in other words, the analysis of data with a structure to it, usually in the form of variables or columns, by records or rows. However, there is a huge amount of data in an unstructured format, such as documents, emails, and blogs, which is generally textual. Hence the term text analysis to try to analyze this unstructured content. It is said (nobody knows by whom, but no one challenges it) that up to 90% of enterprise-relevant information originates in unstructured data residing inside or outside an organization, such as in blogs, forum postings, social media such as Twitter, Facebook, Google+, Xing, in wikis, emails, contact-center notes, surveys, service entries, warranty claims, etc. The list is almost endless. The challenge, as with data mining, is to extract useful information.

16.1   Introduction

In this chapter we use the term text analysis for the extraction of information from text, in other words, the adding of some structure to the unstructured data; we use the term text mining for the application of predictive analysis algorithms to the extracted structured data. Data mining is concerned with looking for patterns in data; similarly, text mining is about looking for patterns in text.

Text mining is more challenging than data mining in the sense that text is unstructured, potentially ambiguous, expressive, and hard to interpret, when compared to the unemotional nature of structured data. Therefore, extracting useful information to improve business process will be more difficult in text mining compared to data mining; however, it is the ever-increasing volume of textual data and the suspected nuggets of information contained therein that makes text mining so important.

Figure 16.1 shows an example of a CAR ISSUES table, where the detailed information is hidden in the text.

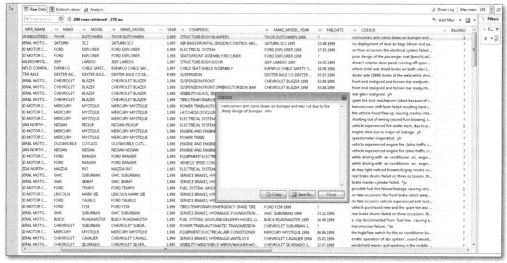

Figure 16.1 An Example of the Text "Hidden" within a Database Table

SAP HANA offers three broad capabilities: full text search, fuzzy search, and text analysis, as well as, in combination with the PAL and PA, text mining.

We describe each in detail, following an overview of the applications of text analysis and text mining.

16.2   Applications

Given the prevalence of text, there are many applications of text analysis and text mining. Examples include:

▶ Filtering out junk email and spam, based on certain terms or words that are unlikely to appear in legitimate messages.

▶ Automatically classifying messages to be routed to the most appropriate destination, for example, email messages with complaints or specific requests.

▶ Screening of email and messages for inappropriate content.

▶ Analyzing open-ended responses. Open-ended survey questions encourage unconstrained responses that may yield comments that structured surveys might miss.

▶ Analyzing insurance claims.

▶ Analyzing warranty claims to help identify common problems and complaints.

▶ Medical diagnosis where open-ended descriptions by patients of their own symptoms might yield useful clues for the actual medical diagnosis.

▶ Monitoring public opinions, for example in blogs or review sites.

▶ Automatic labeling of documents for later retrieval.

▶ Sentiment analysis using blogs, comments, etc.

▶ Fraud detection by analyzing claim contents.

▶ Preventing cyberbullying or cybercrime in instant messages, chat, and social networks.

▶ Social network analysis.

The list is almost endless.

We start our discussion of this topic by looking at the full text search capabilities of SAP HANA which form the basis of text analysis.

16.3 Full Text Search

Massive amounts of unstructured data are captured in operational business processes, CRM systems, maintenance applications, in R&D, in call center systems, as well as social media, blogs, forums, emails, documents, etc.

Companies are struggling to search on unstructured text related content, to extract meaningful structured information from the unstructured text, to find and analyze the content, and to combine unstructured with structured data.

Full Text Search in SAP HANA provides:

▶ Native full text search

▶ In-database text analysis

▶ Graphical modeling of search models

▶ Simple Info Access (SInA) API for JavaScript

▶ Info Access (InA) toolkit for HTML5 UIs

A high-level architecture diagram is shown in Figure 16.2. At the core of the architecture is SAP HANA and the tables that store the data. Pre-processing is done with linguistic analysis, and entity and fact extraction. The search engine provides full text search and fuzzy search. SAP HANA Studio provides the developer workbench, while the SAP HANA Extended Application Services provide the basis for end user applications.

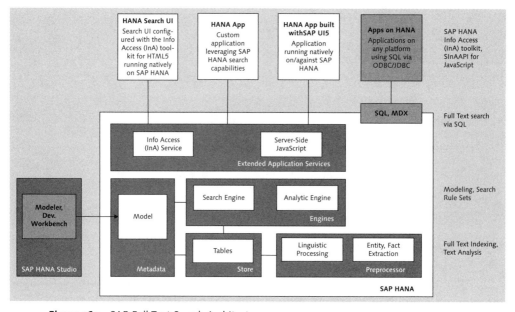

Figure 16.2 SAP Full Text Search Architecture

The steps to create a search-based application reflect the architecture:

1. Load the data into an SAP HANA table.

2. Create a full text index using SAP HANA Studio to enable full text search.

3. Run text analysis using SAP HANA Studio to extract salient information from text.

4. Optionally, create a search model using SAP HANA Studio to define search models and to specify search behavior.

5. Optionally, develop an application using the Info Access (InA) toolkit to define layout and data for search UIs, and the Simple Info Access (SInA) API for Javascript and SAP UI5 to develop search applications.

The full text index enables the full text search, and is an index that is created implicitly or explicitly. It gets created implicitly when you use the column data type TEXT or SHORTTEXT, and explicitly when you create an index of type full text in the table definition editor or via issuing a CREATE FULLTEXT INDEX SQL statement.

When a FULLTEXT INDEX is created, binary file types like .pdf, .ppt are converted into plain text. Then linguistic analysis is performed, consisting of tokenization, which decomposes word sequences, e.g., "the quick brown fox" becomes "the" "quick" "brown" "fox"; stemming, which is the reduction of tokens to linguistic base form, e.g., "houses" becomes "house," "ran" becomes "run"; and part-of-speech identification, e.g., quick: adjective; houses: noun-plural. The full text index is attached to the table column, as shown in Listing 16.1.

```
CREATE FULLTEXT INDEX [INDEX NAME] ON [SCHEMA].[TABLE]([COLUMN]);
```
Listing 16.1 Creating a Full Text Index on a Table Column

The full text index is updated, automatically reflecting changes in the table column.

You can use SAP HANA Studio to create what are called search models, which are similar to analytic models and comprise multiple tables. The search properties control the search behavior of your model, either freestyle search or using weights for ranking, with a range from 0 to 1.

Within SQLScript you use the SQL CONTAINS predicate to run a full text search against a table or a search model. See Listing 16.2.

```
SELECT * FROM [TABLE or MODEL]
   WHERE CONTAINS([COLUMN_NAME], '[SEARCH TERMS]');
```
Listing 16.2 Full Text Search of a Table via SQLScript

Listing 16.3 includes fuzzy search and ranking, which we will discuss shortly.

```
-- Search model
SELECT DISTINCT SCORE(), CMPLID, MAKE, MODEL, CDESCR
FROM "_SYS_BIC"."nhtsa/J_COMPLAINTS"

-- Filter condition
WHERE CONTAINS (*, 'throttle engine', FUZZY(0.8))   AND MAKE = 'FORD')

-- sort by relevance
ORDER BY SCORE() DESC;
```

Listing 16.3 Full Text Search of a Search Model via SQL Example

The output is shown in Figure 16.3.

	SCORE	CMPLID	MAKE	MODEL	CDESCR
1	0,7608278393745422	948.417	FORD	FREESTYLE	lost power from the engine causing lost speed. unable to accelerate. engine sputtered. sinc...
2	0,7588242292404175	931.449	FORD	FUSION	pulling into traffic car lost all throttle control wrench light came on engine still running sta...
3	0,758563756942749	930.477	FORD	ESCAPE	while driving at normal speeds on ice-glazed winter roads in fairbanks, ak, i approached an...
4	0,757868230342865	933.918	FORD	TAURUS	i pushed the accelerator into passing gear to go around a vehicle in the passing zone on a ...
5	0,7575799822807312	929.191	FORD	EXPEDITI...	tl* the contact owns a 2006 ford expedition. the contact stated that while driving 70 mph t...
6	0,7573421597480774	947.937	FORD	FIVE HU...	was driving my 2005 five hundred today. i pulled off the highway and stopped at a red ligh...
7	0,7571542859077454	921.228	FORD	F-150	while entering a highway via an on-ramp doing about approximately 45 miles per hour i at...
8	0,7567934393882751	922.051	FORD	FUSION	going about 75 mph with cruise on when problem occurred. the wrench light comes on a...
9	0,7567836046218872	948.263	FORD	TAURUS	entered highway on-ramp. as i merged onto highway at approximately 55 mph, i notice th...
10	0,7561171650886536	933.441	FORD	F-150	at roughly 800 miles i attempted to pass on a rainy afternoon and while applying enough l...

Figure 16.3 The Output from the SQLScript in Listing 16.3

There are four options to develop search-based applications on SAP HANA, ranging from the simplest to the most flexible:

▶ Use the SAP HANA Info Access (InA) toolkit for HTML5, a template for the configuration of SAP HANA search UI. It is fast and simple, but has a fixed layout.

▶ Use the Simple Info Access (SInA) API for JavaScript, and optionally SAP UI5. This is a client-side API for browser-based applications, with specific support to handle search requests.

▶ Use the SAP Extended Application Services and optionally SAP UI5.

▶ For any platform, use SQL over ODBC/JDBC.

Figure 16.4 provides an example of using the SAP HANA Info Access (InA) toolkit for HTML5. The toolkit enables you to configure modern, highly interactive search UIs, and is shipped with SAP HANA.

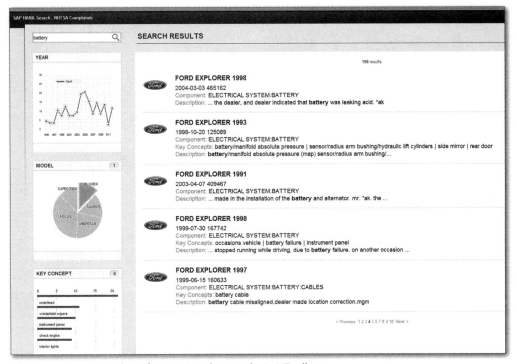

Figure 16.4 An Example UI for Text Search using the InA Toolkit

The SAP HANA Simple Info Access (SInA) API for JavaScript is a client-side or frontend JavaScript API for developing browser-based search UIs. It provides a simplified set of features of the SAP HANA Info Access (InA) HTTP service, including connecting to an attribute view in SAP HANA, freestyle search and filter conditions, suggestions of possible search terms, and the handling of result sets for lists for simple charts. The high-level architecture is shown in Figure 16.5.

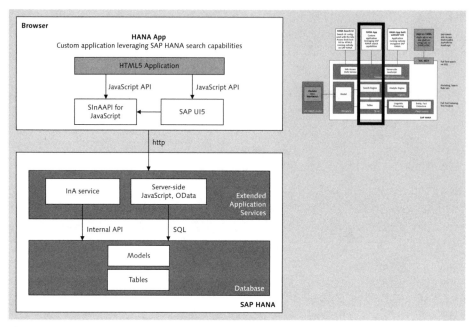

Figure 16.5 SAP HANA Simple Info Access (SInA) API for JavaScript

An example of the JavaScript is shown in Listing 16.4.

```
...
var sina = global.sap.bc.ina.api.sina;
var dataSource = {
    "objectName"  : {"value":"J_COMPLAINTS"} ,
    "packageName" : {"value":"nhtsa"}
    };
var query = sina.createSearchQuery()
  .dataSource(dataSource)
  .top(10);
query.addResponseAttribute("CMPLID")
  .addResponseAttribute("MAKE")
  .addResponseAttribute("MODEL")
  .addResponseAttribute("CDESCR")
  .setSearchTerms("throttle engine");
  .addFilterCondition("MAKE", "=", "FORD");
var resultSet = query.getResultSetSync();
var elements = resultSet.getElements();
...
```

Listing 16.4 SAP HANA Simple Info Access API for JavaScript Example

Following on from full text search is the less demanding, but more practical, fuzzy search.

16.4 Fuzzy Search

Fuzzy search is used to find database content similar to the search terms or with typographic errors. It is used for incomplete search terms and searching with synonyms, also referred to as term mapping.

Examples of fuzzy search are shown in Listing 16.5, where we have used the FUZZY argument in the SQLScript. We are looking for the text "ploti," which, because it is a fuzzy search, includes the return of the text pilot in the example as shown in Figure 16.6.

```
-- Fuzzy search error-tolerant search, e.g. "ploti"
SELECT * FROM AT_NARRATIVES
WHERE CONTAINS (NARR_ACCP,'ploti', FUZZY (0.9));

-- Relevance ranking. Calculate a score per result based on attribute
relevance, fuzziness and text-rank

SELECT SCORE(),*
FROM AT_NARRATIVES …
```

Listing 16.5 Fuzzy Search Example

An example of the output is shown in Figure 16.6.

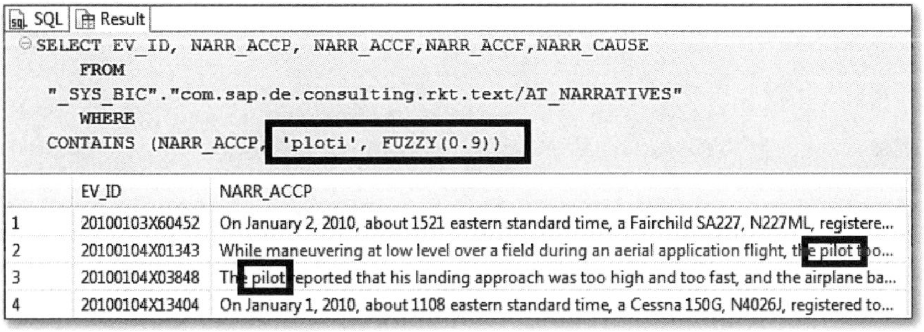

Figure 16.6 The Results of a Fuzzy Search

Fuzzy Search provides a fault tolerant comparison of terms, e.g.

"Gremelspacher" vs. "Kremelsbacher" vs. "Gremelsbacker."

The degree of fuzziness can be defined, ranging from 0 to 1, with supported SQL types of VARCHAR, NVARCHAR, TEXT, SHORTTEXT, FULLTEXT INDEX, and DATE.

Additional index structures can be defined to make fuzzy search faster, as shown in the example in Listing 16.6. Note that the FUZZY SEARCH INDEX needs additional memory.

```
CREATE COLUMN TABLE mytable
(
  firstname NVARCHAR(100) FUZZY SEARCH INDEX OFF,
  lastname  NVARCHAR(100) FUZZY SEARCH INDEX ON
);


-- Get the status of fuzzy search indexes:
SELECT table_name, column_name, fuzzy_search_index
FROM table_columns
WHERE table_name = 'MYTABLE';



-- Enable/disable fuzzy search index on an existing column:
ALTER TABLE mytable ALTER
(
  firstname NVARCHAR(100) FUZZY SEARCH INDEX ON
);
```

Listing 16.6 Enable Fuzzy Search Index Functionality

Some data domains need specific search algorithms, so fuzzy search supports postcode, house number, and date of birth. An example of house number fuzzy search is shown in Listing 16.7, where we want to be able to search beyond simple house numbers such as 10 to include house numbers with additions, such as 10a App 920.

```
CREATE COLUMN TABLE mytab
(
  postcode NVARCHAR(20) FUZZY SEARCH MODE 'postcode',
  housenumber NVARCHAR(50)
);


ALTER TABLE mytab ALTER
(
 housenumber NVARCHAR(50) FUZZY SEARCH MODE    'housenumber'
);
```

```
SELECT * FROM mytab
WHERE CONTAINS(housenumber, '10a App 920', FUZZY(0.8));
```
Listing 16.7 An Example of Fuzzy Search of House Numbers

Substring search is also supported; see the example in Listing 16.8.where we show finding the entry Coca Cola Company within a substring.

```
SELECT TO_DECIMAL(SCORE(),3,2) score, company FROM customers WHERE
CONTAINS( company, 'Cola Comp.',
   FUZZY(0.8,'similarcalculationmode=substringsearch'))
   order by SCORE() DESC;
```
Listing 16.8 Substring Fuzzy Search

SAP HANA supports search rules, for example, an application wishes to search for all persons similar to a given set of data, searching for possible duplicates before saving a new record to a CRM system, e.g., find all records that have the same name + address or the same name + date of birth or the same last name + address.

Search rules can define criteria for two records to be considered similar and which records are to be returned. Multiple sets of rules can be defined for different use cases.

Search rules are called using the EXECUTE_SEARCH_RULE_SET function, with all the rules executed in a single call. The result set contains the results of all rules. This removes the need to write complex SQL. Applications can share the same rules and can choose from multiple sets of rules. An example is shown in Figure 16.7.

```
CALL EXECUTE_SEARCH_RULE_SET('
  <query>
    <ruleset name="documentation.sps5::FindDuplicates.searchruleset" />
    <column name="FIRSTNAME">claus</column>
    <column name="LASTNAME">muller</column>
    <column name="STREETNAME">Mezstr.</column>
    <column name="HOUSENUMBER">18</column>
    <column name="POSTCODE">10701</column>
    <column name="CITYNAME">berlin</column>
    <column name="PHONE">+493012345678</column>
    <column name="DATEOFBIRTH">1980-02-01</column>
  </query>
')
```

	_SCORE	_RULE_ID	ID	FIRSTNAME	LASTNAME	STREETNAME	HOUSENUMBER	POSTCODE	CITYNAME	PHONE
1	0.893...	SamePerson	12300001	Klaus	Müller	Metzstr.	18	10707	Berlin	+493012345678
2	0.810...	SamePerson	9760901	Klaus Peter	Müller	Metzstr.	18	10707	Berlin	<?>
3	0.783...	SamePhone	12300002	Klaus	Müller	Bahnhofstr.	102	10543	Berlin	+493012345678
4	0.735...	Family	12300004	Claudia	Müller	Metzstr.	18	10707	Berlin	<?>

Figure 16.7 Search Rule Sets in SAP HANA

Full Text search and fuzzy search are user driven activities to find information in databases. SAP HANA Text Analysis is data driven, in the sense that information is automatically extracted from text using such concepts as linguistic processing, entity extraction, and fact extraction.

It is analogous to cluster analysis, where we have ABC analysis for user defined and driven cluster analysis, and K-Means and Kohonen SOMs for data driven cluster analysis.

16.5 Text Mining and Text Analysis

Text analysis is concerned with extracting useful information from unstructured data, for example, using named entity recognition and subjective information extraction such as positive or negative sentiments contained in text.

Example use cases include brand or product monitoring of sentiment, and determining the primary reasons for failures or defects in a product or service.

SAP HANA supports in-database text analysis, as an optional process in conjunction with full text indexing. The results from a text analysis are stored in a table. There is no data replication and no transformation outside of the SAP HANA database. Text analysis feeds from and writes to SAP HANA tables

During text analysis, the following text pre-processing steps may be executed:

- File filtering, which consists of converting binary document formats such as .pdf, .ppt to text/HTML.
- Tokenization, which involves decomposing word sequences, e.g., "the quick brown fox" -> "the" "quick" "brown" "fox".
- Stemming, which is the reduction of tokens to linguistic base form, e.g., houses -> house; ran -> run.
- Linguistic analysis, which comprises part-of-speech identification, e.g., quick: Adjective; houses: Noun-Plural.
- Entity extraction, which involves extracting entities form text, e.g., persons, locations, dates, etc.
- Fact extraction voice of the customer, e.g., sentiments, requests, topics, etc.

Because these pre-processing steps are also required to create a full text index for search purposes, text analysis is implemented as an optional configuration of the full text index.

SAP HANA Text Analysis supports 31 languages, with automatic language identification from content. Additional fact types for voice of the customer now include:

▶ Profanity: defines a set of pejorative vocabulary.

▶ Emoticons: expressions of someone's feelings about the whole sentence or situation.

▶ Weak positive: Loving my new iPad J No XYZ needed over here.

▶ Strong positive: The show was hilarious -:).

▶ Weak negative: I hate this phone I'm using :-(.

▶ Strong negative: The Dow Jones fell 200 points :-(((.

▶ Social slang: e.g., GR8, LOL, luv, etc.

The Text Analysis processes run inside the SAP HANA database, with a high-level architecture diagram shown in Figure 16.8. The process starts with the data stored in SAP HANA, which is accessed and analyzed by the text analysis engine, before being made available to various user interfaces, such as HTML 5 client applications.

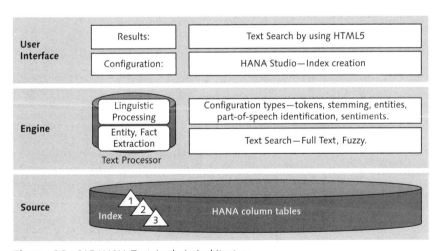

Figure 16.8 SAP HANA Text Analysis Architecture

Technically, the text analysis is performed by the Text Analysis SDK, the same natural language processing technology found in Text Data Processing on Data Services, formally known as Inxight. As the text analysis process is coupled with the full text indexing process, text analysis inherits some of its behavior, such as changes to the source table resulting in automatic updates in the text analysis result table.

Altering the full text index may result in an index re-build, and dropping the full text index will also drop the TA result table.

The full text index and the processing queue can be monitored via:

```
SELECT * FROM SYS.FULLTEXT_INDEXES;
SELECT * FROM SYS.M_FULLTEXT_QUEUES;
```

During full text indexing, a full text index is created, which is attached to the indexed table column in SAP HANA. This index is accessed indirectly, when a full text search is performed. In contrast, the results of text analysis are stored in a table, which can then provide input for further analysis and mining.

Text analysis is configured via SQLScript:

```
CREATE FULLTEXT INDEX [INDEX NAME] ON [SCHEMA].[TABLE]([COLUMN])
CONFIGURATION '[CONFIGURATION FILE NAME]' TEXT ANALYSIS ON;
```

The [CONFIGURATION FILE NAME] refers to pre-defined, standard SAP configuration files shipped with SAP HANA:

LINGANALYSIS_BASIC; LINGANALYSIS_STEMS; LINGANALYSIS_FULL

The text analysis results in terms of the tokens; tokens and stems; tokens, stems, and POS tags are contained here:

EXTRACTION_CORE

The text analysis results in terms of predefined entities, noun groups etc., are stored here:

EXTRACTION_CORE_VOICEOFCUSTOMER

For example:

```
CREATE FULLTEXT INDEX myIndex ON myTable(myColumn) CONFIGURATION 'EXTRAC-
TION_CORE' TEXT ANALYSIS ON;
```

This creates a full text index for the table myTable on column myColumn.

16.5.1 Examples

In this section we look at several different examples of text analysis and text mining.

Example 1: Entity Index Extraction

For this example, the database record is as shown in Figure 16.9, and comprises an example record and text for a car warranty application. We wish to search and analyze this textual information.

Figure 16.9 Example SAP HANA Database Record

After running SAP HANA Text Analysis, the extracted the entity index is as shown in Figure 16.10.

CMPLID	RULE	COUNTER	TOKEN	LANGUAGE	TYPE
923.158	Entity Extra...	1	ford	en	ORGANIZATION/COMMERCIAL
923.158	Entity Extra...	2	2001	en	YEAR
923.158	Entity Extra...	3	safety recall notice 11s24	en	NOUN_GROUP
923.158	Entity Extra...	4	recall notice	en	NOUN_GROUP
923.158	Entity Extra...	5	jan 2012	en	DATE
923.158	Entity Extra...	6	safety recall	en	NOUN_GROUP
923.158	Entity Extra...	7	ford	en	ORGANIZATION/COMMERCIAL
923.158	Entity Extra...	8	$1900	en	CURRENCY
923.158	Entity Extra...	9	catalytic converter	en	NOUN_GROUP
923.158	Entity Extra...	10	exhaust manifold	en	NOUN_GROUP
923.158	Entity Extra...	11	master cylinder	en	NOUN_GROUP
923.158	Entity Extra...	12	brake line booster	en	NOUN_GROUP
923.158	Entity Extra...	13	tie rods	en	NOUN_GROUP
923.158	Entity Extra...	14	intake manifold	en	NOUN_GROUP
923.158	Entity Extra...	15	air bag	en	NOUN_GROUP
923.158	Entity Extra...	16	rear passenger door handle fell	en	NOUN_GROUP
923.158	Entity Extra...	17	oil pan	en	NOUN_GROUP
923.158	Entity Extra...	18	air condition	en	NOUN_GROUP
923.158	Entity Extra...	19	rear shock	en	NOUN_GROUP

Figure 16.10 Extracted Entity Index for the Record Shown in Figure 16.9

Next we show an example of linguistic index extraction.

Example 2: Linguistic Index Extraction

Using the data shown in Figure 16.9, the results of a linguistic index extraction are shown in Figure 16.11.

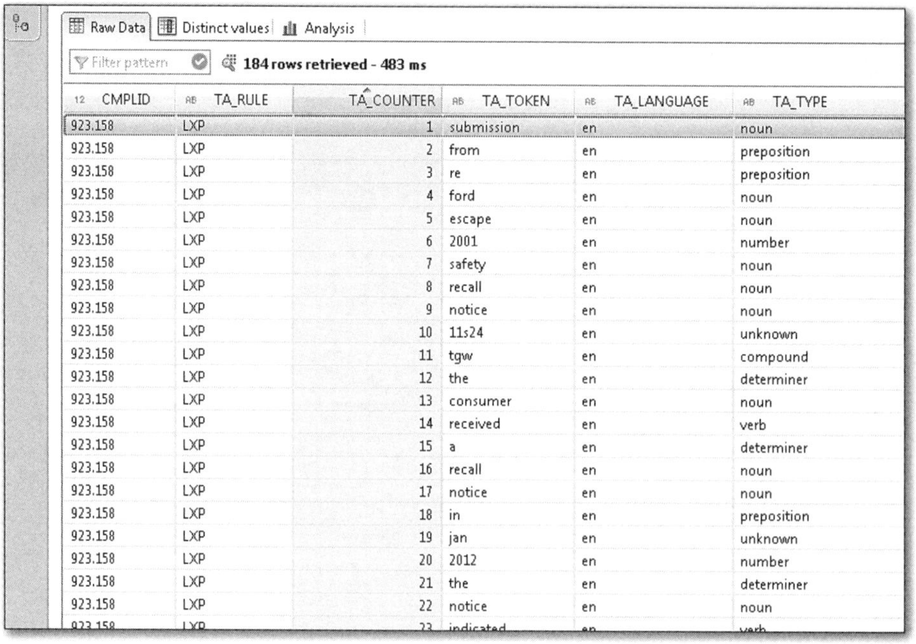

Raw Data | Distinct values | Analysis

Filter pattern | 184 rows retrieved - 483 ms

CMPLID	TA_RULE	TA_COUNTER	TA_TOKEN	TA_LANGUAGE	TA_TYPE
923.158	LXP	1	submission	en	noun
923.158	LXP	2	from	en	preposition
923.158	LXP	3	re	en	preposition
923.158	LXP	4	ford	en	noun
923.158	LXP	5	escape	en	noun
923.158	LXP	6	2001	en	number
923.158	LXP	7	safety	en	noun
923.158	LXP	8	recall	en	noun
923.158	LXP	9	notice	en	noun
923.158	LXP	10	11s24	en	unknown
923.158	LXP	11	tgw	en	compound
923.158	LXP	12	the	en	determiner
923.158	LXP	13	consumer	en	noun
923.158	LXP	14	received	en	verb
923.158	LXP	15	a	en	determiner
923.158	LXP	16	recall	en	noun
923.158	LXP	17	notice	en	noun
923.158	LXP	18	in	en	preposition
923.158	LXP	19	jan	en	unknown
923.158	LXP	20	2012	en	number
923.158	LXP	21	the	en	determiner
923.158	LXP	22	notice	en	noun
923.158	LXP	23	indicated	en	verb

Figure 16.11 Extracted Linguistic Index for the Record Shown in Figure 16.9

In the next example, we look at the popular topic of sentiment analysis.

Example 3: Voice of the Customer–Sentiment Analysis

In this example, shown in Figure 16.12, we use the same data input; however, the extraction is in terms of sentiment extraction, for use in voice of the customer analysis.

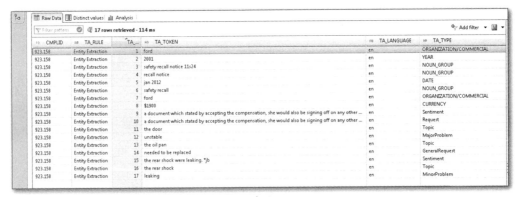

Figure 16.12 Voice of the Customer Sentiment Analysis

Example 4: Text Analysis and Tag Cloud Charts

The text output can be very usefully presented in a tag cloud chart, as shown in Figure 16.13.

Figure 16.13 Tag Cloud Chart of Text Data in SAP HANA Studio

Example 5: Text Analysis Token Extraction Visualization in PA

We can, of course, bring the data from SAP HANA into PA. The example, in Figure 16.14 shows how a bubble plot helps identify the major problem areas in the vehicle maintenance database.

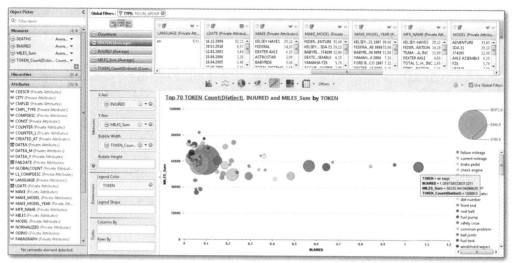

Figure 16.14 Bubble Plot in PA of Extracted Tokens using SAP Text Analysis

In the next example we look at custom dictionaries, whereby users can define their own extraction text.

Example 6: Custom Dictionaries

Custom dictionaries can be defined for specific text entity extraction, as shown in the Listing 16.9.

```
<entity_category name="engine components">
   <entity_name standard_form="wastegate">
      <variant name ="waste gate"/>
   </entity_name>

   <entity_name standard_form="turbocharger">
<variant name ="twin scroll turbo"/>
<variant name ="turbosupercharging"/>
   </entity_name>
<entity_category>
```

Listing 16.9 Custom Dictionaries Example in SAP Text Analysis

An example of the output is shown in Figure 16.15.

	CMPLID	TA_RULE	TA_COUNTER	TA_TOKEN	TA_LANGUAGE	TA_TYPE	TA_NORMALIZED
1	700686	Entity Extraction	4	coolant	en	engine cooling systems	coolant
2	700687	Entity Extraction	4	coolant	en	engine cooling systems	coolant
3	700704	Entity Extraction	4	fuel pump	en	engine components	fuel pump
4	700705	Entity Extraction	4	fuel pump	en	engine components	fuel pump
5	700738	Entity Extraction	1	turbo	en	engine components	turbo
6	700738	Entity Extraction	8	turbo	en	engine components	turbo
7	700748	Entity Extraction	4	crank shaft	en	engine components	crank shaft
8	700748	Entity Extraction	13	crankshaft	en	engine components	crankshaft

Figure 16.15 SAP Text Analysis with Customer Dictionaries

Example 7: Text Mining in PA using the Text Analysis from SAP HANA

We defined text analysis as the extraction of structure from unstructured data, and text mining as then applying predictive analysis algorithms to that data, usually augmented by other structured data.

Here is an example using the results of a customer sentiment analysis from SAP HANA Text Analysis, combined with data for each customer on their income, expenditure, and loyalty. The objective of the analysis is to determine the characteristics of customers with strong positive and negative sentiments regarding our product.

The data from the SAP HANA Text Analysis customer sentiment analysis is shown in Figure 16.16, with the first 20 records displayed.

ID	Customer	Sentiment
1	William Lucas	Negative
2	Morris Allen	Neutral
3	Hugh Smith	Negative
4	Henry Rufoote	Positive
5	Thomas Phevens	Very Positive
6	John Stilman	Very Negative
7	Edmund Walden	Very Positive
8	Humphrey Little	Neutral
9	Kelley Edward	Negative
10	Christopher Cross	Positive
11	Stevenson Charles	Negative
12	Stilman John	Very Negative
13	Powell Edward	Very Positive
14	Willett Richard	Neutral
15	Nicholas Petman	Positive
16	Roger Pratt	Positive
17	Willie Clancy	Negative
18	Johnny Doran	Neutral
19	Thomas Smith	Very Positive
20	Richard Taverner	Positive

Figure 16.16 Sample Output from SAP HANA Text Analysis Sentiment Analysis

We merge this data, using the PREPARE VIEW MERGE option in PA, with the customer data shown in Figure 16.17, with again only the first 20 records displayed.

ID	Customer	Lifespend	Newspend	Income	Loyalty
1	William Lucas	7.2	3.6	6.1	2.5
2	Morris Allen	5.4	3.4	1.5	0.4
3	Hugh Smith	6.9	3.2	5.7	2.3
4	Henry Rufoote	5.5	2.3	4.0	1.3
5	Thomas Phevens	6.1	2.9	4.7	1.4
6	John Stilman	5.0	3.3	1.4	0.2
7	Edmund Walden	5.8	2.7	5.1	1.9
8	Humphrey Little	5.1	3.4	1.5	0.2
9	Kelley Edward	6.4	3.2	5.3	2.3
10	Christopher Cross	5.7	2.8	4.5	1.3
11	Stevenson Charles	6.8	3.0	5.5	2.1
12	Stilman John	4.3	3.0	1.1	0.1
13	Powell Edward	7.0	3.2	4.7	1.4
14	Willett Richard	5.4	3.4	1.7	0.2
15	Nicholas Petman	5.4	3.0	4.5	1.5
16	Roger Pratt	5.7	2.9	4.2	1.3
17	Willie Clancy	6.3	2.9	5.6	1.8
18	Johnny Doran	5.1	3.7	1.5	0.4
19	Thomas Smith	6.3	2.8	5.1	1.5
20	Richard Taverner	5.6	2.5	3.9	1.1

Figure 16.17 Sample Output of the Structured Customer Data

We use PA to merge the data, as shown in Figure 16.18.

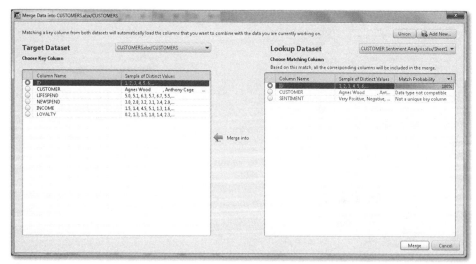

Figure 16.18 The Merging of the Sentiment Analysis and Customer Data

The data can then be viewed in PA PREPARE VIEW, as shown in Figure 16.19.

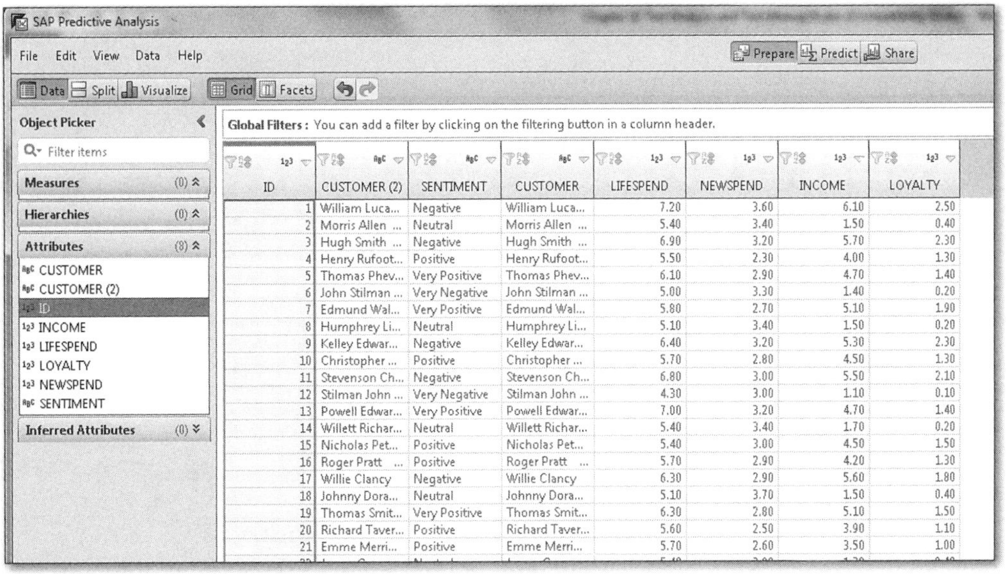

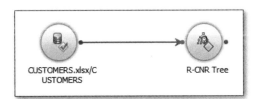

Figure 16.19 The Merged Data in PA

We want to try to determine the characteristics of customers in each sentiment group. To do this, we will use a decision tree, where the input variables are lifespend, newspend, income and loyalty; and the target variable is sentiment.

We define the analysis in PA as shown in Figure 16.20.

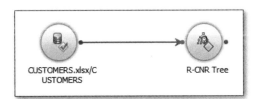

Figure 16.20 Sentiment Analysis in PA

After we run the analysis in PA, we can view the decision tree, as shown in Figure 16.21, to try to extract the rules and characteristics of customers in the different sentiment groups.

It broadly appears that income is the main decider between customer sentiment, with the split at the value 2.45 between positive and negative sentiment.

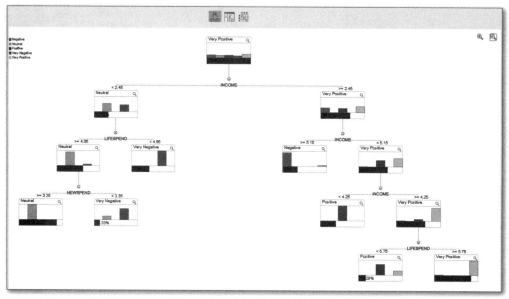

Figure 16.21 The Decision Tree Output from the Sentiment Analysis in PA

We can also look at the quality of the model in PA, by viewing the Classifier Confusion Matrix, which shows a very strong model, as shown in Figure 16.22.

The VISUALIZE option of PA allows us to create ad hoc charts such as the trellis chart shown in Figure 16.23, which shows a scatter chart of customer income and lifespend, and how it varies by sentiment.

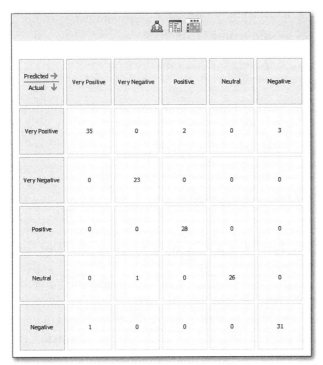

Predicted → Actual ↓	Very Positive	Very Negative	Positive	Neutral	Negative
Very Positive	35	0	2	0	3
Very Negative	0	23	0	0	0
Positive	0	0	28	0	0
Neutral	0	1	0	26	0
Negative	1	0	0	0	31

Figure 16.22 The Classifier Confusion Matrix for the Sentiment Analysis

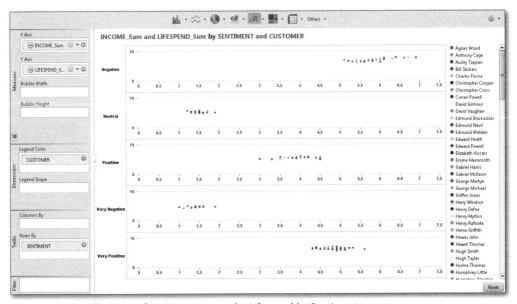

Figure 16.23 Trellis Chart of Customer Income by Lifespend by Sentiment

There are many other examples of text mining where we can combine the extracted entities from unstructured data with structured data:

▶ Perform a logistic regression to see whether we can predict who is most likely to have a positive or negative sentiment.

▶ Time series analysis on a text count or sentiment. What is the trend and projection?

▶ Cluster analysis of documents using similarity indexes.

Finally, it should be noted that with the integration of R, the wealth of text analysis in R is also available to users of SAP HANA and PA.

16.6 The Business Case for Text Analysis and Text Mining

The prevalence of text, and the promise of useful information contained therein, has led to many business applications, as described in Section 16.2. The explosive growth in email and the emergence of social media has fuelled even greater interest in text analysis. Compared to structured data analysis, unstructured data analysis is a relatively new discipline. The potential business benefits are very significant but with the caveat that it is harder to find interesting patterns in unstructured data, compared to structured data. The extension of text analysis to text mining, where we combine the two data classes, shows the greater promise, as then we are using the information in structured data sources and augmenting it with unstructured data.

16.7 Summary

In this chapter, we addressed the topics of text analysis and text mining, starting with full text indexing for text search, and then extending that to fuzzy search. Using various examples we looked at the functionality in SAP HANA for in-database text analysis. Finally, we described an example combining the output from SAP HANA text analysis with structured data in PA, and using decision tree analysis to analyze the characteristics of groups of customers by sentiment.

In the next and final chapter, we review the many examples of the use of the previously described predictive analysis algorithms by our customers.

This chapter describes the various applications of SAP predictive analysis products by SAP customers, starting with specific examples, and then a wide range of use cases by industry.

17   Customer Applications

Although the use of SAP predictive analysis products by SAP customers is quite recent, given the relative newness of the products, there are already many examples. We can specifically name some of the customers, while others prefer not to be named either for competitive reasons or because the often lengthy process of agreeing upon a named reference is not yet complete. However, it is still very interesting to know of these "unnamed" but real customer applications, and therefore they are included in this chapter. A name is interesting, but it is not critical to appreciating the use case. We start with six named customers and then list the many case studies where predictive analysis has proven very beneficial for SAP customers, grouped by industry.

17.1   eBay

With more than 100 million active users globally, eBay is the world's largest online marketplace, where practically anyone can buy and sell practically anything. The collective impact on ecommerce is staggering: in 2012, the total value of goods sold on eBay was $175 billion; eBay predicts that number to grow over the next three years to $300 billion: more than the gross domestic product of all but 33 of the world's countries. In addition, eBay owns PayPal. With more than 128 million active users in 193 markets and 25 currencies around the world, PayPal enables global commerce. PayPal's net total payment volume for 2012, the total value of transactions, was $145 billion.

The eBay CFO describes his company as a dynamic self-regulating economy, similar to how the free-market based economy of a country operates. Just as the Federal Reserve Chairman can manage the US economy by manipulating monetary policies such as changing interest rates, the eBay CFO believes they can manage the eBay economy as well, by modifying variables at a micro and macro level, such as listing rates, policies, etc.

To achieve this goal, eBay's vision is to build a system that has four components:

▶ Track several thousand business metrics forecast for one day in the future and, if there is significant deviation between forecast and actual, send an alert or a signal.

▶ Determine causality once a signal or deviation from forecast is detected. The system needs to automate the process of root-cause analysis as much as possible.

▶ Generate near-term, mid-term, and long-term forecasts, from one day to eighteen months in the future, with differing confidence levels.

▶ Run simulations to visualize the impact of decisions on the eBay economy.

eBay has more than 300 analysts tracking the metrics. Even then, the key issue was still how to distinguish the signal from the noise. In addition, the eBay team was concerned about the impact of any added workload on the central Enterprise Data Warehouse and potentially slowing down the rest of the critical eBay operational reporting.

SAP successfully delivered the first phase of the project as part of a proof of concept using the SAP HANA Platform and the SAP Performance and Insight Optimization (PIO) consulting services group, who are specialists in the field of predictive analysis. The solution involved building a comprehensive early signal detection system that can automatically handle any of the thousands of time series metrics that eBay tracks on a daily basis by combining the following features:

▶ Data cleansing operations to remove duplicates and fill in missing data for planned and unplanned events.

▶ Determination of time series characteristics such as multiple seasonal cycles.

▶ A library of different time series models that consider the trend, seasonality, lagged effects, as well as correlation with holidays and promotions.

▶ A decision tree based framework that determines the best time series model to use for different metrics.

▶ A dashboard for business users that helps them find the signals within a day and understand the strength of the signals based on the probability of the metric value being an outlier on any single day.

By using the signal detection system, eBay analysts can focus on the most important variations within a day rather than spending weeks before learning about potential problems. SAP is now working with eBay on executing the remaining phases of the project.

You can hear David Schwarzbach, VP and CFO eBay North America, describe the application in this YouTube video: *http://www.youtube.com/watch?v=hS-0ZadT6so*

17.2   MKI Japan

With headquarters in Tokyo, Japan, MKI has a revenue budget of 48.26 billion yen in 2013.

Its business challenges were to reduce delays and minimize the costs associated with new drug discovery, by optimizing the process for genome analysis. MKI also wanted to improve and accelerate decision making for hospitals that conduct cancer detection based on DNA sequence matching.

The technical implementations leveraged the combination of SAP HANA, R, and Hadoop to store, pre-process, compute, and analyze huge amounts of data.

The key benefit was derived by reducing genome analysis from several days to only twenty minutes, making real-time cancer/drug screening possible.

You can hear Dr. Carlos Bustamonte, Professor of Genetics at Stanford University and Yukihisa Kato, CTO and Director of MKI, describe how SAP HANA can improve and revolutionize genome analysis in this YouTube video:

http://www.youtube.com/watch?v=Y-zOq3nKjaA

17.3   CISCO

Cisco Systems, Inc. (*www.cisco.com*) with headquarters in San Jose, California, is a leading high-tech company with over 66,000 employees and revenues of over $45 billion. The key business challenges were to provide sales teams with real-time insights to enable them to make better decisions through better data delivery to improve the business and drive topline growth. There was also a lack of understanding of underlying sales performance drivers and the seasonality of buying patterns.

The technical challenge was to transform the results of predictive analysis into actionable insights.

For Cisco, the key benefits were to

▶ Better respond to customers and deliver tangible business value.

▶ Reduce the time taken to transform information into insights.

▶ Improvement in the quality of decision-making on those insights.

▶ Ultimately drive higher profitability and growth.

The SAP HANA platform at Cisco has been used to deliver near real-time insights to their executives, and the integration with R allows Cisco to combine the predictive algorithms in R with this near real-time data from SAP HANA. The net impact is that Cisco is able to take this capability, which previously took weeks and months to put together, and deliver just-in-time as the business is changing.

You can hear Jeff McKittrick, Director of Strategic Initiatives at Cisco, and Piyush Bhargava, Distinguished Engineer IT, Cisco Systems, describe the application in this YouTube video:

https://www.youtube.com/watch?v=HLg9L-2bkec#at=12

17.4   CIR Foods

CIR Foods is a food service and restaurant business that provides catering services to schools, hospitals and healthcare facilities, businesses, and military communities. Its 1,200 facilities and 11,000 employees worldwide include restaurant managers and staff, dieticians and nutritionists, who develop healthy menus, dishes, and culinary methods.

A significant problem for CIR Foods is trying to balance staff numbers across restaurants, given the daily fluctuations in demand, resulting in some restaurants having too many employees and others having too few.

Already a user of business intelligence to analyze its business, CIR Foods chose to move beyond providing real-time information to its executives and restaurant managers. The company saw the need and value in more accurately predicting the fluctuations in demand and the habits of customers, in order to optimize restaurant operations and employee allocation of different tasks.

The company spends over Euros 130M per year buying food, so a small percentage saving will yield significant results. They focused on schools and predicting how many children will be at each school, from which they can reduce the number of dishes for that school and reduce waste.

Predictive analytics helps CIR Foods improve business functions by:

▸ Providing demand forecasts and predicting restaurant attendance fluctuations.

▸ Improving staff allocation planning by allocating employees to the appropriate restaurants and food service functions.

▸ Optimizing food purchases, which are approximately 30% of turnover, to reduce waste.

You can hear Giorgio Spaggiari, CTO CIR Foods, and Davide Rota, Founder B4C Consulting, describe the application in this YouTube video:

http://www.youtube.com/watch?v=AjUvMMsOREk

17.5   Home Shopping Europe 24

Home Shopping Europe (HSE24) uses SAP Customer Engagement Intelligence (CEI), a high performance application, developed on SAP HANA. It has rich functionality for the analysis of customer relationship and customer contribution, and supports targeted sales and marketing activities. CEI includes SAP Predictive Analysis to enrich the standard CEI functionality with predictive content and enable the HSE24 marketing department to base their activities on predictive analytics.

HSE24 sells more than a million products to about eight million customers in Germany, Switzerland and Austria. The company is growing successfully, mainly because customers can chose from a broad range of products and return products if they don't meet expectations, at no extra cost.

To keep and grow market share is a major challenge for online retailers, where margins are low, freight and handling costs are high and have a direct impact. SAP Performance and Insight Optimization (PIO) services supported the application where SAP Predictive Analysis is used to gain new insights, and SAP Audience Discovery & Targeting (ADT) within CEI provides access to the analytics to design target customer groups. Data mining experts, data analysts and business users with no data mining expertise are able to work collaboratively in generating and deploying insight.

PIO created 25 clusters based on a data set of 1.3 million customer transactions from one year with about 30 attributes. The high number of clusters was required to have discriminating customer segments that qualify for specific campaigns. The results at cluster level were imported into SAP Predictive Analysis to analyze the patterns and enrich the data even further. The clusters were published in ADT to enable business users to integrate this information with a high number of further attributes when designing target groups. ADT finally exported the target group into CRM and closed the loop from analysis to operational process.

You can hear Michael Kuenzl, Vice President of IT, HSE24, describe the application in this YouTube video:

http://www.youtube.com/watch?v=2-TuA6Q6QiQ

17.6   Bigpoint

With headquarters in San Francisco, California, revenues over \$350 million, and a user community of over 300 million, Bigpoint is a leading player in the virtual gaming industry, with well-known products such as Battlestar Galactica, Space Invasion, and Pirate Storm.

With SAP HANA, gaming companies can analyze player behavior patterns to deliver personalized, context-relevant offers to players and thereby increase the conversion rate from free to paying players.

For example, with Bigpoint, when a player is engaged in intense battle and their ship is being destroyed, there is a few seconds break before the player can resume playing. During this time, the SAP HANA system analyzes the player's historical and transaction behavioral data and delivers a personalized context relevant offer to the player that is specifically designed to achieve Bigpoint's revenue objectives.

The business challenges were to increase conversion rates from free to paying players and increase the average revenue per paying player, while also decreasing churn by keeping paying players playing longer.

The technical implementation involved real-time data processing with more than 5,000 events in the game per second loaded into SAP HANA. Predictive classification algorithms from the R Integration for SAP HANA were developed to deliver personalized context-relevant offers to players through the analysis of vast amounts of historical and transactional data to forecast player behavior patterns.

The key benefits are real-time insights with per player profitability analysis and an increased understanding of player behavior. The increased data volume and processing capabilities enable Bigpoint to communicate personalized messages to players. Overall, the objective is to increase a game's revenue by 10-30%.

You can hear Michael Gutsmann, CFO, Bigpoint, describe the application in this YouTube video:

http://www.youtube.com/watch?v=N6orDVq61wo

17.7 Other Customer Use Cases

SAP has many customers who use predictive analysis but who prefer not to be named here, as they would rather keep their analysis and competitive advantage to themselves. In this section we briefly describe many of these applications developed by the SAP Performance and Insight Optimization (PIO) organization. PIO works collaboratively with customers on their predictive analysis applications, leveraging their expertise in predictive analysis and the power of SAP HANA's in-memory technology to solve complex business challenges. The PIO organization comprises advanced analytical experts, mathematicians, data scientists, industry experts, and developers who combine their knowledge with technologies such as SAP's predictive assets and SAP HANA to analyze massive amounts of data.

We present these predictive use cases by industry – retail, manufacturing, transport and logistics, banking, public sector, high tech, oil and gas, and utilities. In each of these industries, we present the most common predictive analysis projects undertaken, the use case challenges, and the business benefits.

17.7.1 Retail

Table 17.1 lists some of the predictive projects undertaken by PIO in the retail industry. As we saw in Chapter 1, this is a major area of application of predictive analysis.

Applications in Retail	Use Case Challenges	Benefits
Affinity Insight	Determine product affinities to drive increased average transaction size, increased average number of items, and consequently increased revenue, at both a geographical and store group level.	Increased profit through leveraging point of sale data to develop and assess product and affinity strategies. Increased sales through discovering the true financial impact of product drag-along effects.
Price Optimization	Retail price optimization requires the development of product lifecycle pricing strategy, maximizing revenue through efficient promotion execution, and measuring price sensitivity by market segment.	Rapid ROI on sales and increased profitability, enhanced efficiency and lower costs through reduced inventory levels. Increased product profitability through prolonged product lifecycles and improved forecast accuracy.
Zone Optimization	Determination of single versus multiple zone pricing strategy. Grouping of retail stores into manageable sets of pricing zones.	Increase profits by aligning zones with customer price sensitivity. Increase sales by aligning zones with customer demand.
Size Optimization	Determining optimal size profiles for purchasing and distribution by aligning product supply with shopper demand by size and by store.	Mitigate lost sales caused by not having the correct product sizes in stores. Accurately forecast product demand by size. Maximize profitability by reducing markdowns.
Demand Modelling and Forecasting	Ad-hoc methods lead to a significant loss in revenue in what is a highly competitive environment with tight margins. Time constrained to operate strategically with large volumes of complex data.	Better forecasting at the product level across all stores with the best forecast MAPEs in the order of 10-20%. At the category level the best results were forecast MAPEs on the order of 15%.

Table 17.1 SAP Customer Applications of Predictive in Retail

17.7.2 Manufacturing

Table 17.2 lists some of the predictive projects undertaken by PIO in the manufacturing industry, including the classic areas of inventory control, demand forecasting and production optimization.

Applications in Manufacturing	Use Case Challenges	Benefits
Spare Parts Inventory Optimization	Spare part inventory optimization needs to consider the operational practices applied to purchasing, ordering and goods movements. Various demand patterns for parts which can exhibit both random and systematic effects. Special cases like dangerous goods, perishable goods, etc.	Reduce inventory cost whilst increase service levels. Optimize inventory policies to achieve best possible trade-offs between service level and inventory holding cost.
Demand Modelling for Configurable Products	Demand depends on the combination of product characteristics, e.g., the number of cars with GPS system and A/C. It's an ever changing portfolio with new configuration options, the discontinuation of variants or extra equipment, the mandatory bundling of extra equipment	Improved production planning and accuracy of parts procurement. Reduction of production bottlenecks. Optimization of stock levels.
Segmenting Materials by the most precise Sales Forecasting Method	SAP Advanced Planner and Optimizer (APO) offers several alternative material forecasting algorithms. By doing an evaluation of historic material data from the customer, give a recommendation which forecasting algorithm is most suited to provide the best forecast.	The configuration of APO has been pre-evaluated based on historic material data and a "best suited configuration" has been suggested to the customer. APO running more effectively to meet customer demands and the material forecasting performance has been maximized.

Table 17.2 SAP Customer Applications of Predictive in Manufacturing

Applications in Manufacturing	Use Case Challenges	Benefits
Production Capacity Optimization with Linear Optimization	Difficulty in planning production capacities and workforce schedules. Limited information on hand relative to production when making purchasing decisions and the complex nature of the articles built.	Increased utilization of manufacturing equipment. Higher throughput and increase efficiency through the manufacturing process and supply chain.

Table 17.2 SAP Customer Applications of Predictive in Manufacturing (Cont.)

17.7.3 Transport and Logistics

Table 17.3 lists some of the predictive projects undertaken by PIO in the transport and logistics industry, including predictive maintenance, which is a current hot topic given the vast volumes of telemetry data involved and the power of SAP HANA.

Applications in Transport and Logistics	Use Case Challenges	Benefits
Passenger Recovery	Rescheduling and accommodating stranded passengers needs to be done quickly. The aftermath of airline disruption for example, from bad weather, sudden mechanical problems, or crew unavailability, can result in significant costs and customer frustration. The ability to quickly calculate alternative passenger itineraries after major flight schedule disturbances can result in significant savings and competitive advantage.	Performance improvement from on average 20 minutes to around 10 seconds translates into millions in savings. Extend to future use cases for aircraft and crew recovery.

Table 17.3 SAP Customer Applications of Predictive in Transport and Logistics

Applications in Transport and Logistics	Use Case Challenges	Benefits
Spare Parts Inventory Optimization	Spare part inventory optimization needs to consider the operational practices applied to purchasing, ordering and goods movements, and the specific parameters that can be changed and optimized in inventory policies.	Reduce inventory holding costs whilst increasing service levels.
Predictive Maintenance	Massive amounts of historical maintenance data and sensor data. Also known as preventive maintenance, to prevent costly failures before they happen.	Detailed analysis of historical maintenance data with performance rankings and key insights related to maintenance decisions. Identification of key factors related to variations in performance.

Table 17.3 SAP Customer Applications of Predictive in Transport and Logistics (Cont.)

17.7.4 Banking

Table 17.4 lists some of the predictive projects undertaken by PIO in the banking industry. Here the analysis of customer behavior dominates with analytic CRM.

Applications in Banking	Use Case Challenges	Benefits
Analytical CRM – Campaign Portfolio Optimization	Selling the right product to the right customer through the right channel at the right time.	Increased campaign response rates. Gain intimate customer insight. Be prepared for future requirements.

Table 17.4 SAP Customer Applications of Predictive in Banking

Applications in Banking	Use Case Challenges	Benefits
Analytical CRM – Customer Segmentation	Ability to better target the right customers. Driving higher response rates from marketing and sales campaigns	Improved forecasting of customer response. Increased productivity of marketing and sales. Insight into potential drivers for customer retention, cross-selling and campaign management.
Analytical CRM – Customer Retention	Retaining existing customers in a competitive environment. Understanding customer behaviour to improve sales and service management.	Improved return on marketing investment. Cost savings: it is 5-10 times more expensive to acquire new customers than to keep existing customers. Increased revenue stream from the customer base.
Analytical CRM – Cross-selling and Up-selling	Reduce the sales cycle while increasing order size. Expanding on existing customer relationships in competitive markets. Focusing on the right customers to drive additional sales.	Increased productivity for sales and marketing Increased profitability from existing customer base . Insight into market demand for product bundling Increased market share
Analytical CRM –Customer Lifetime Value (CLV)	Having deep knowledge about current customers and keeping pace with quickly changing market conditions and customer demands. Broaden and deepen insight into customer relationships and business operations.	Cost savings through concentration on the most valuable customers. Increased profitability from existing customer base. Insight into market demand for product bundling.
Multidimensional Workforce Simulation.	Understanding and planning for future workforce demand. Ensuring planned HR measures meet the desired staffing needs.	Generate optimized project plans based on performance, planning horizon, planning strategy and business rules for maximized resource planning. Evaluate employee turnover.

Table 17.4 SAP Customer Applications of Predictive in Banking (Cont.)

17.7.5 Public Sector

Table 17.5 lists some of the predictive projects undertaken by PIO in the public sector. Here tax analysis and the prevention of fraud figure prominently.

Applications in Public Sector	Use Case Challenges	Benefits
Fraud, Waste and Abuse Detection	Governments are overwhelmed when attempting to address fraud, waste and abuse. Government agencies struggle with massive amounts of data, silos and unchecked data sets, and limited resources.	Produce a larger pipeline of discovery leads in real time, day by day. Empower a broader pool of staff to act on the information. Establish better business processes for more consistent follow-ups.
Tax Gap Discovery	Tax administration process has been very focused on tax return processing and validation. Errors were detected and acted on sometimes years after refund cheques were sent and cashed. Taxes could be avoided simply by ensuring that forms were filled out "completely" not necessarily in "compliance". The resulting impact on government agencies was a significant difference between what taxpayers claim they owe and what is truly owed.	Change from the current "Reactive" method of analysis, to a real time "Proactive" method of tax discovery and action. These actions could result in identifying hundreds of millions to billions of dollars annually in potential tax revenue at a time many states desperately need it.
Tax Compliance: Circular Trade and Loop Detection	Commercial tax departments need an intelligent system to help them to do deeper analysis and audit suspected dealers who have been consistently evading tax. Tax departments have difficulty auditing the many places of potential fraud such as interstate transactions, lump sum provisions, unregistered dealers, bogus bills and circular trading .	Empowerment to tax analyst team—to slice and dice the data as per their requirements (finding maximum value add, minimum value add, more set off claimed than VAT paid transactions.) Capability to integrate with multiple tax data sources.

Table 17.5 SAP Customer Applications of Predictive in the Public Sector

17.7.6 High Tech

Table 17.6 lists some of the predictive projects undertaken by PIO in the high tech industry. Here forecasting and customer analysis dominate.

Applications in High Tech	Use Case Challenges	Benefits
Sales Forecasting	Understanding the impact on cash flow in a highly seasonal business, made more complex by the delays between bookings and billings. Accurately forecasting revenues and margin to identify underperforming parts of the business. Taking advantage of each supplier's/buyer's unique seasonal behaviour. Understanding demand for parts vs. products vs. bundled solutions, and any cannibalization effects.	Better respond to customers and deliver tangible business value. Reduce time to transform information into insights and improvement in the quality of decision-making on those insights. Ultimately drive higher profitability and growth.
Book to Bill Forecast and Analysis	Holistic management of manufacturing parts, product options, and services, in a complex supply chain. Reliance on outsourcing and globalization in volatile geopolitical climates. Unreliable forecasting methods.	More accurate forecasts and faster response, ultimately leading to better management of the business, from cash flow through to risk. Reduce the time spent on consolidations, reporting, reconciliations and financial close. Increase gross margin through improved planning and forecasting.
Strategic Customer Stratification	Hundreds of thousands of daily customer interactions across multiple customer touch points and systems. Hard to view complete account information on a single version of the truth.	Improve margins and profitability. Recognize customer trends and order patterns. Drive sales and improve product line penetration.

Table 17.6 SAP Customer Applications of Predictive in High Tech

Applications in High Tech	Use Case Challenges	Benefits
	Hard to aggregate mass volumes of data to visualize customer profitability, duration, sentiment, and satisfaction	
	Hard to understand where to focus; what to do next to grow revenue and profit in an account.	

Table 17.6 SAP Customer Applications of Predictive in High Tech (Cont.)

17.7.7 Oil and Gas

Table 17.7 lists some of the predictive projects undertaken by PIO in the oil and gas industry, with optimization models playing an important part.

Applications in Oil and Gas	Use Case Challenges
Marine Scheduling Optimization	Core aspects of the business problem include balancing the constant oil production at the production harbour, with contracts with customers defining amount and type of oil to be shipped. Added to which, the limited storage capacity at the production harbour, the limited number of ships that can be filled up at the same time, and limited ship capacity.
Blend Optimization	Various different types of crude oil to be produced based on a multitude of characteristics such as API, sulphur, viscosity, etc. Then there is the customer specific ranges of quality required, resulting in the need to blend different types of crude oil to reach that quality. This further complicated by the need for the ability to allow calculations for more characteristics freely defined by the user.

Table 17.7 SAP Customer Applications of Predictive in Oil and Gas

17.7.8 Utilities

Table 17.8 lists some of the predictive projects undertaken by PIO in the utilities industry, where demand planning is an important topic.

Applications in Utilities	Use Case Challenges	Benefits
Outage Management	Unplanned distribution outages create long equipment outages, dissatisfied customers and unexpected large costs.	Reduce outage costs such as overtime, repair costs and megawatt hours lost. Improve response to outages, e.g., recommendations made on potential crew shift changes to reduce costs. Increased customer satisfaction through improvement in the reliability KPIs.
Data Mining to improve Asset Register	For historic reasons asset registers are usually incomplete, whilst regulatory requirements require them to be complete. The challenge is to find a promising data mining-based approach to complete the asset register.	Data mining-based methods can complete the asset register in general at higher levels of accuracy compared to other approaches. Completeness and accuracy of asset register is a significant lever to reduce operational costs.
Peak Load Forecasting	Peak Load Forecasting is a critical function for maintaining safe operations and driving investment decisions for asset replacement. The current manual process takes around 2–3 months to complete. The challenge is to reduce the process time, improve forecast accuracy and increase the analysis frequency.	Improved effectiveness of the process through increase in forecast accuracy and frequency of calculations. Efficiency gains by automating some of the manual tasks and making the process more flexible. Regulatory compliance by ensuring auditability of the process.
Load Demand Modelling and Forecasting	Predict peak power demand for various customer groups. Design effective demand response programs and improve network reliability and reduce blackouts.	Improve forecast accuracy from 0.5% up to 1% with highest predictive ability. Produce short term demand forecasts for each distinct customer profile. Increase control over operational costs.

Table 17.8 SAP Customer Applications of Predictive in Utilities

Although we have not been able to name the customers, the thirty-one projects listed above demonstrate the depth and breadth of the predictive applications being undertaken by SAP.

17.8   Summary

In this chapter we focused on customers of SAP using SAP predictive analysis products and customers engaging our data scientists from the SAP Performance and Insight Optimization group. We described significant applications of SAP predictive products at eBay, MKI Japan, Cisco, CIR Foods, HSE 24, and Bigpoint. We then summarized thirty-one predictive projects undertaken by PIO, grouped by industry sector. In summary, SAP has significantly accelerated its predictive offerings and involvement in predictive projects, across all regions of the world and all industry sectors.

A   References and Resources

This appendix brings together all the references in the book, and includes links to resources on the web and material produced by industry analysts.

A.1   References

Chatfield, C. (1995) *Problem Solving: A Statistician's Guide,* Chapman & Hall/CRC Texts in Statistical Science.

Dallal, Gerald E. Ph.D, "Causality: Cause and Effect." *The Little Handbook of Statistical Practice*, Last Modified May 22, 2012, *http://www.jerrydallal.com/LHSP/cause.htm*

Everitt, Brian S., Landau, Sabine, Leese Morven and Stahl, Daniel. (2011) *Cluster Analysis, 5th edition*, Wiley, Series in Probability and Statistics.

Gualtieri, Mike, Powers, Stephen, and Brown, Vivian. "The Forrester Wave: Big Data Predictive Analytics Solutions, Q1 2013" Forrester Research Inc. last modified: February 4, 2013. *http://www.forrester.com/The+Forrester+Wave+Big+Data+Predictive +Analytics+Solutions+Q1+2013/fulltext/-/E-RES85601*.

Huff, Darrel and Geis, Irving. (1954) *How to Lie with Statistics*, Norton, W. W. & Company, Inc.

IDC. "IDC's Business Value from Predictive Analytics Survey", IDC Research., June 2011. Available from IDC Research, accessed October 13, 2013.

KD Nuggets. "Algorithms for Data Analysis/Data Mining." Poll, 2011. Last modified: November 2011. *http://www.kdnuggets.com/polls/2011/algorithms-analytics-data-mining.html*.

KD Nuggets. "Hottest Analytics/Data Mining Topics in 2012." Poll, 2012. Last modified: January 2012. *http://www.kdnuggets.com/polls/2012/hottest-analytics-data-mining-topics.html*

Linden, A. "The 1999 Magic Quadrant on Data Mining Workbenches" Gartner, Inc. 1 August 16, 1999. Available from Gartner, Inc. accessed October 13, 2013.

Linoff, G.S and M.J. Berry. (2011) *Data Mining Techniques: For Marketing, Sales, and Customer Relationship*, Wiley.

Makridakis, S.G and S.C. Wheelwright and R.J. Hyndman (1997) *Forecasting: Methods and Applications*, Wiley.

Playfair, W. (1786) *The Commercial and Political Atlas*, Cambridge University Press.

Rexer, Karl. "2011 Data Miner Survey" Rexer Analytics. January 2011. Available from Rexer Analytics. *http://www.rexeranalytics.com/Data-Miner-Survey-Results-2011. html*. accessed October 13, 2013.

Tufte, E.R. (2001) *The Visual Display of Quantitative Information*, Graphics Press.

Tukey, J. (1977) *Exploratory Data Analysis*, Addison-Wesley.

Ventana Research. "Predictive Analytics: Improving Performance by Making the Future More Visible" 2012. Available from SAP AG. *https://www54.sap.com/content/ dam/site/sapcom/global/usa/en_us/assetmgt/docs/2013/02-feb/05/18/predictive-analytics- improving-performance-by-making-the-future-more-visible.PDF*. accessed October 13, 2013.

Wonnacott, T.H and R.J. Wonnacott (1990) *Introductory Statistics*, Wiley.

A.2 Additional Resources

There are several excellent resources that inform the Predictive analysis process. This list is by no means exhaustive.

An excellent overall web resource for data mining is the KDnuggets web site. *http://www.kdnuggets.com/*

The Karl Rexer Data Miner Surveys are another valuable resource. *http://www.rexeranalytics.com/*

For an excellent selection of data sets, see the University of California Machine Learning Repository. *http://archive.ics.uci.edu/ml/*

To learn more about PMML, go to the Data Mining Group website. *http://www.dmg.org/*

For the SAP HANA Predictive Analysis Library Guide, see *http://help.sap.com/hana/SAP_HANA_Predictive_Analysis_Library_PAL_en.pdf*

For the SAP HANA R Integration Guide, see
http://help.sap.com/hana/SAP_HANA_R_Integration_Guide_en.pdf

For the SAP Predictive Analysis Online Help, see
http://help.sap.com/businessobject/product_guides/SAPpa10/en/pa1_0_11_user_en.pdf

The R manual is located here:
http://cran.r-project.org/doc/manuals/R-intro.html

A good site for beginners is
http://www.statmethods.net/

Other Resources that may be helpful are:
http://www.ats.ucla.edu/stat/R/
http://www.r-bloggers.com/
http://www.inside-r.org/r-resources-web

B   The Author

John MacGregor graduated with a Master's Degree in Operations Research from Lancaster University, England, and then spent several years as a management consultant in Unilever's UK Operations Research Group. He then joined Birds Eye Foods, a Unilever subsidiary, as Operations Research Manager, before becoming the Strategic Planning Manager, and finally the Commercial Manager of the Confectionery Group.

John then joined the University of North London as a Senior Lecturer in Statistics and Operations Research. At the same time he worked with the first BI products and OLAP servers before both acronyms were even coined.

John then emigrated to Sydney, Australia to jointly start and run a software distributorship company, also covering New Zealand and Southeast Asia. He then joined Pilot Software, which had acquired his company, as joint Managing Director, Australia & New Zealand. John then joined Gentia Software, Australia & New Zealand, as Managing Director, and subsequently assumed the position of Managing Director, Gentia Software, UK.

Upon returning to Australia, John became Regional Director, Crystal Decisions, Australia & New Zealand.

John holds several patents including "OLAP Data Mining", with over a dozen in application, and was an External Examiner, Master's Program, Centre for Decision Support, Monash University, Melbourne, Australia.

John is currently based in the UK, as Vice President and Head of the Centre for Predictive Analytics, coming to SAP through their acquisition of BusinessObjects, which had acquired Crystal Decisions. In his career at Crystal and SAP BusinessObjects, he has been a Solution Manager, a Product Manager, and a Program Manager, focused on OLAP tools, business applications, and predictive analysis.

Index

■ Learn the basic principles and
concepts of BW

■ Get step-by-step instructions for
performing BW tasks

■ Download sample data and
recreate a real-life business scenario
to get hands-on experience

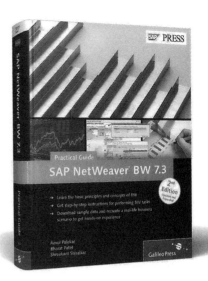

Amol Palekar, Bharat Patel, Shreekant Shiralkar

SAP NetWeaver BW 7.3 — Practical Guide

Business analytics remains one of the hottest and most dynamic topics in
enterprise software—so don't be left behind. With this comprehensive
reference, you can get up to speed and stay up to date on the principles of SAP
NetWeaver BW 7.3, from the basics to the advanced concepts. Thanks to a
practical example that is carried throughout the course of the book, you'll do
more than learn what DSOs, InfoCubes, or InfoProviders are: You'll learn what
you can do with them, and how. If you want to master BW, this book is what
you need.

789 pp., 2. edition 2013, 69,95 Euro / US$ 69.95
ISBN 978-1-59229-444-2
www.sap-press.com

Galileo Press

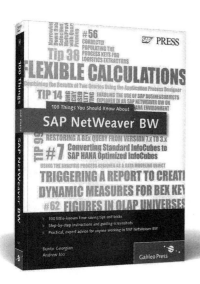

- 100 little-known time-saving tips and tricks

- Step-by-step instructions and guiding screenshots

- Practical, expert advice for anyone working in SAP NetWeaver BW

Buntic Georgian, Andrew Joo

SAP NetWeaver BW

100 Things You Should Know About...

If you're looking to take your knowledge of SAP NetWeaver BW to the next level, then this is the book for you! You'll benefit from expert information that reveals the secrets of SAP NetWeaver BW gurus as they provide the most useful tricks of working with the major task areas in SAP NetWeaver BW. These "100 Things" provide detailed screenshots, easy instructions, and a hands-on approach to quickly working with SAP NetWeaver BW.

367 pp., 2013, 49,95 Euro / US$ 49.95
ISBN 978-1-59229-447-3
www.sap-press.com